Land of Silver Rain

Vol. 2

MIRA LEE

NETCOMICS

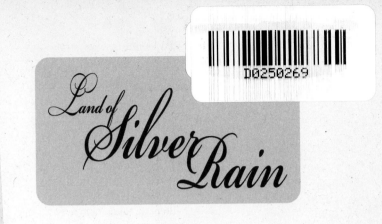

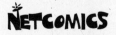

Land of Silver Rain Vol. 2

Story and Art by Mira Lee

English translation rights in USA,
Canada, UK, NZ, Australia arranged by
Ecomix Media Company
395-21 Seogyo-dong, Mapo-gu, Seoul, Korea 121-840
info@ecomixmedia.com

- Produced by **Ecomix Media Company**
- Translator **Jennifer Park**
- Pre-Press Manager **Yesook Ahn**
- Graphic Designer **Eunsoon Cheon**
- Editor **Wanda Albano**
- Managing Editor **Soyoung Jung**
- President & Publisher **Heewoon Chung**

P.O.Box 16484, Jersey City, NJ 07306
info@netcomics.com
www.NETCOMICS.com

ISBN: 1-60009-046-X

First printing: April 2006
10 9 8 7 6 5 4 3 2 1
Printed in Korea

Land of Silver Rain

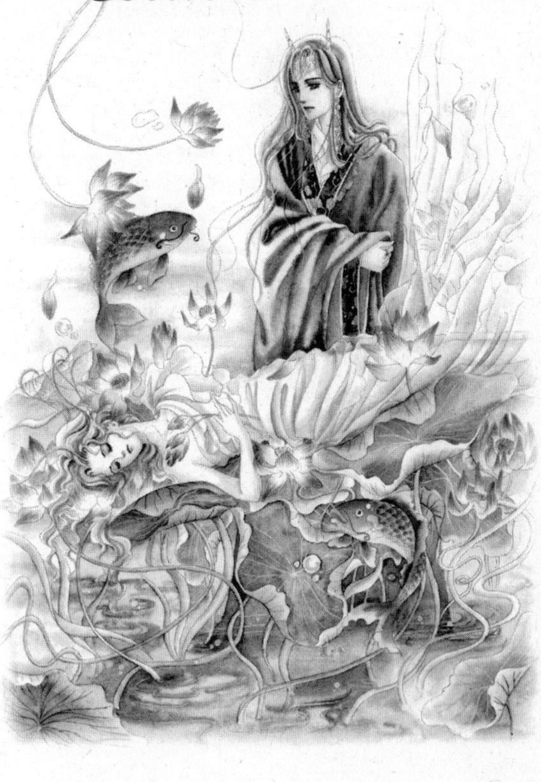

Vol. 2

MIRA LEE

Contents

PART 1 LAND OF THE GODS

PART 2 LAND OF HUMANS

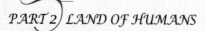

PART 1 LAND OF THE GODS

CHAPTER 5
MISTY-RAIN LEAVES THE DOKEBI LAND

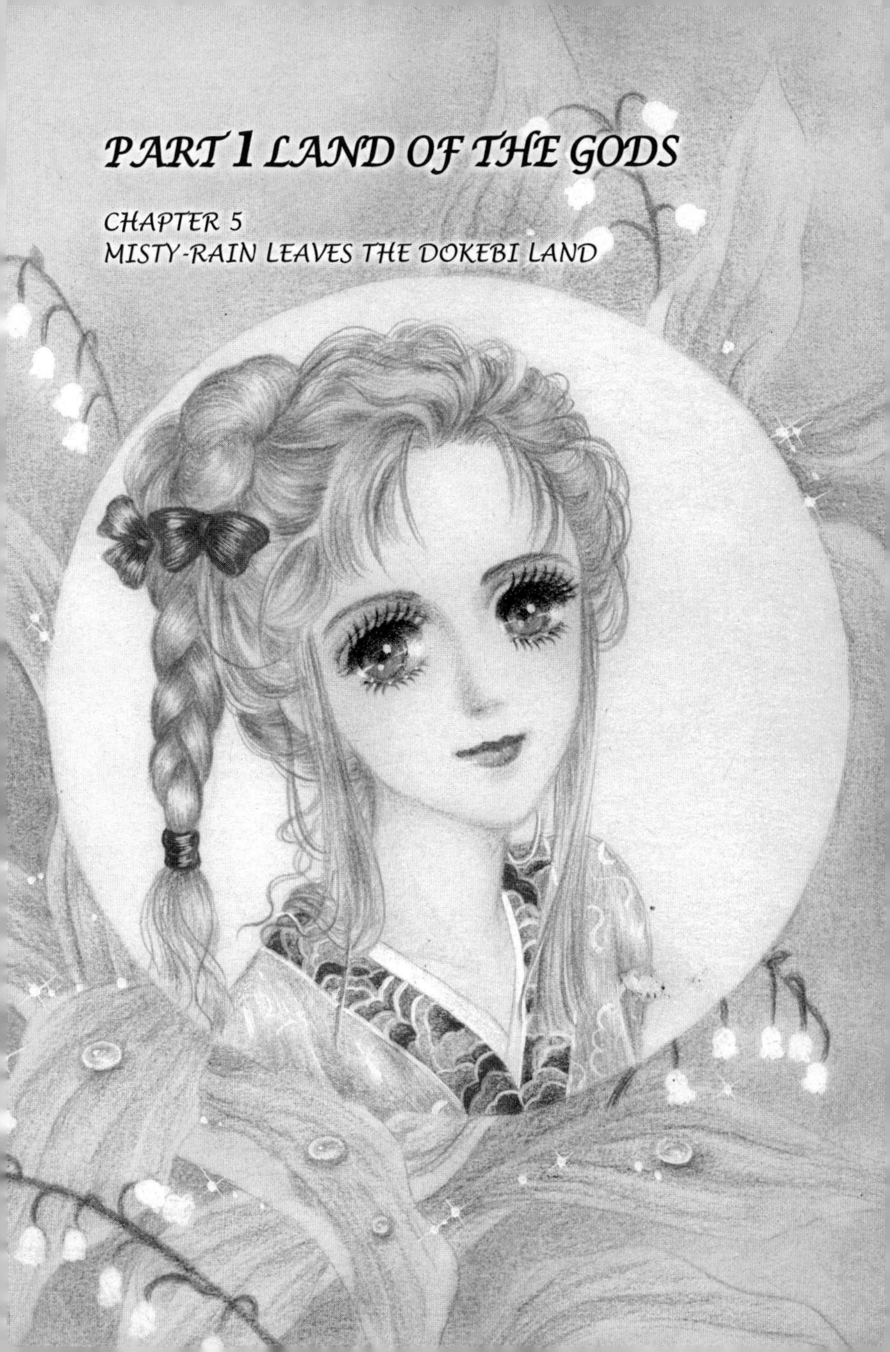

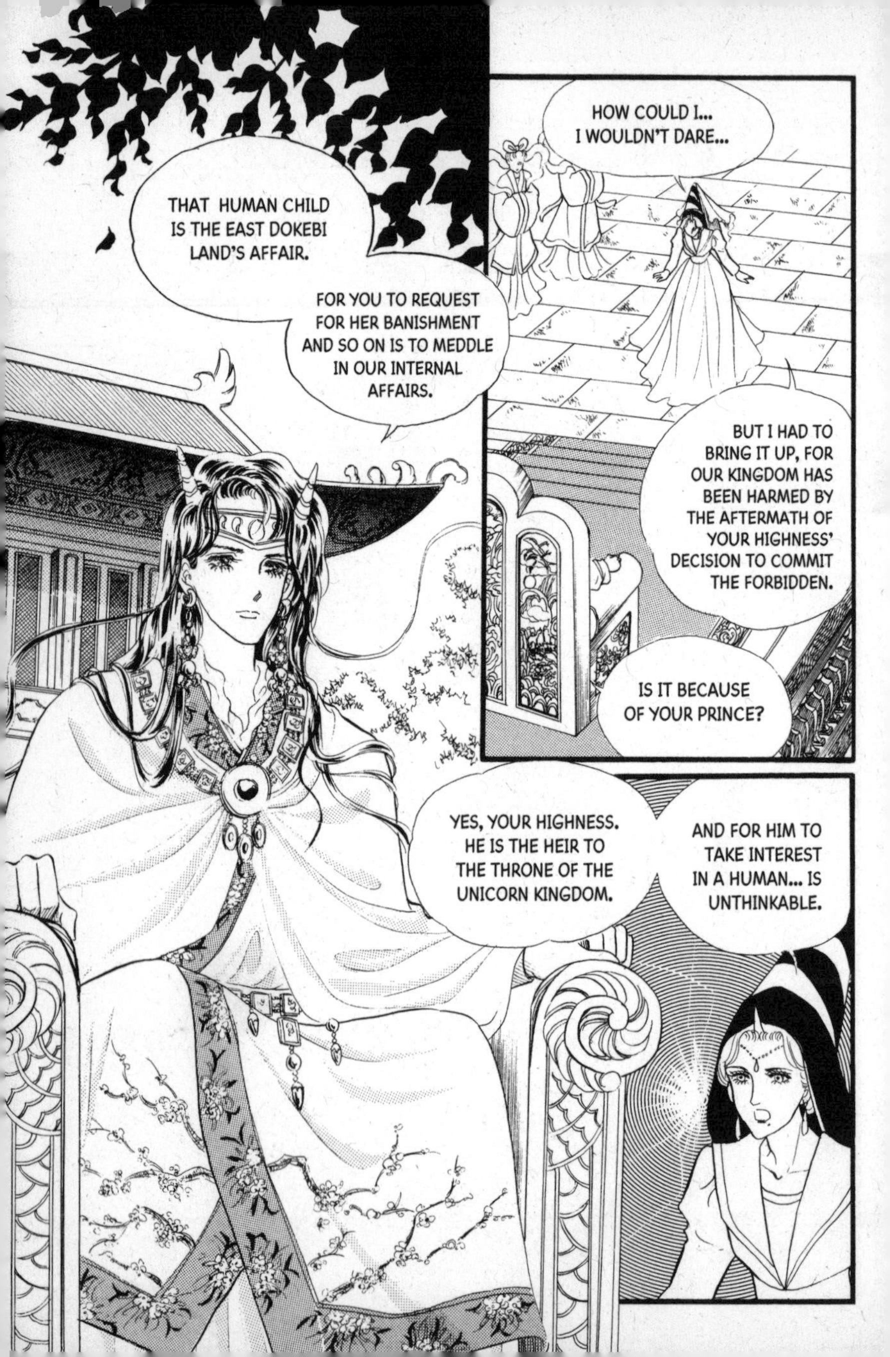
THAT HUMAN CHILD IS THE EAST DOKEBI LAND'S AFFAIR.
FOR YOU TO REQUEST FOR HER BANISHMENT AND SO ON IS TO MEDDLE IN OUR INTERNAL AFFAIRS.
HOW COULD I... I WOULDN'T DARE...
BUT I HAD TO BRING IT UP, FOR OUR KINGDOM HAS BEEN HARMED BY THE AFTERMATH OF YOUR HIGHNESS' DECISION TO COMMIT THE FORBIDDEN.
IS IT BECAUSE OF YOUR PRINCE?
YES, YOUR HIGHNESS. HE IS THE HEIR TO THE THRONE OF THE UNICORN KINGDOM.
AND FOR HIM TO TAKE INTEREST IN A HUMAN... IS UNTHINKABLE.

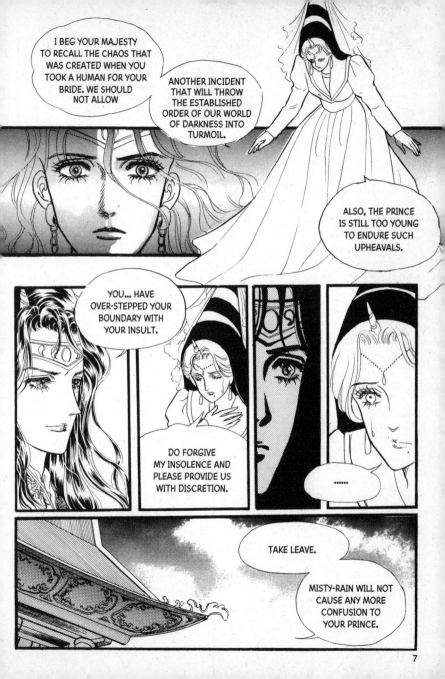

I BEG YOUR MAJESTY TO RECALL THE CHAOS THAT WAS CREATED WHEN YOU TOOK A HUMAN FOR YOUR BRIDE. WE SHOULD NOT ALLOW

ANOTHER INCIDENT THAT WILL THROW THE ESTABLISHED ORDER OF OUR WORLD OF DARKNESS INTO TURMOIL.

ALSO, THE PRINCE IS STILL TOO YOUNG TO ENDURE SUCH UPHEAVALS.

YOU... HAVE OVER-STEPPED YOUR BOUNDARY WITH YOUR INSULT.

DO FORGIVE MY INSOLENCE AND PLEASE PROVIDE US WITH DISCRETION.

......

TAKE LEAVE.

MISTY-RAIN WILL NOT CAUSE ANY MORE CONFUSION TO YOUR PRINCE.

7

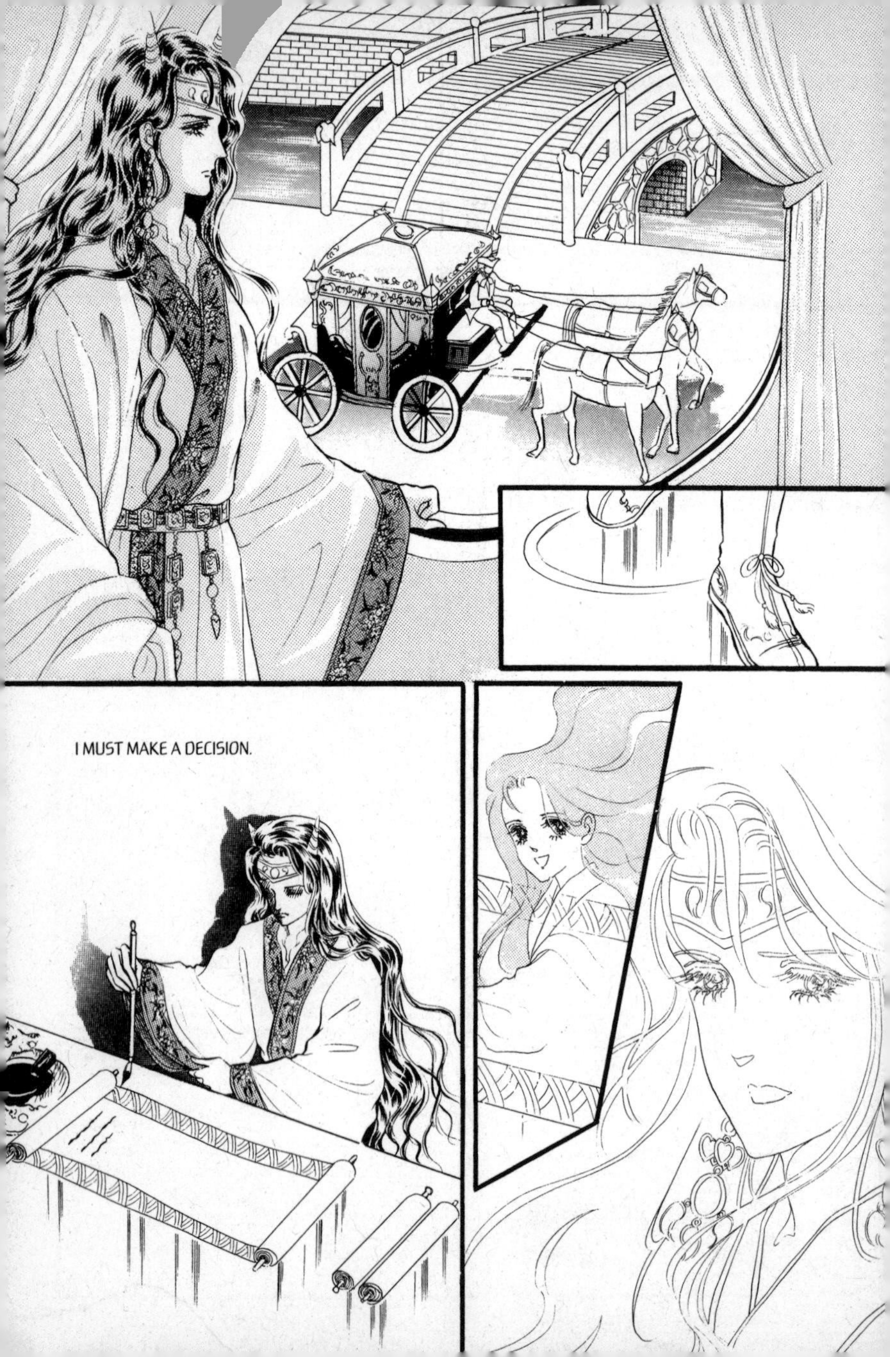
I MUST MAKE A DECISION.

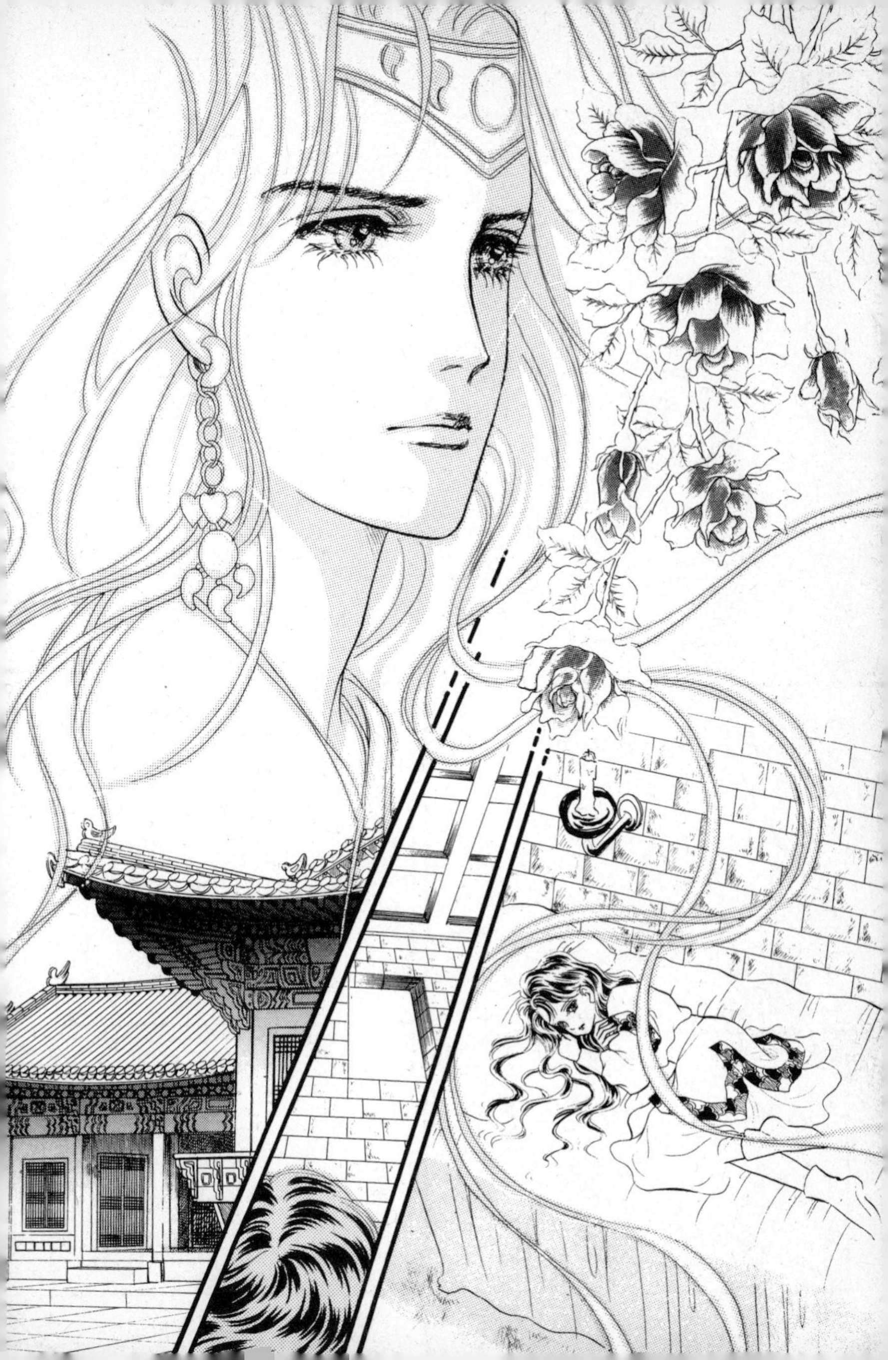

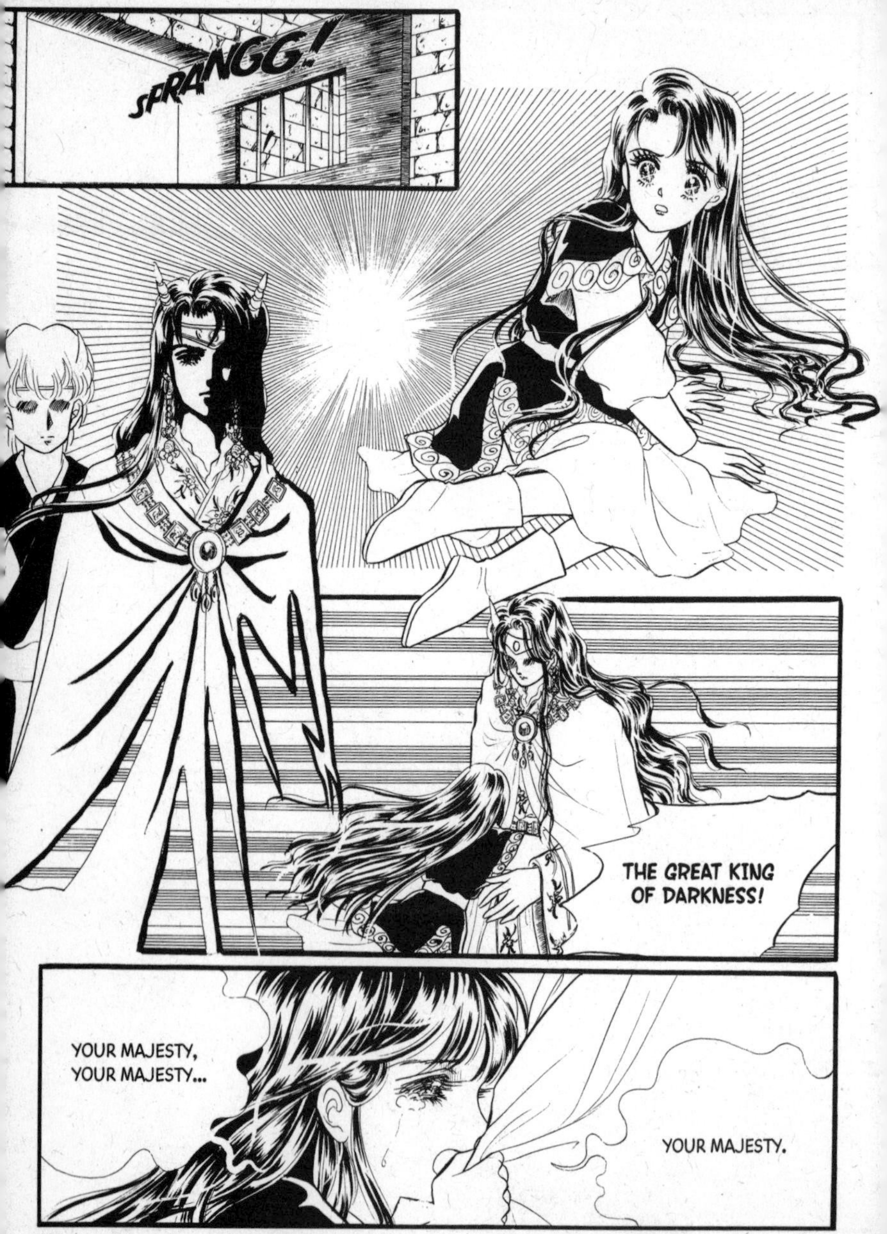
SPRANGG!
THE GREAT KING
OF DARKNESS!
YOUR MAJESTY,
YOUR MAJESTY...
YOUR MAJESTY.

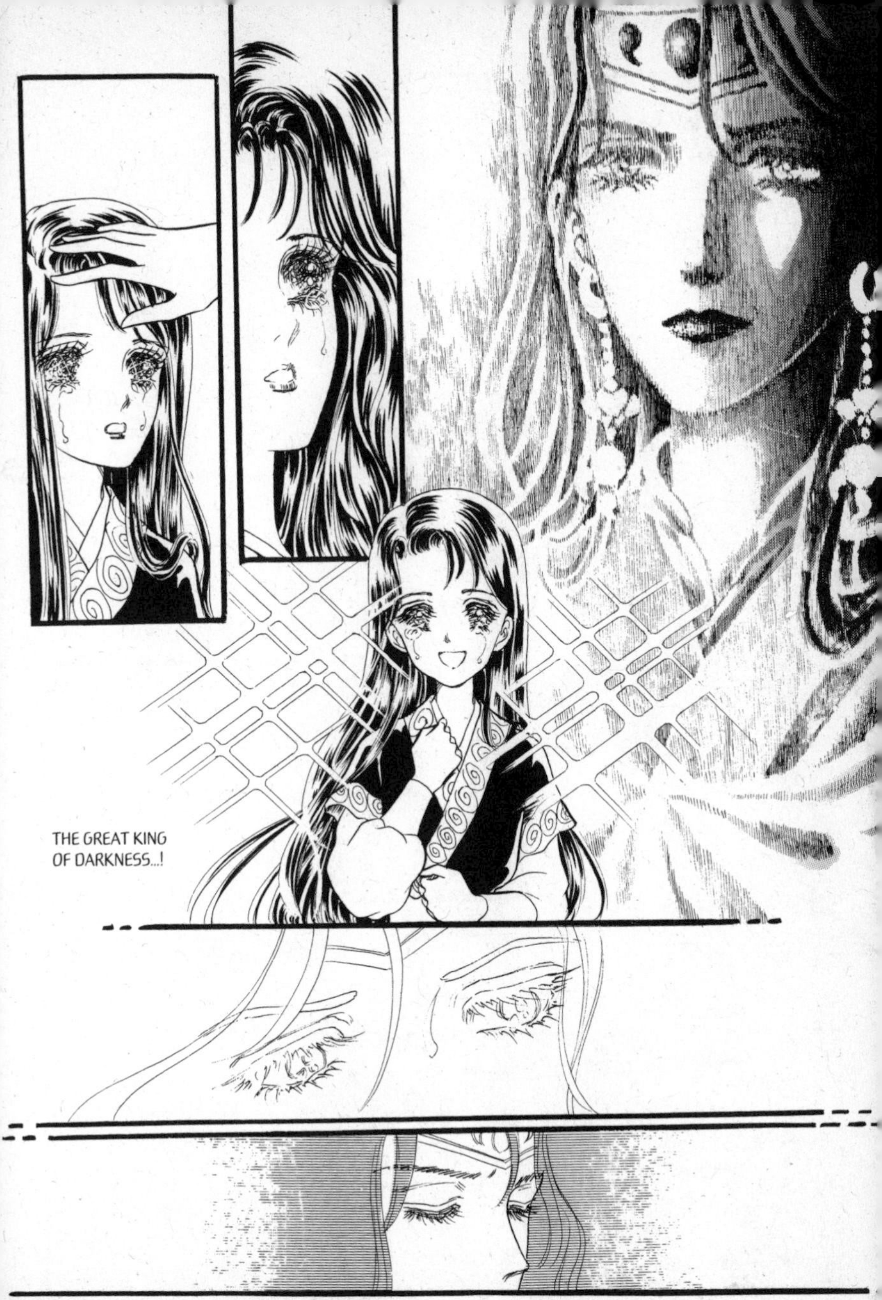
THE GREAT KING
OF DARKNESS...!

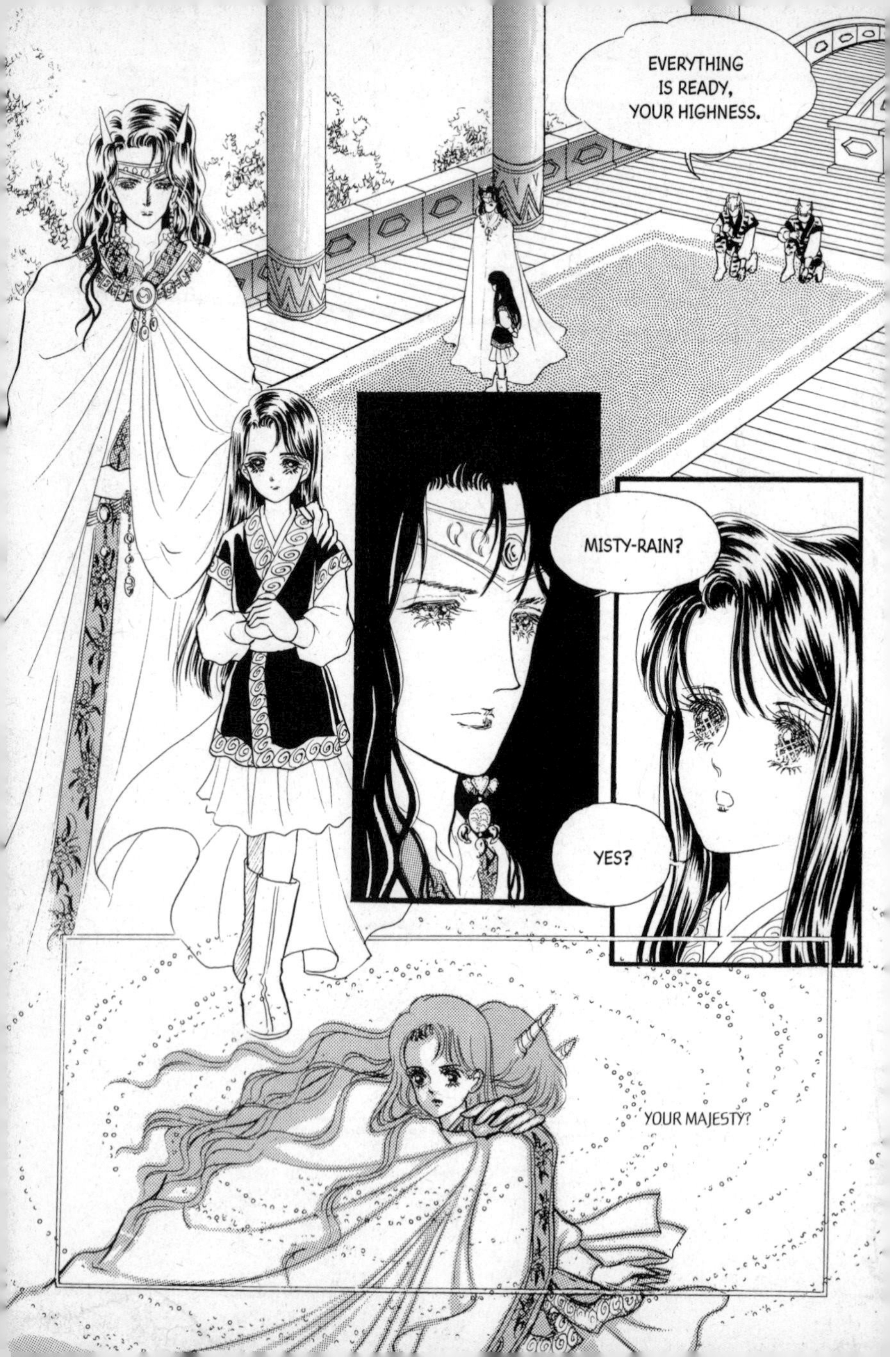
EVERYTHING IS READY, YOUR HIGHNESS.
MISTY-RAIN?
YES?
YOUR MAJESTY?

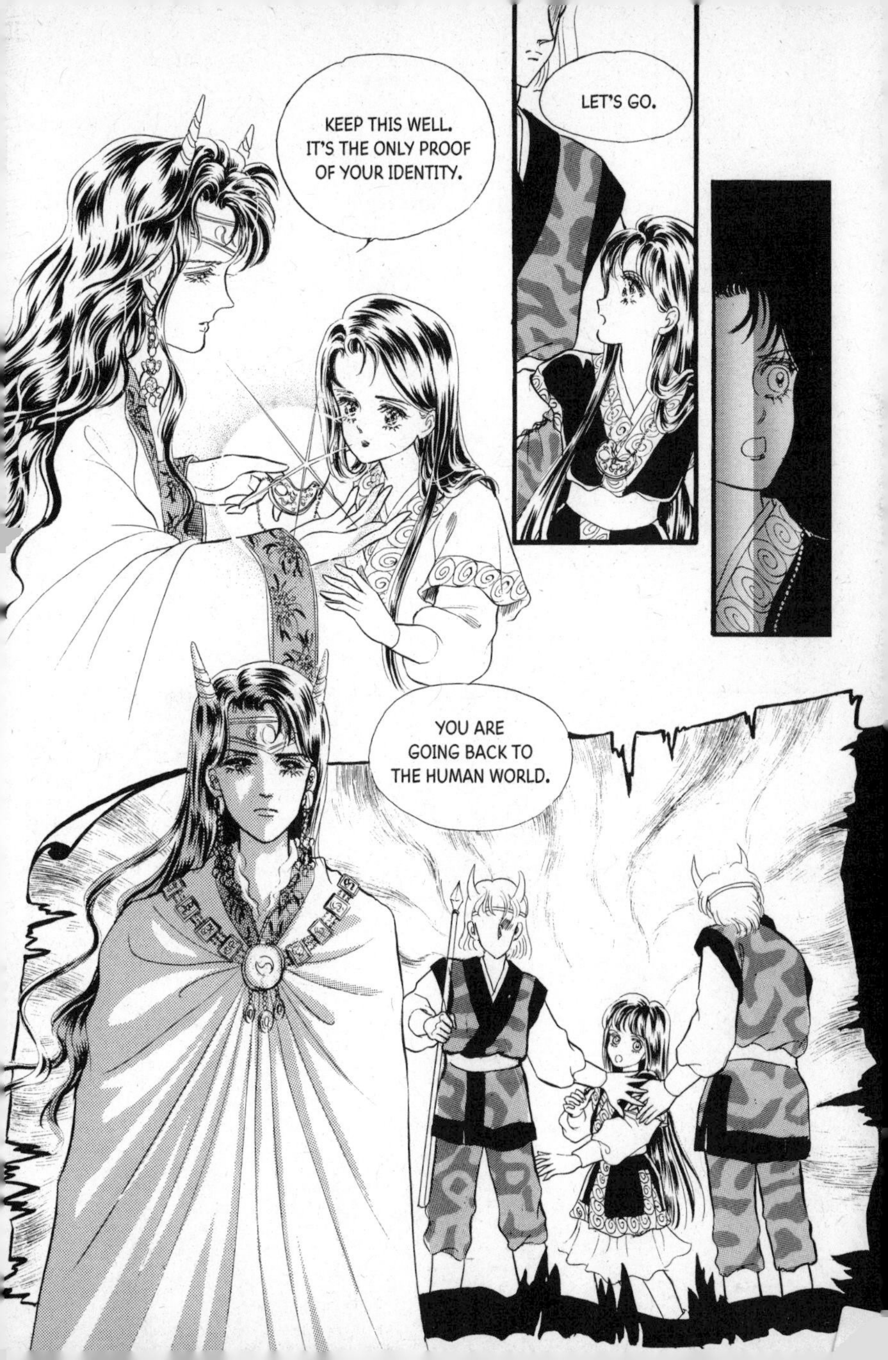
KEEP THIS WELL. IT'S THE ONLY PROOF OF YOUR IDENTITY.
LET'S GO.
YOU ARE GOING BACK TO THE HUMAN WORLD.

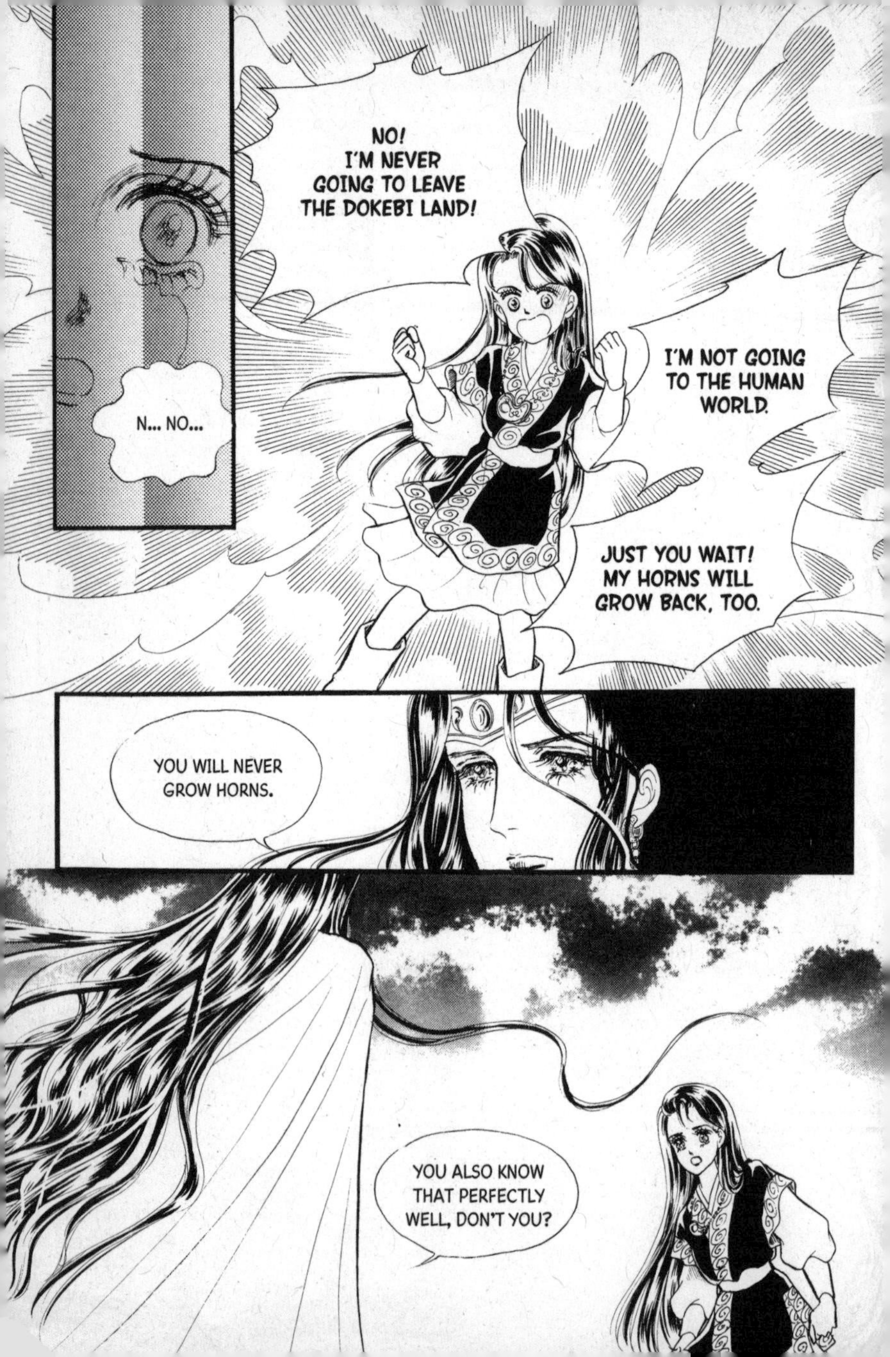
N... NO...
NO! I'M NEVER GOING TO LEAVE THE DOKEBI LAND!
I'M NOT GOING TO THE HUMAN WORLD.
JUST YOU WAIT! MY HORNS WILL GROW BACK, TOO.
YOU WILL NEVER GROW HORNS.
YOU ALSO KNOW THAT PERFECTLY WELL, DON'T YOU?

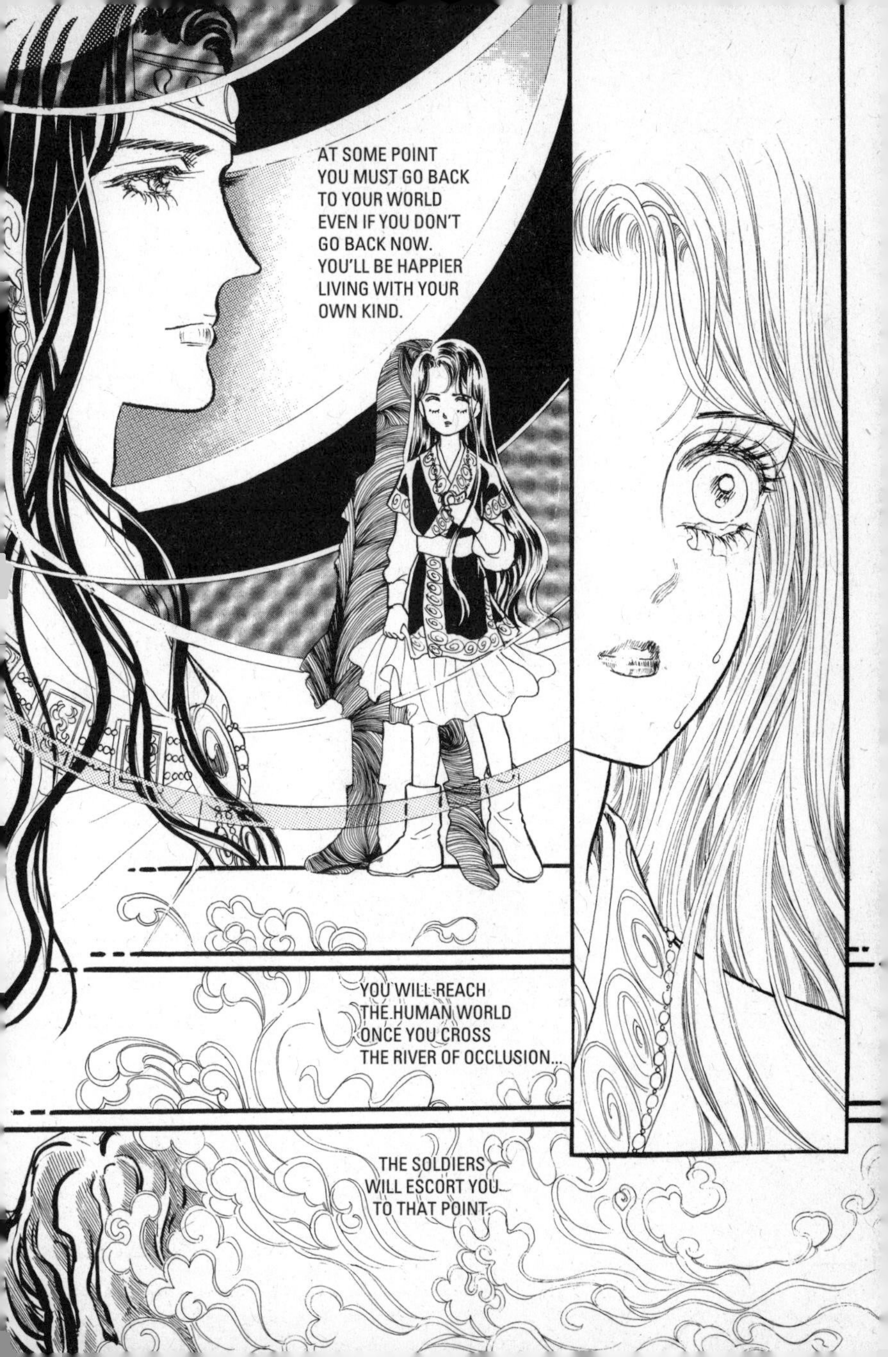
AT SOME POINT YOU MUST GO BACK TO YOUR WORLD EVEN IF YOU DON'T GO BACK NOW. YOU'LL BE HAPPIER LIVING WITH YOUR OWN KIND.
YOU WILL REACH THE HUMAN WORLD ONCE YOU CROSS THE RIVER OF OCCLUSION...
THE SOLDIERS WILL ESCORT YOU TO THAT POINT.

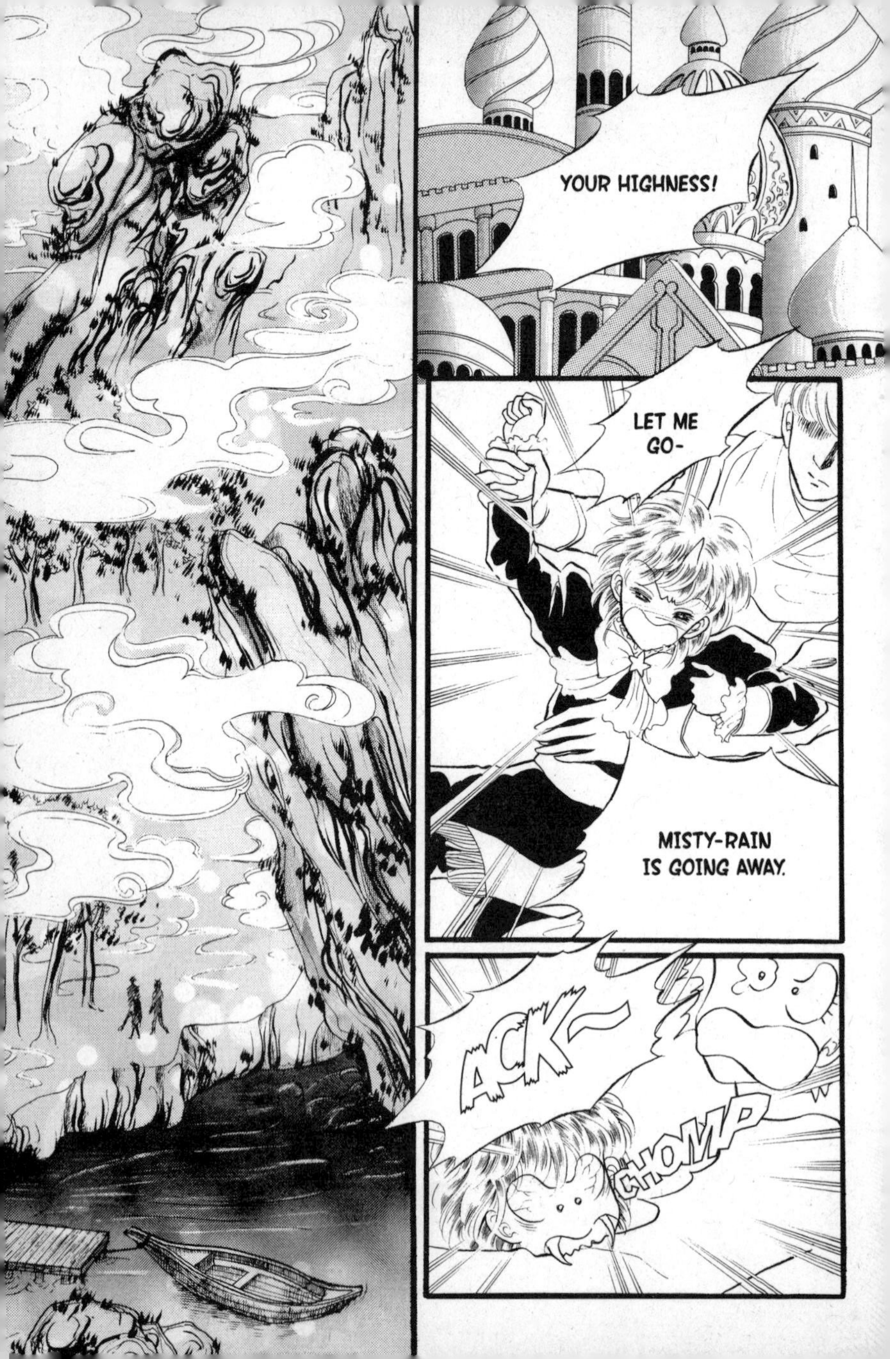
YOUR HIGHNESS!
LET ME GO-
MISTY-RAIN IS GOING AWAY.
ACK~
CHOMP

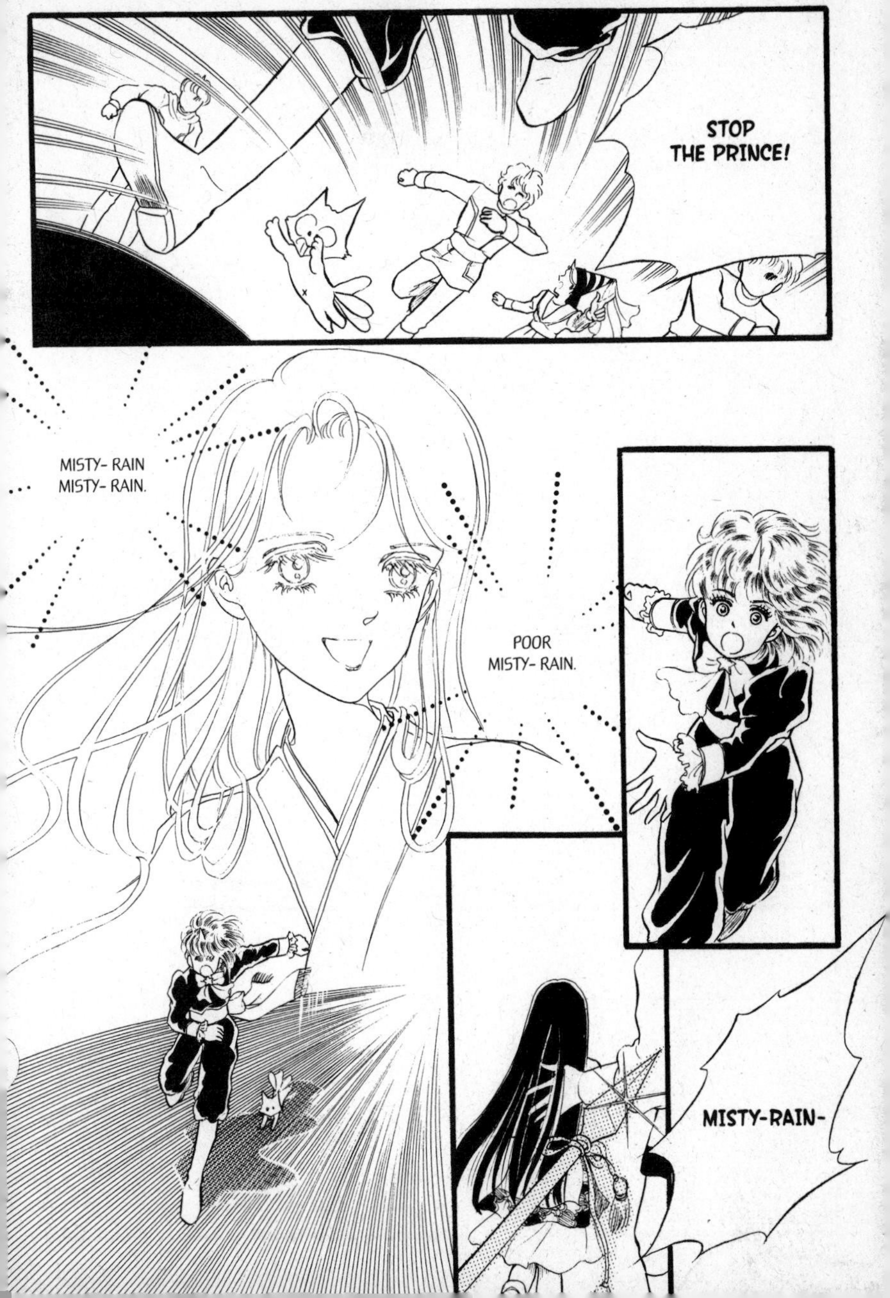
STOP THE PRINCE!
MISTY- RAIN MISTY- RAIN.
POOR MISTY- RAIN.
MISTY-RAIN-

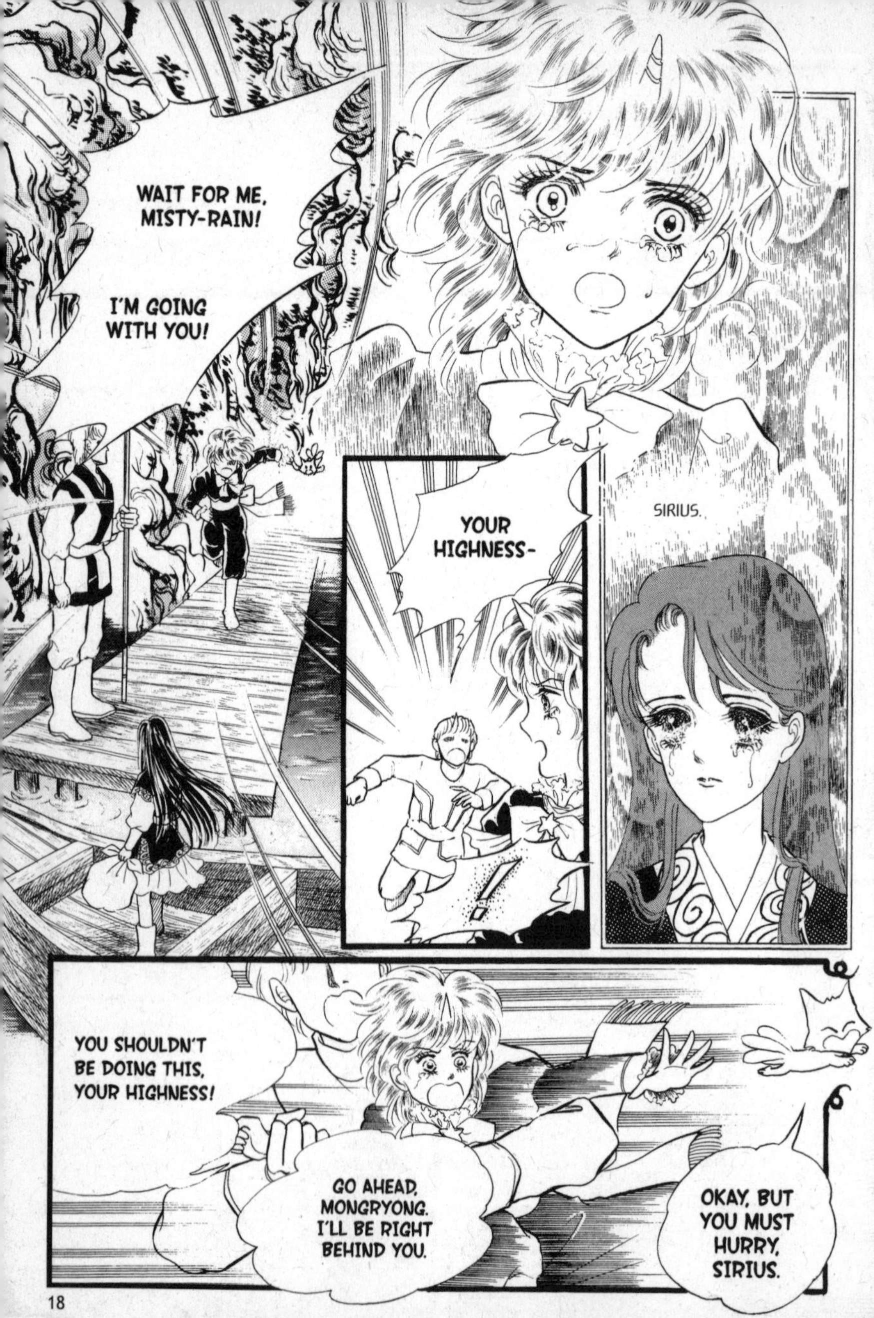
WAIT FOR ME, MISTY-RAIN!
I'M GOING WITH YOU!
YOUR HIGHNESS-
SIRIUS.
YOU SHOULDN'T BE DOING THIS, YOUR HIGHNESS!
GO AHEAD, MONGRYONG. I'LL BE RIGHT BEHIND YOU.
OKAY, BUT YOU MUST HURRY, SIRIUS.

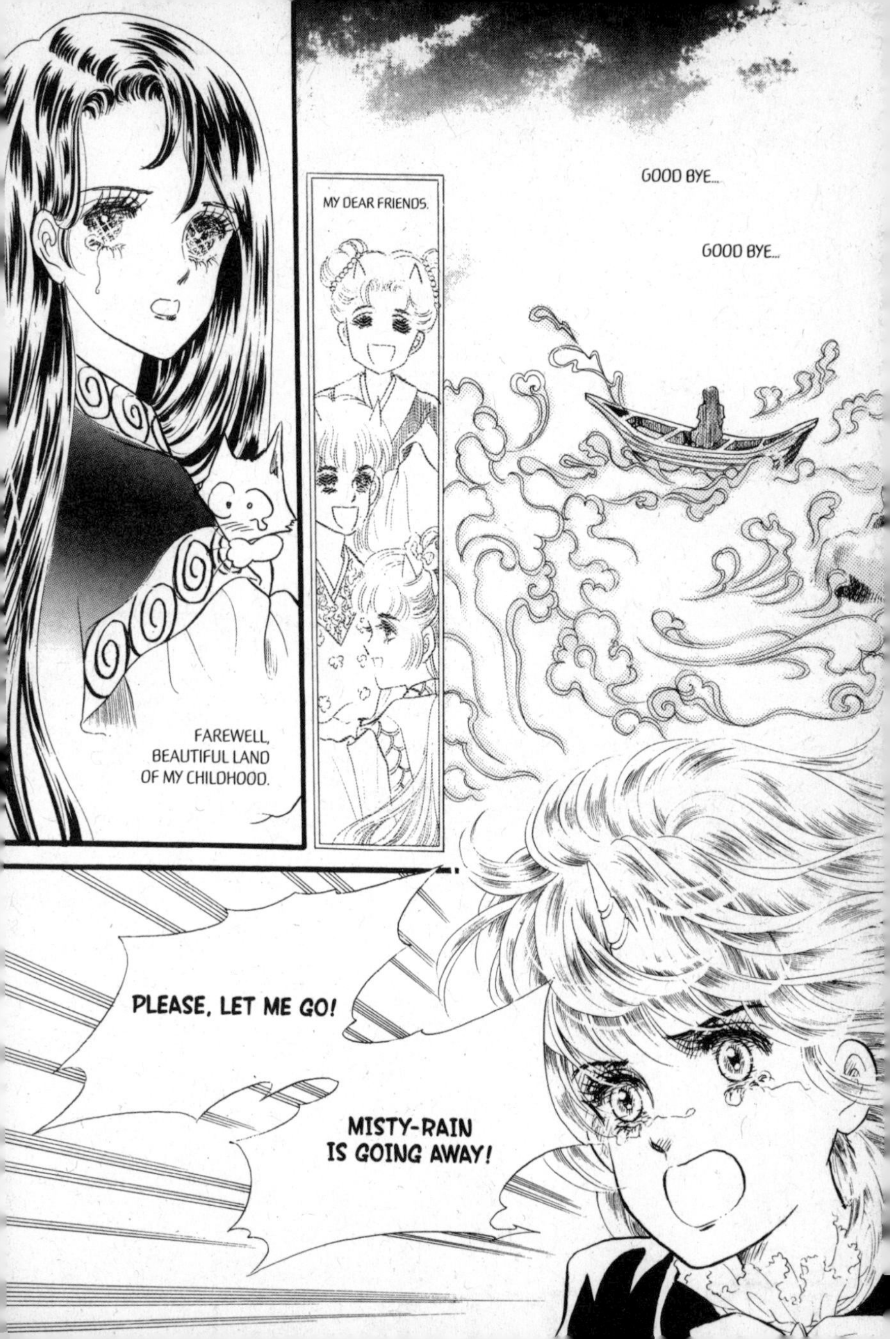
FAREWELL, BEAUTIFUL LAND OF MY CHILDHOOD.
MY DEAR FRIENDS.
GOOD BYE...
GOOD BYE...
PLEASE, LET ME GO!
MISTY-RAIN IS GOING AWAY!

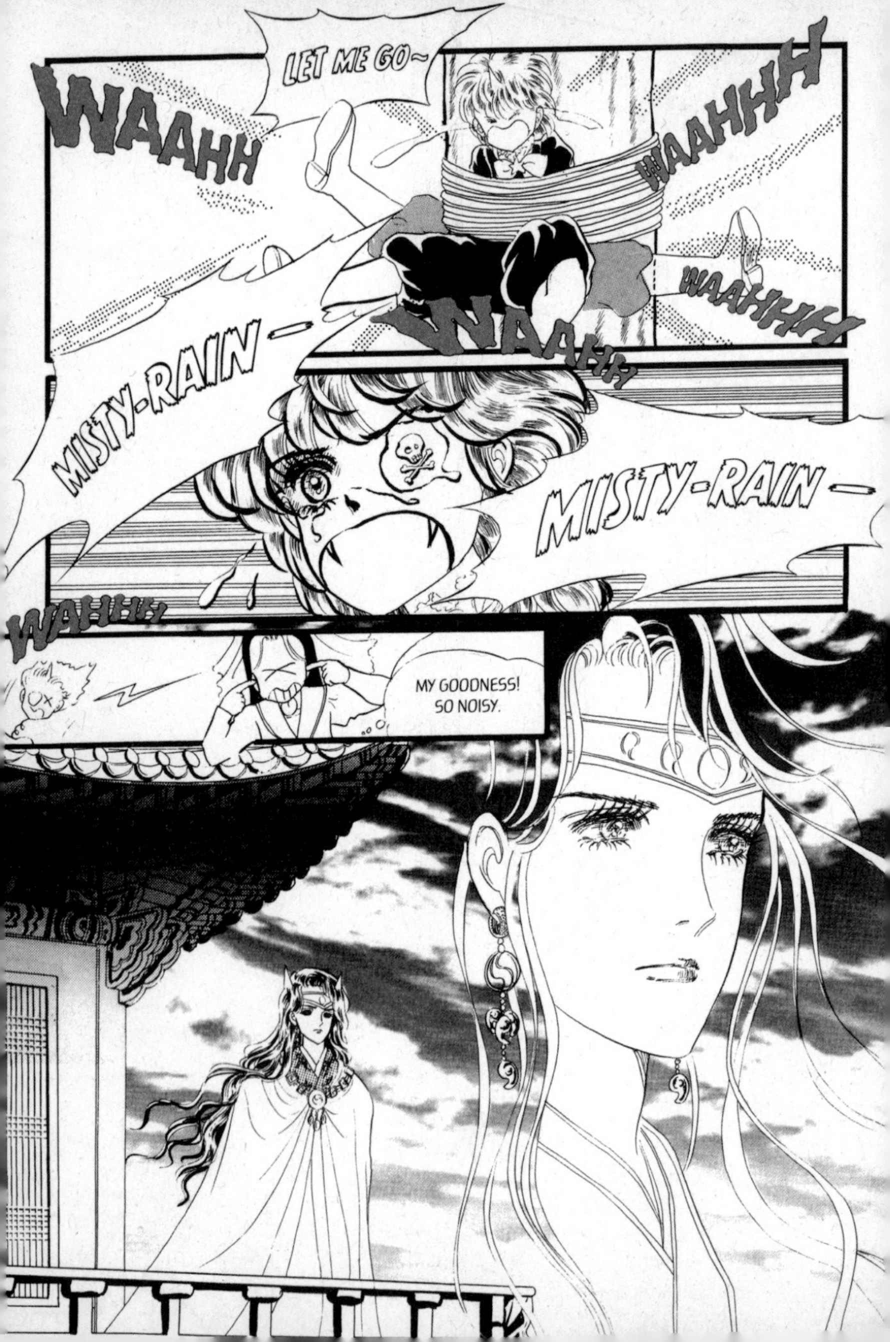

LET ME GO~
WAAHH
WAAHHH
WAAHHH
WAAHH
MISTY-RAIN-
MISTY-RAIN-
WAHHH
MY GOODNESS! SO NOISY.

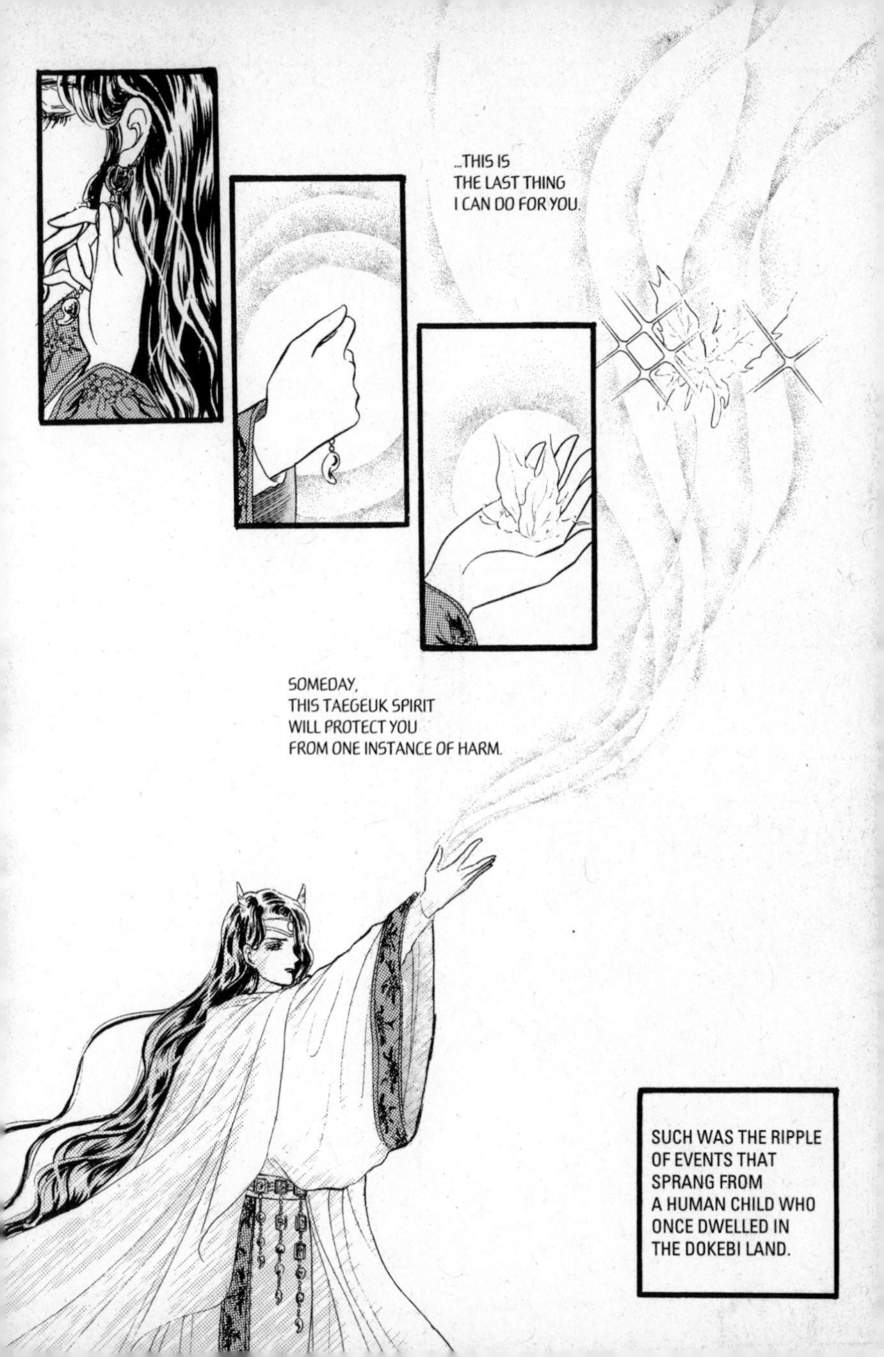
...THIS IS
THE LAST THING
I CAN DO FOR YOU.
SOMEDAY,
THIS TAEGEUK SPIRIT
WILL PROTECT YOU
FROM ONE INSTANCE OF HARM.
SUCH WAS THE RIPPLE
OF EVENTS THAT
SPRANG FROM
A HUMAN CHILD WHO
ONCE DWELLED IN
THE DOKEBI LAND.

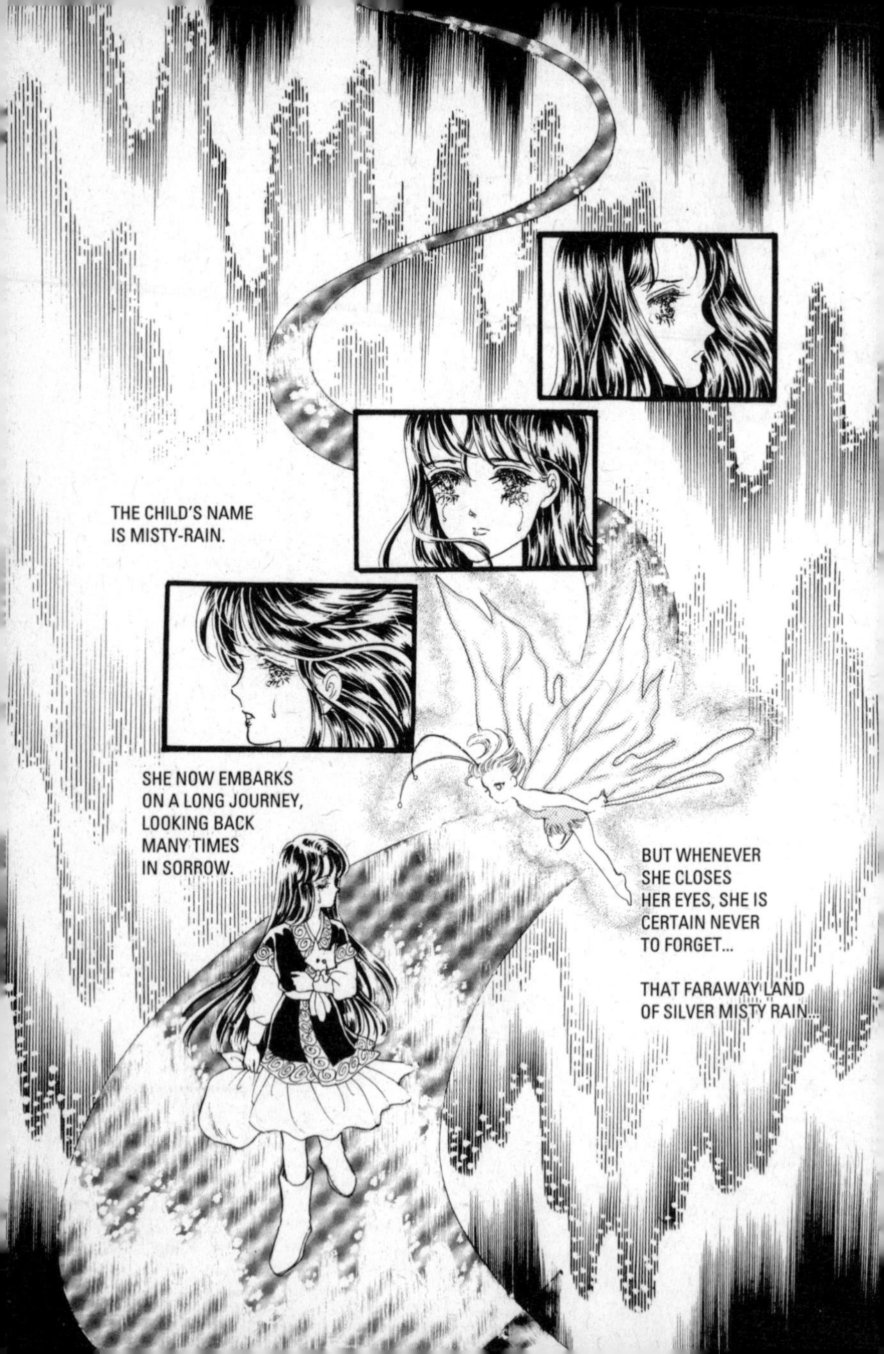
THE CHILD'S NAME IS MISTY-RAIN.
SHE NOW EMBARKS ON A LONG JOURNEY, LOOKING BACK MANY TIMES IN SORROW.
BUT WHENEVER SHE CLOSES HER EYES, SHE IS CERTAIN NEVER TO FORGET...
THAT FARAWAY LAND OF SILVER MISTY RAIN...

PART 1 LAND OF THE GODS

CHAPTER 6
SIRIUS FORGETS MISTY-RAIN

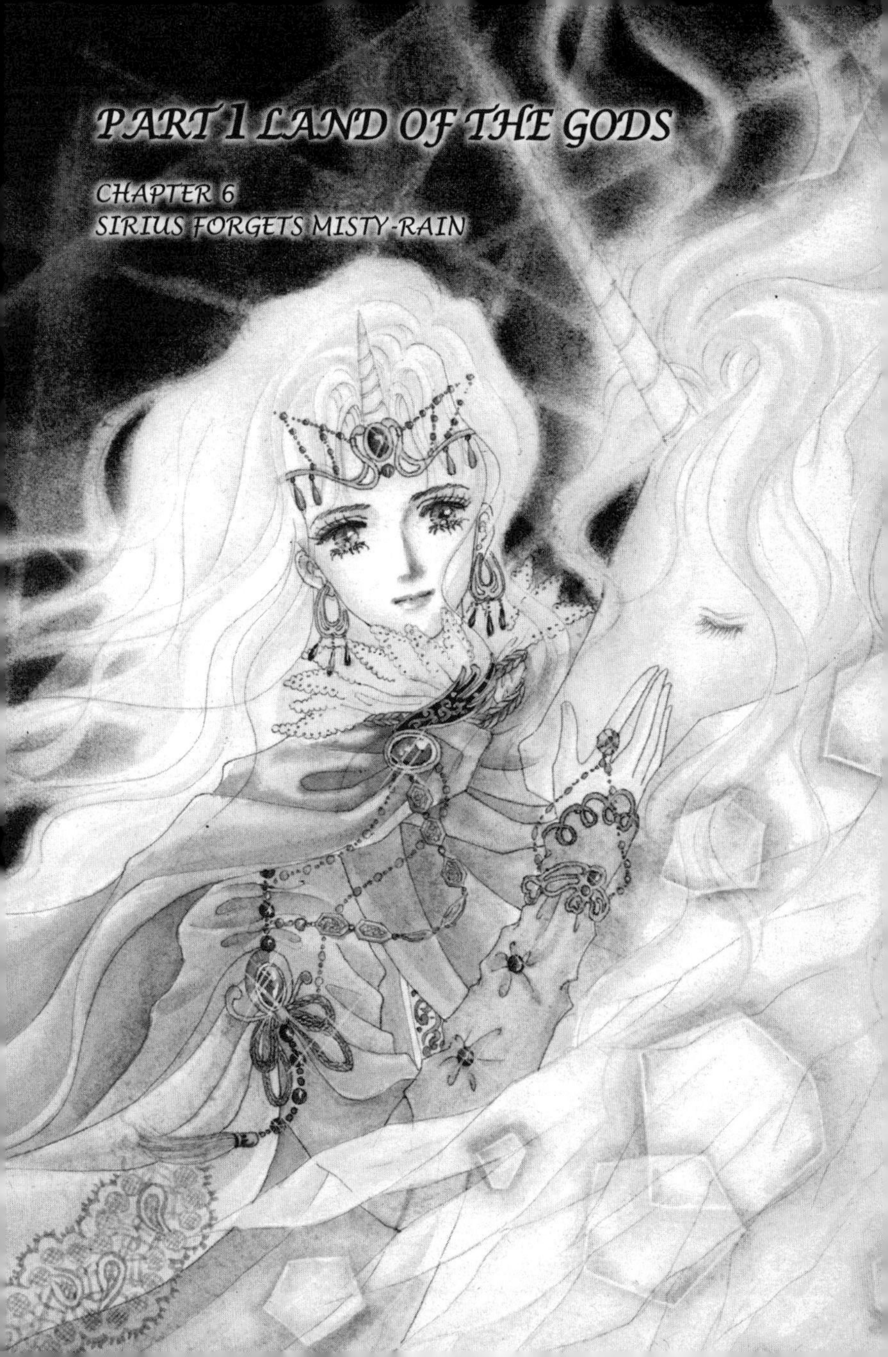

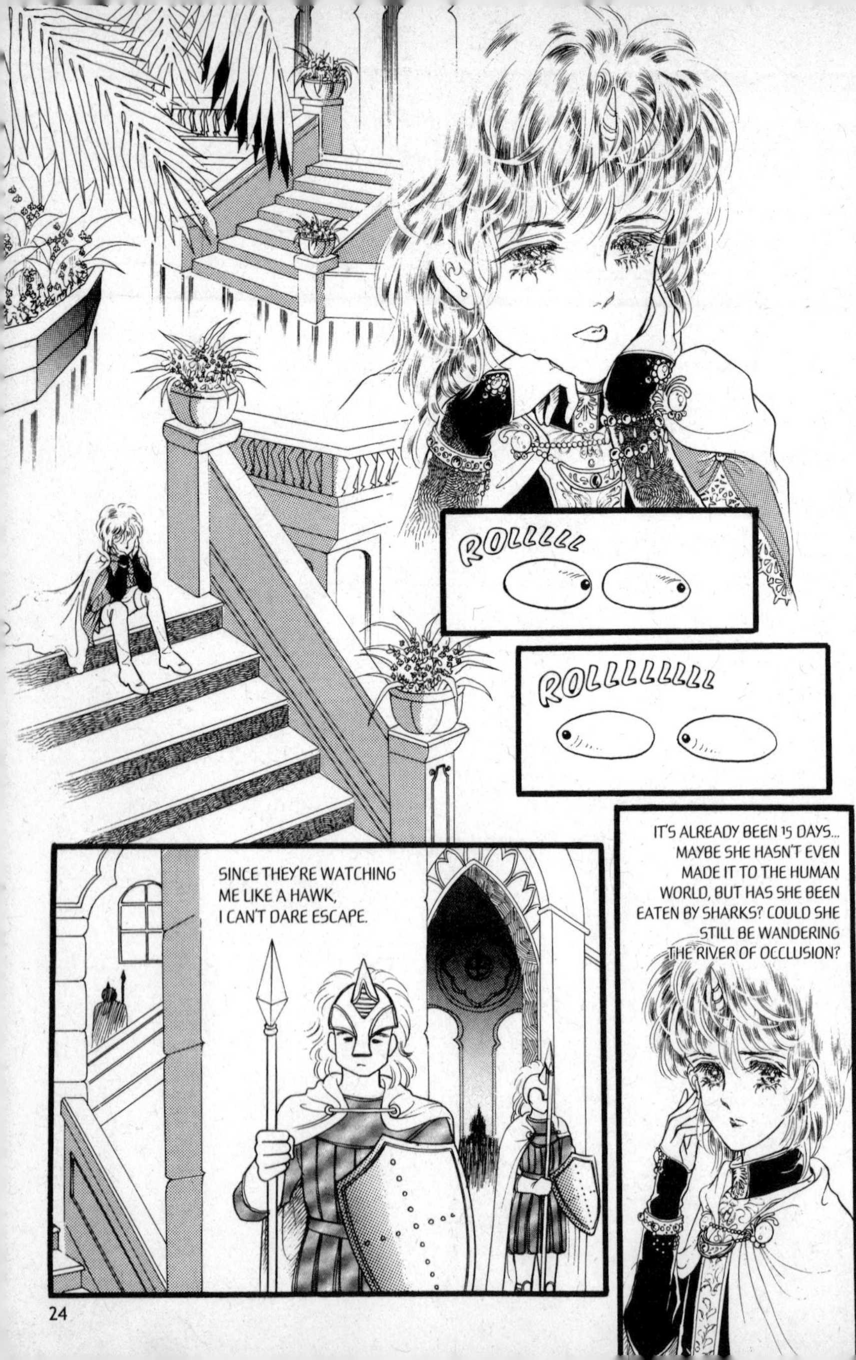

ROLLLLL
ROLLLLLLLL
SINCE THEY'RE WATCHING ME LIKE A HAWK, I CAN'T DARE ESCAPE.
IT'S ALREADY BEEN 15 DAYS... MAYBE SHE HASN'T EVEN MADE IT TO THE HUMAN WORLD, BUT HAS SHE BEEN EATEN BY SHARKS? COULD SHE STILL BE WANDERING THE RIVER OF OCCLUSION?

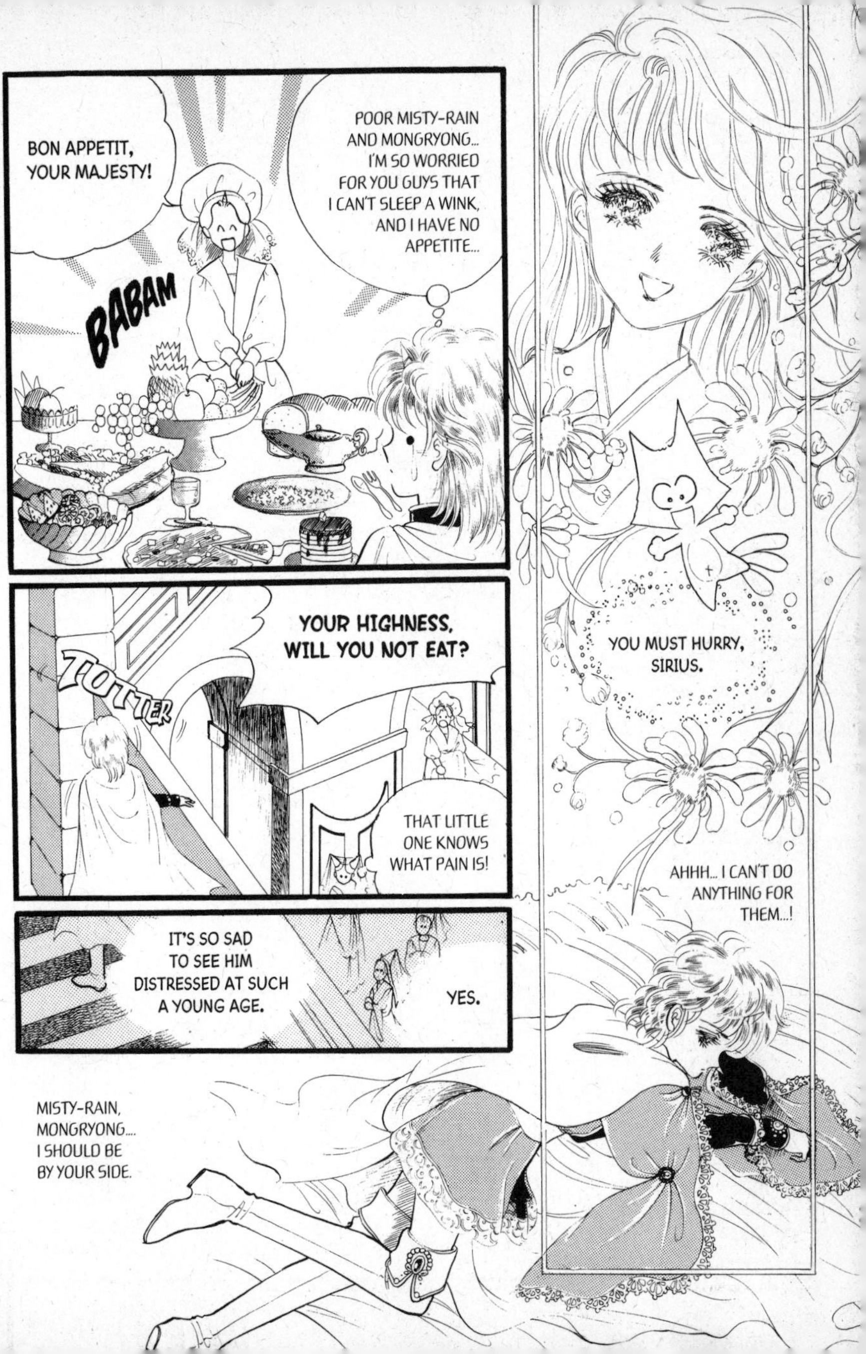
BON APPETIT, YOUR MAJESTY!
POOR MISTY-RAIN AND MONGRYONG... I'M SO WORRIED FOR YOU GUYS THAT I CAN'T SLEEP A WINK, AND I HAVE NO APPETITE...
BABAM
YOUR HIGHNESS, WILL YOU NOT EAT?
TOTTER
THAT LITTLE ONE KNOWS WHAT PAIN IS!
IT'S SO SAD TO SEE HIM DISTRESSED AT SUCH A YOUNG AGE.
YES.
YOU MUST HURRY, SIRIUS.
AHHH... I CAN'T DO ANYTHING FOR THEM...!
MISTY-RAIN, MONGRYONG.... I SHOULD BE BY YOUR SIDE.

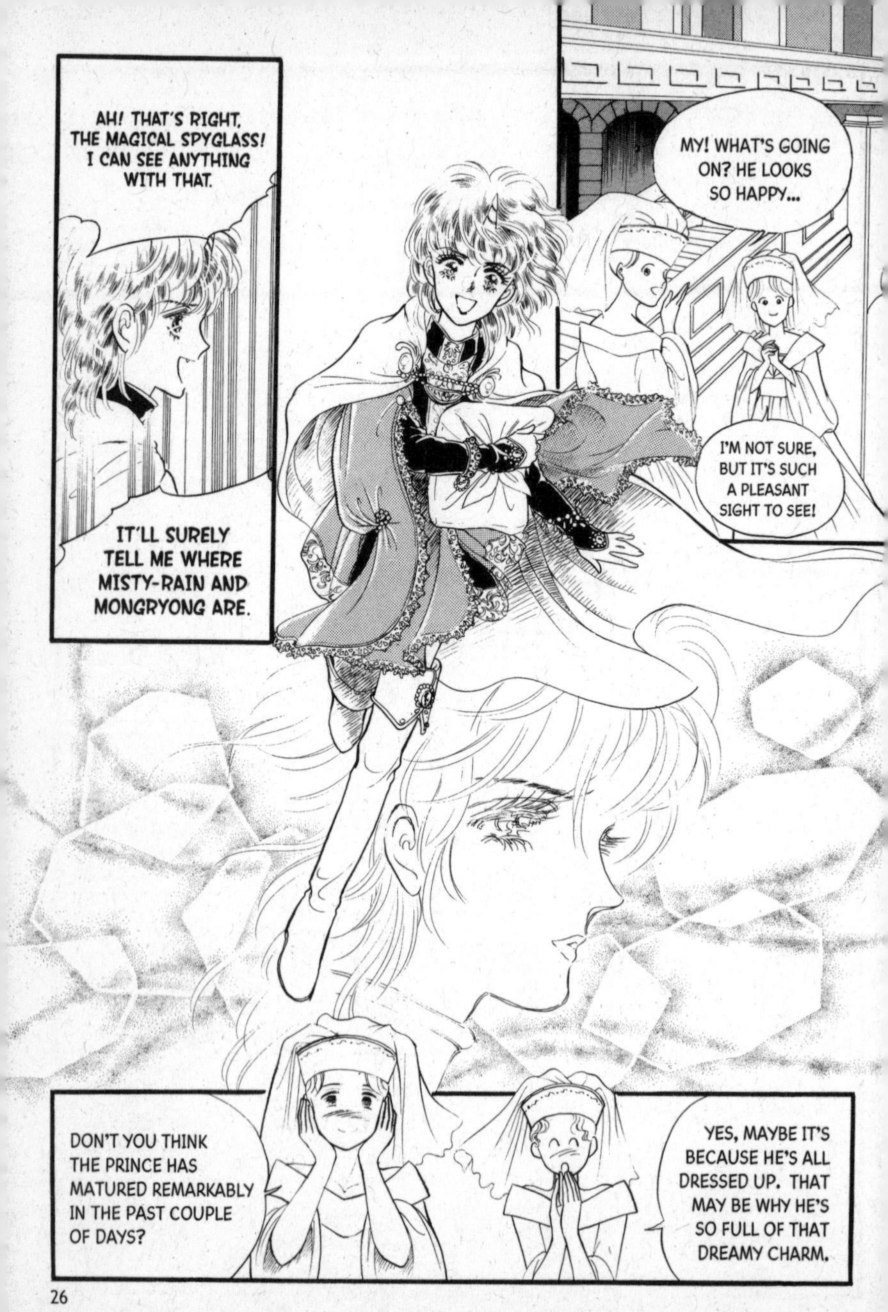
AH! THAT'S RIGHT, THE MAGICAL SPYGLASS! I CAN SEE ANYTHING WITH THAT.
IT'LL SURELY TELL ME WHERE MISTY-RAIN AND MONGRYONG ARE.
MY! WHAT'S GOING ON? HE LOOKS SO HAPPY...
I'M NOT SURE, BUT IT'S SUCH A PLEASANT SIGHT TO SEE!
DON'T YOU THINK THE PRINCE HAS MATURED REMARKABLY IN THE PAST COUPLE OF DAYS?
YES, MAYBE IT'S BECAUSE HE'S ALL DRESSED UP. THAT MAY BE WHY HE'S SO FULL OF THAT DREAMY CHARM.

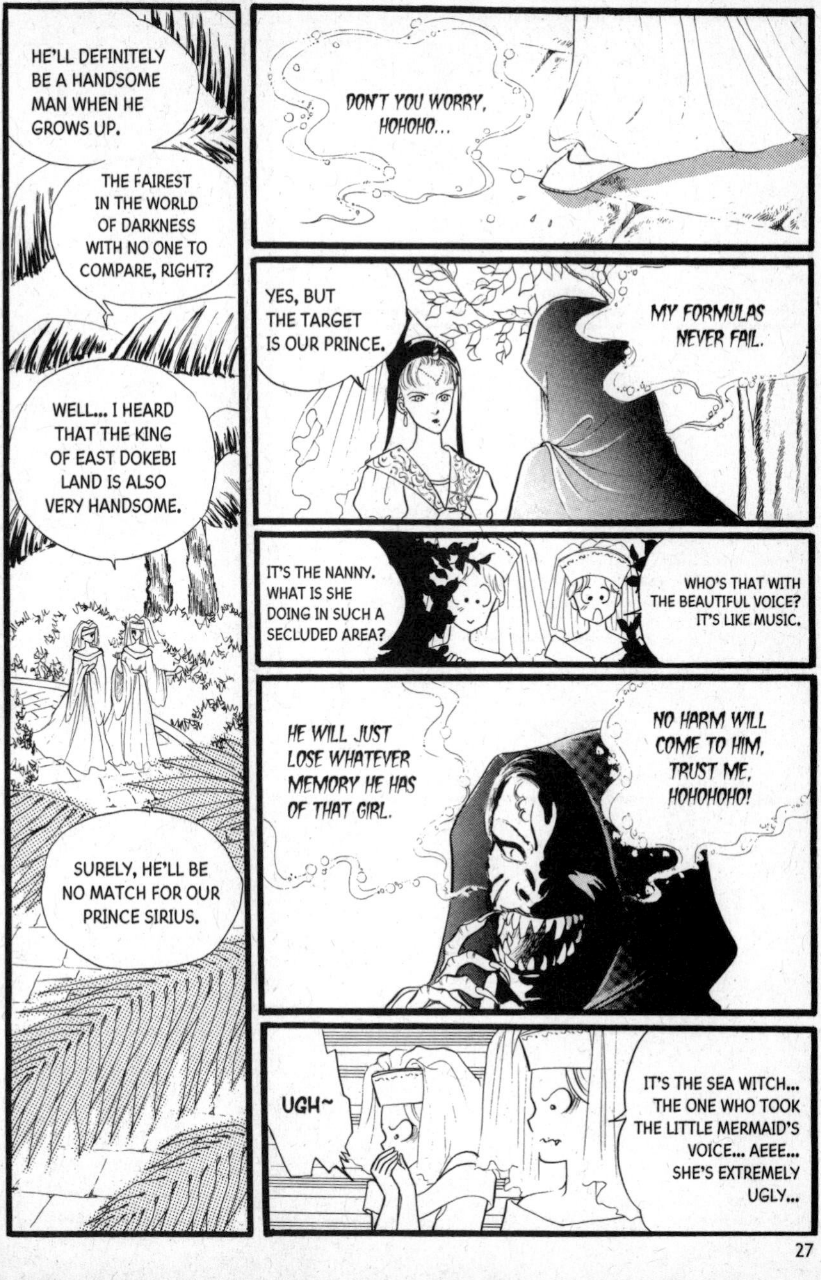
HE'LL DEFINITELY BE A HANDSOME MAN WHEN HE GROWS UP.
THE FAIREST IN THE WORLD OF DARKNESS WITH NO ONE TO COMPARE, RIGHT?
WELL... I HEARD THAT THE KING OF EAST DOKEBI LAND IS ALSO VERY HANDSOME.
SURELY, HE'LL BE NO MATCH FOR OUR PRINCE SIRIUS.
DON'T YOU WORRY, HOHOHO...
YES, BUT THE TARGET IS OUR PRINCE.
MY FORMULAS NEVER FAIL.
IT'S THE NANNY. WHAT IS SHE DOING IN SUCH A SECLUDED AREA?
WHO'S THAT WITH THE BEAUTIFUL VOICE? IT'S LIKE MUSIC.
HE WILL JUST LOSE WHATEVER MEMORY HE HAS OF THAT GIRL.
NO HARM WILL COME TO HIM, TRUST ME, HOHOHOHO!
UGH~
IT'S THE SEA WITCH... THE ONE WHO TOOK THE LITTLE MERMAID'S VOICE... AEEE... SHE'S EXTREMELY UGLY...

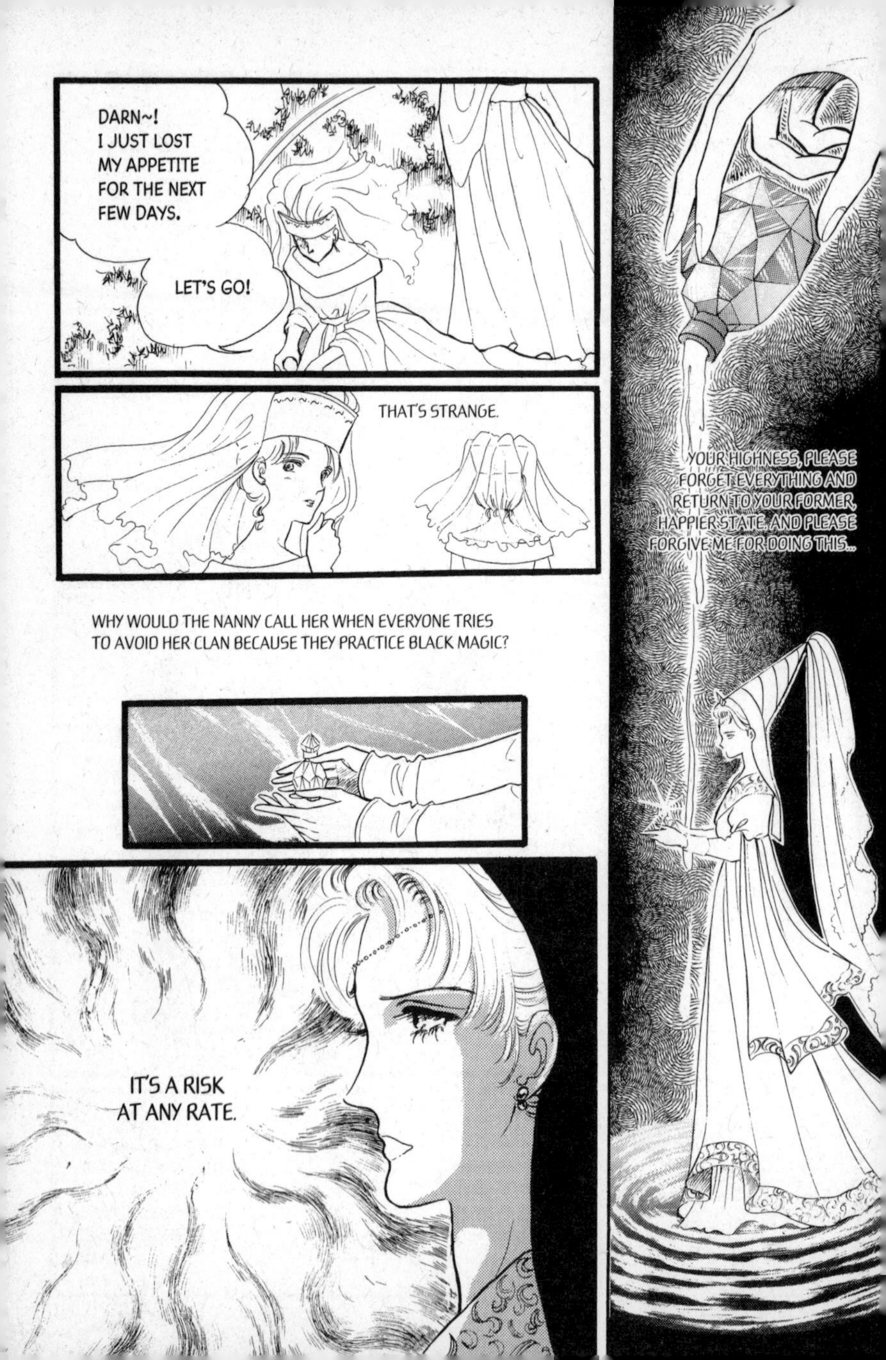
DARN~! I JUST LOST MY APPETITE FOR THE NEXT FEW DAYS.
LET'S GO!
THAT'S STRANGE.
WHY WOULD THE NANNY CALL HER WHEN EVERYONE TRIES TO AVOID HER CLAN BECAUSE THEY PRACTICE BLACK MAGIC?
IT'S A RISK AT ANY RATE.
YOUR HIGHNESS, PLEASE FORGET EVERYTHING AND RETURN TO YOUR FORMER, HAPPIER STATE. AND PLEASE FORGIVE ME FOR DOING THIS...

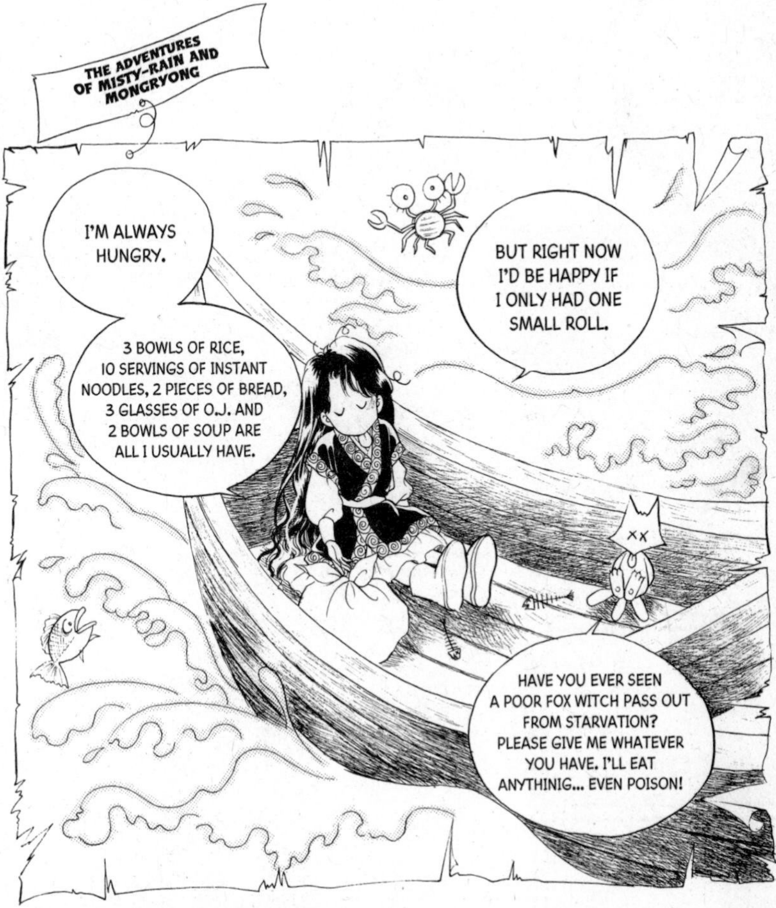
THE ADVENTURES OF MISTY-RAIN AND MONGRYONG
I'M ALWAYS HUNGRY.
3 BOWLS OF RICE, 10 SERVINGS OF INSTANT NOODLES, 2 PIECES OF BREAD, 3 GLASSES OF O.J. AND 2 BOWLS OF SOUP ARE ALL I USUALLY HAVE.
BUT RIGHT NOW I'D BE HAPPY IF I ONLY HAD ONE SMALL ROLL.
HAVE YOU EVER SEEN A POOR FOX WITCH PASS OUT FROM STARVATION? PLEASE GIVE ME WHATEVER YOU HAVE. I'LL EAT ANYTHINIG... EVEN POISON!

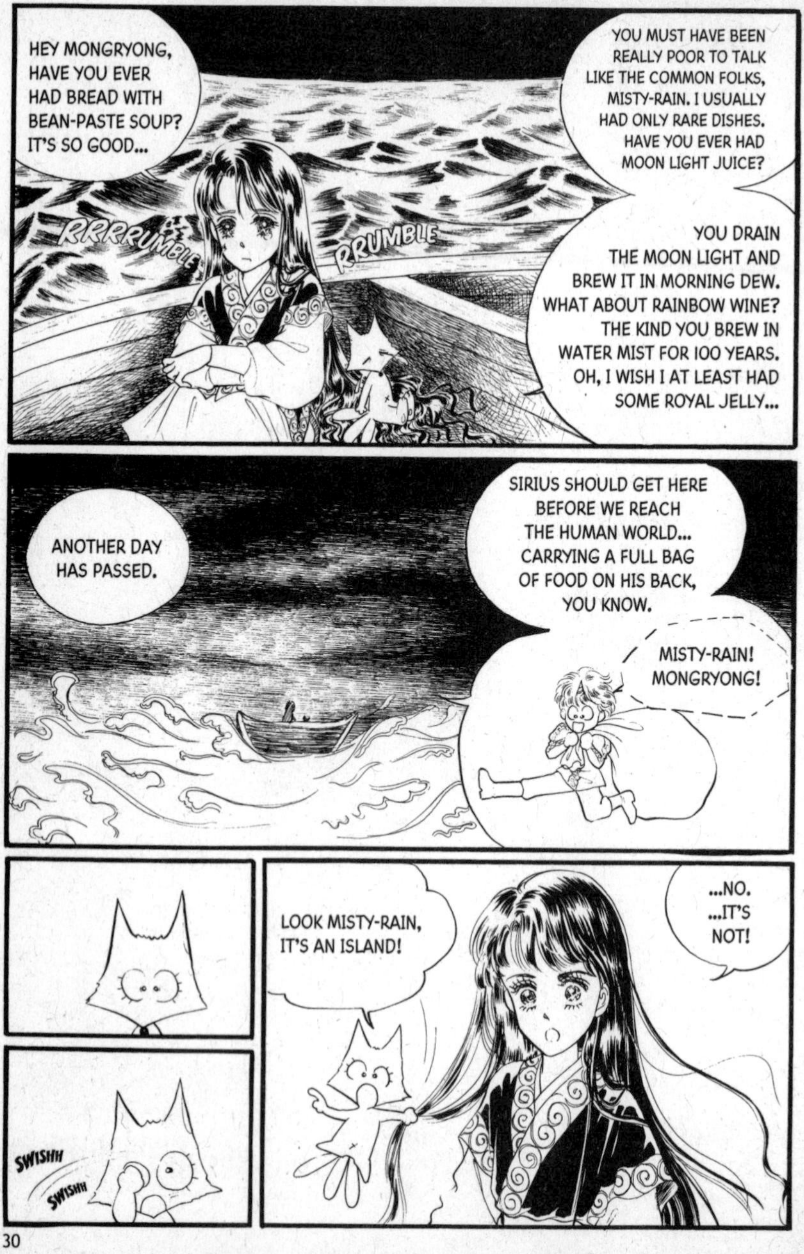
HEY MONGRYONG, HAVE YOU EVER HAD BREAD WITH BEAN-PASTE SOUP? IT'S SO GOOD...
YOU MUST HAVE BEEN REALLY POOR TO TALK LIKE THE COMMON FOLKS, MISTY-RAIN. I USUALLY HAD ONLY RARE DISHES. HAVE YOU EVER HAD MOON LIGHT JUICE?
RRRRUMBLE
RRUMBLE
YOU DRAIN THE MOON LIGHT AND BREW IT IN MORNING DEW. WHAT ABOUT RAINBOW WINE? THE KIND YOU BREW IN WATER MIST FOR 100 YEARS. OH, I WISH I AT LEAST HAD SOME ROYAL JELLY...
ANOTHER DAY HAS PASSED.
SIRIUS SHOULD GET HERE BEFORE WE REACH THE HUMAN WORLD... CARRYING A FULL BAG OF FOOD ON HIS BACK, YOU KNOW.
MISTY-RAIN! MONGRYONG!
SWISHH
SWISHH
LOOK MISTY-RAIN, IT'S AN ISLAND!
...NO. ...IT'S NOT!

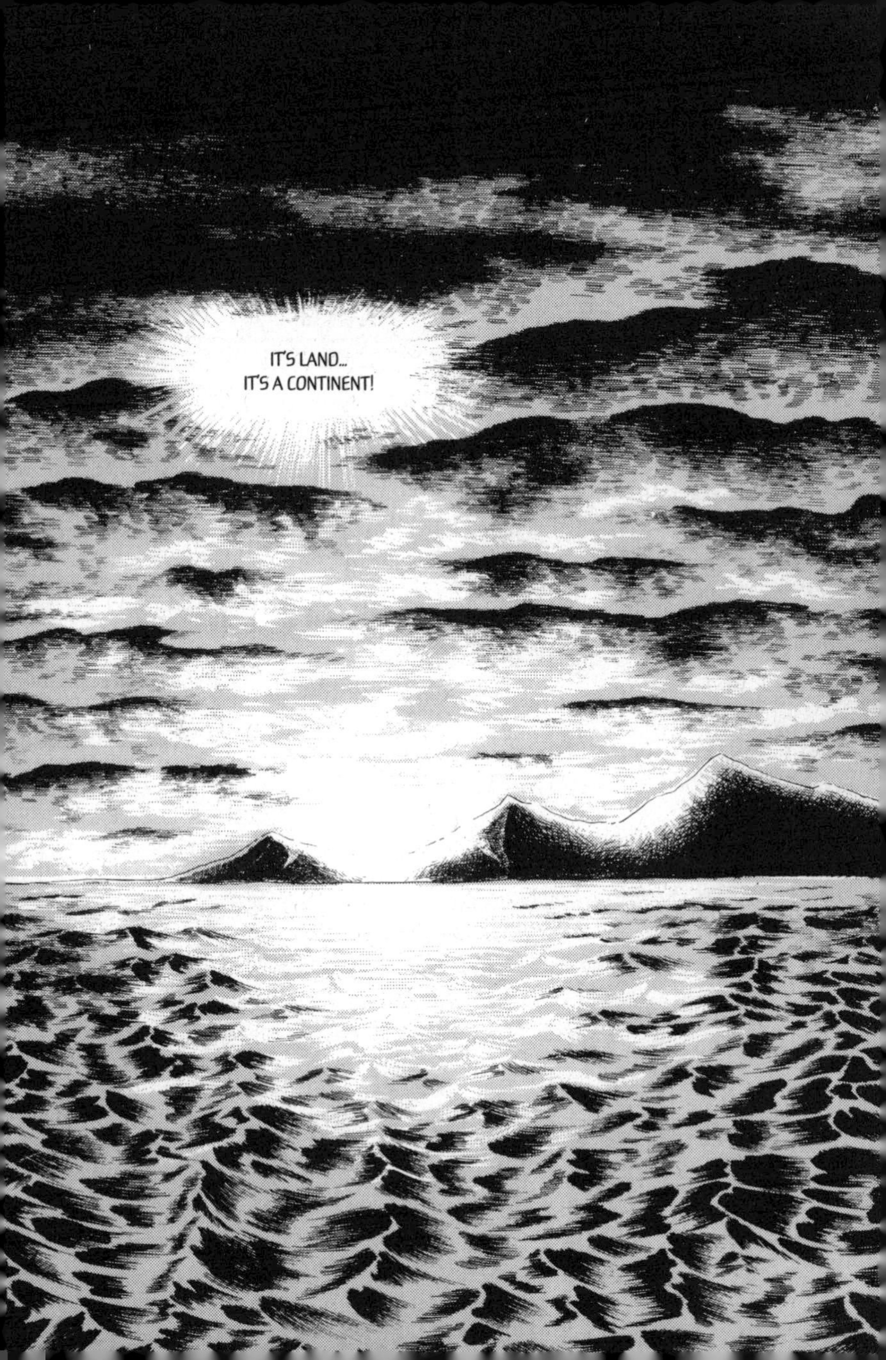
IT'S LAND...
IT'S A CONTINENT!

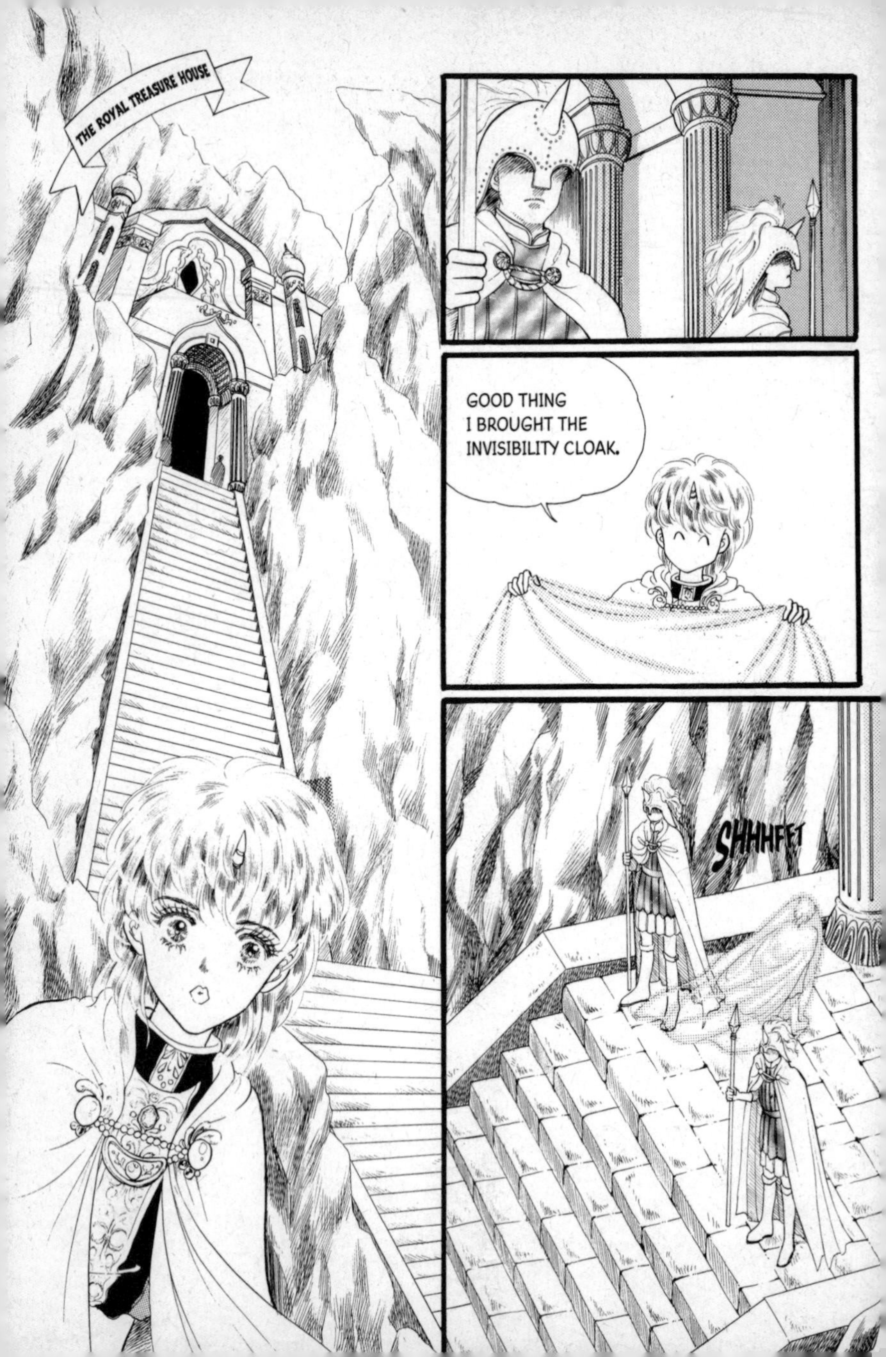
THE ROYAL TREASURE HOUSE
GOOD THING I BROUGHT THE INVISIBILITY CLOAK.
SHHHFFT

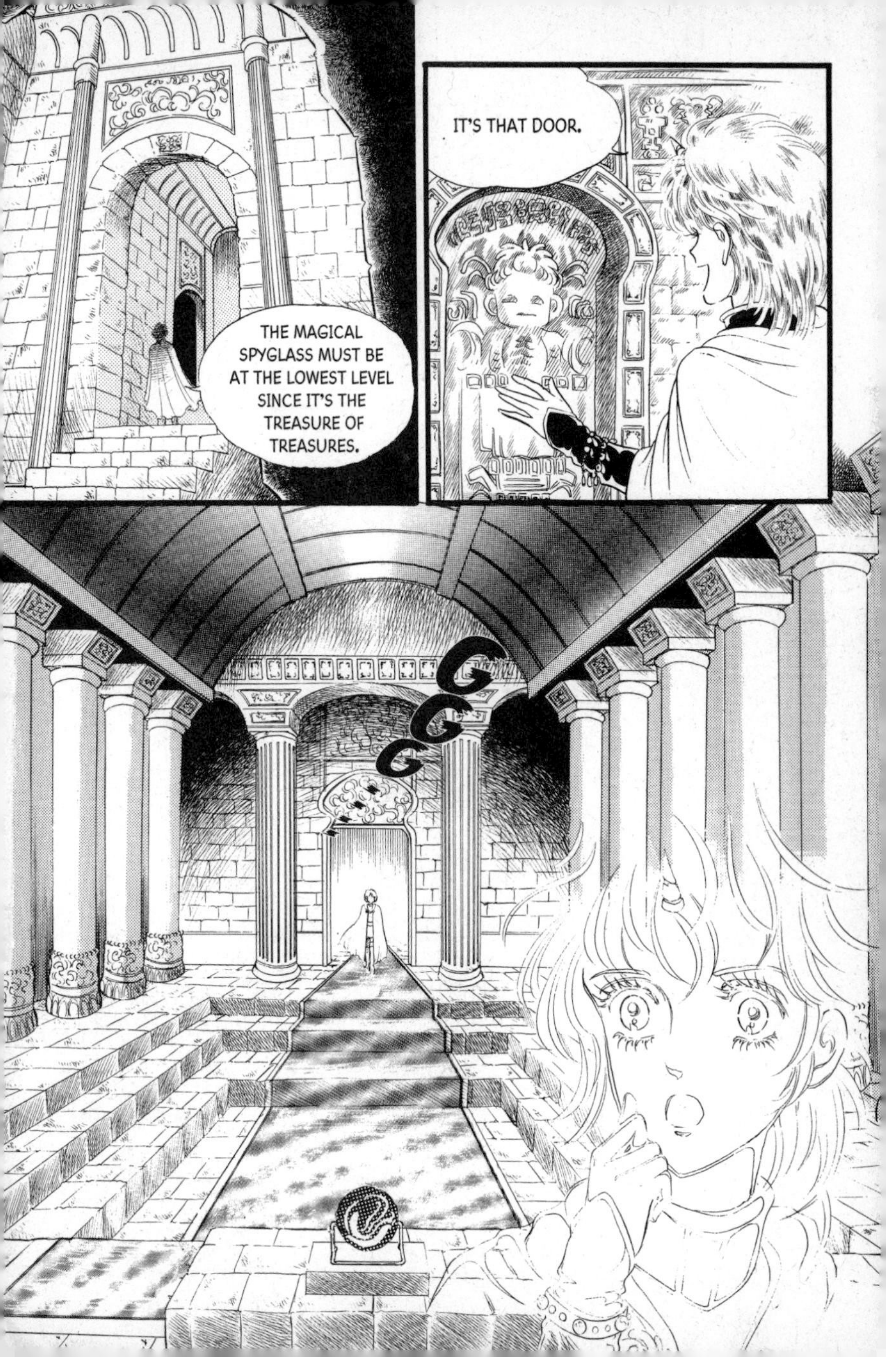
THE MAGICAL SPYGLASS MUST BE AT THE LOWEST LEVEL SINCE IT'S THE TREASURE OF TREASURES.
IT'S THAT DOOR.
GGG

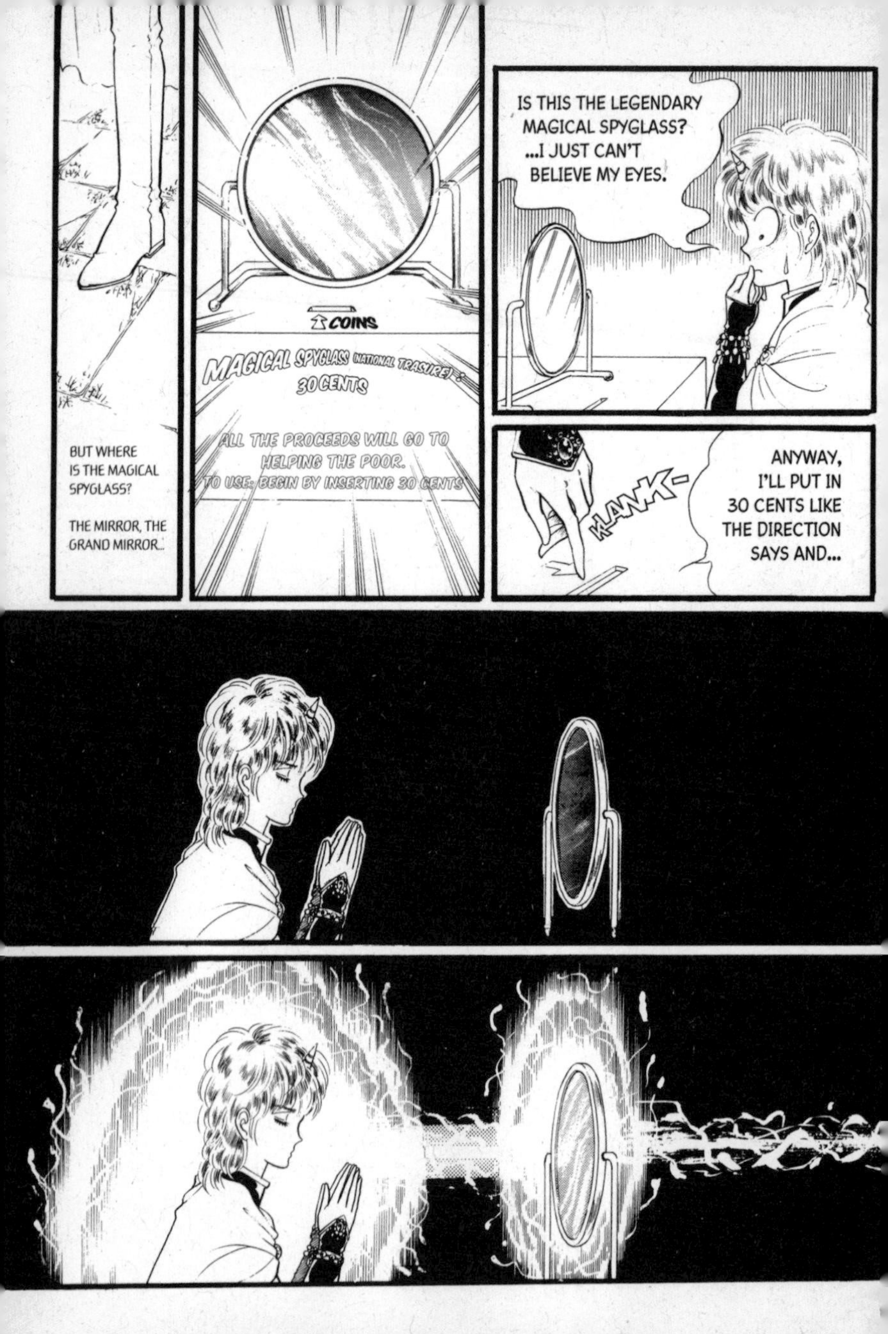
BUT WHERE IS THE MAGICAL SPYGLASS?
THE MIRROR, THE GRAND MIRROR...
COINS
MAGICAL SPYGLASS (NATIONAL TRASURE): 30 CENTS
ALL THE PROCEEDS WILL GO TO HELPING THE POOR.
TO USE: BEGIN BY INSERTING 30 CENTS
IS THIS THE LEGENDARY MAGICAL SPYGLASS? ...I JUST CAN'T BELIEVE MY EYES.
KLANK-
ANYWAY, I'LL PUT IN 30 CENTS LIKE THE DIRECTION SAYS AND...

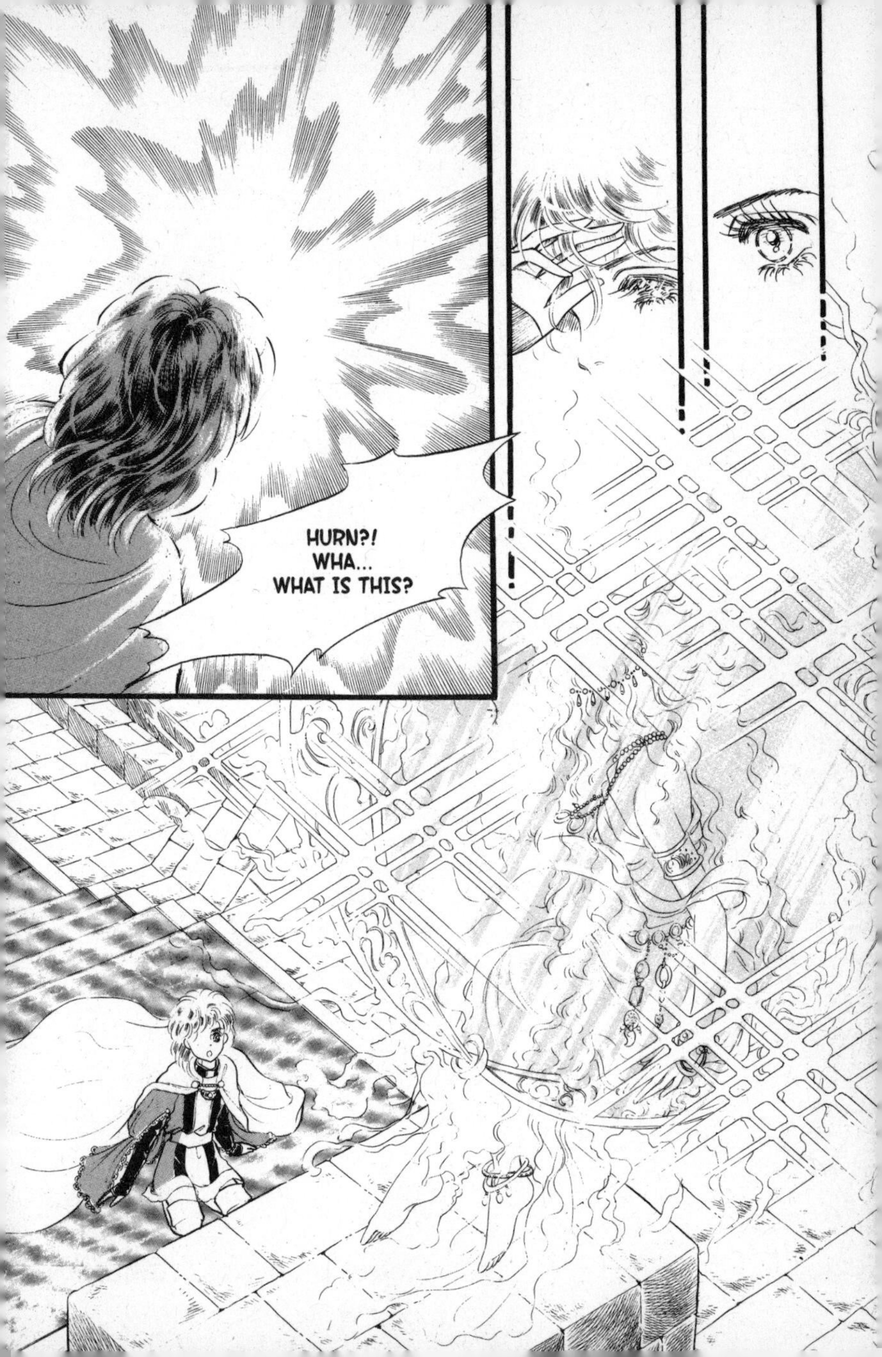
HURN?!
WHA...
WHAT IS THIS?

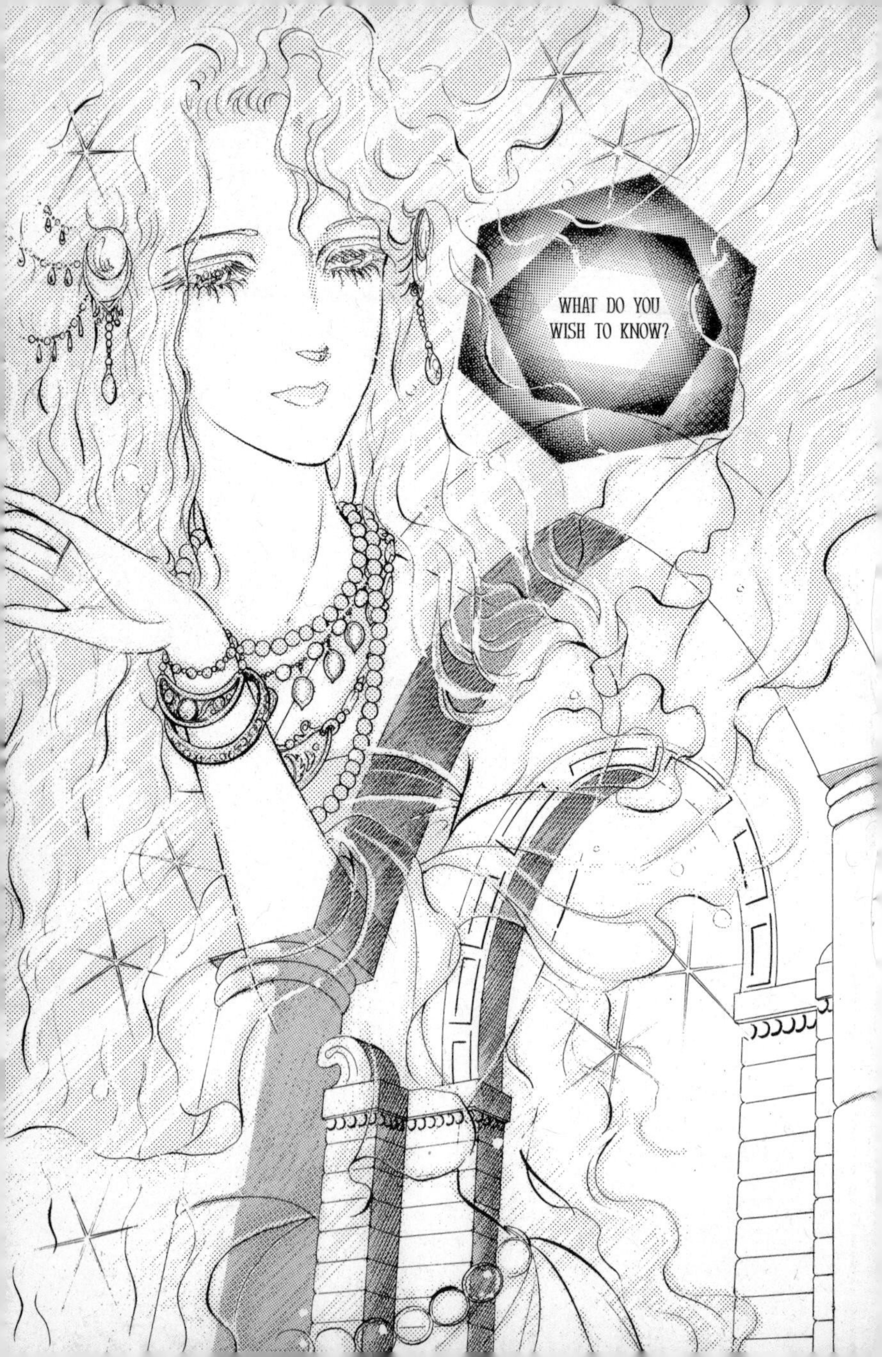
WHAT DO YOU WISH TO KNOW?

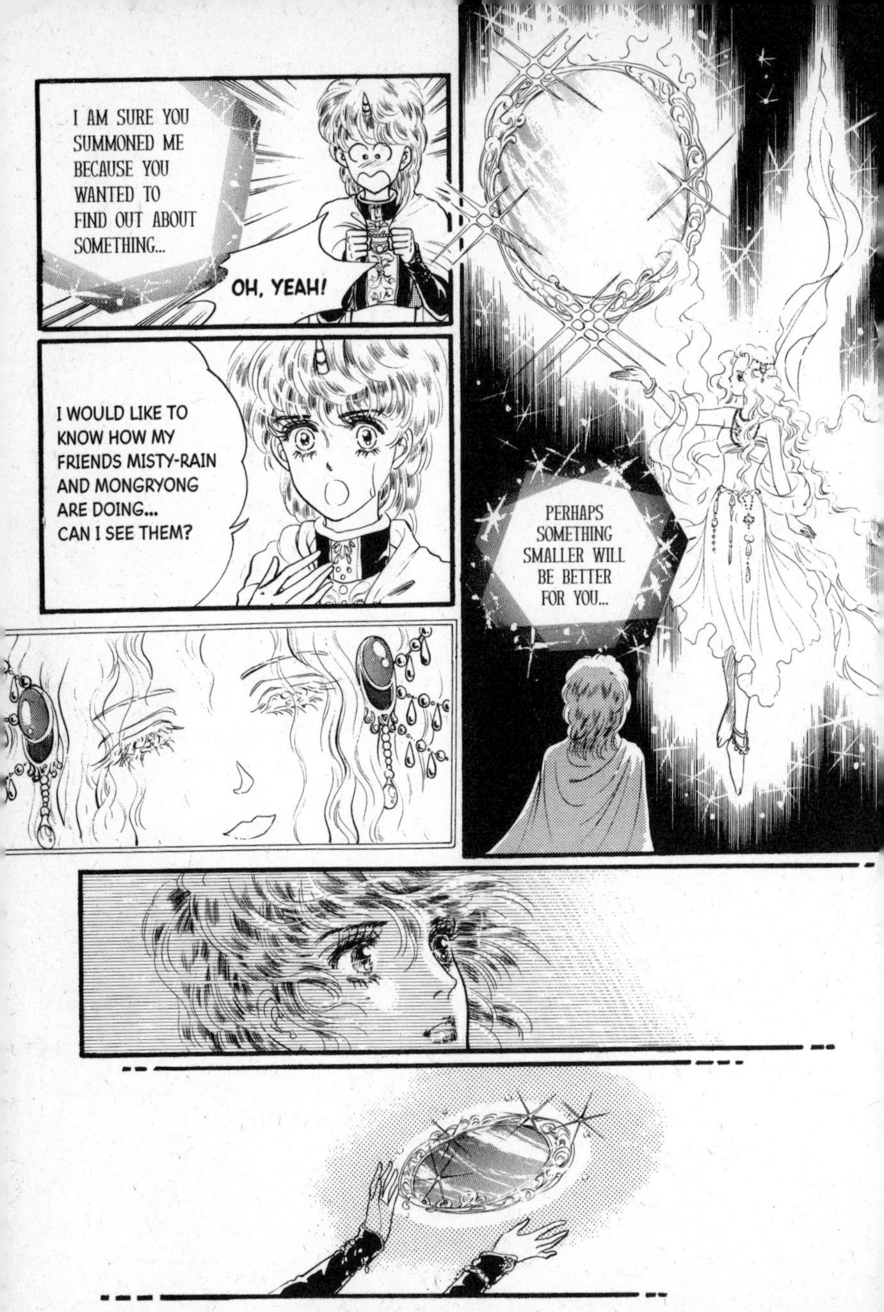
I AM SURE YOU SUMMONED ME BECAUSE YOU WANTED TO FIND OUT ABOUT SOMETHING...
OH, YEAH!
I WOULD LIKE TO KNOW HOW MY FRIENDS MISTY-RAIN AND MONGRYONG ARE DOING... CAN I SEE THEM?
PERHAPS SOMETHING SMALLER WILL BE BETTER FOR YOU...

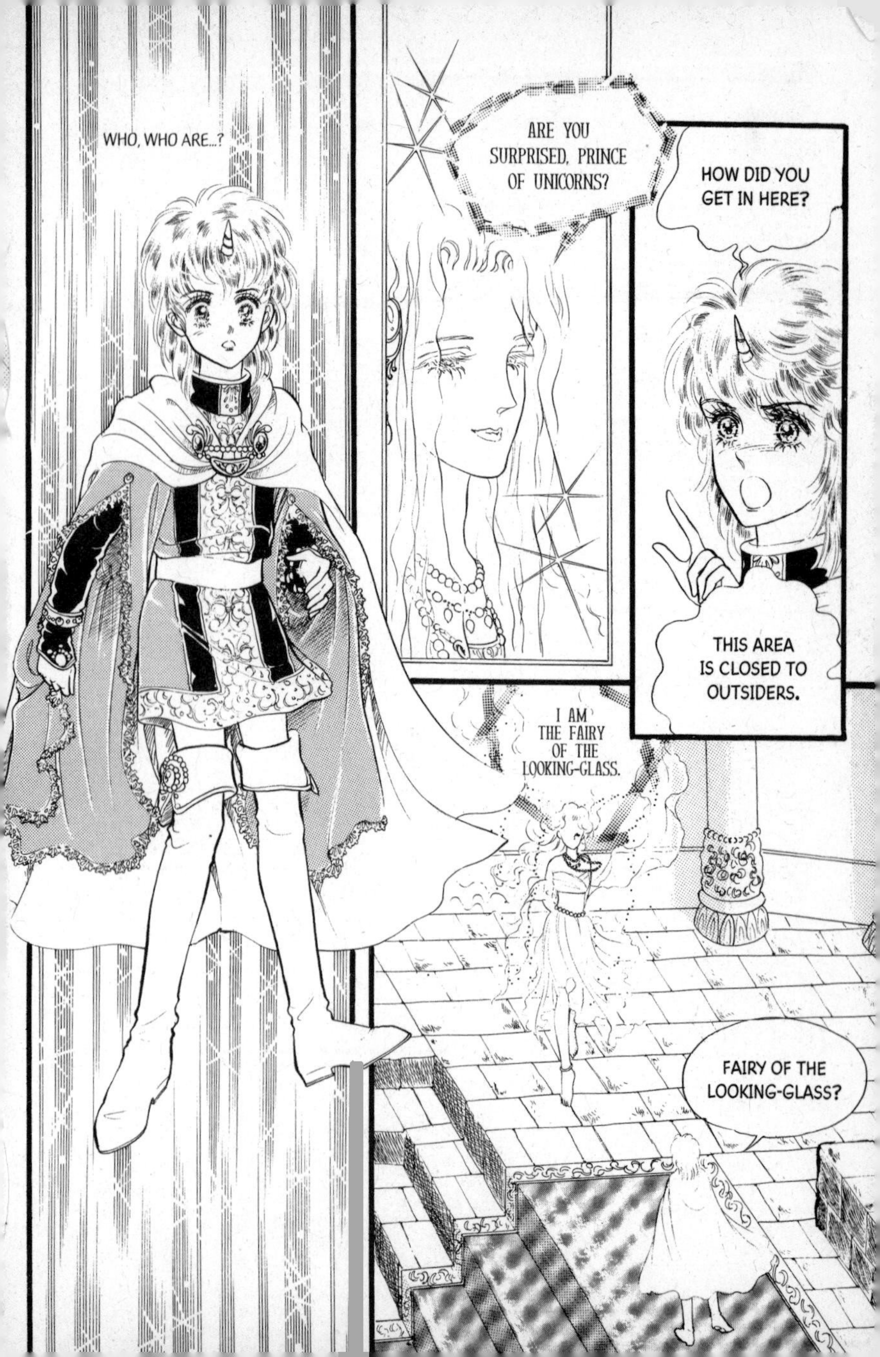
WHO, WHO ARE...?
ARE YOU SURPRISED, PRINCE OF UNICORNS?
HOW DID YOU GET IN HERE?
THIS AREA IS CLOSED TO OUTSIDERS.
I AM THE FAIRY OF THE LOOKING-GLASS.
FAIRY OF THE LOOKING-GLASS?

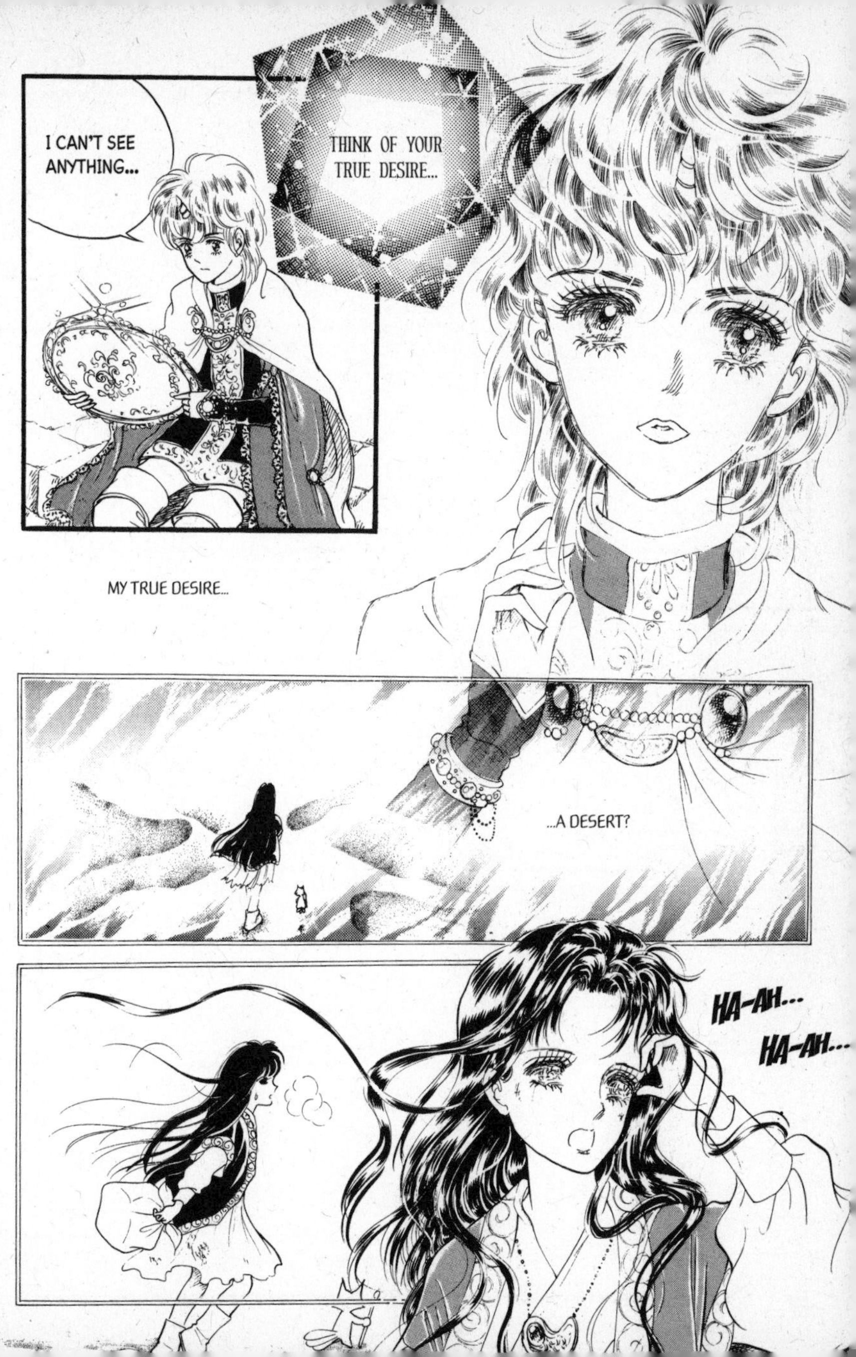
I CAN'T SEE ANYTHING...
THINK OF YOUR TRUE DESIRE...
MY TRUE DESIRE...
...A DESERT?
HA-AH...
HA-AH...

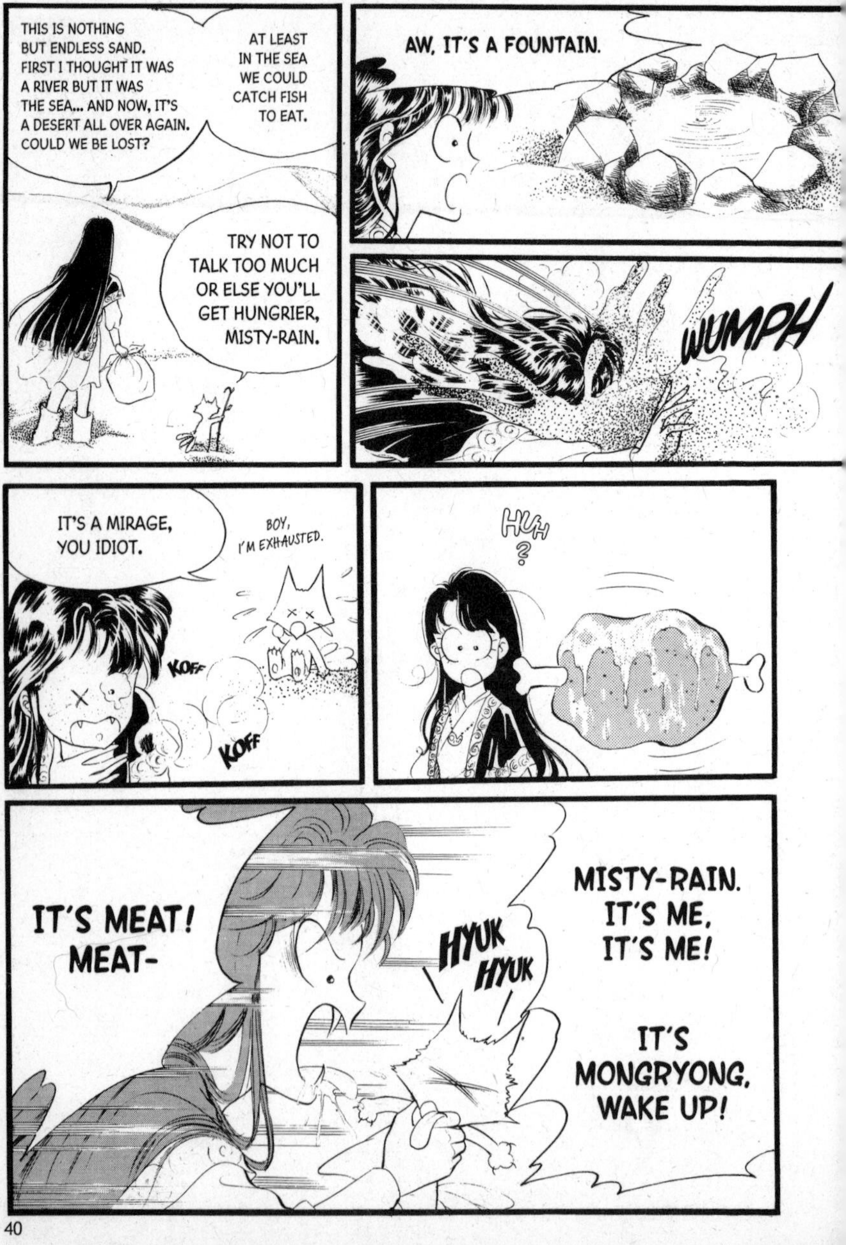
THIS IS NOTHING BUT ENDLESS SAND. FIRST I THOUGHT IT WAS A RIVER BUT IT WAS THE SEA... AND NOW, IT'S A DESERT ALL OVER AGAIN. COULD WE BE LOST?
AT LEAST IN THE SEA WE COULD CATCH FISH TO EAT.
TRY NOT TO TALK TOO MUCH OR ELSE YOU'LL GET HUNGRIER, MISTY-RAIN.
AW, IT'S A FOUNTAIN.
WUMPH
IT'S A MIRAGE, YOU IDIOT.
BOY, I'M EXHAUSTED.
KOFF
KOFF
HUH ?
IT'S MEAT! MEAT-
HYUK HYUK
MISTY-RAIN. IT'S ME, IT'S ME!
IT'S MONGRYONG, WAKE UP!

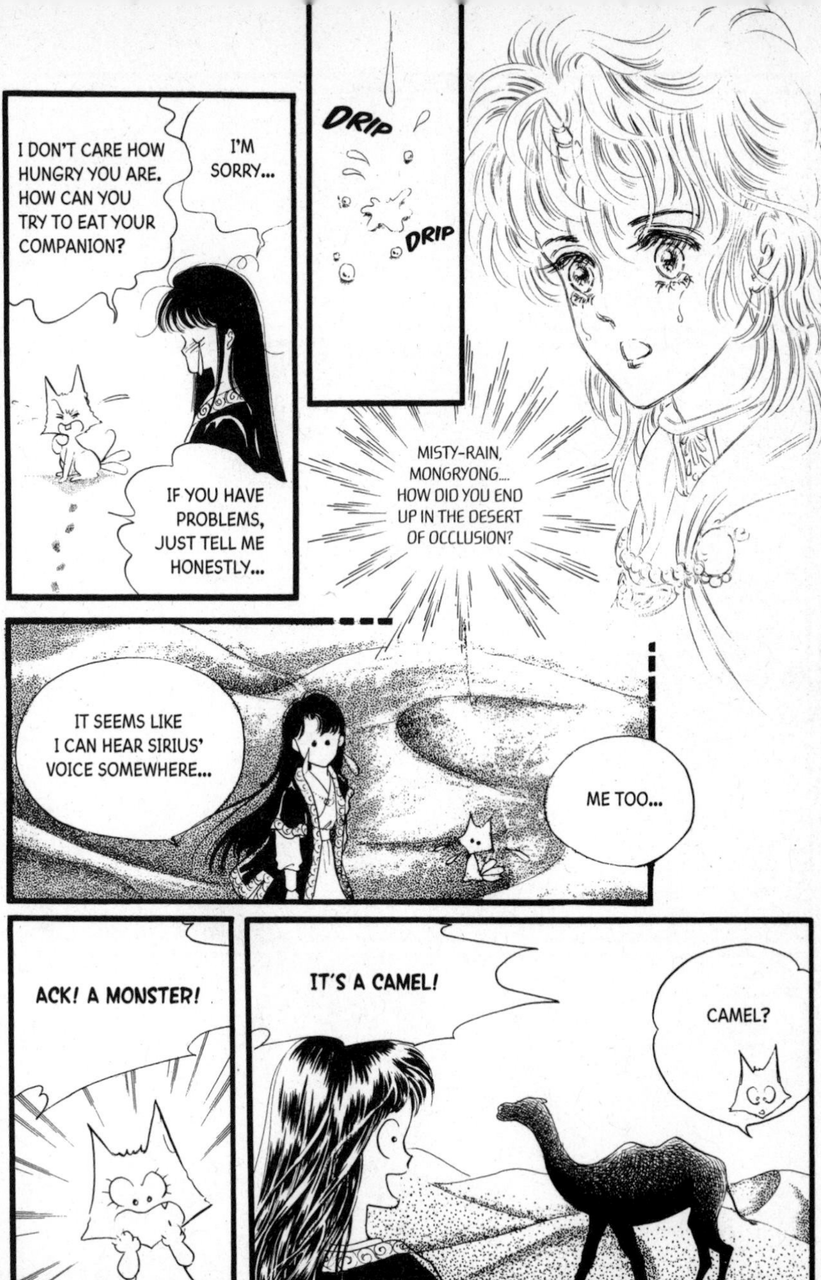
I DON'T CARE HOW HUNGRY YOU ARE. HOW CAN YOU TRY TO EAT YOUR COMPANION?
I'M SORRY...
IF YOU HAVE PROBLEMS, JUST TELL ME HONESTLY...
DRIP
DRIP
MISTY-RAIN, MONGRYONG.... HOW DID YOU END UP IN THE DESERT OF OCCLUSION?
IT SEEMS LIKE I CAN HEAR SIRIUS' VOICE SOMEWHERE...
ME TOO...
ACK! A MONSTER!
IT'S A CAMEL!
CAMEL?

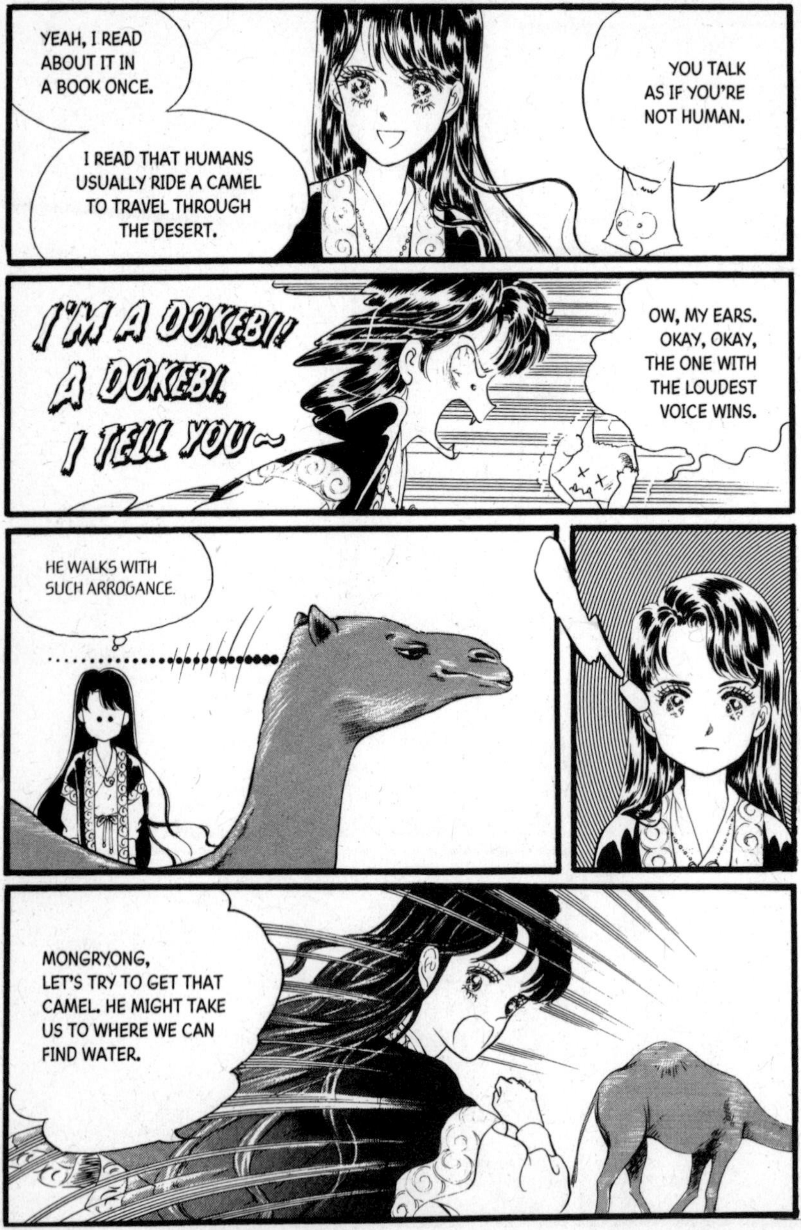
YEAH, I READ ABOUT IT IN A BOOK ONCE.
I READ THAT HUMANS USUALLY RIDE A CAMEL TO TRAVEL THROUGH THE DESERT.
YOU TALK AS IF YOU'RE NOT HUMAN.
I'M A DOKEBI! A DOKEBI, I TELL YOU~
OW, MY EARS. OKAY, OKAY, THE ONE WITH THE LOUDEST VOICE WINS.
HE WALKS WITH SUCH ARROGANCE.
MONGRYONG, LET'S TRY TO GET THAT CAMEL. HE MIGHT TAKE US TO WHERE WE CAN FIND WATER.

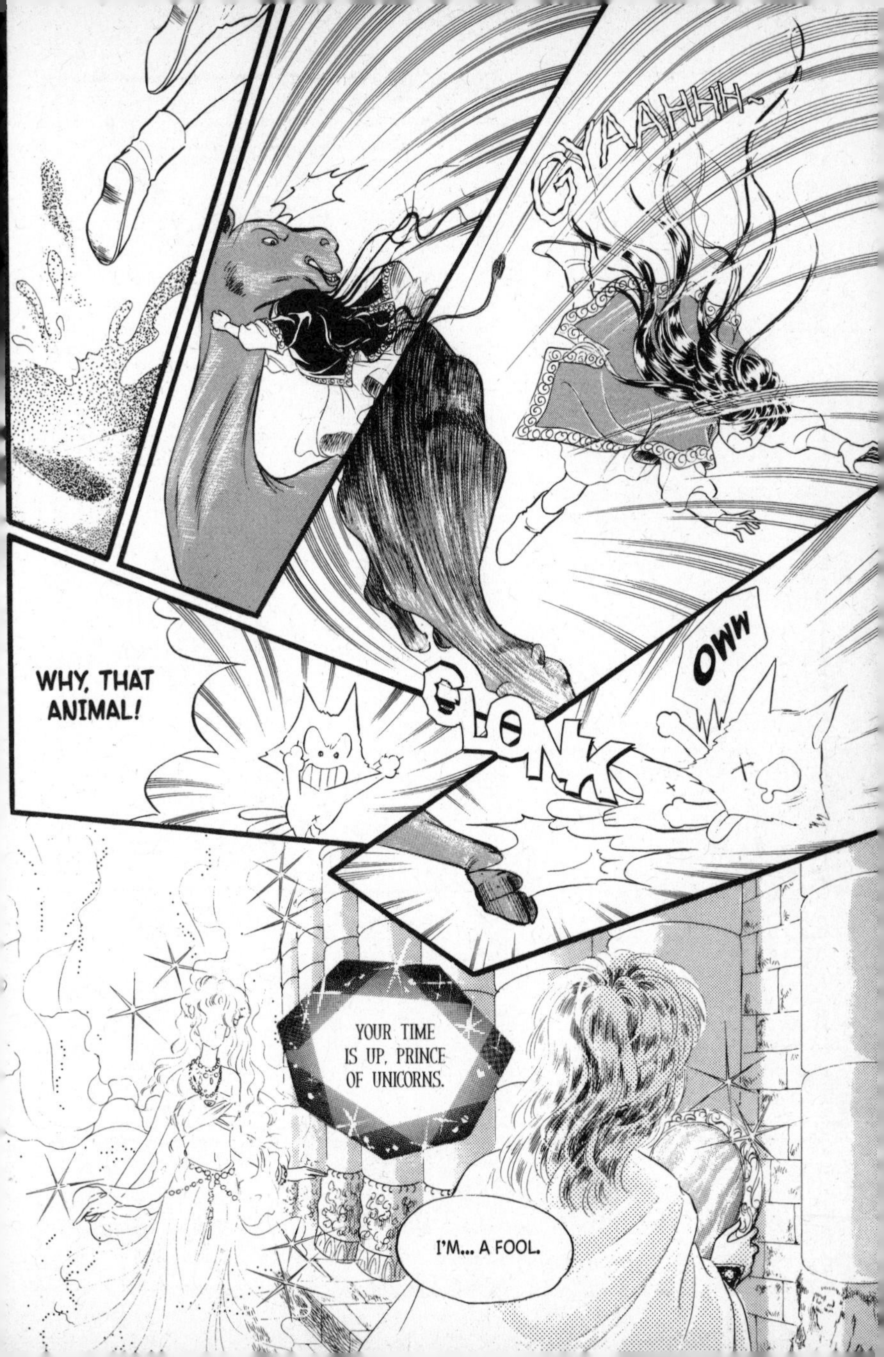
GYAAHHH
WHY, THAT ANIMAL!
CLONK
OWW
YOUR TIME IS UP, PRINCE OF UNICORNS.
I'M... A FOOL.

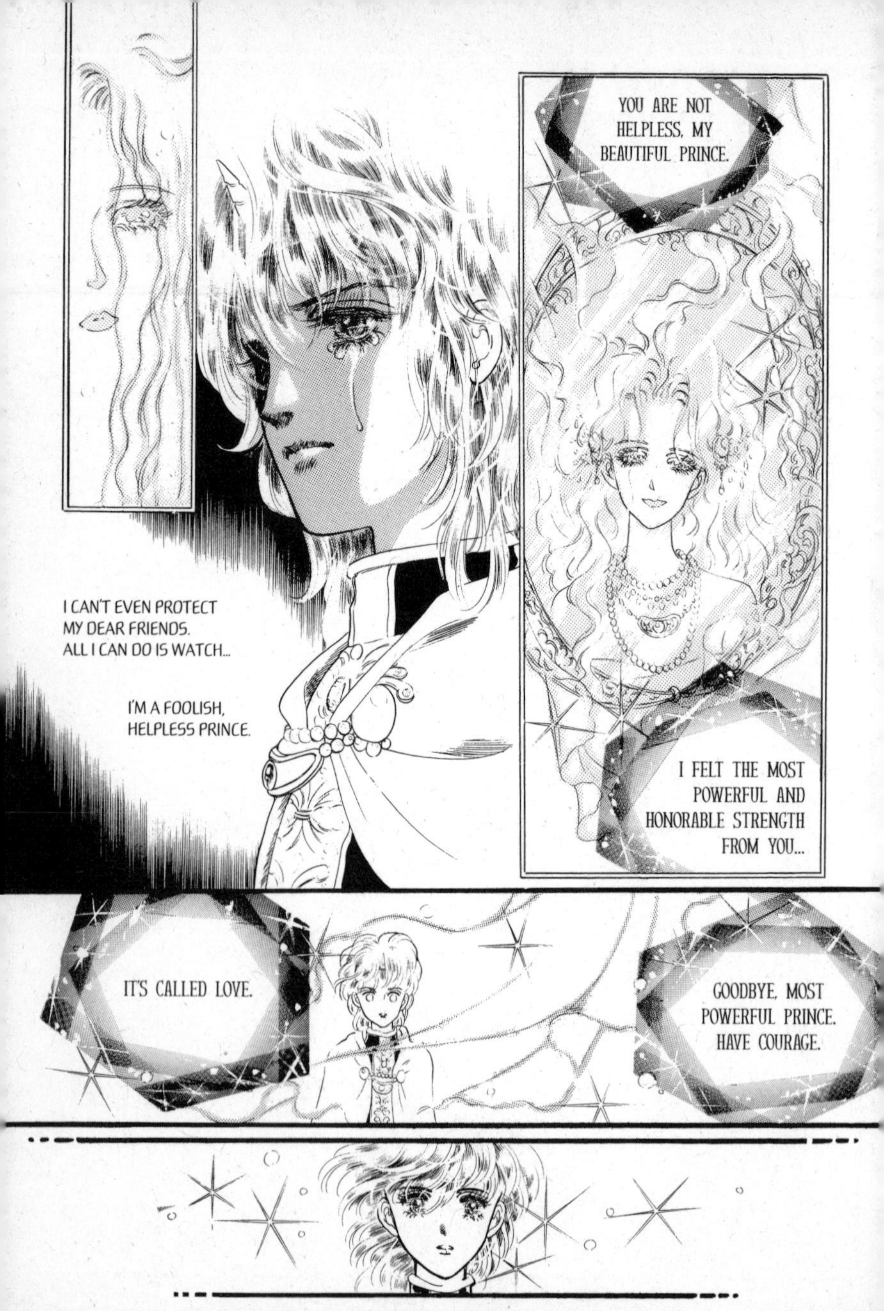
I CAN'T EVEN PROTECT MY DEAR FRIENDS. ALL I CAN DO IS WATCH...
I'M A FOOLISH, HELPLESS PRINCE.
YOU ARE NOT HELPLESS, MY BEAUTIFUL PRINCE.
I FELT THE MOST POWERFUL AND HONORABLE STRENGTH FROM YOU...
IT'S CALLED LOVE.
GOODBYE, MOST POWERFUL PRINCE. HAVE COURAGE.

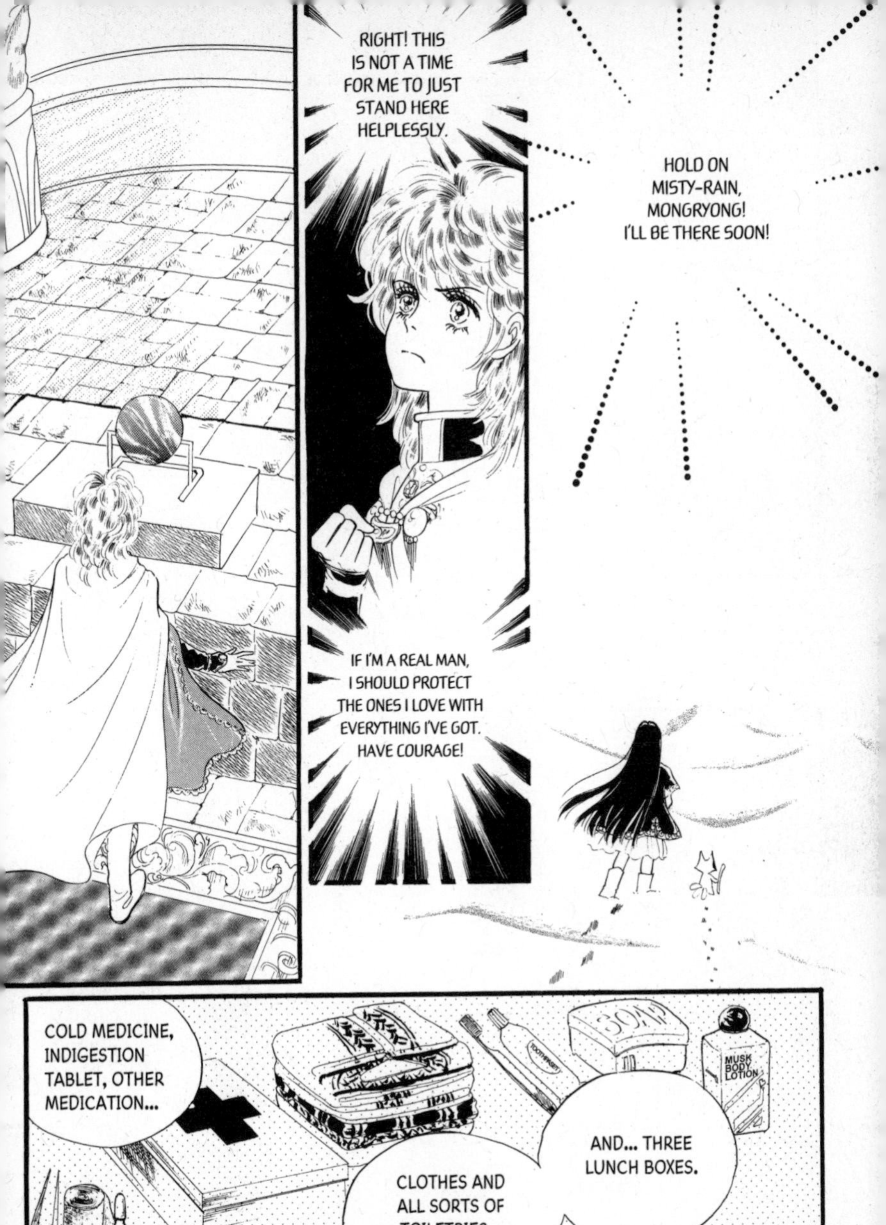
RIGHT! THIS IS NOT A TIME FOR ME TO JUST STAND HERE HELPLESSLY.
IF I'M A REAL MAN, I SHOULD PROTECT THE ONES I LOVE WITH EVERYTHING I'VE GOT. HAVE COURAGE!
HOLD ON MISTY-RAIN, MONGRYONG! I'LL BE THERE SOON!
COLD MEDICINE, INDIGESTION TABLET, OTHER MEDICATION...
SOAP
MUSK BODY LOTION
CLOTHES AND ALL SORTS OF TOILETRIES...
AND... THREE LUNCH BOXES.

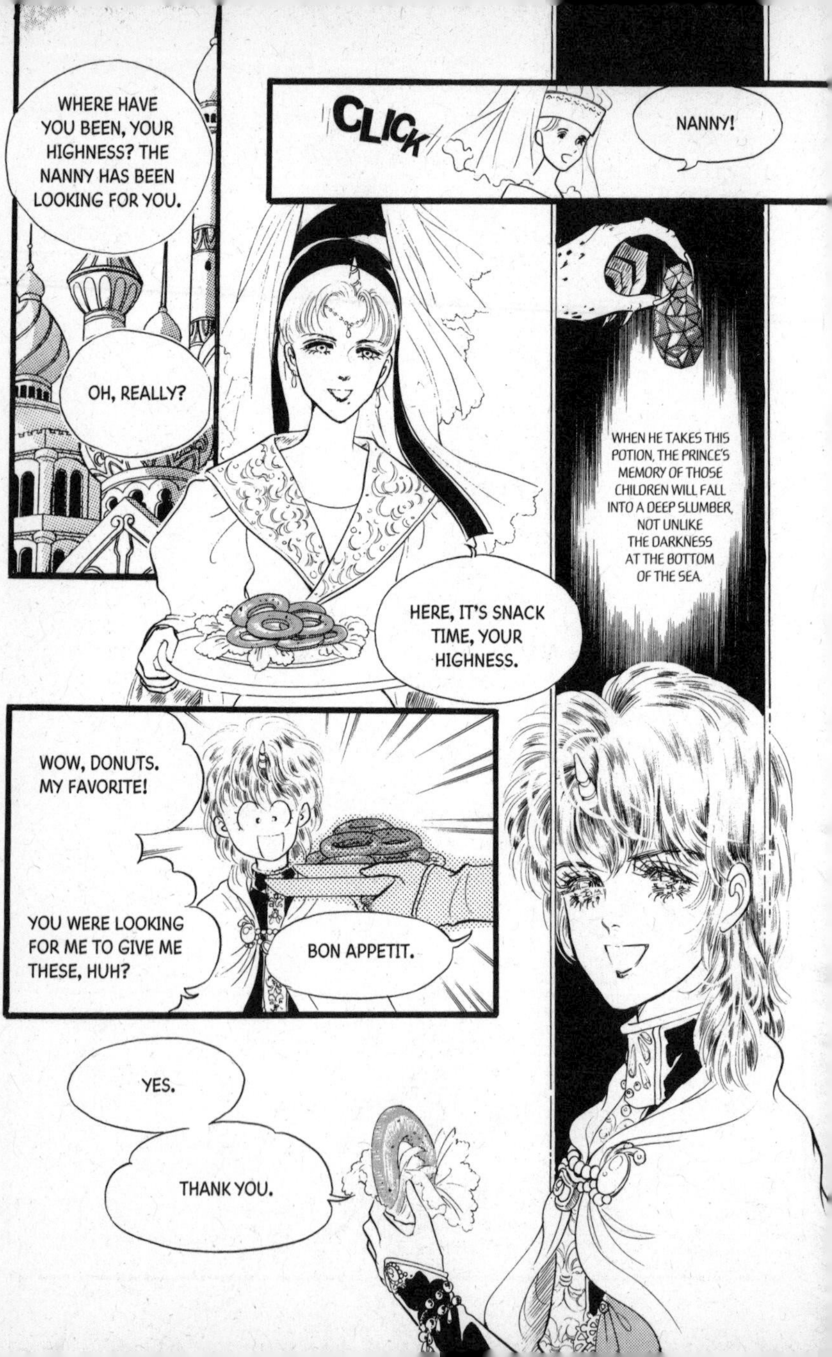
WHERE HAVE YOU BEEN, YOUR HIGHNESS? THE NANNY HAS BEEN LOOKING FOR YOU.
OH, REALLY?
CLICK
NANNY!
HERE, IT'S SNACK TIME, YOUR HIGHNESS.
WHEN HE TAKES THIS POTION, THE PRINCE'S MEMORY OF THOSE CHILDREN WILL FALL INTO A DEEP SLUMBER, NOT UNLIKE THE DARKNESS AT THE BOTTOM OF THE SEA.
WOW, DONUTS. MY FAVORITE!
YOU WERE LOOKING FOR ME TO GIVE ME THESE, HUH?
BON APPETIT.
YES.
THANK YOU.

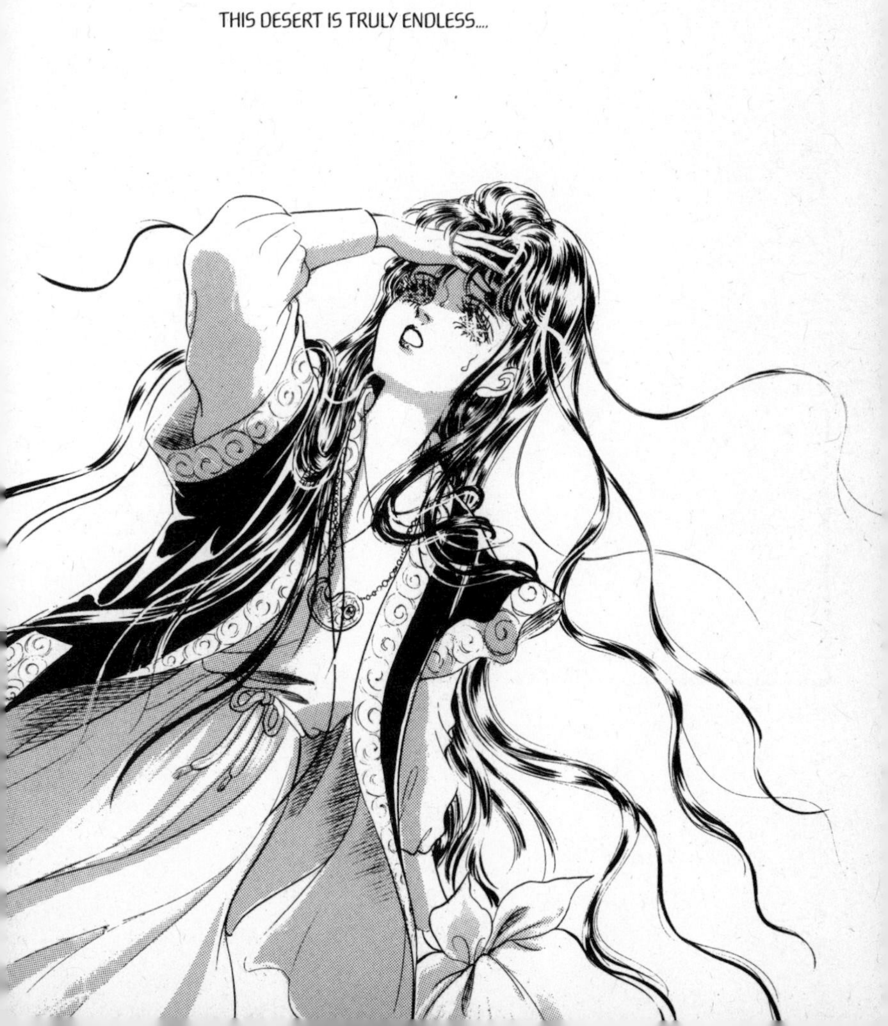
THIS DESERT IS TRULY ENDLESS....

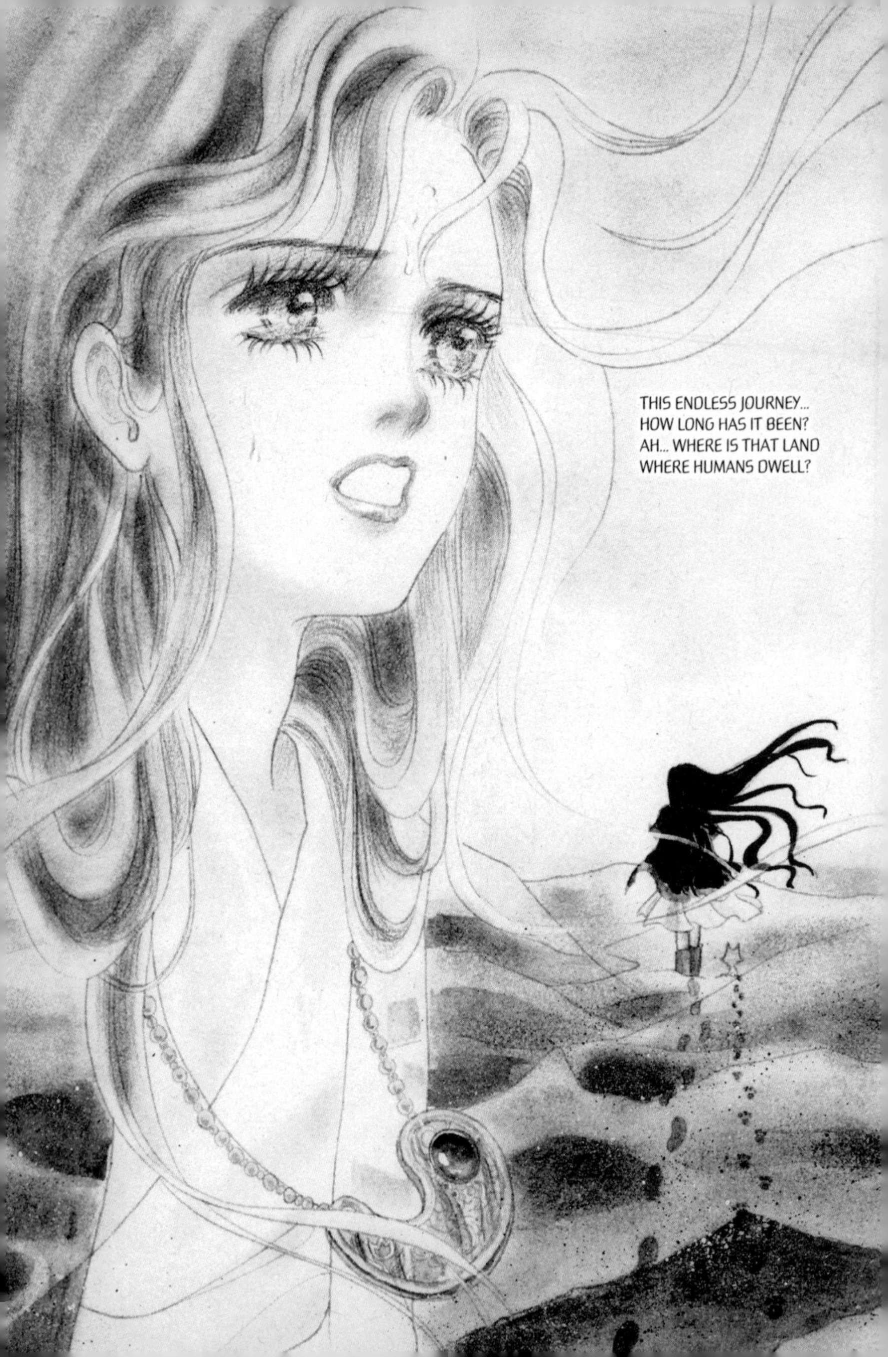
THIS ENDLESS JOURNEY... HOW LONG HAS IT BEEN? AH... WHERE IS THAT LAND WHERE HUMANS DWELL?

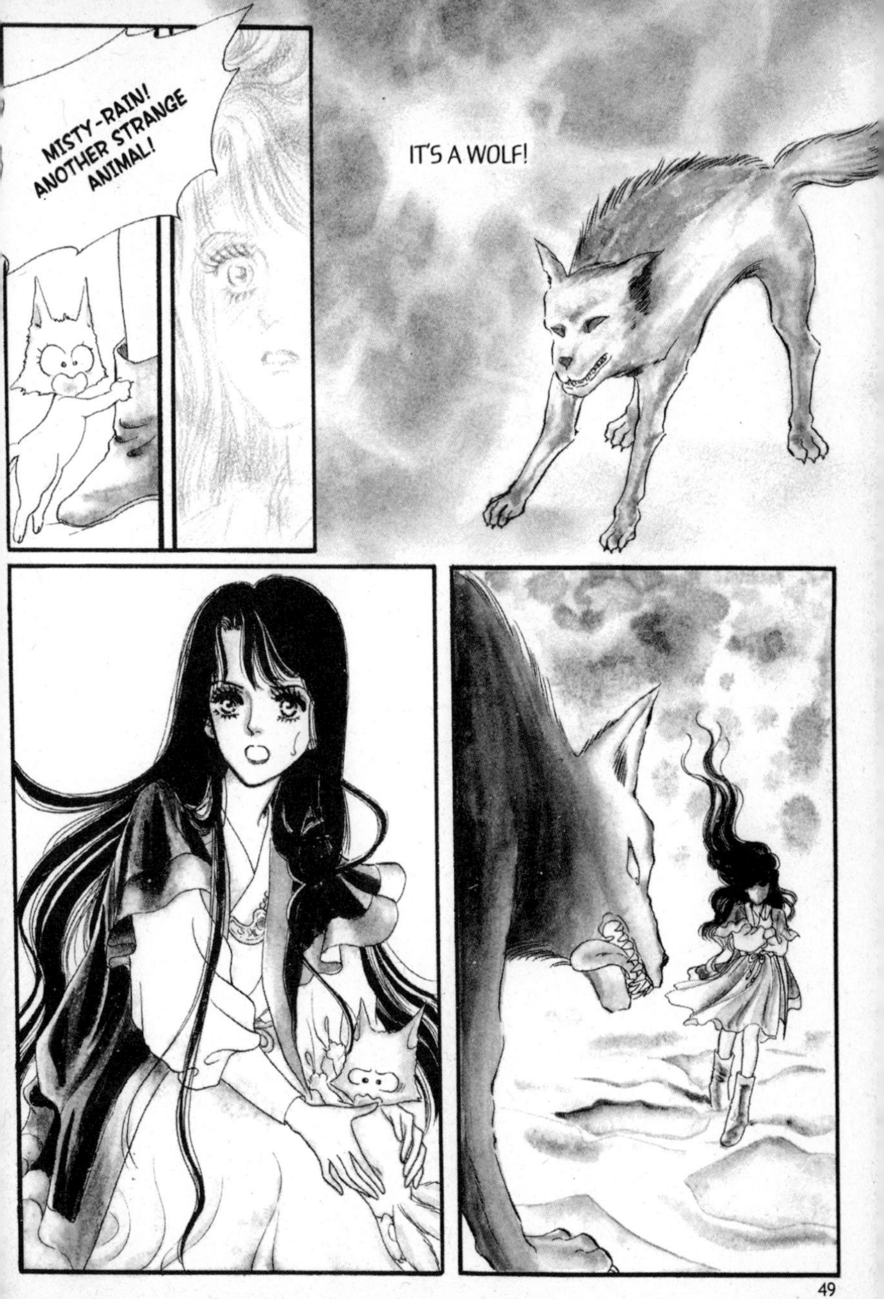

MISTY-RAIN! ANOTHER STRANGE ANIMAL!
IT'S A WOLF!

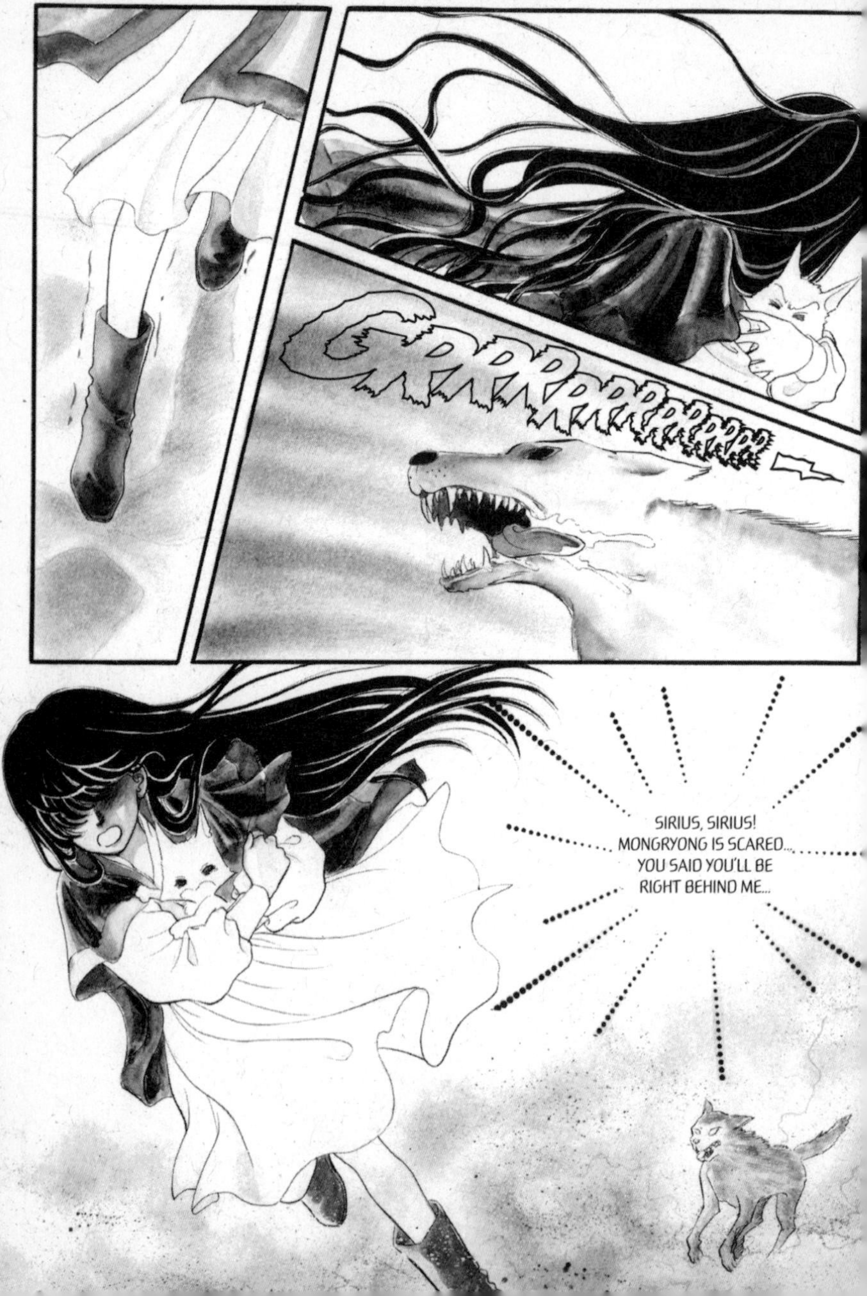
GRRRRRRRRRRR
SIRIUS, SIRIUS!
MONGRYONG IS SCARED...
YOU SAID YOU'LL BE
RIGHT BEHIND ME...

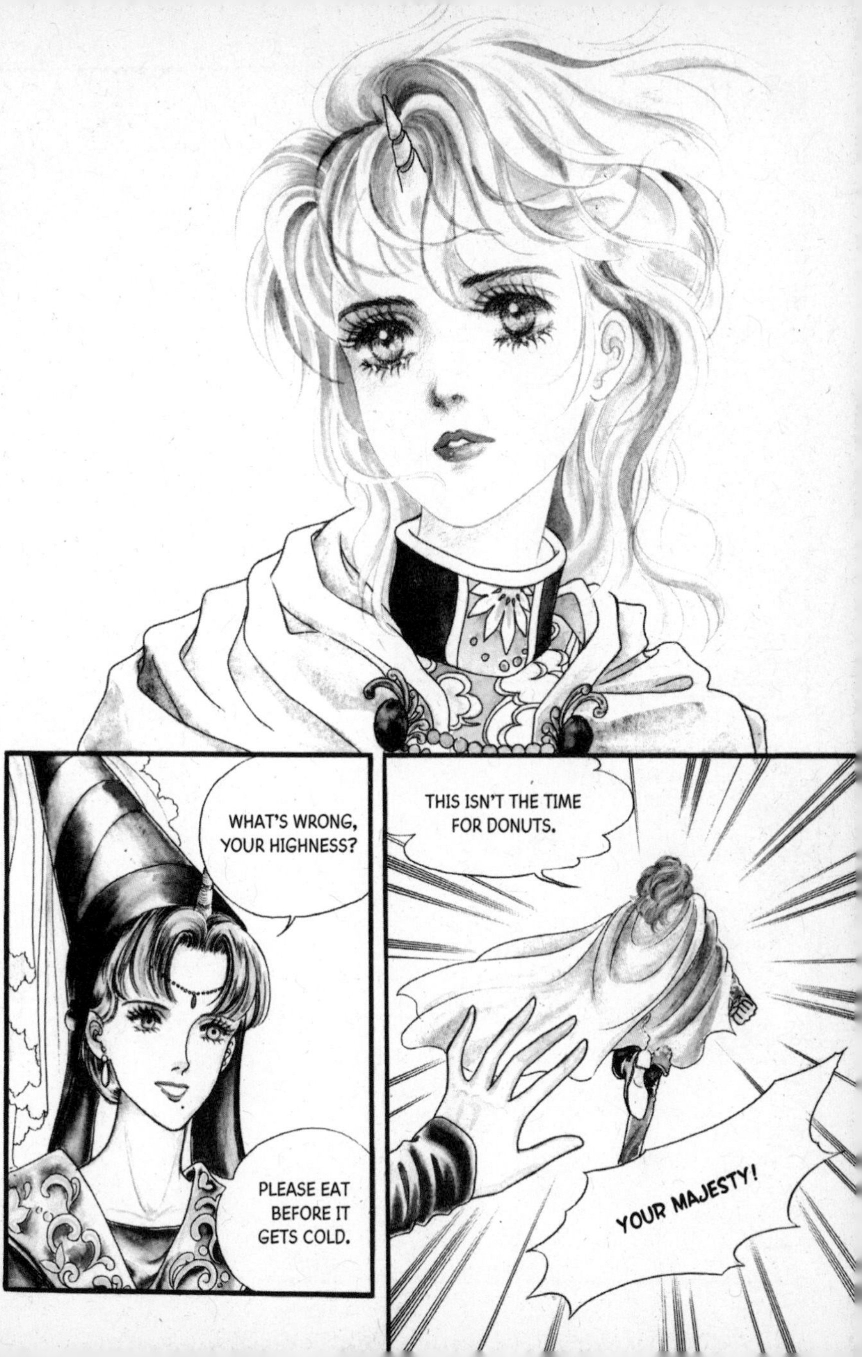
WHAT'S WRONG, YOUR HIGHNESS?
PLEASE EAT BEFORE IT GETS COLD.
THIS ISN'T THE TIME FOR DONUTS.
YOUR MAJESTY!

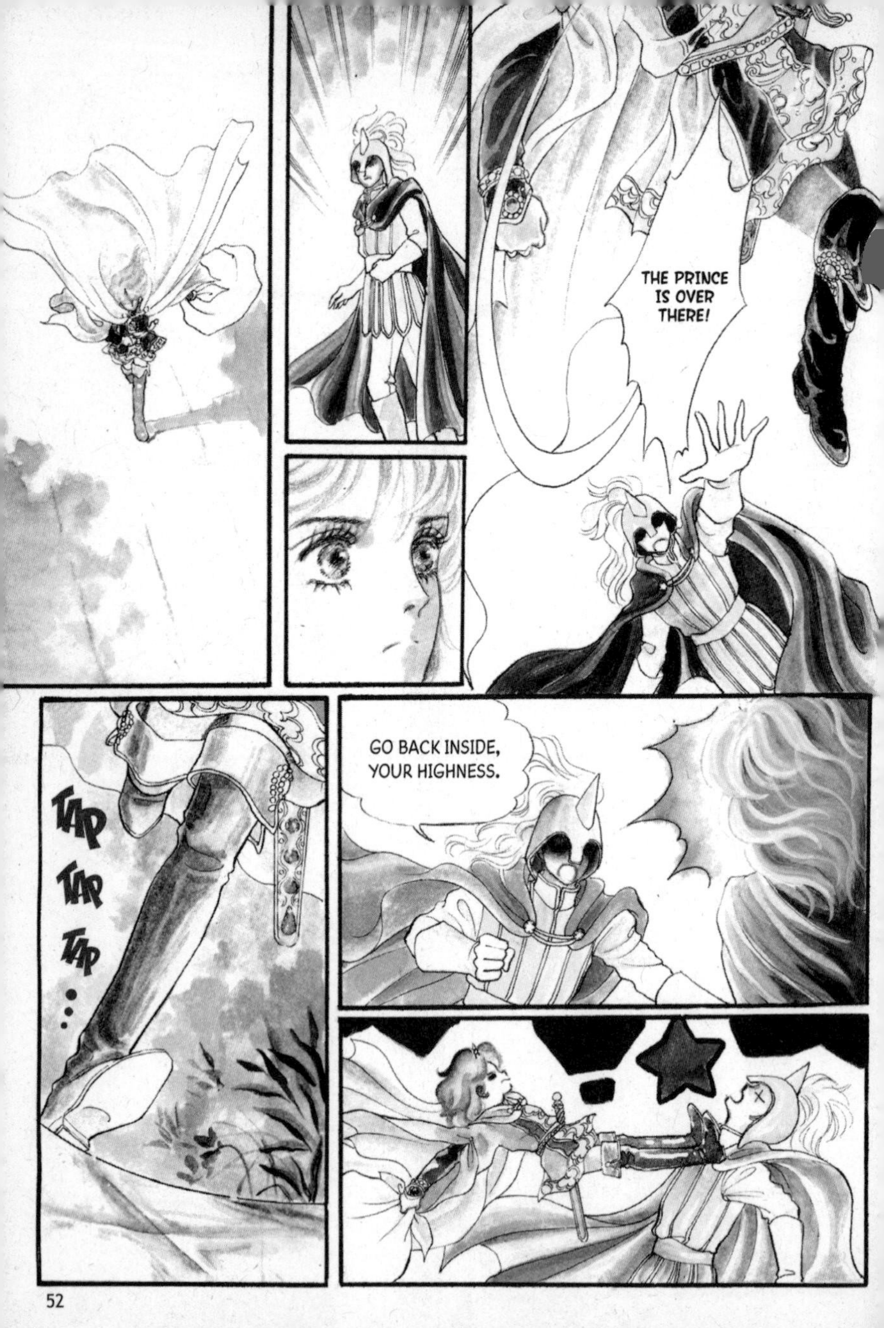
THE PRINCE IS OVER THERE!
TAP TAP TAP...
GO BACK INSIDE, YOUR HIGHNESS.

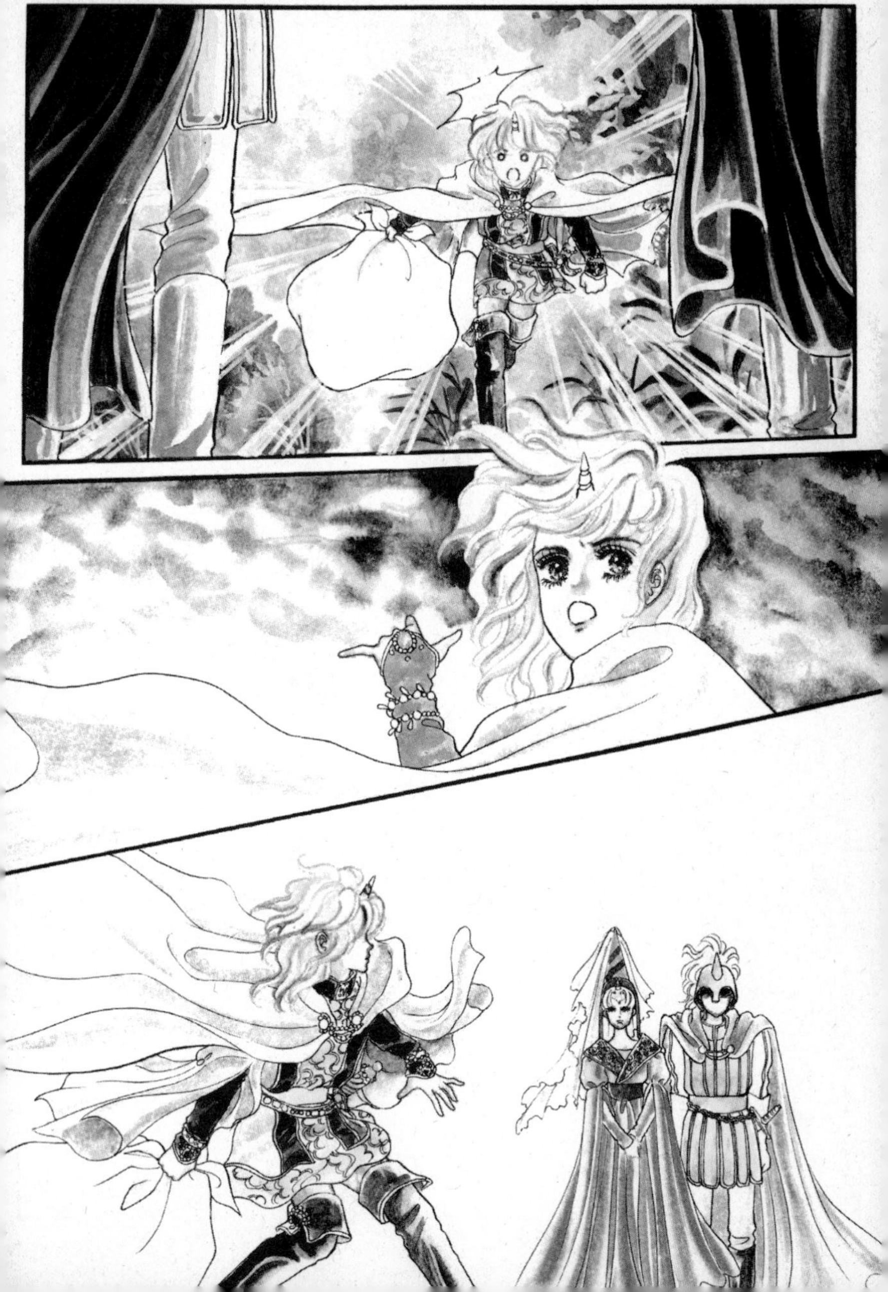

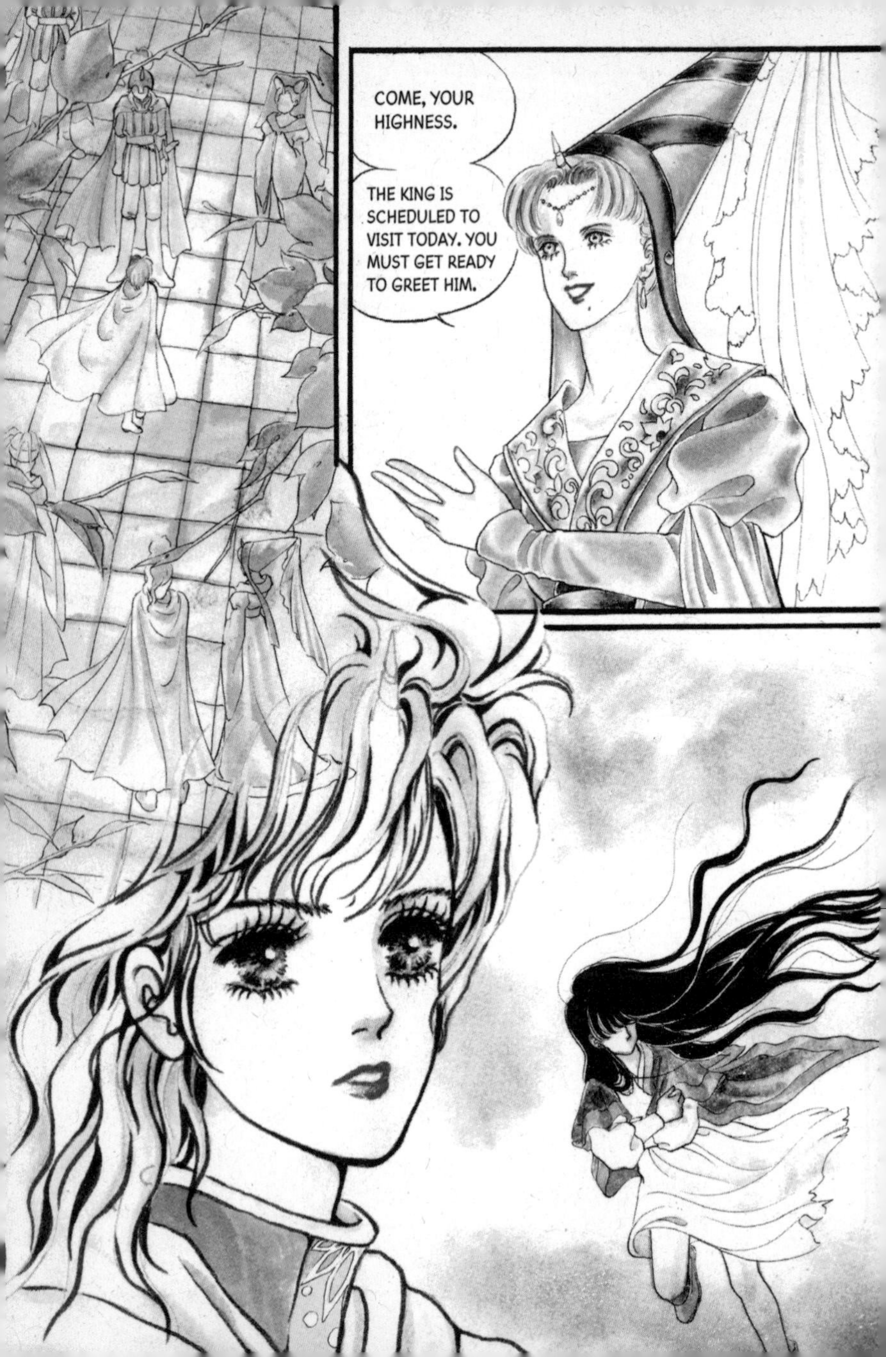
COME, YOUR HIGHNESS.
THE KING IS SCHEDULED TO VISIT TODAY. YOU MUST GET READY TO GREET HIM.

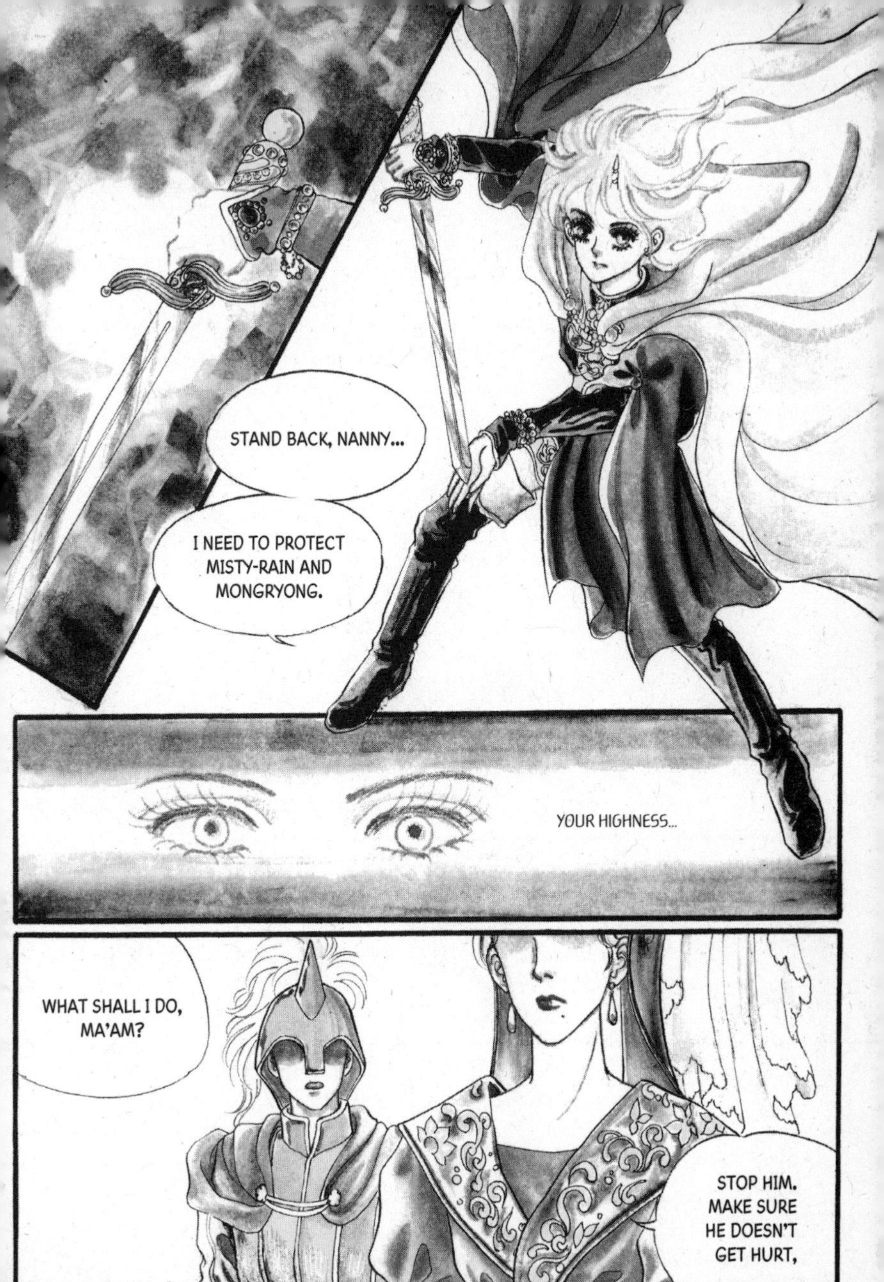
STAND BACK, NANNY...
I NEED TO PROTECT MISTY-RAIN AND MONGRYONG.
YOUR HIGHNESS...
WHAT SHALL I DO, MA'AM?
STOP HIM. MAKE SURE HE DOESN'T GET HURT,

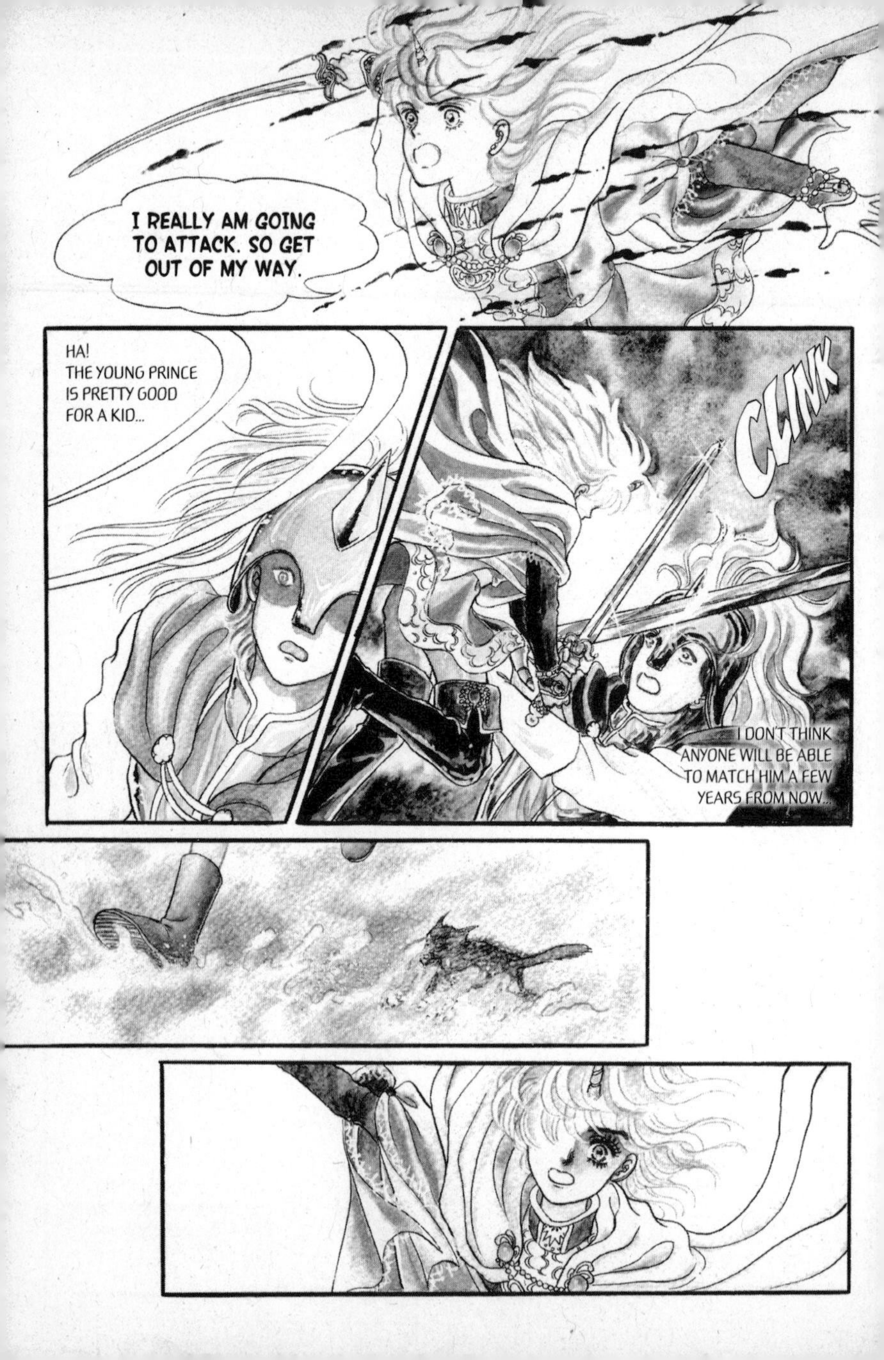
I REALLY AM GOING TO ATTACK. SO GET OUT OF MY WAY.
HA! THE YOUNG PRINCE IS PRETTY GOOD FOR A KID...
CLINK
I DON'T THINK ANYONE WILL BE ABLE TO MATCH HIM A FEW YEARS FROM NOW...

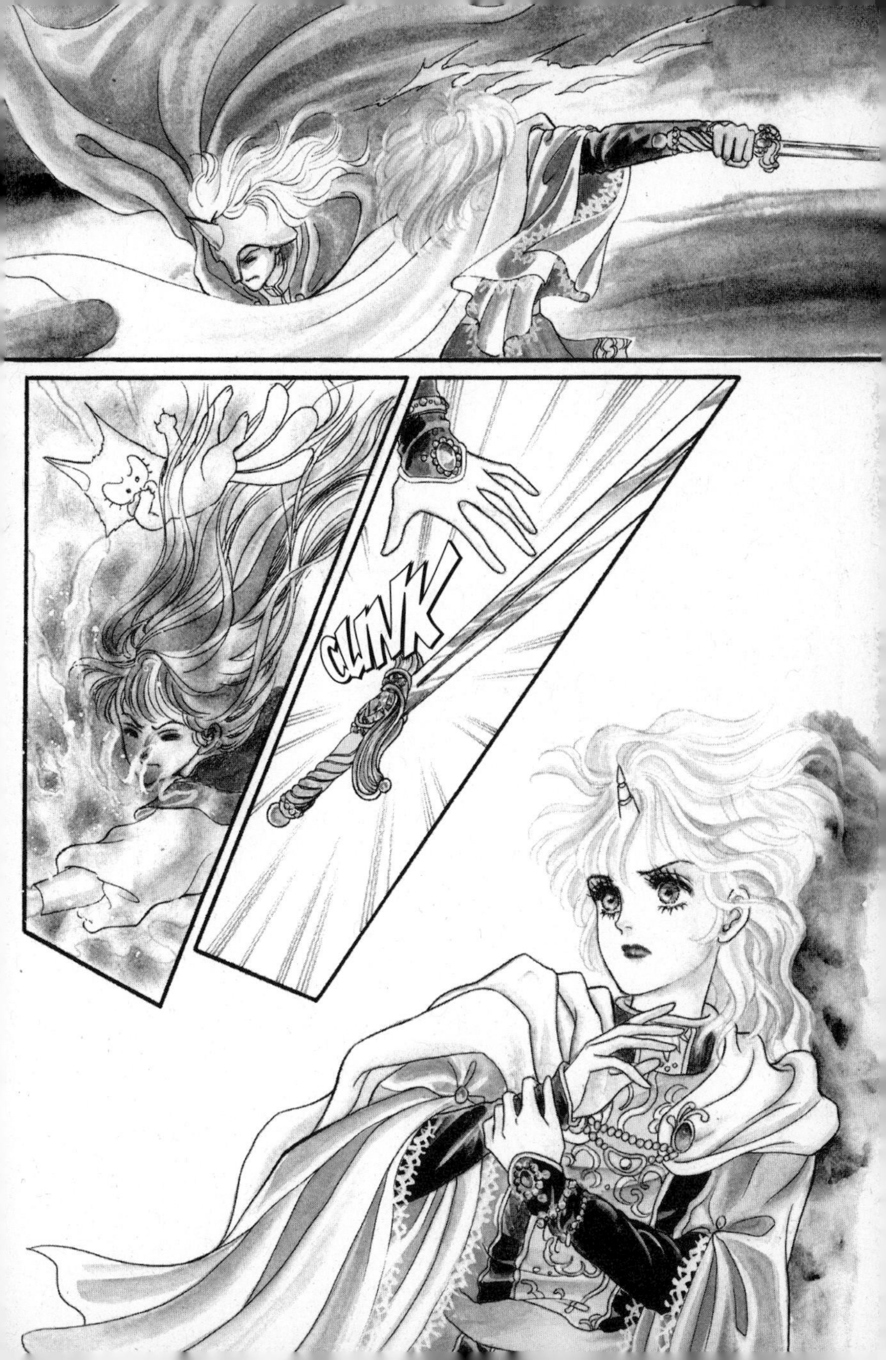
CLINK!

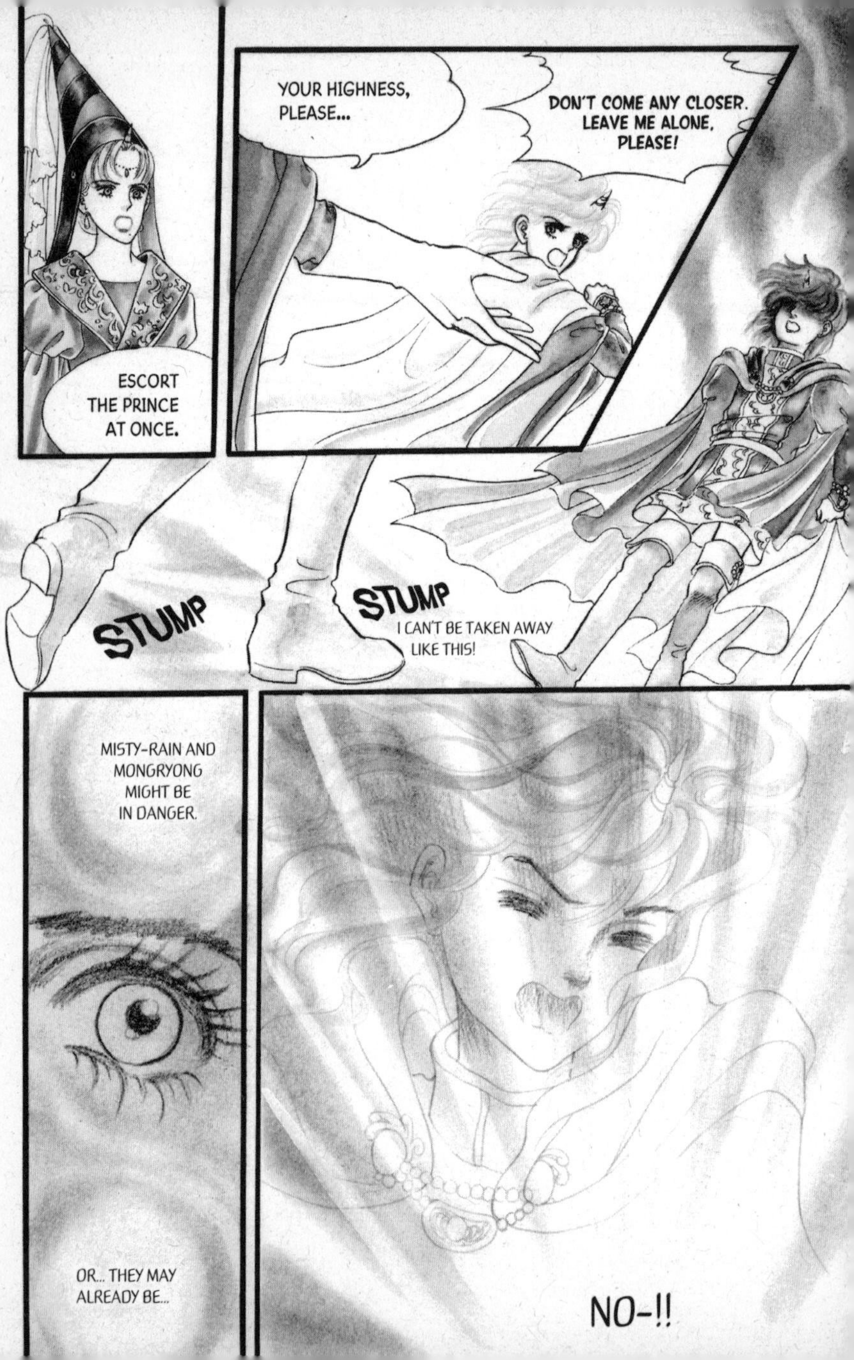
ESCORT THE PRINCE AT ONCE.
YOUR HIGHNESS, PLEASE...
DON'T COME ANY CLOSER. LEAVE ME ALONE, PLEASE!
STUMP
STUMP
I CAN'T BE TAKEN AWAY LIKE THIS!
MISTY-RAIN AND MONGRYONG MIGHT BE IN DANGER.
OR... THEY MAY ALREADY BE...
NO-!!

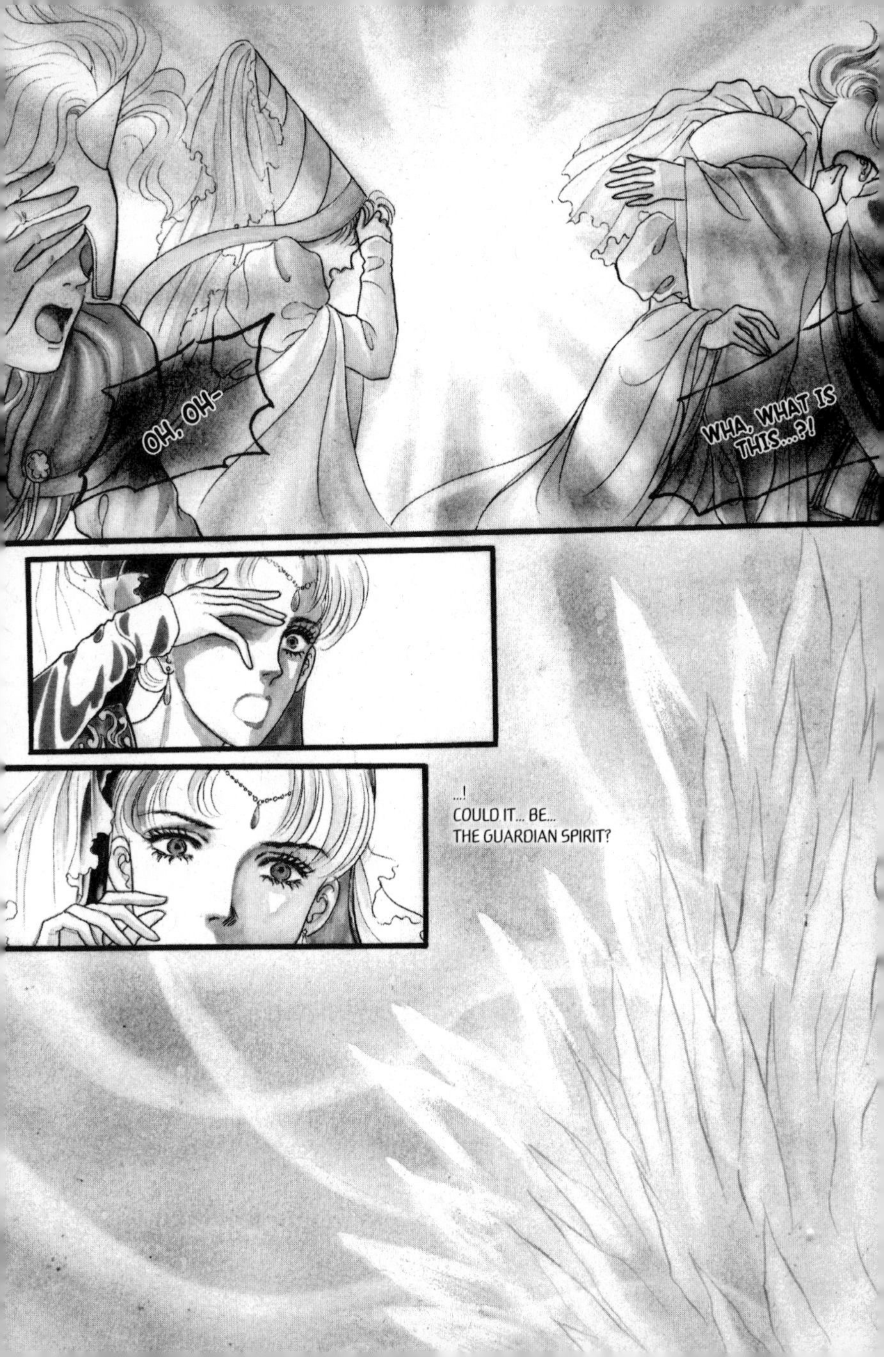
OH, OH-
WHA, WHAT IS THIS...?!
...!
COULD IT... BE...
THE GUARDIAN SPIRIT?

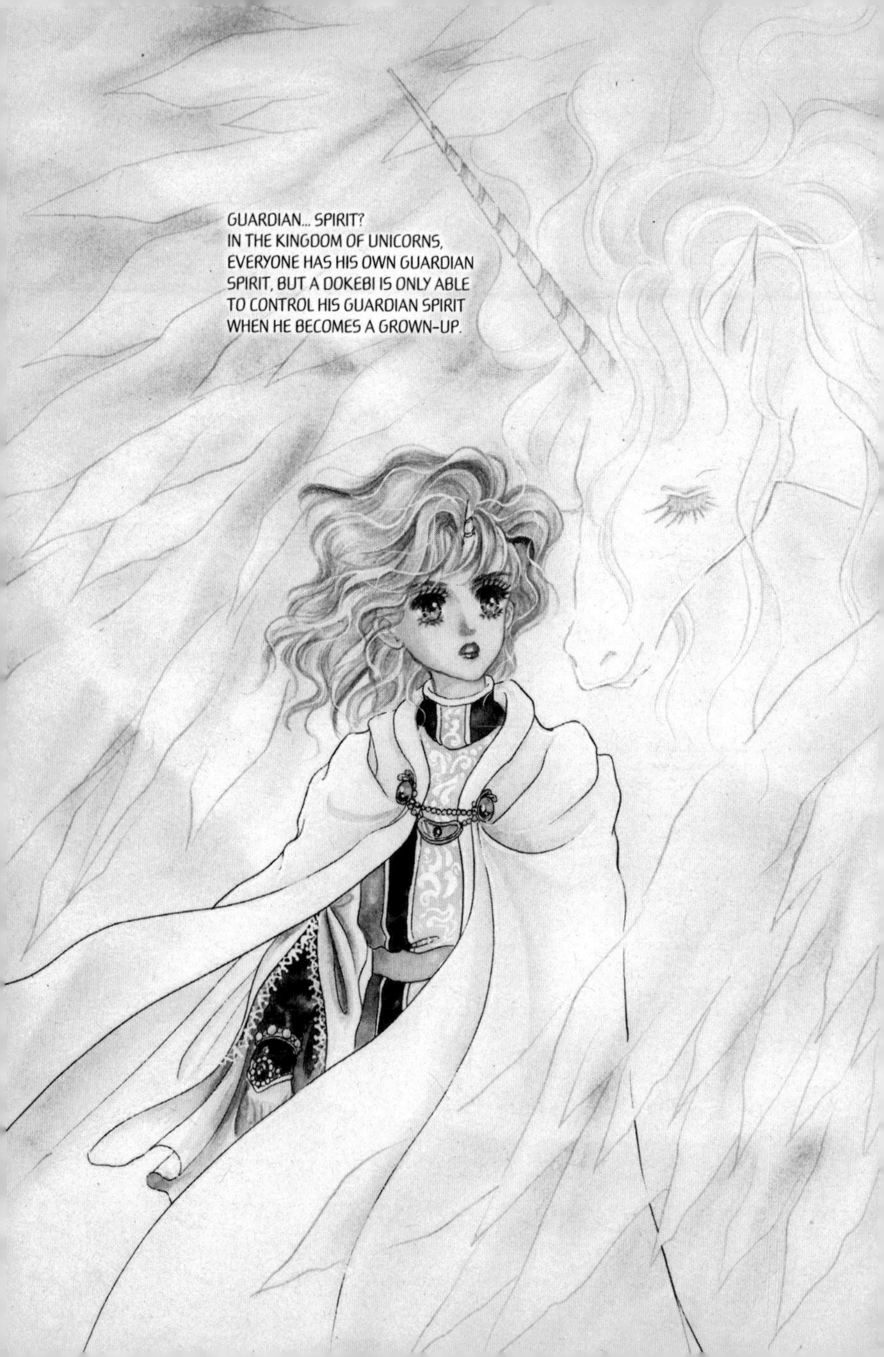
GUARDIAN... SPIRIT?
IN THE KINGDOM OF UNICORNS, EVERYONE HAS HIS OWN GUARDIAN SPIRIT, BUT A DOKEBI IS ONLY ABLE TO CONTROL HIS GUARDIAN SPIRIT WHEN HE BECOMES A GROWN-UP.

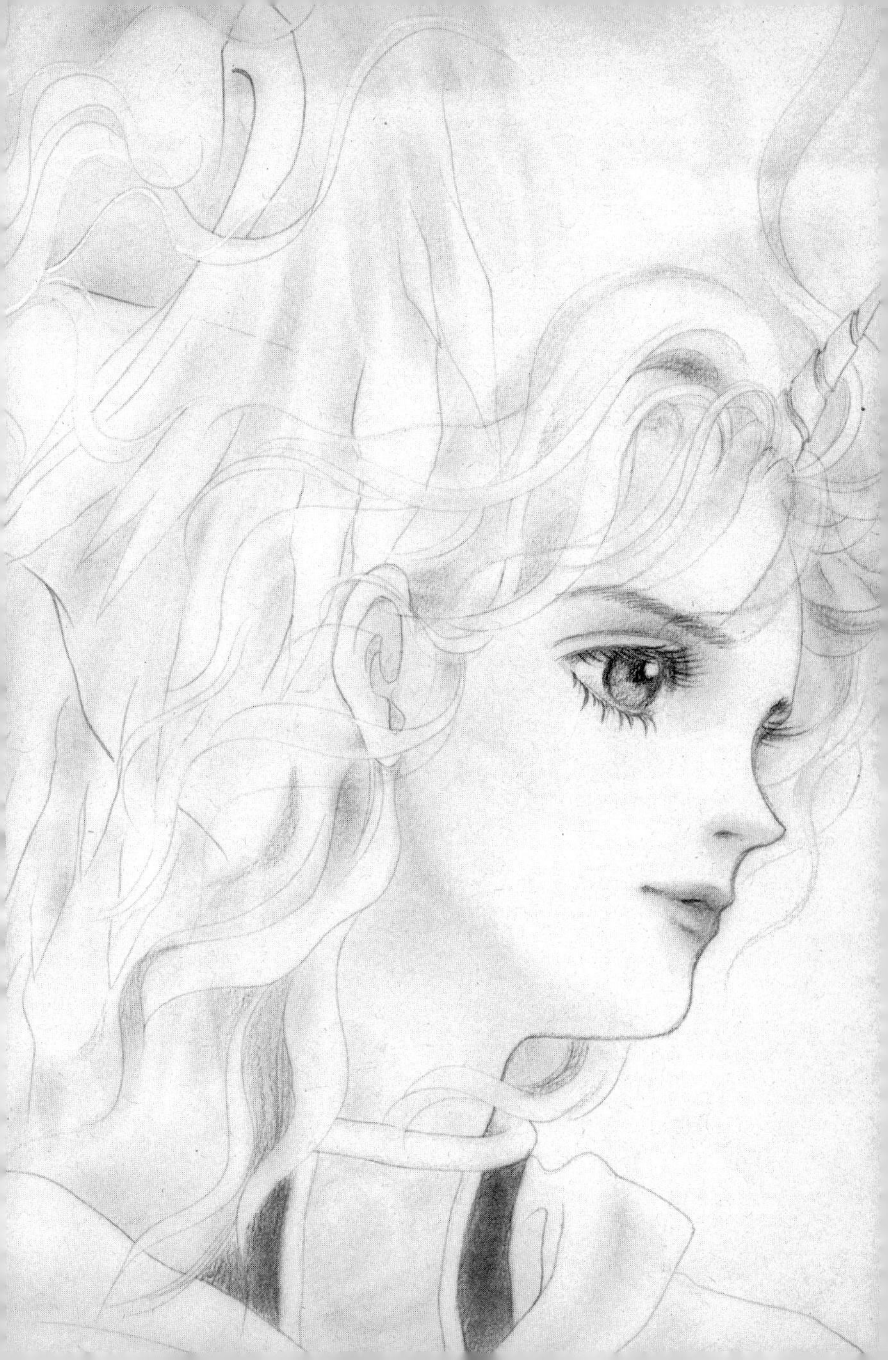

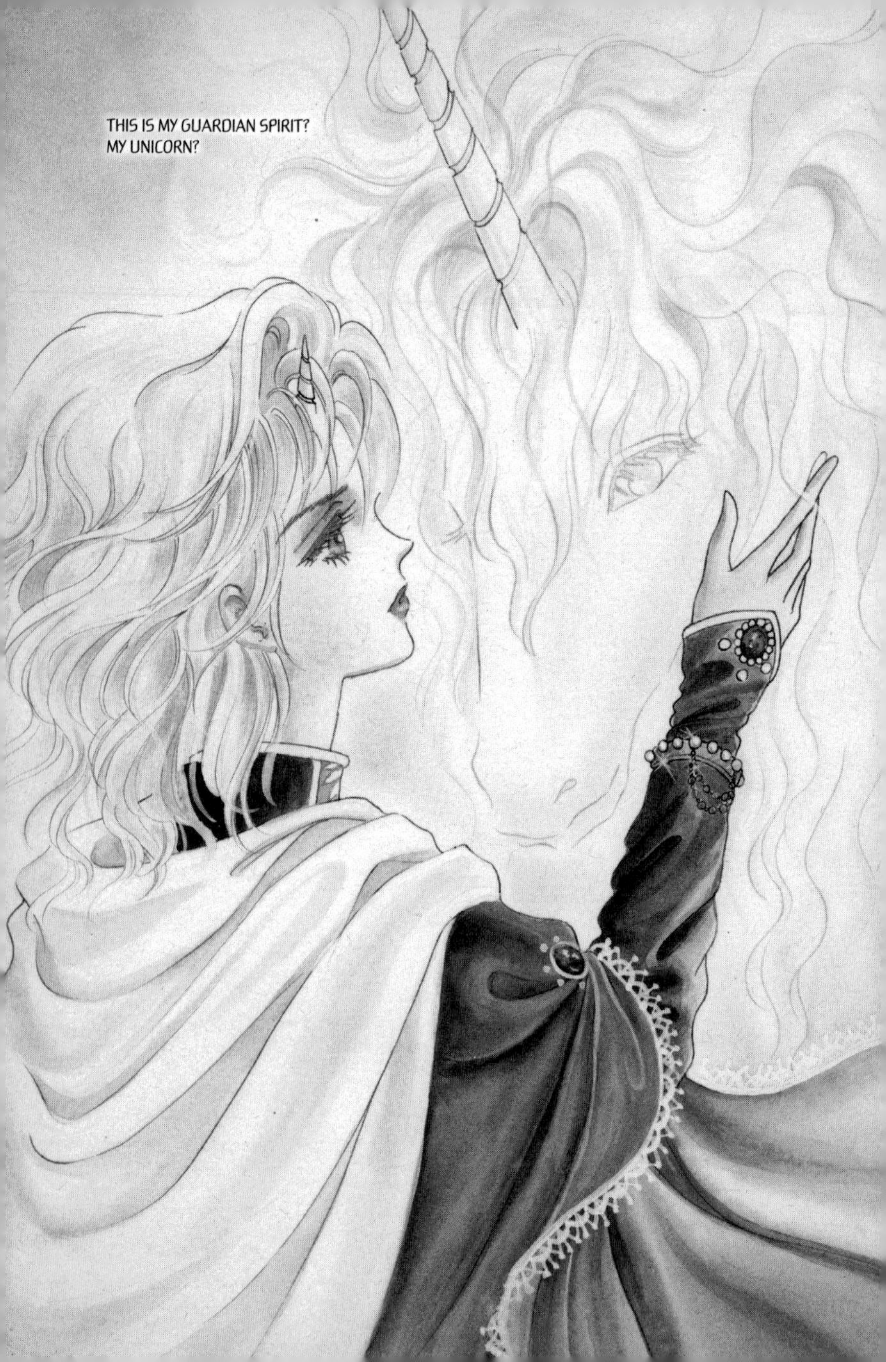
THIS IS MY GUARDIAN SPIRIT?
MY UNICORN?

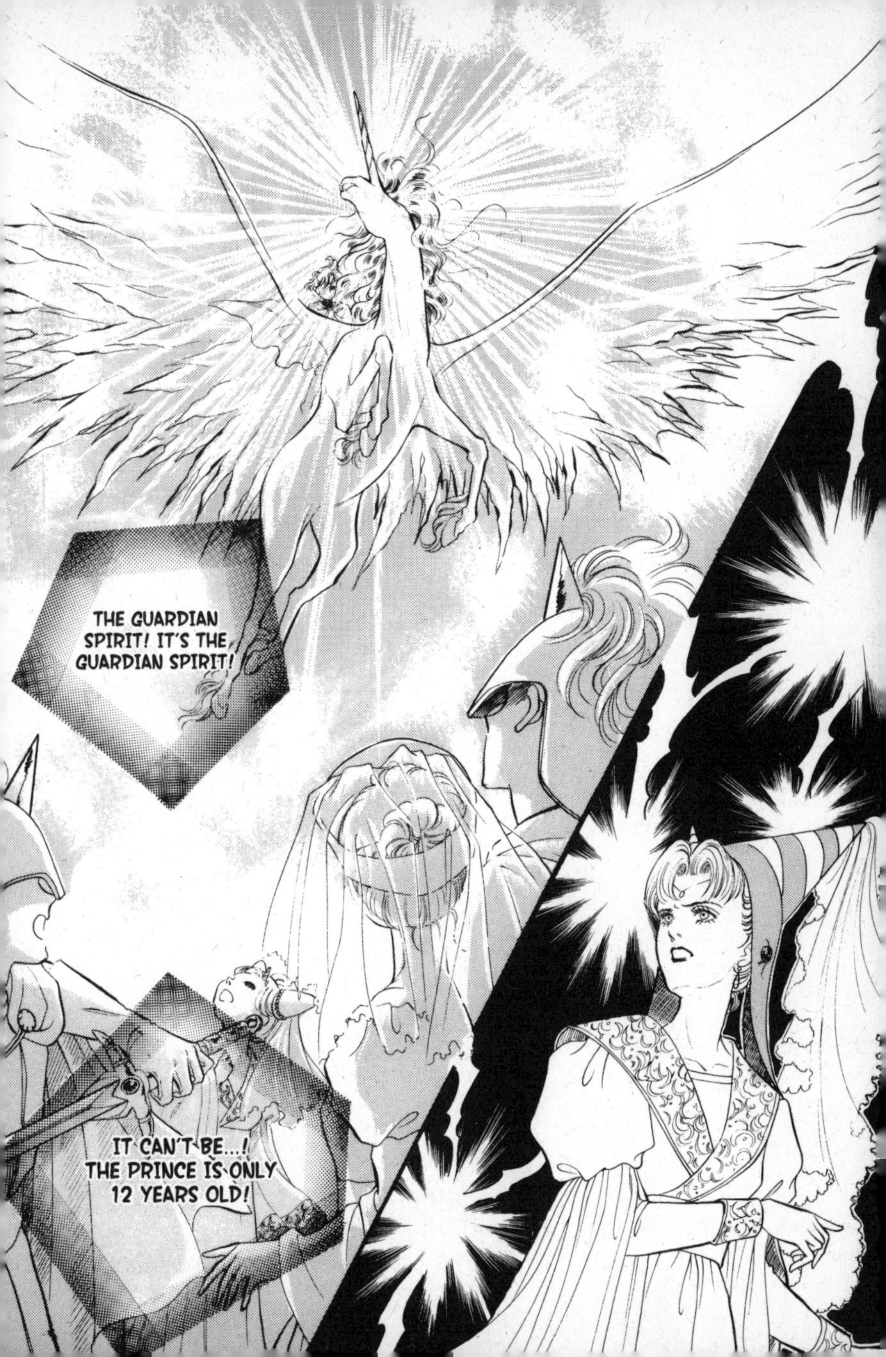
THE GUARDIAN SPIRIT! IT'S THE GUARDIAN SPIRIT!
IT CAN'T BE...! THE PRINCE IS ONLY 12 YEARS OLD!

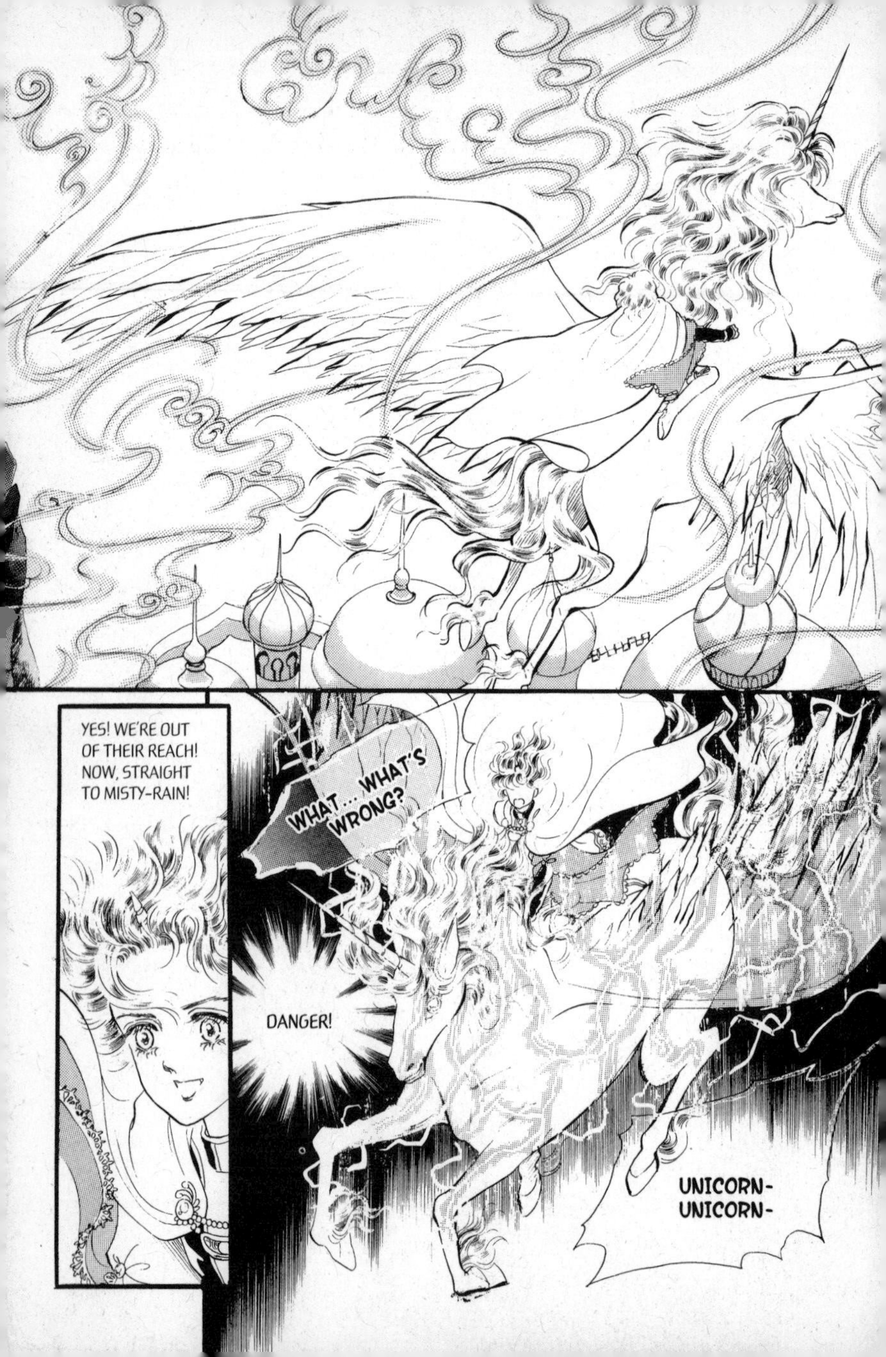
YES! WE'RE OUT OF THEIR REACH! NOW, STRAIGHT TO MISTY-RAIN!
WHAT... WHAT'S WRONG?
DANGER!
UNICORN-
UNICORN-

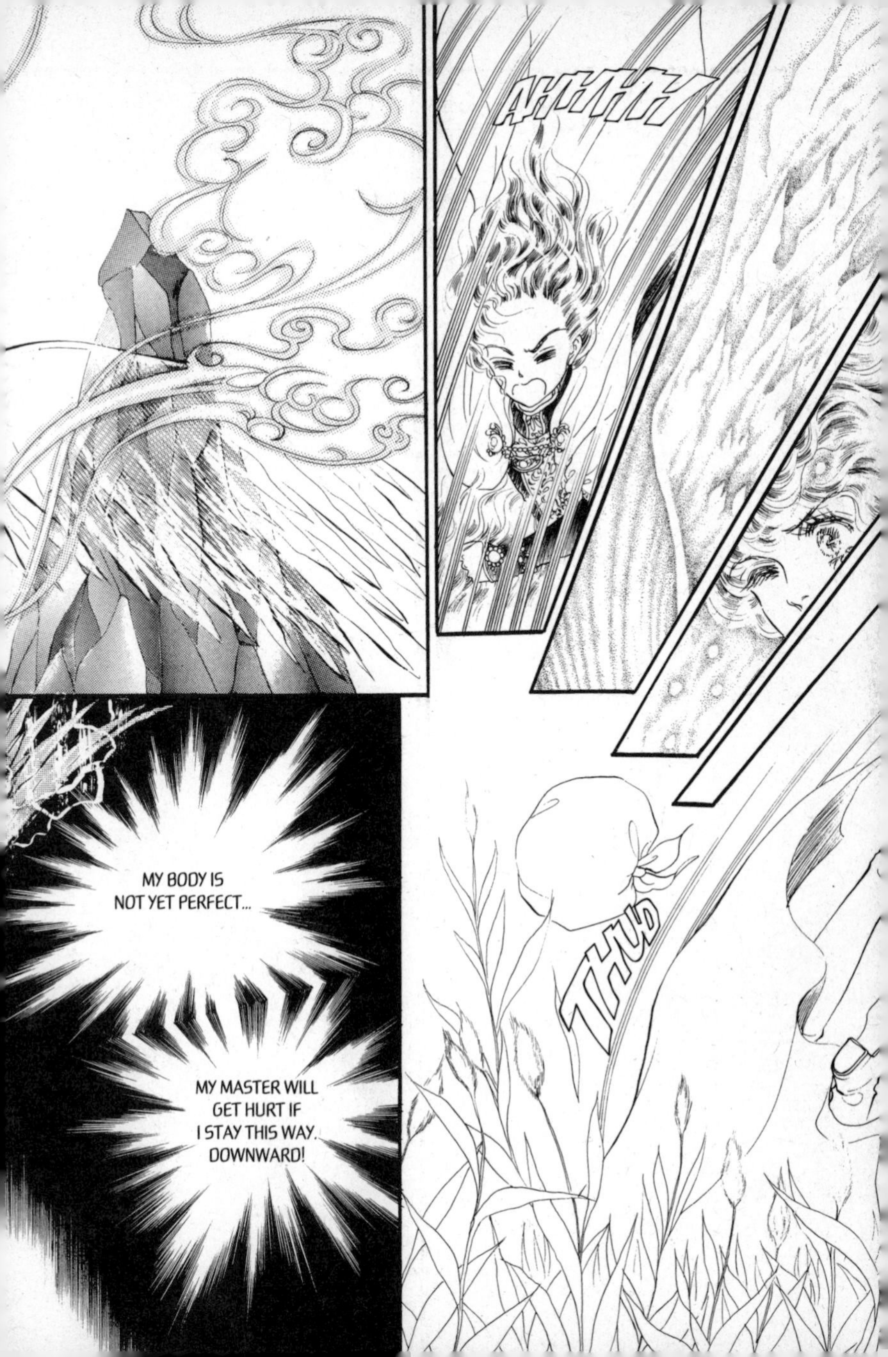
MY BODY IS NOT YET PERFECT...
MY MASTER WILL GET HURT IF I STAY THIS WAY. DOWNWARD!
THUD

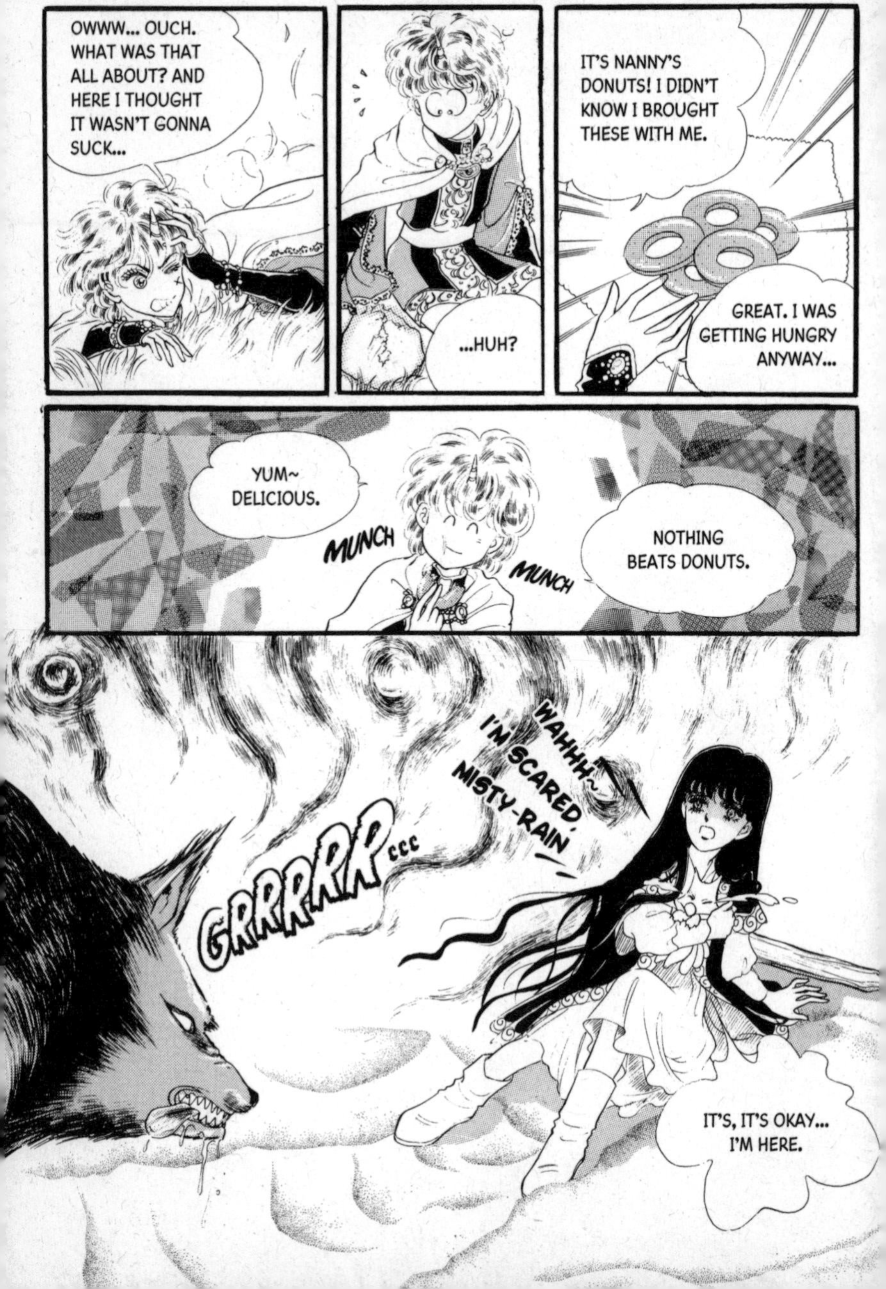
OWWW... OUCH. WHAT WAS THAT ALL ABOUT? AND HERE I THOUGHT IT WASN'T GONNA SUCK...
...HUH?
IT'S NANNY'S DONUTS! I DIDN'T KNOW I BROUGHT THESE WITH ME.
GREAT. I WAS GETTING HUNGRY ANYWAY...
YUM~ DELICIOUS.
MUNCH
MUNCH
NOTHING BEATS DONUTS.
GRRRRRP
WAHHH~ I'M SCARED, MISTY-RAIN
IT'S, IT'S OKAY... I'M HERE.

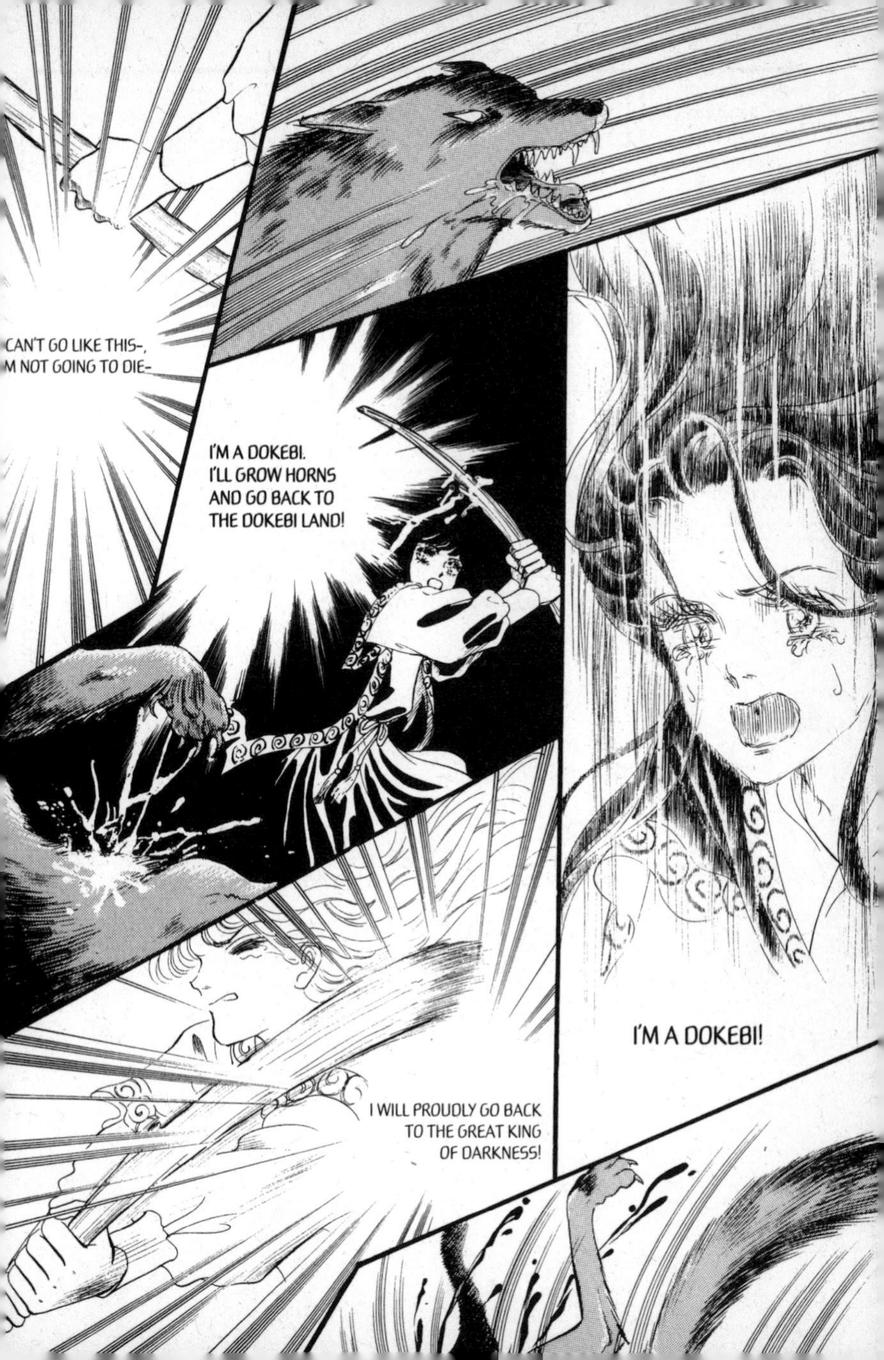
CAN'T GO LIKE THIS-,
M NOT GOING TO DIE-
I'M A DOKEBI. I'LL GROW HORNS AND GO BACK TO THE DOKEBI LAND!
I WILL PROUDLY GO BACK TO THE GREAT KING OF DARKNESS!
I'M A DOKEBI!

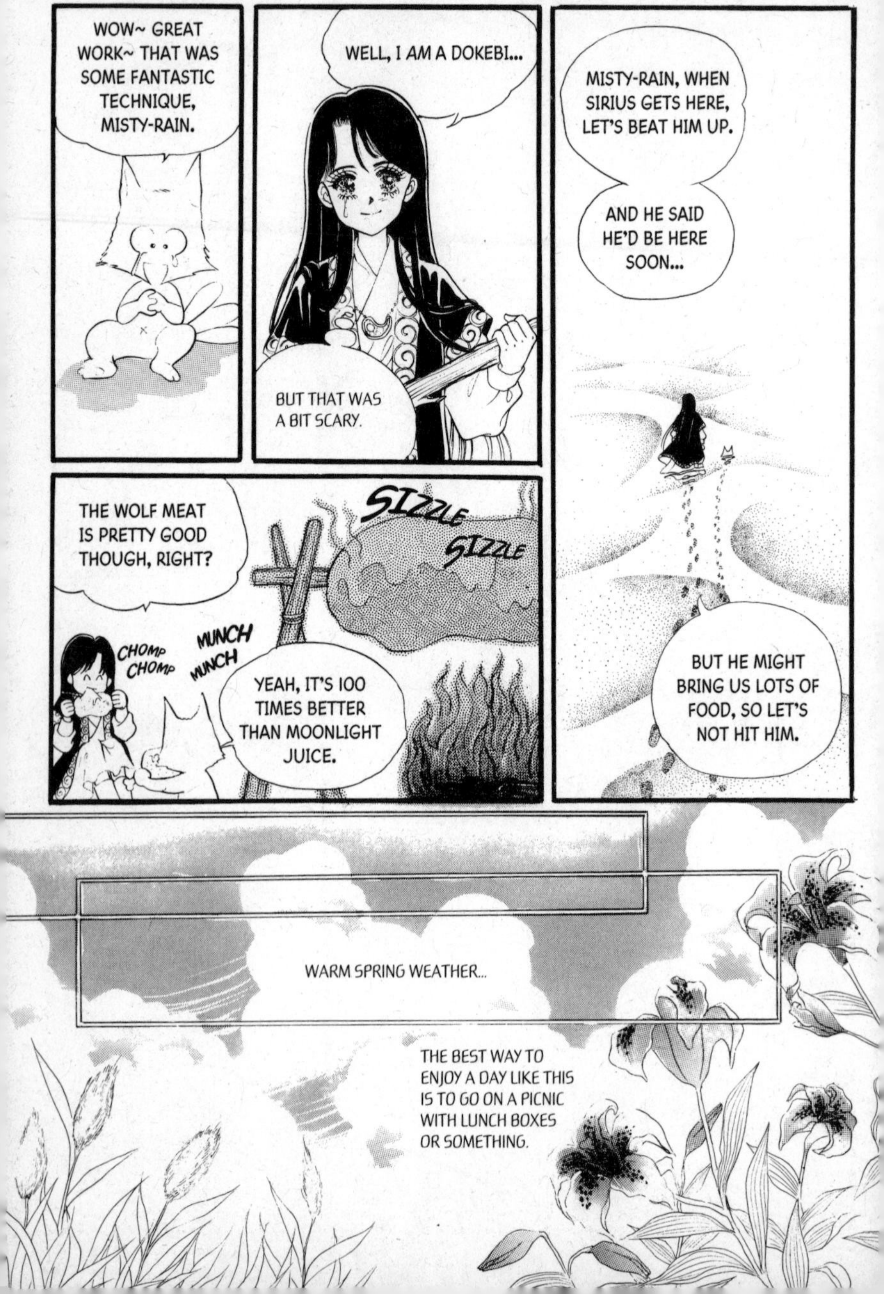
WOW~ GREAT WORK~ THAT WAS SOME FANTASTIC TECHNIQUE, MISTY-RAIN.
WELL, I *AM* A DOKEBI...
BUT THAT WAS A BIT SCARY.
MISTY-RAIN, WHEN SIRIUS GETS HERE, LET'S BEAT HIM UP.
AND HE SAID HE'D BE HERE SOON...
THE WOLF MEAT IS PRETTY GOOD THOUGH, RIGHT?
SIZZLE
SIZZLE
CHOMP CHOMP
MUNCH MUNCH
YEAH, IT'S 100 TIMES BETTER THAN MOONLIGHT JUICE.
BUT HE MIGHT BRING US LOTS OF FOOD, SO LET'S NOT HIT HIM.
WARM SPRING WEATHER...
THE BEST WAY TO ENJOY A DAY LIKE THIS IS TO GO ON A PICNIC WITH LUNCH BOXES OR SOMETHING.

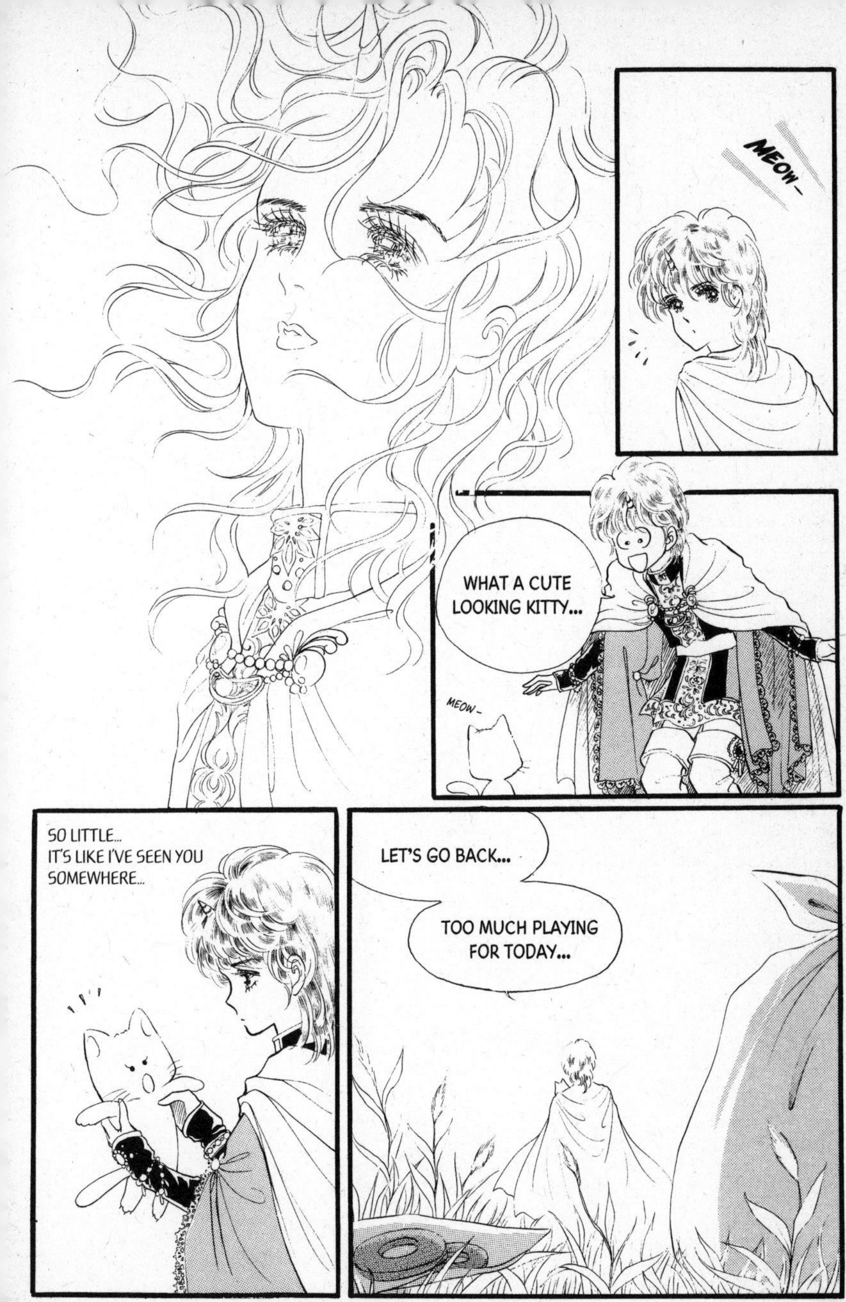
MEOW-
WHAT A CUTE LOOKING KITTY...
MEOW-
SO LITTLE... IT'S LIKE I'VE SEEN YOU SOMEWHERE...
LET'S GO BACK...
TOO MUCH PLAYING FOR TODAY...

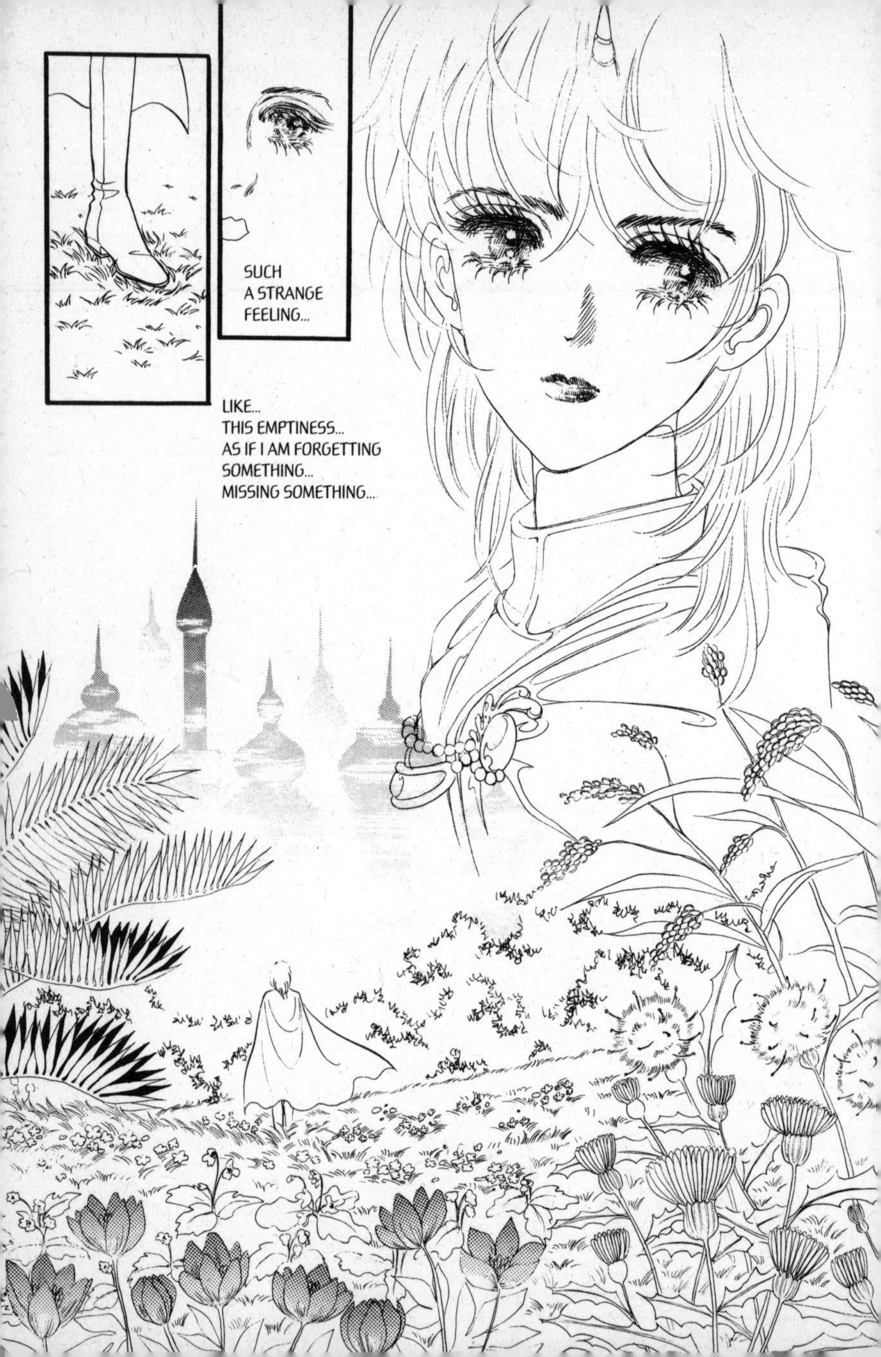
SUCH A STRANGE FEELING...
LIKE... THIS EMPTINESS... AS IF I AM FORGETTING SOMETHING... MISSING SOMETHING...

PART 1 LAND OF THE GODS

CHAPTER 7
MISTY-RAIN COMES TO THE HUMAN WORLD

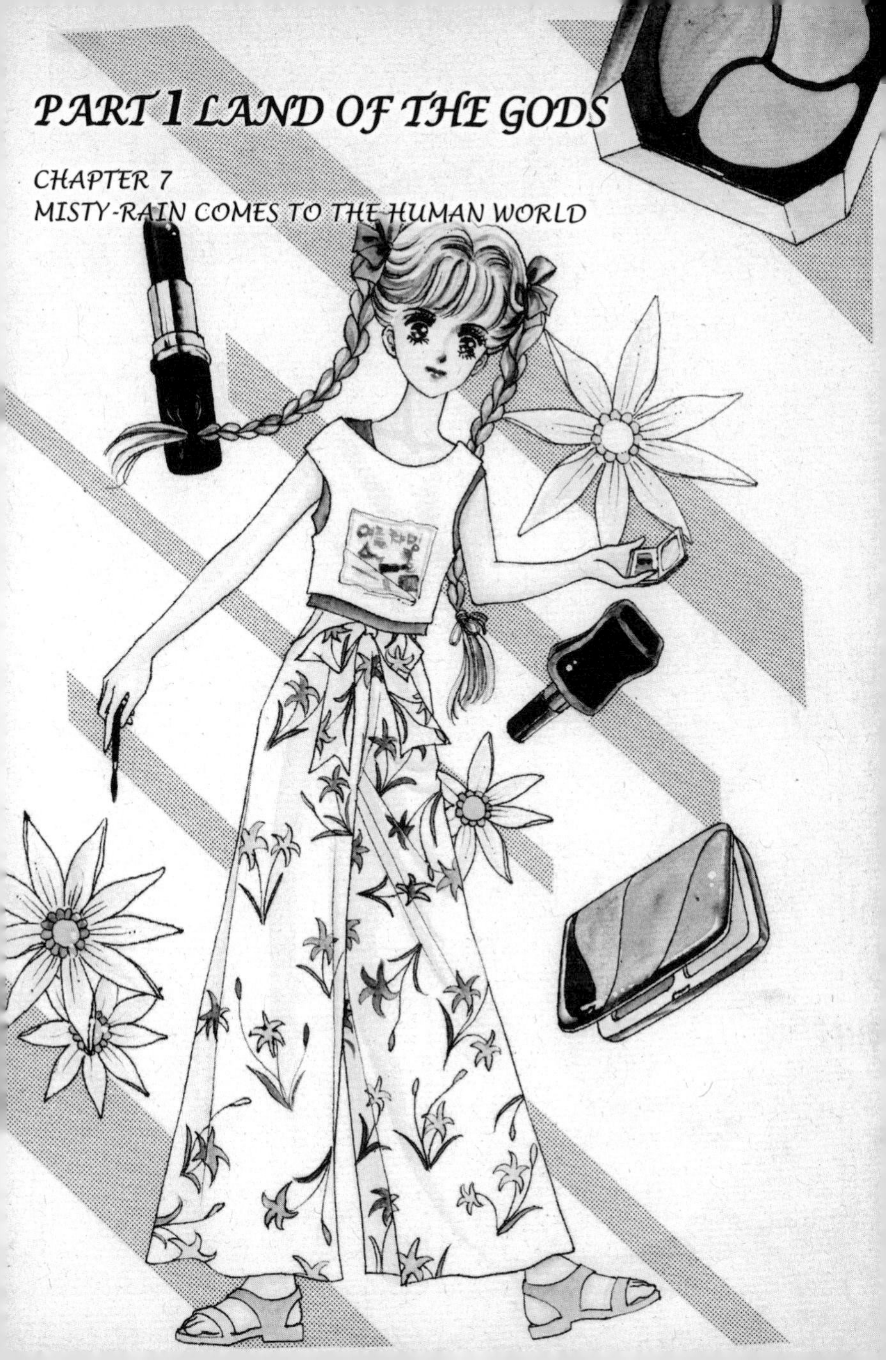

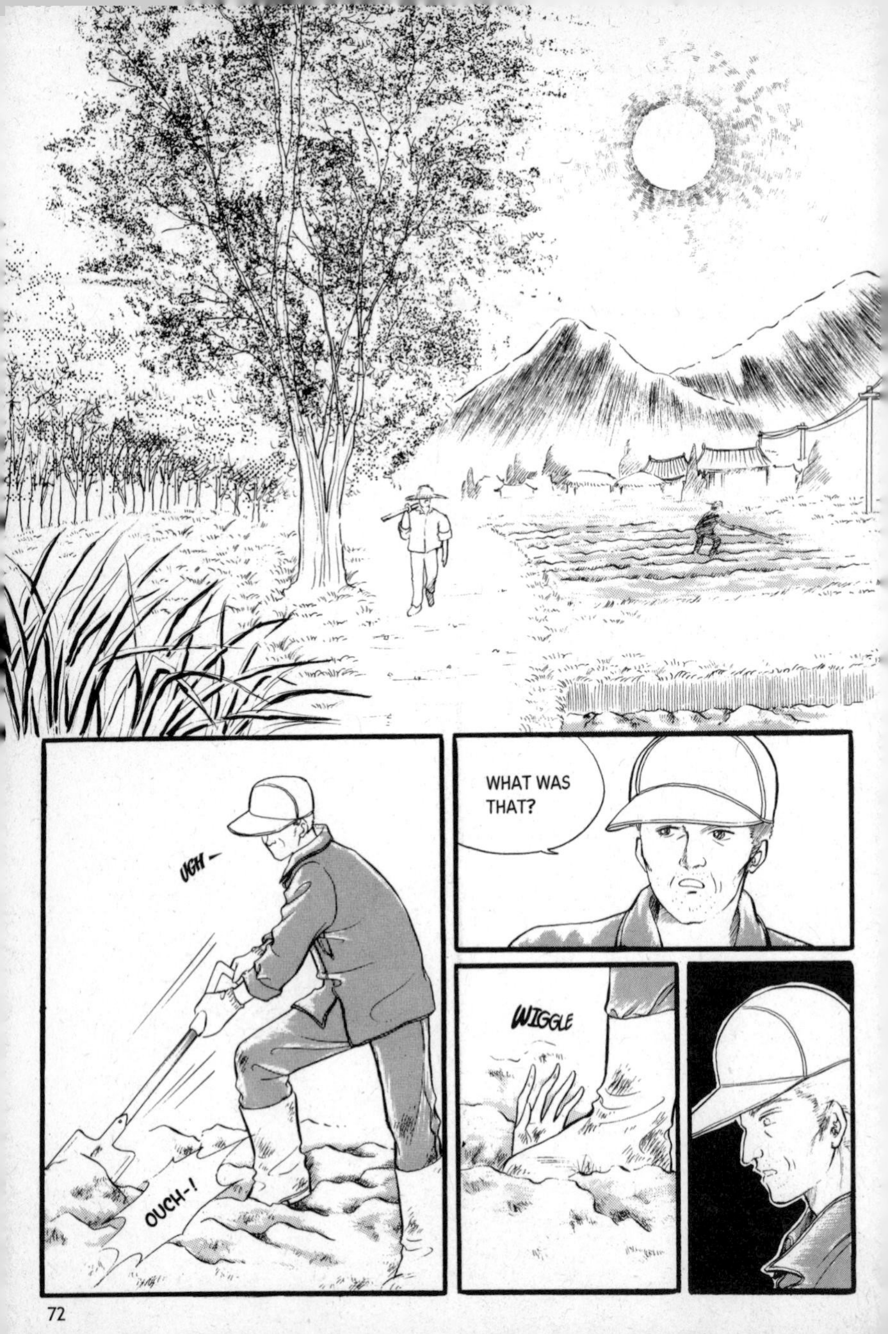
UGH-
OUCH-!
WHAT WAS THAT?
WIGGLE

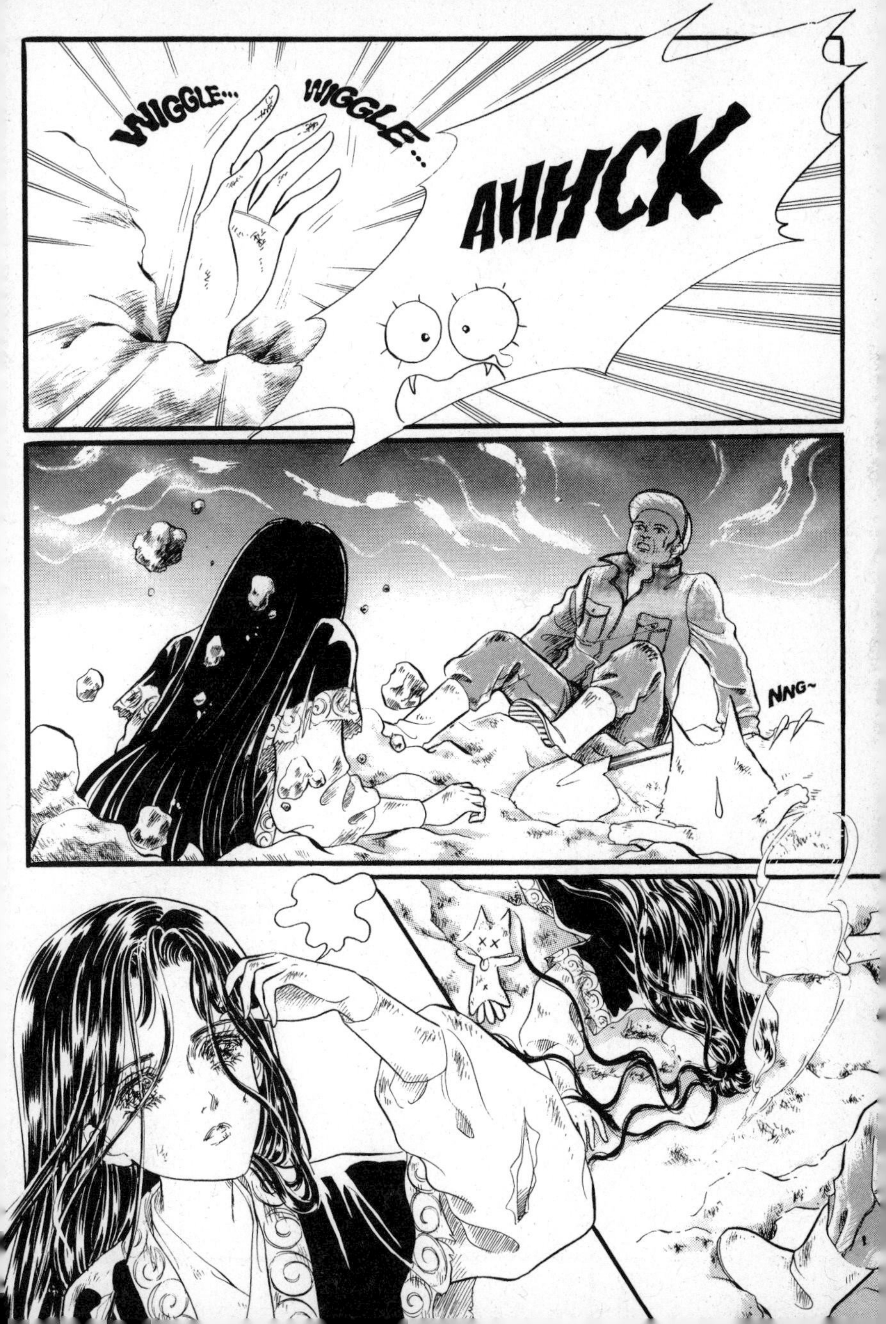
WIGGLE...
WIGGLE...
AHHCK
NNG~

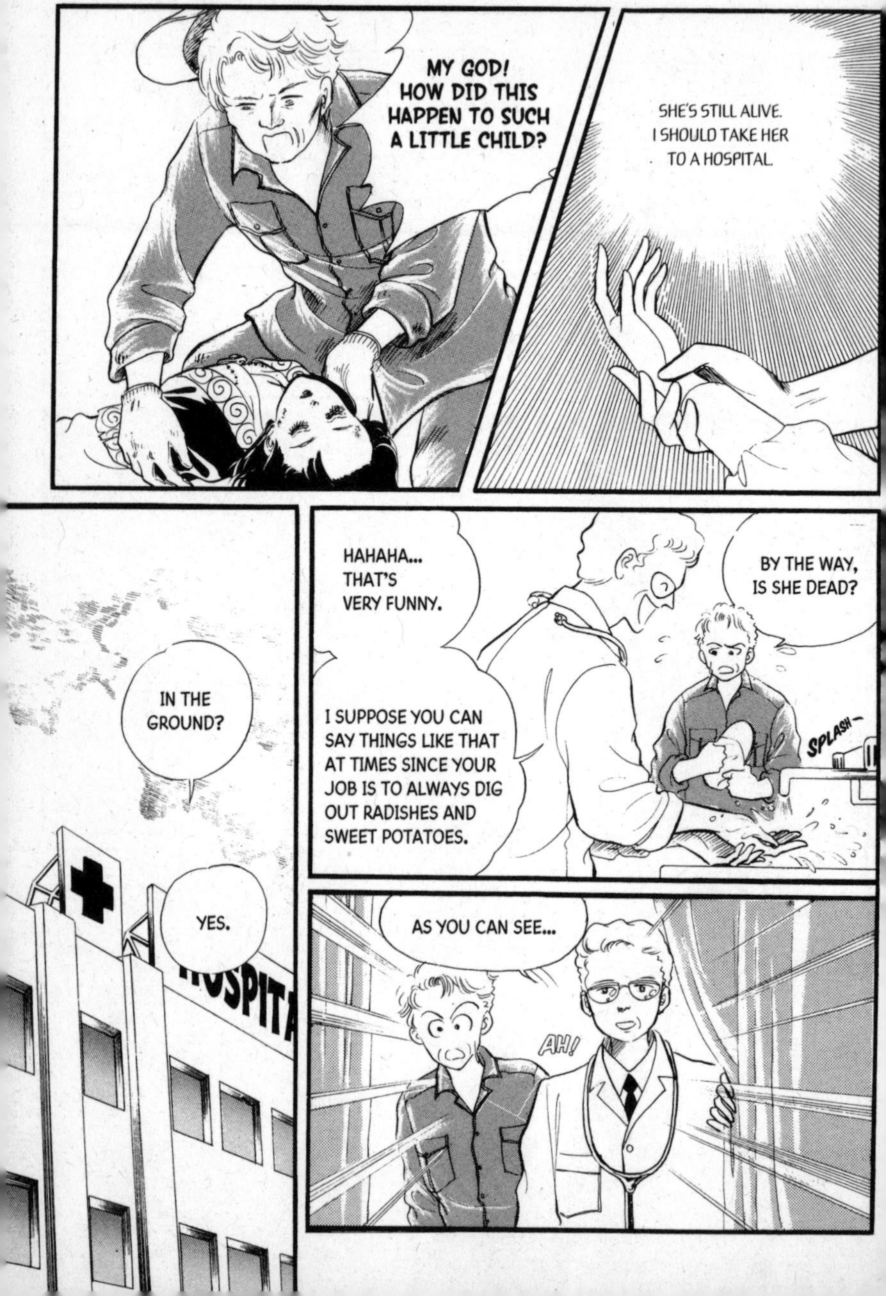
MY GOD! HOW DID THIS HAPPEN TO SUCH A LITTLE CHILD?
SHE'S STILL ALIVE. I SHOULD TAKE HER TO A HOSPITAL.
BY THE WAY, IS SHE DEAD?
HAHAHA... THAT'S VERY FUNNY.
I SUPPOSE YOU CAN SAY THINGS LIKE THAT AT TIMES SINCE YOUR JOB IS TO ALWAYS DIG OUT RADISHES AND SWEET POTATOES.
SPLASH—
IN THE GROUND?
YES.
HOSPITA
AS YOU CAN SEE...
AH!

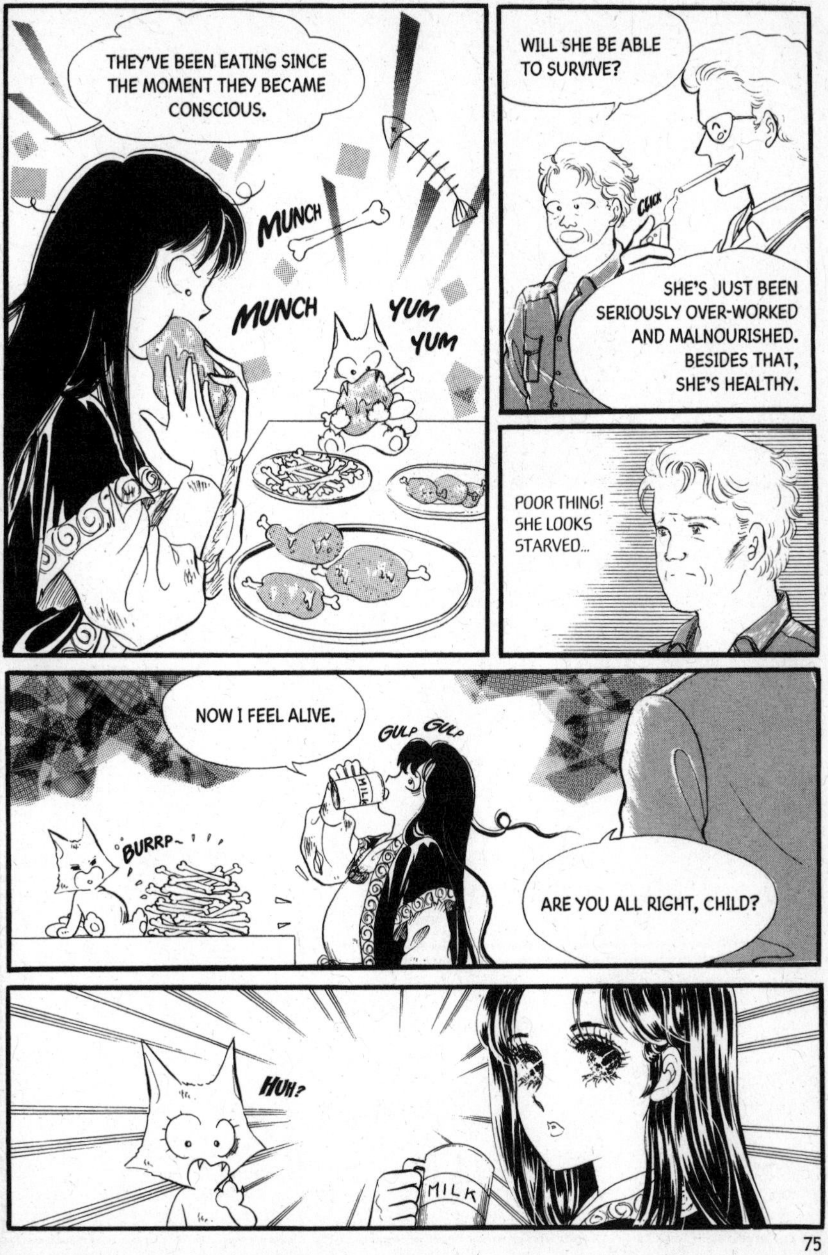
THEY'VE BEEN EATING SINCE THE MOMENT THEY BECAME CONSCIOUS.
MUNCH
MUNCH
YUM YUM
WILL SHE BE ABLE TO SURVIVE?
CLICK
SHE'S JUST BEEN SERIOUSLY OVER-WORKED AND MALNOURISHED. BESIDES THAT, SHE'S HEALTHY.
POOR THING! SHE LOOKS STARVED...
NOW I FEEL ALIVE.
GULP GULP
MILK
BURRP~
ARE YOU ALL RIGHT, CHILD?
HUH?
MILK

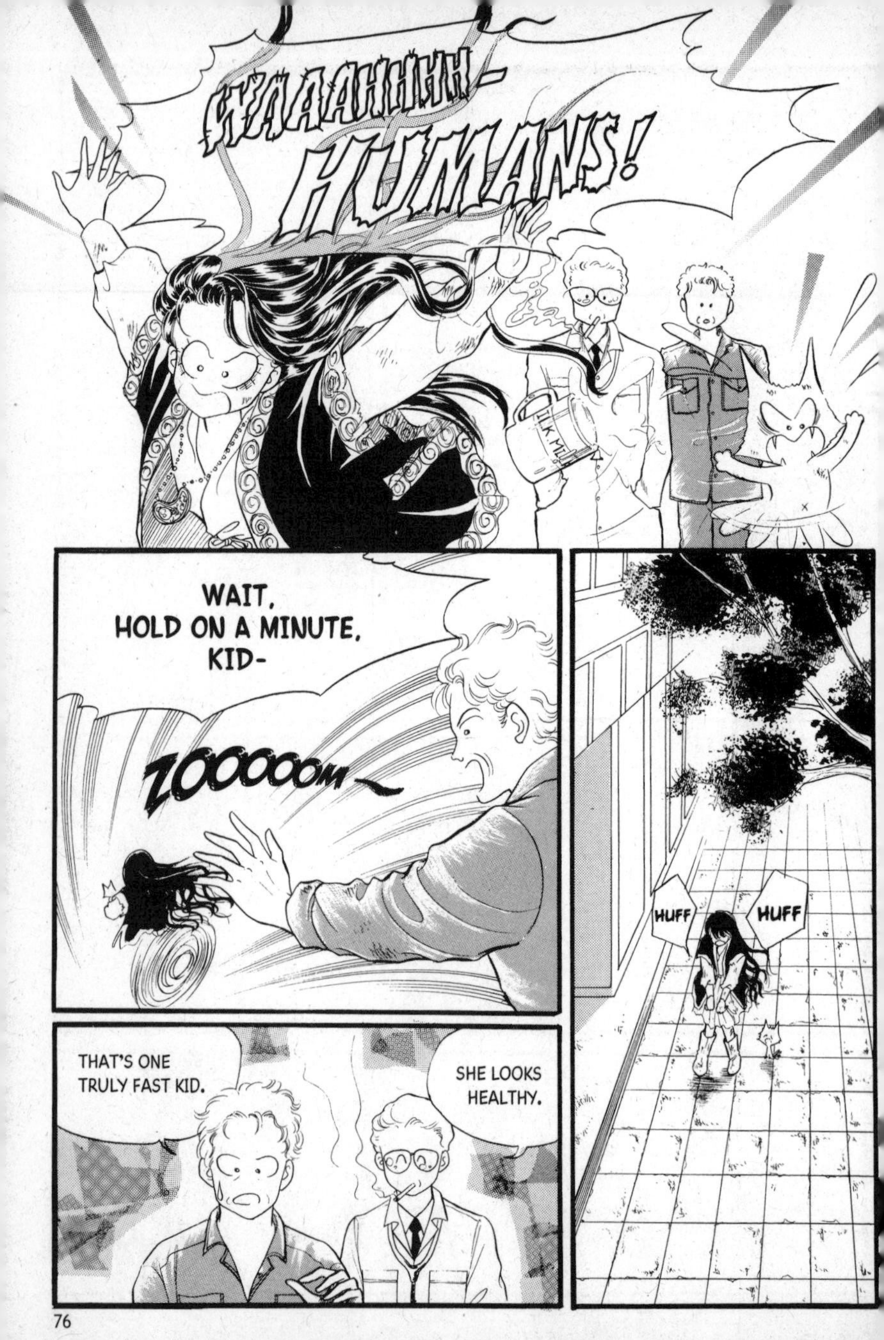
KYAAAHHHH-
HUMANS!
WAIT, HOLD ON A MINUTE, KID-
ZOOOOOM~
THAT'S ONE TRULY FAST KID.
SHE LOOKS HEALTHY.
HUFF
HUFF

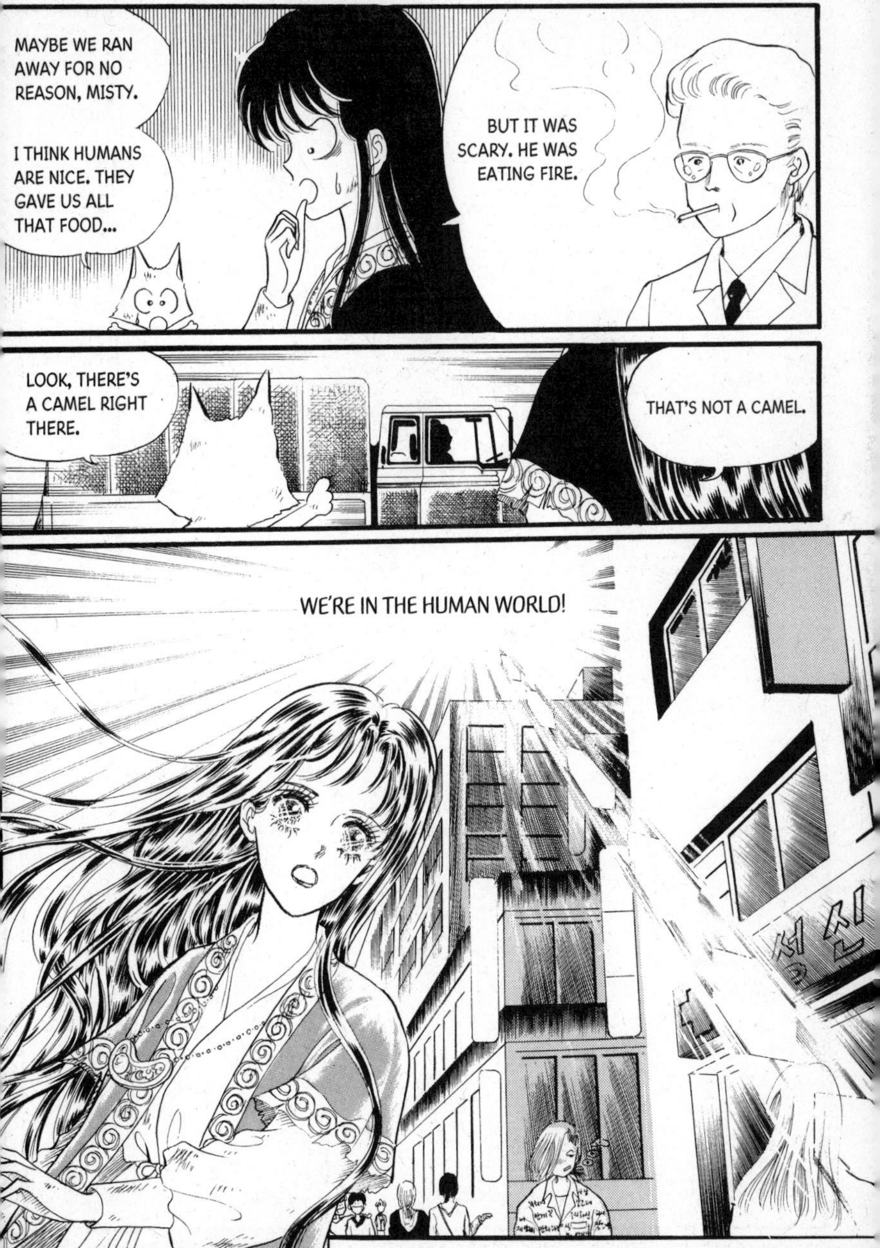
MAYBE WE RAN AWAY FOR NO REASON, MISTY.
I THINK HUMANS ARE NICE. THEY GAVE US ALL THAT FOOD...
BUT IT WAS SCARY. HE WAS EATING FIRE.
LOOK, THERE'S A CAMEL RIGHT THERE.
THAT'S NOT A CAMEL.
WE'RE IN THE HUMAN WORLD!

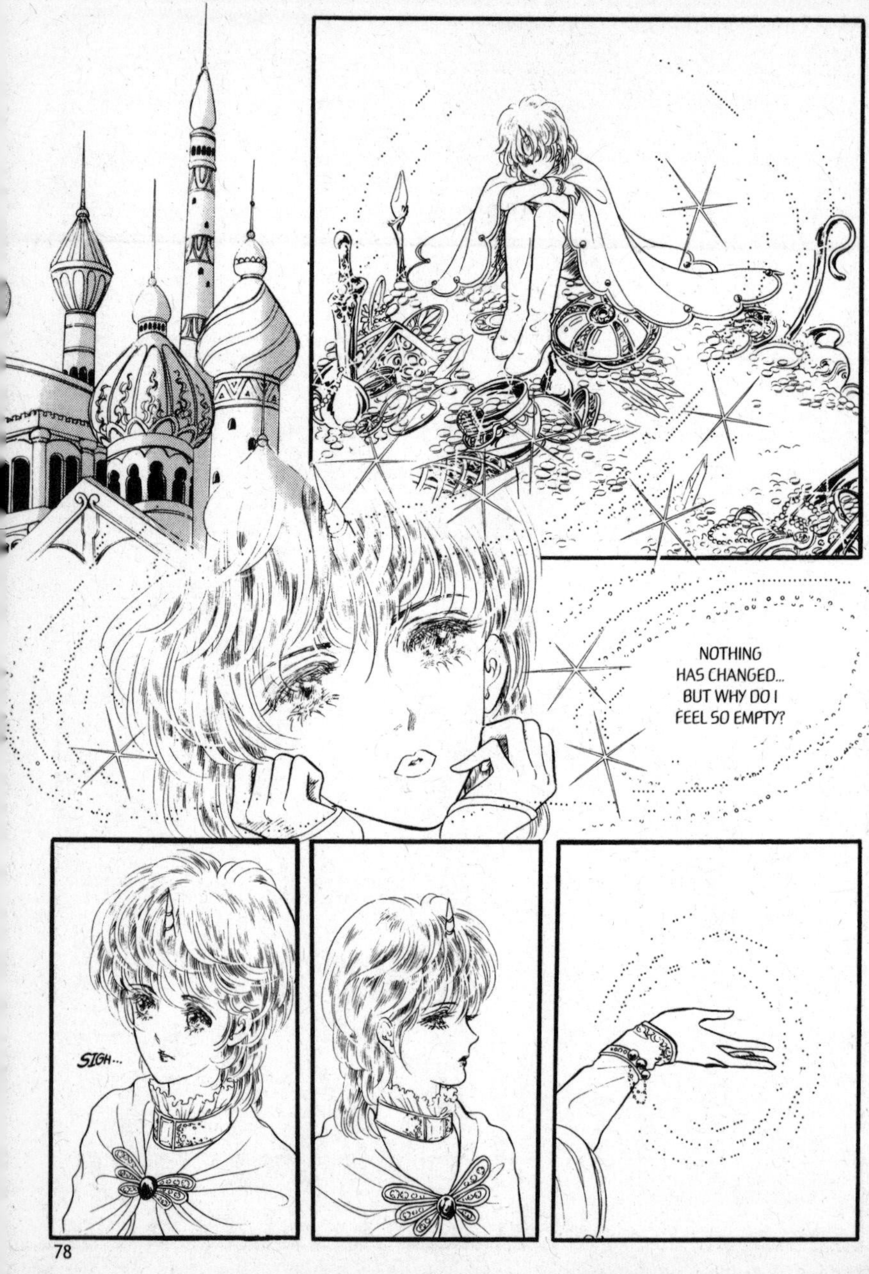
NOTHING HAS CHANGED... BUT WHY DO I FEEL SO EMPTY?
SIGH...

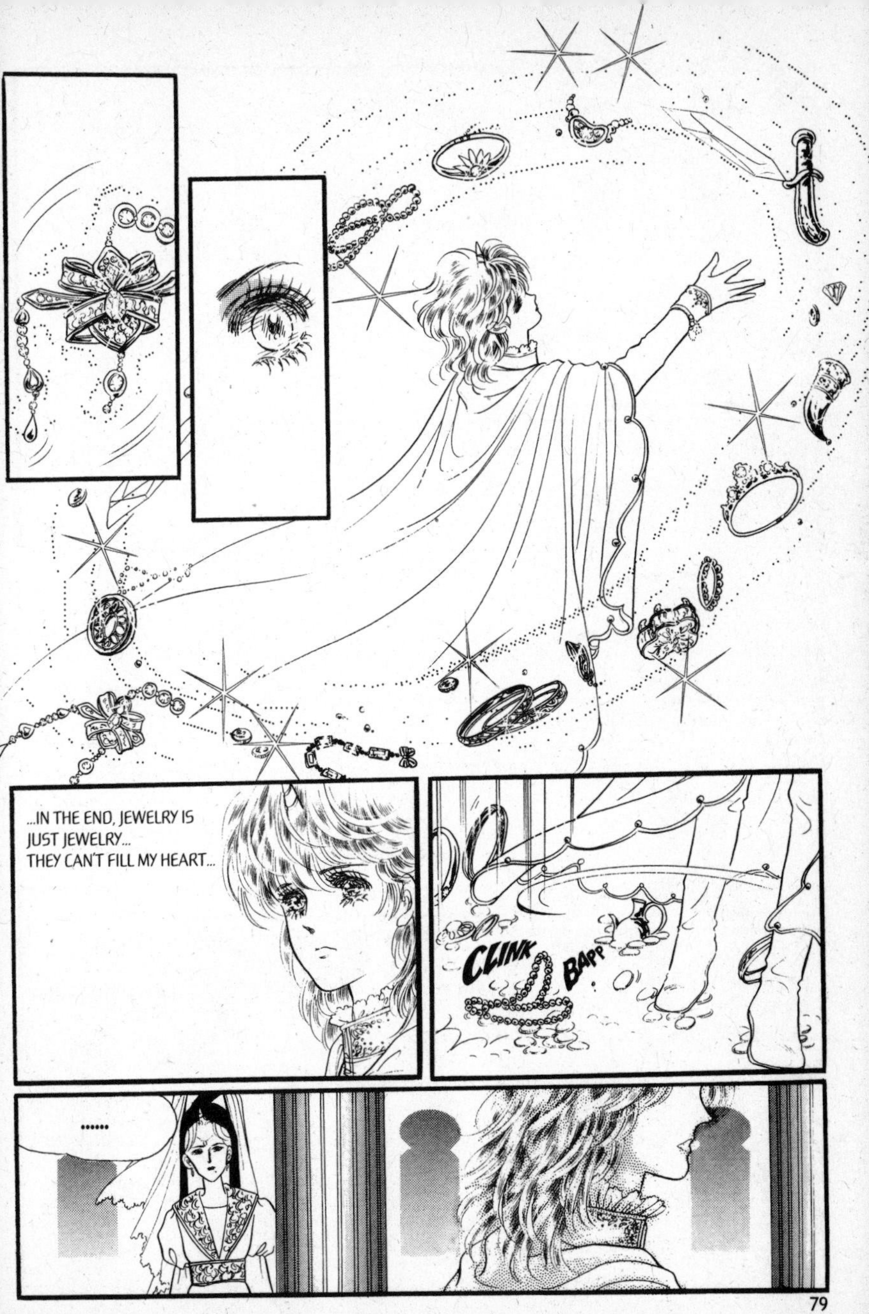
...IN THE END, JEWELRY IS
JUST JEWELRY...
THEY CAN'T FILL MY HEART...
CLINK
BAPP
......

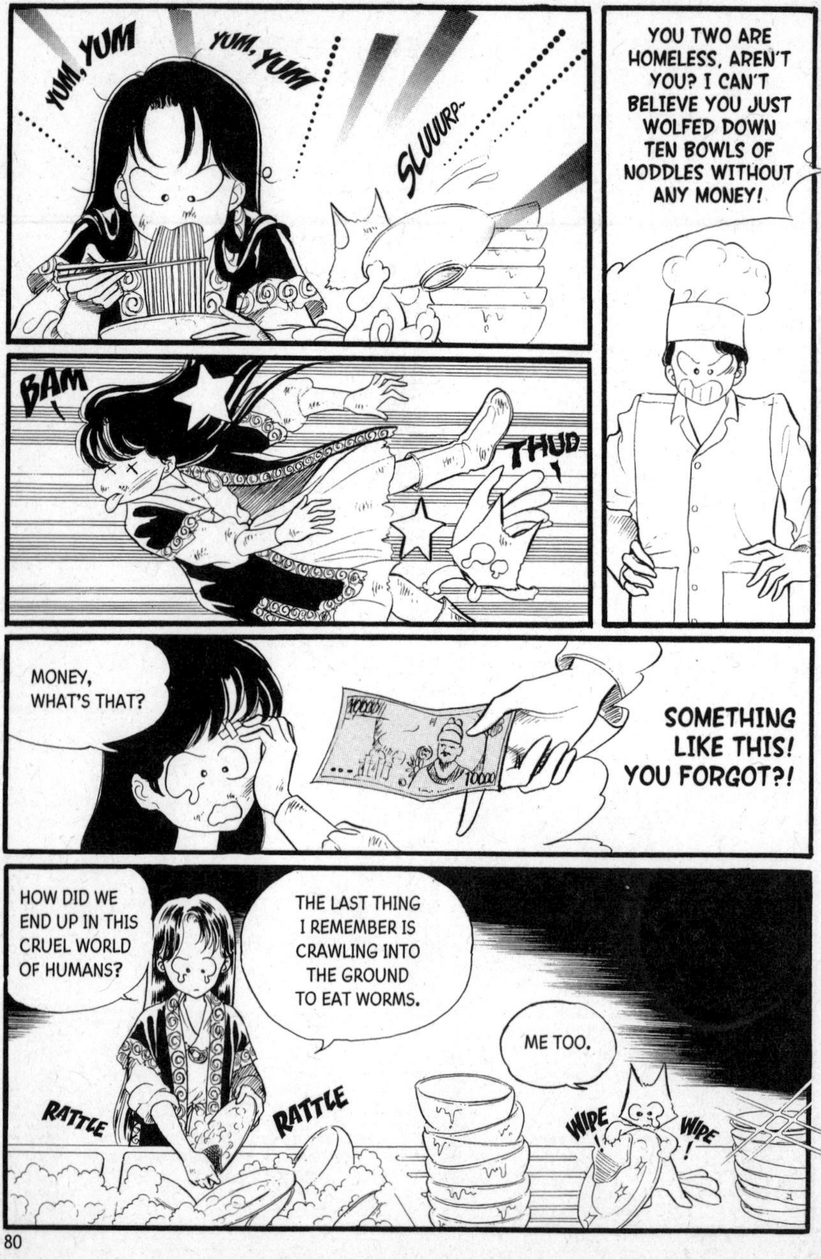
YUM, YUM
YUM, YUM
SLUUURP~
YOU TWO ARE HOMELESS, AREN'T YOU? I CAN'T BELIEVE YOU JUST WOLFED DOWN TEN BOWLS OF NODDLES WITHOUT ANY MONEY!
BAM
THUD
MONEY, WHAT'S THAT?
SOMETHING LIKE THIS! YOU FORGOT?!
HOW DID WE END UP IN THIS CRUEL WORLD OF HUMANS?
THE LAST THING I REMEMBER IS CRAWLING INTO THE GROUND TO EAT WORMS.
ME TOO.
RATTLE
RATTLE
WIPE
WIPE

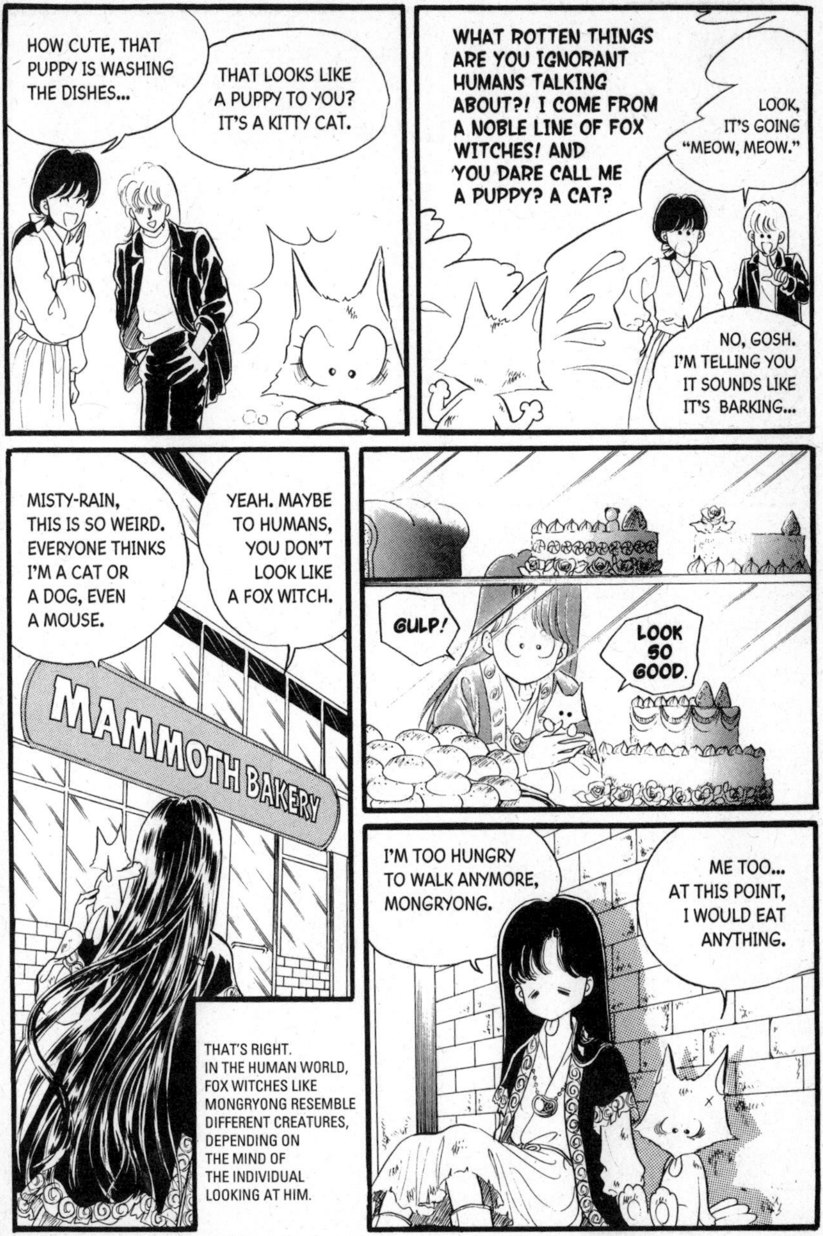
HOW CUTE, THAT PUPPY IS WASHING THE DISHES...
THAT LOOKS LIKE A PUPPY TO YOU? IT'S A KITTY CAT.
WHAT ROTTEN THINGS ARE YOU IGNORANT HUMANS TALKING ABOUT?! I COME FROM A NOBLE LINE OF FOX WITCHES! AND YOU DARE CALL ME A PUPPY? A CAT?
LOOK, IT'S GOING "MEOW, MEOW."
NO, GOSH. I'M TELLING YOU IT SOUNDS LIKE IT'S BARKING...
MISTY-RAIN, THIS IS SO WEIRD. EVERYONE THINKS I'M A CAT OR A DOG, EVEN A MOUSE.
YEAH. MAYBE TO HUMANS, YOU DON'T LOOK LIKE A FOX WITCH.
MAMMOTH BAKERY
THAT'S RIGHT. IN THE HUMAN WORLD, FOX WITCHES LIKE MONGRYONG RESEMBLE DIFFERENT CREATURES, DEPENDING ON THE MIND OF THE INDIVIDUAL LOOKING AT HIM.
GULP!
LOOK SO GOOD.
I'M TOO HUNGRY TO WALK ANYMORE, MONGRYONG.
ME TOO... AT THIS POINT, I WOULD EAT ANYTHING.

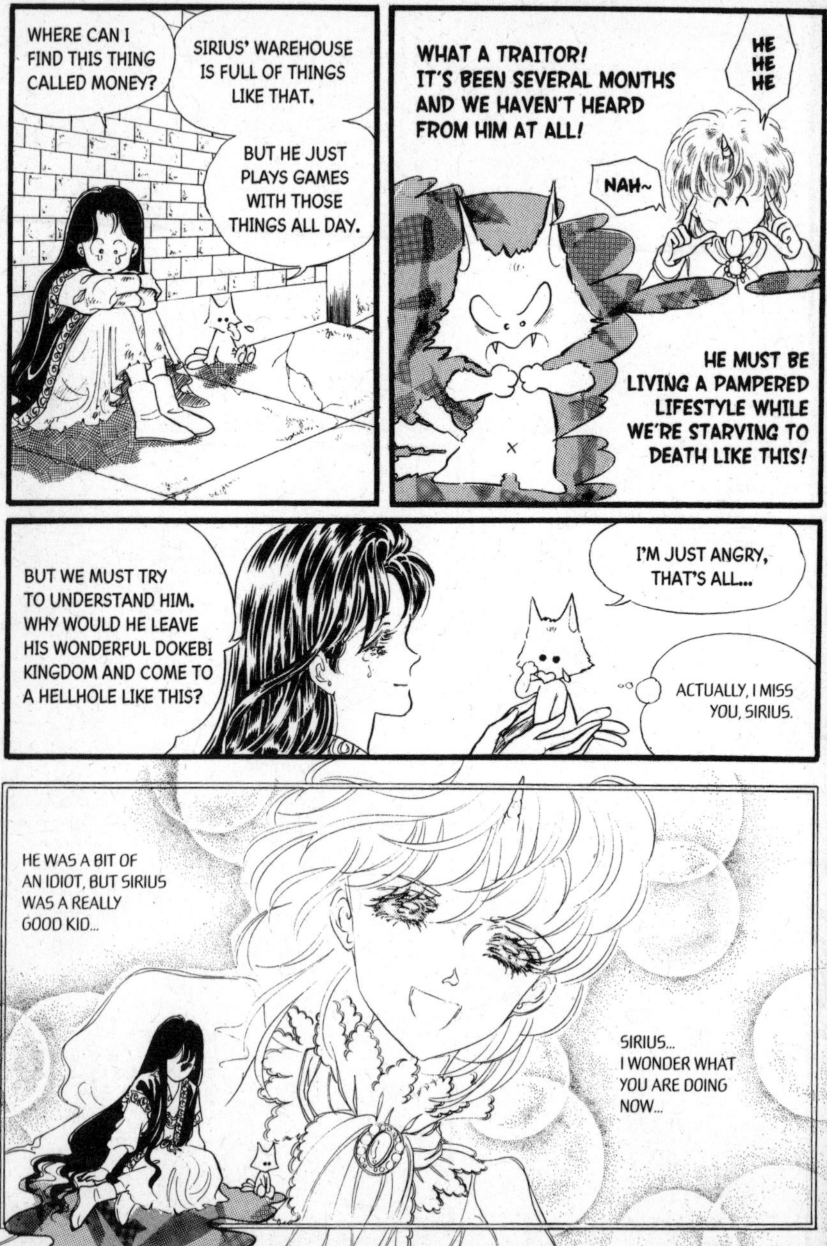
WHERE CAN I FIND THIS THING CALLED MONEY?
SIRIUS' WAREHOUSE IS FULL OF THINGS LIKE THAT.
BUT HE JUST PLAYS GAMES WITH THOSE THINGS ALL DAY.
WHAT A TRAITOR! IT'S BEEN SEVERAL MONTHS AND WE HAVEN'T HEARD FROM HIM AT ALL!
HE HE HE
NAH~
HE MUST BE LIVING A PAMPERED LIFESTYLE WHILE WE'RE STARVING TO DEATH LIKE THIS!
BUT WE MUST TRY TO UNDERSTAND HIM. WHY WOULD HE LEAVE HIS WONDERFUL DOKEBI KINGDOM AND COME TO A HELLHOLE LIKE THIS?
I'M JUST ANGRY, THAT'S ALL...
ACTUALLY, I MISS YOU, SIRIUS.
HE WAS A BIT OF AN IDIOT, BUT SIRIUS WAS A REALLY GOOD KID...
SIRIUS... I WONDER WHAT YOU ARE DOING NOW...

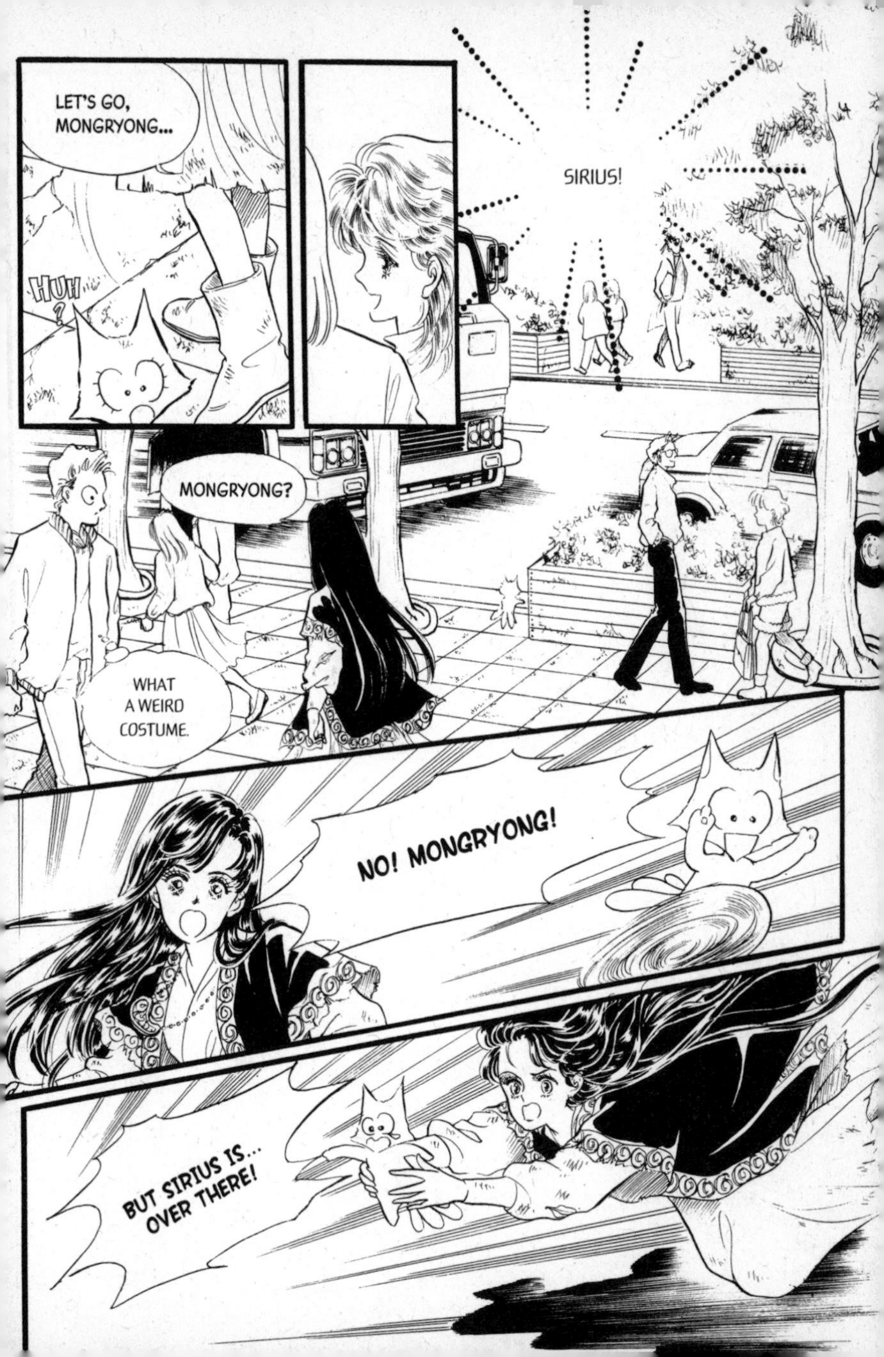
LET'S GO, MONGRYONG...
HUH ?
SIRIUS!
MONGRYONG?
WHAT A WEIRD COSTUME.
NO! MONGRYONG!
BUT SIRIUS IS... OVER THERE!

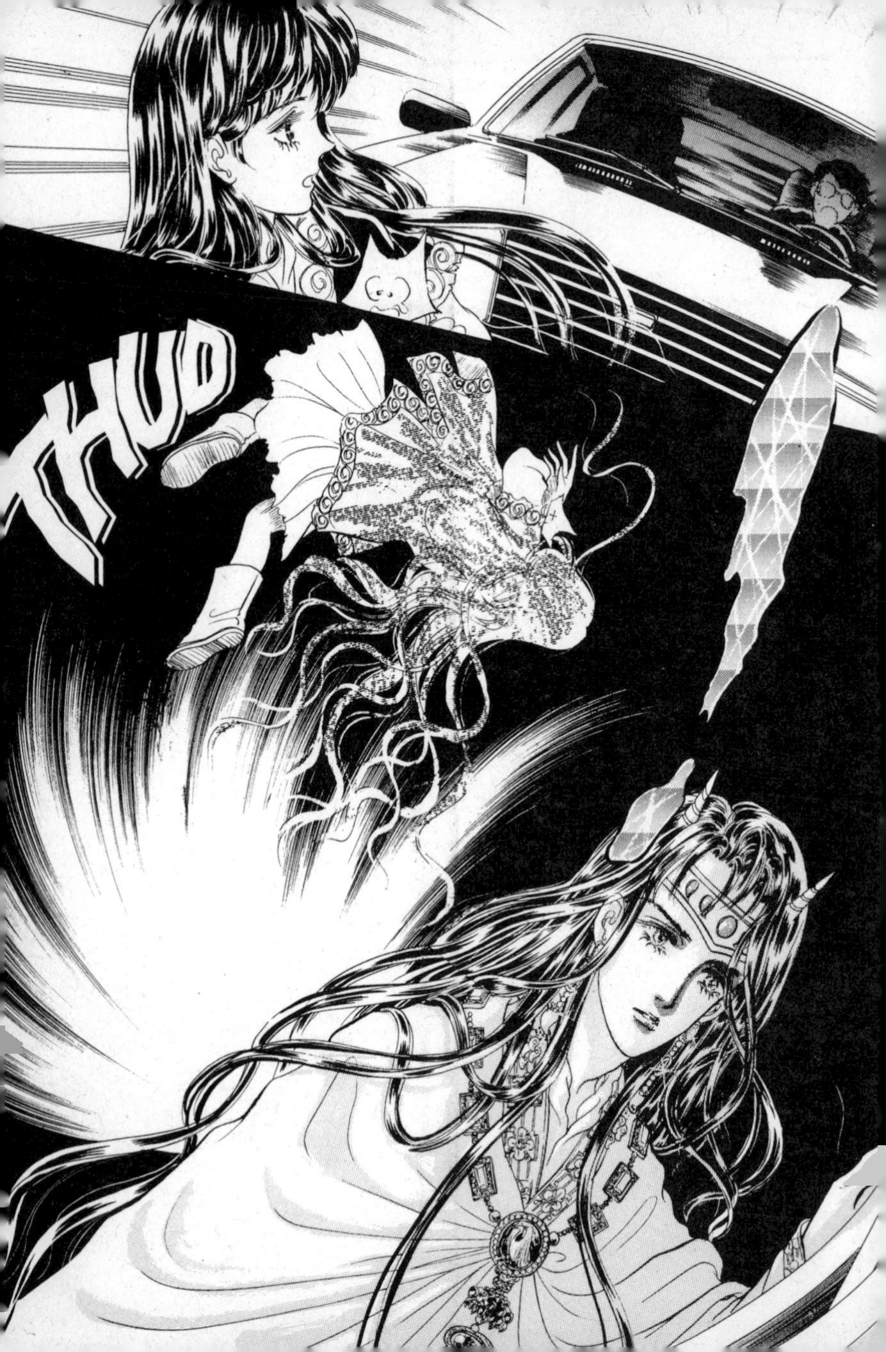
THUD

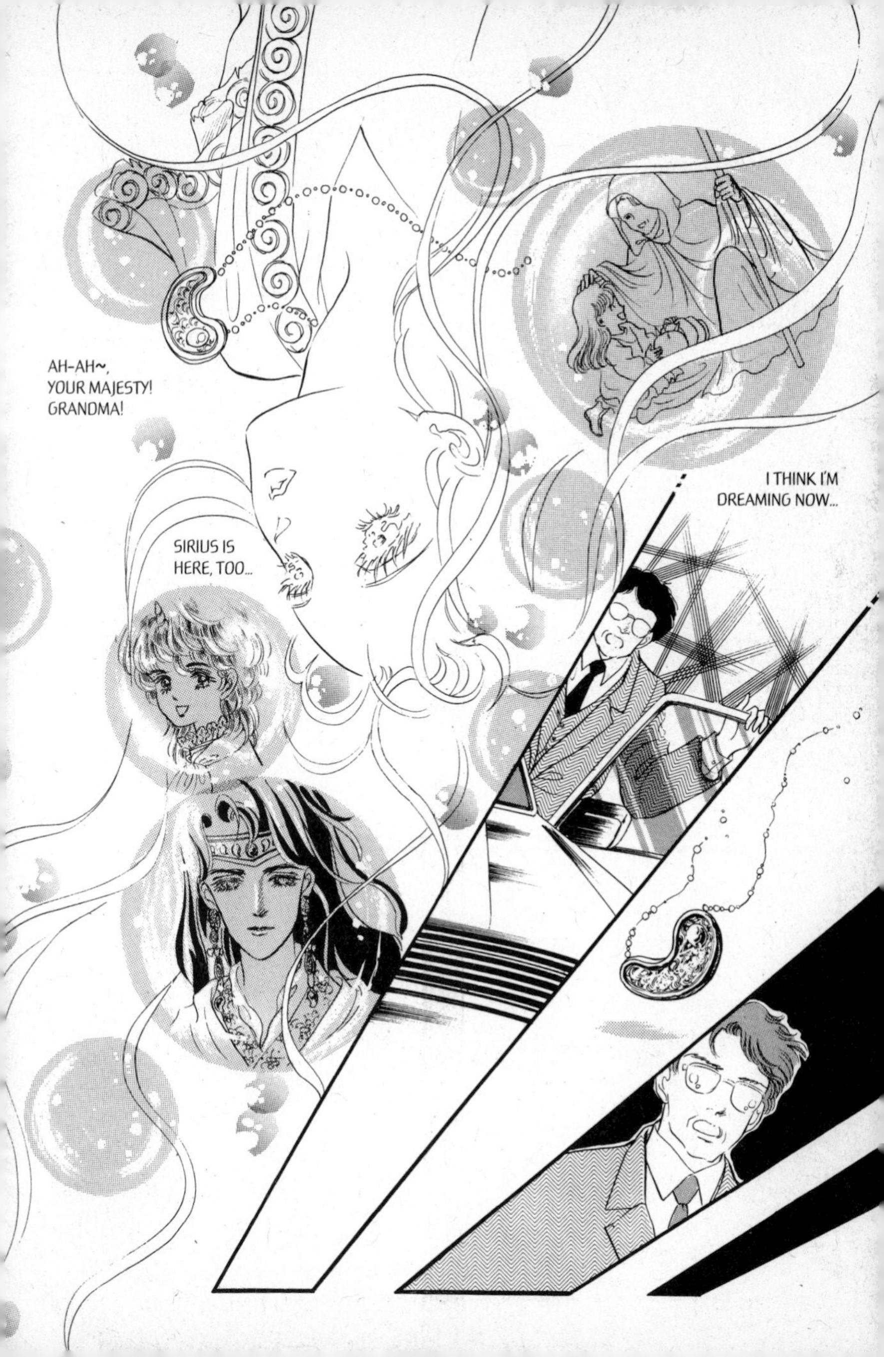
AH-AH~,
YOUR MAJESTY!
GRANDMA!
SIRIUS IS
HERE, TOO...
I THINK I'M
DREAMING NOW...

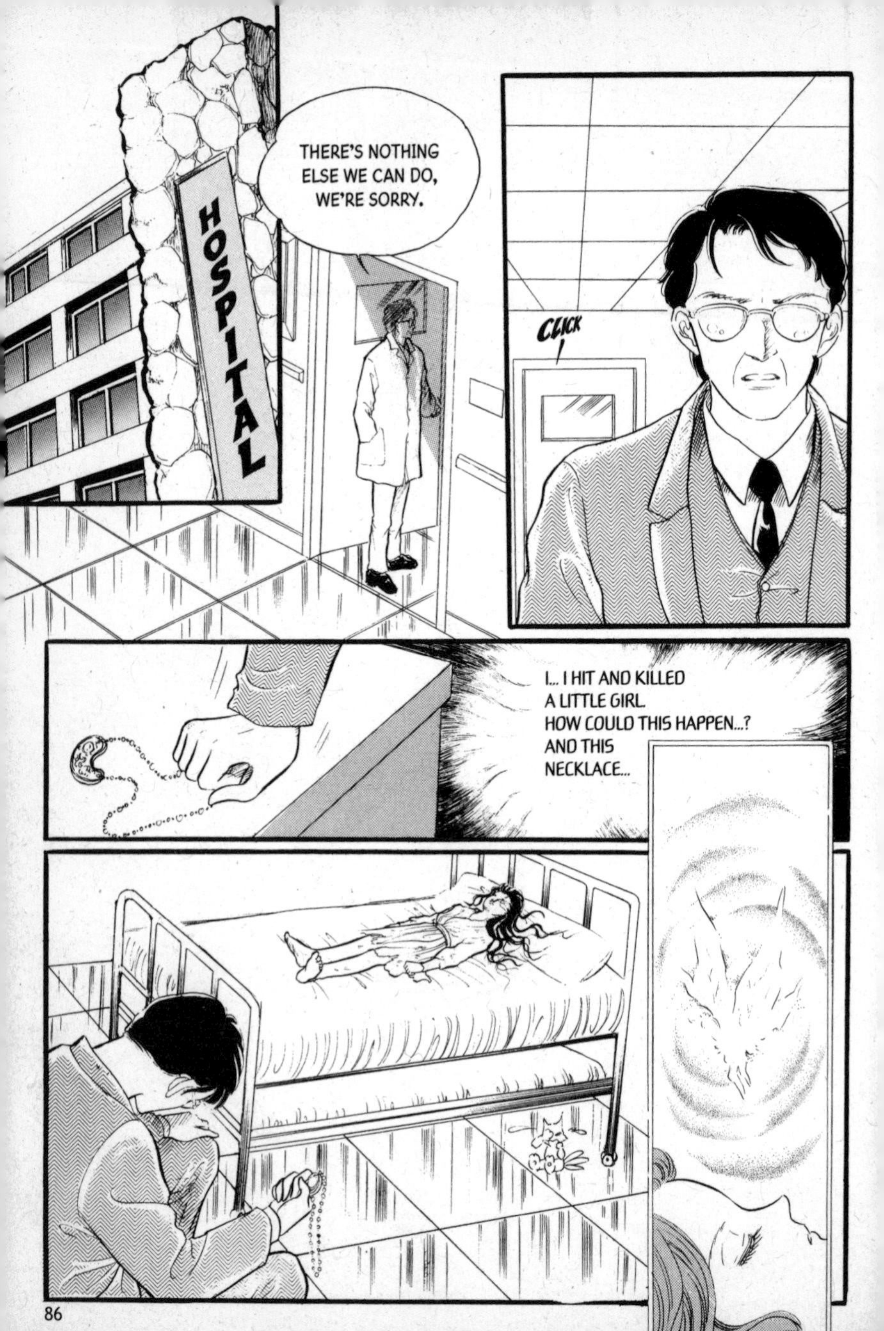
HOSPITAL
THERE'S NOTHING ELSE WE CAN DO, WE'RE SORRY.
CLICK
I... I HIT AND KILLED A LITTLE GIRL. HOW COULD THIS HAPPEN...? AND THIS NECKLACE...

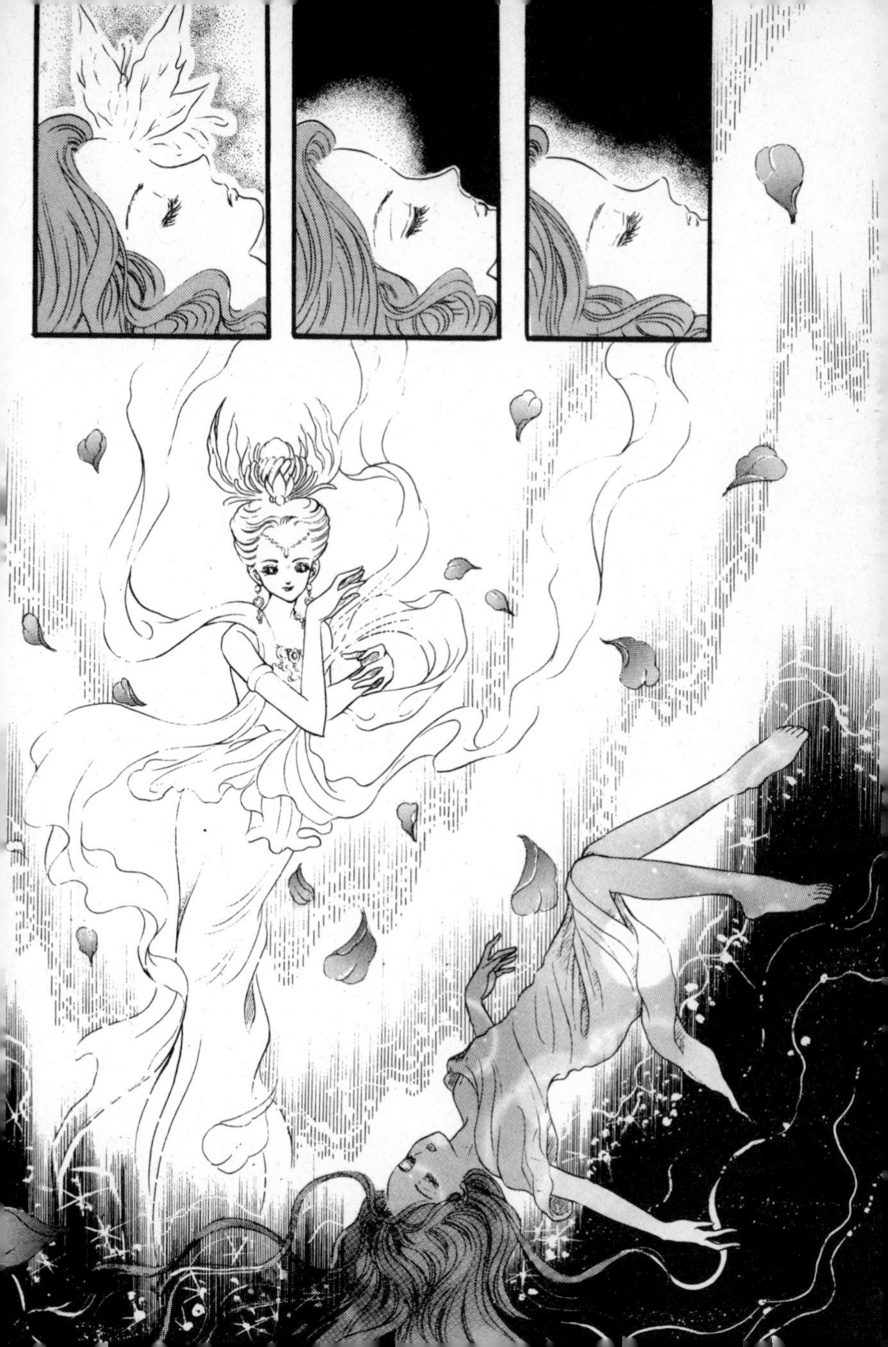

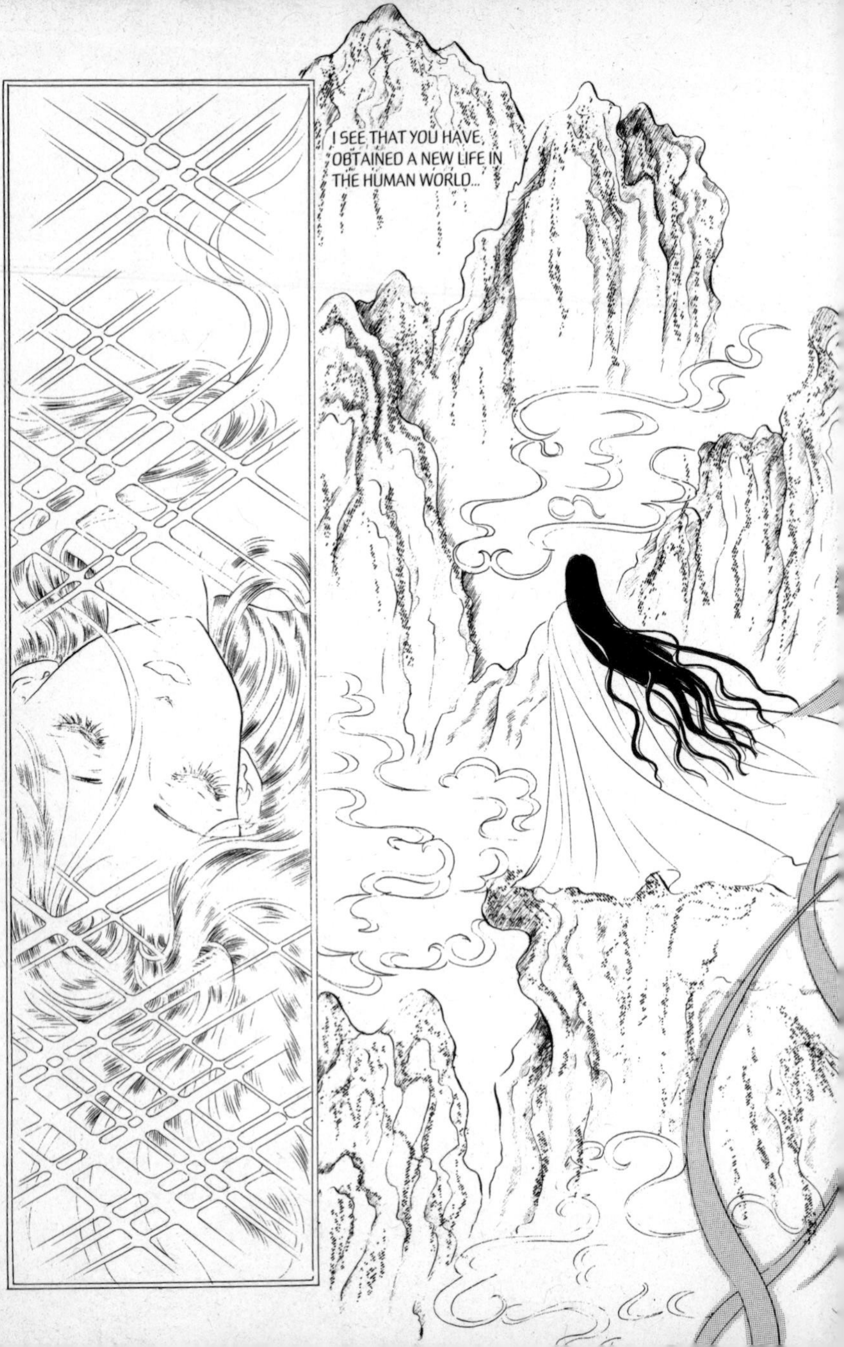
I SEE THAT YOU HAVE OBTAINED A NEW LIFE IN THE HUMAN WORLD...

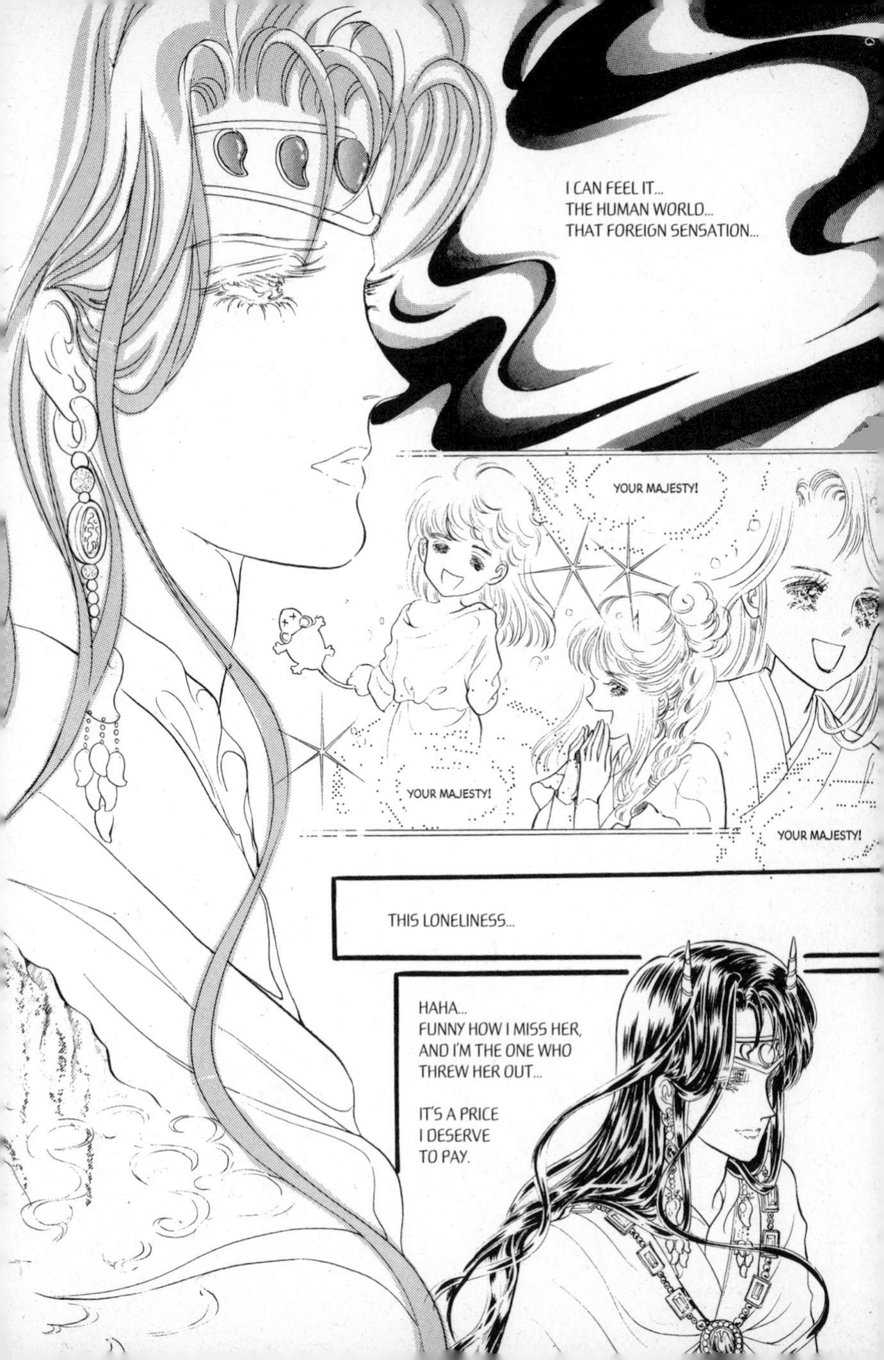
I CAN FEEL IT...
THE HUMAN WORLD...
THAT FOREIGN SENSATION...
YOUR MAJESTY!
YOUR MAJESTY!
YOUR MAJESTY!
THIS LONELINESS...
HAHA...
FUNNY HOW I MISS HER,
AND I'M THE ONE WHO
THREW HER OUT...
IT'S A PRICE
I DESERVE
TO PAY.

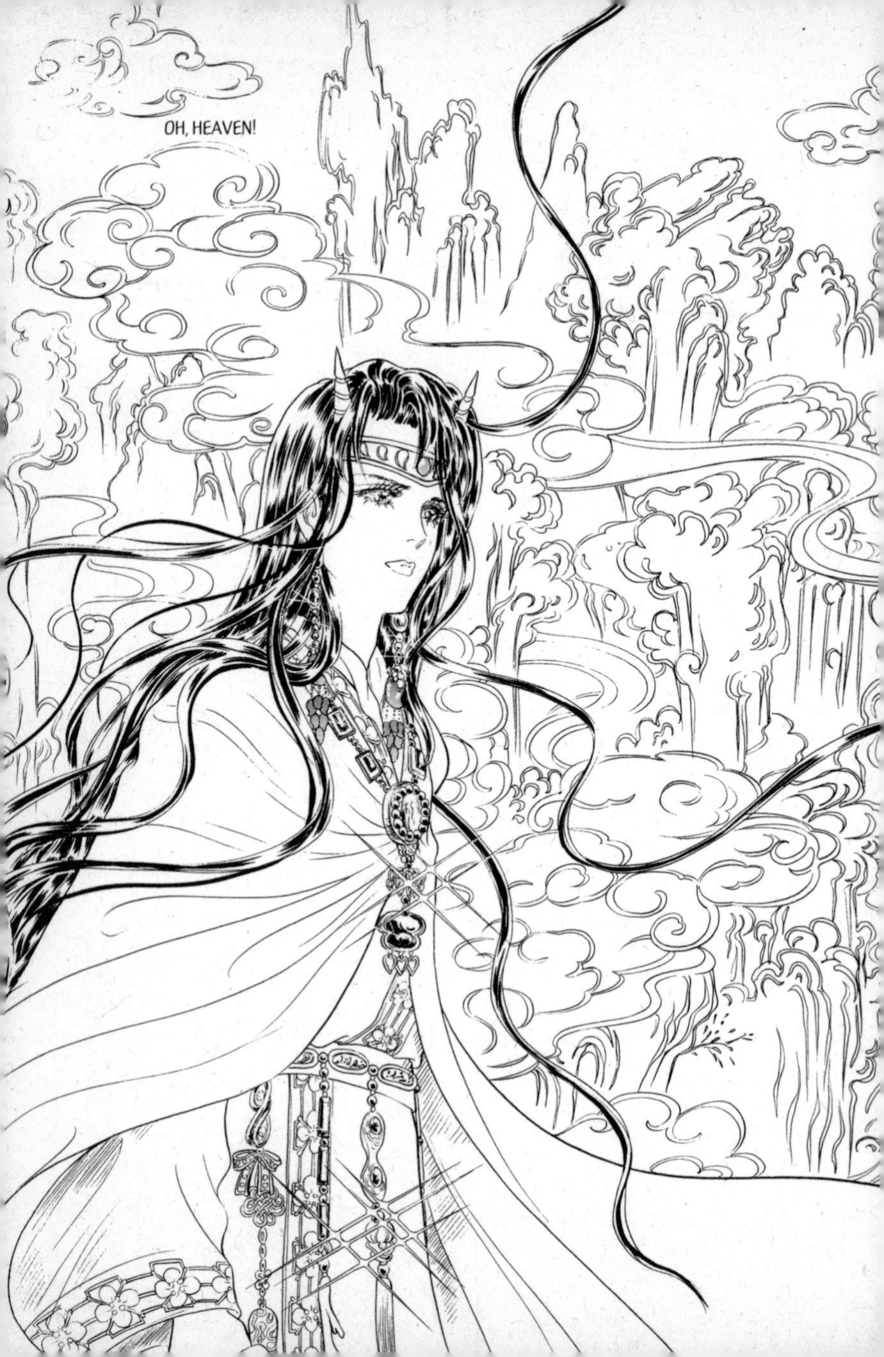
OH, HEAVEN!

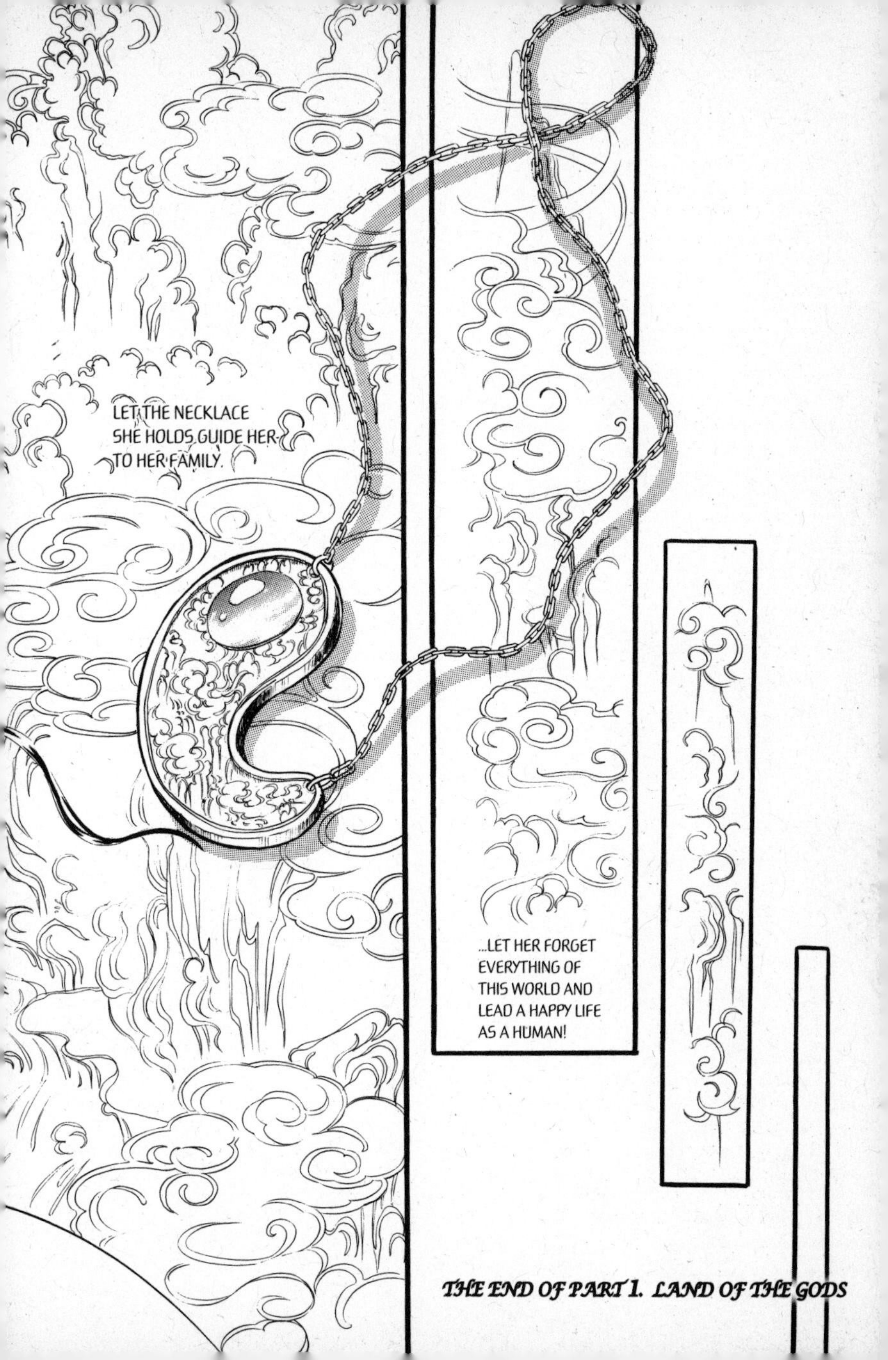
LET THE NECKLACE SHE HOLDS GUIDE HER TO HER FAMILY.
...LET HER FORGET EVERYTHING OF THIS WORLD AND LEAD A HAPPY LIFE AS A HUMAN!
THE END OF PART 1. LAND OF THE GODS

PART 2 LAND OF HUMANS

CHAPTER 1
MISTY-RAIN MEETS HANBIT

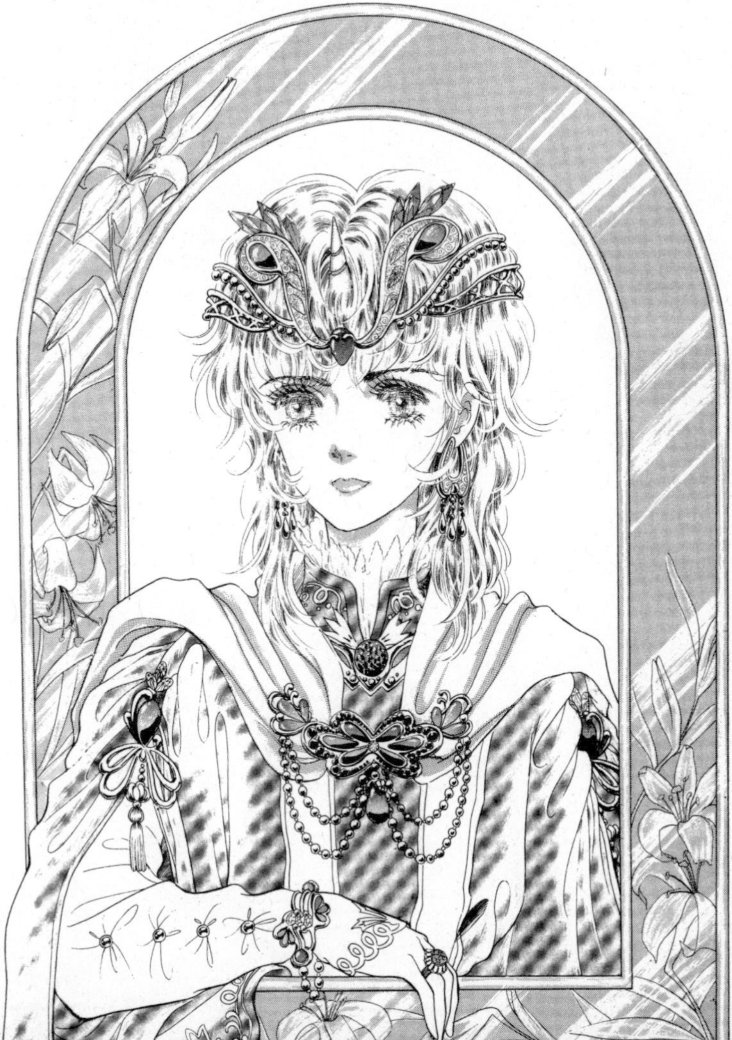

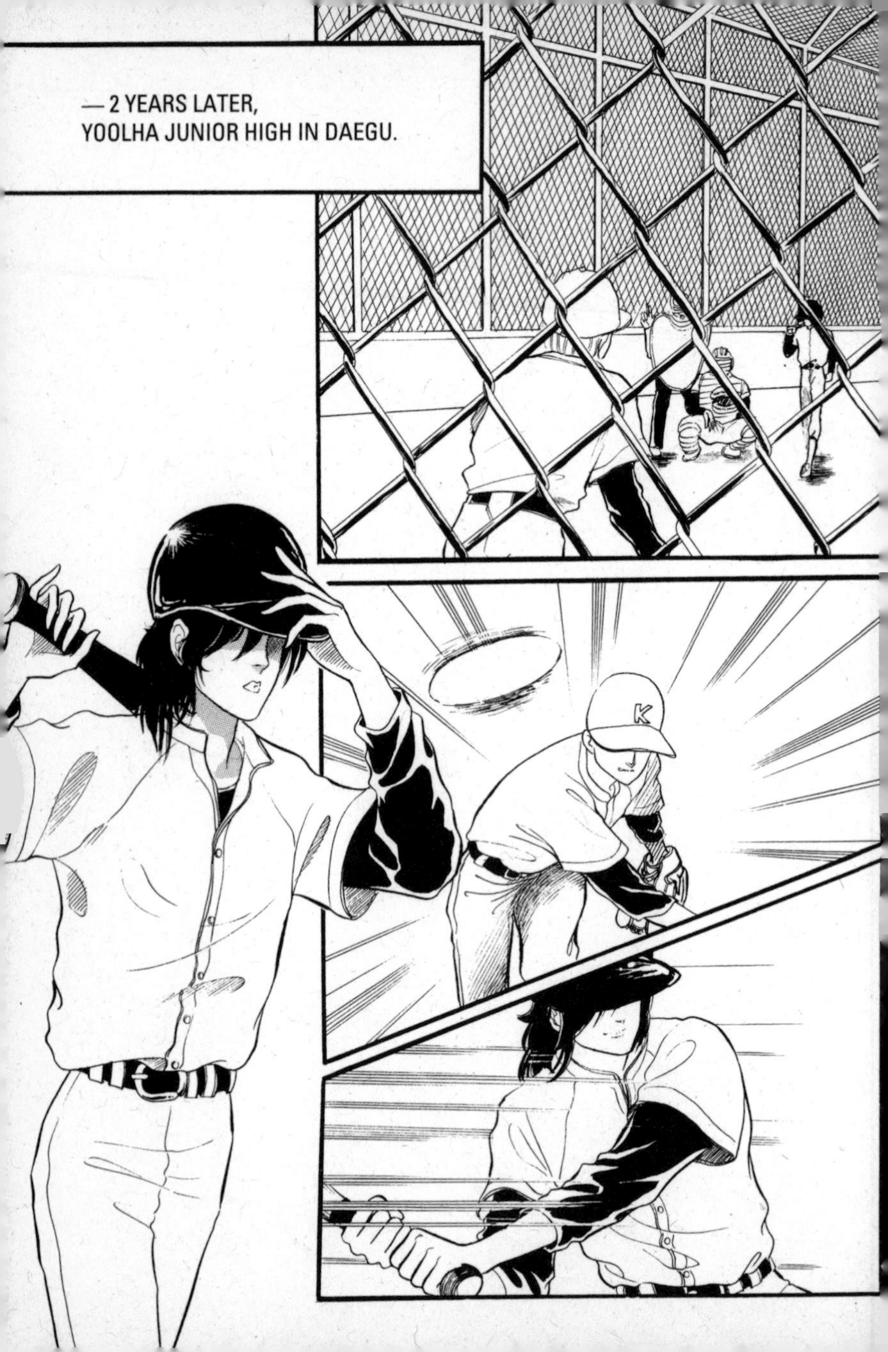
— 2 YEARS LATER,
YOOLHA JUNIOR HIGH IN DAEGU.
K

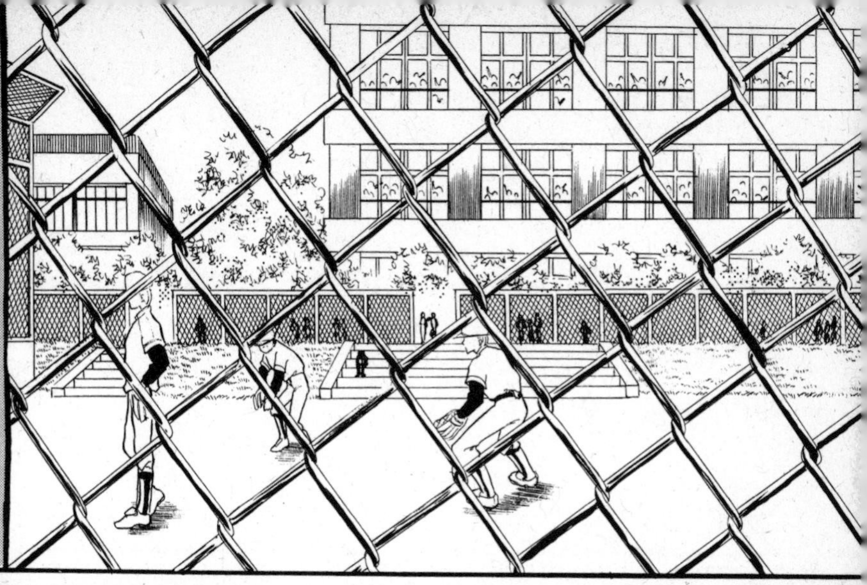
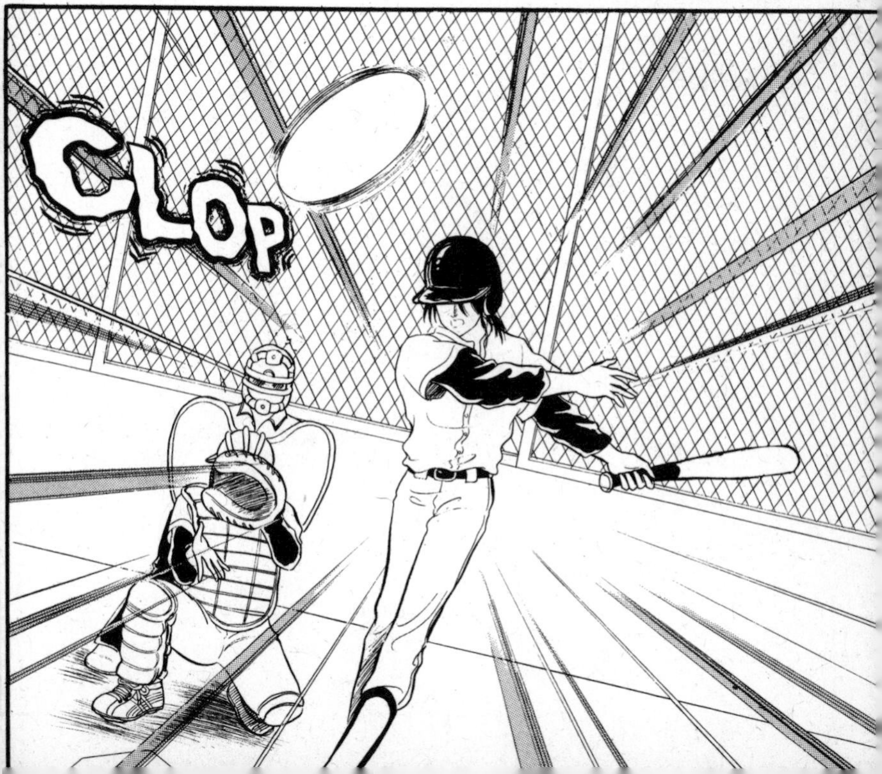
CLOP

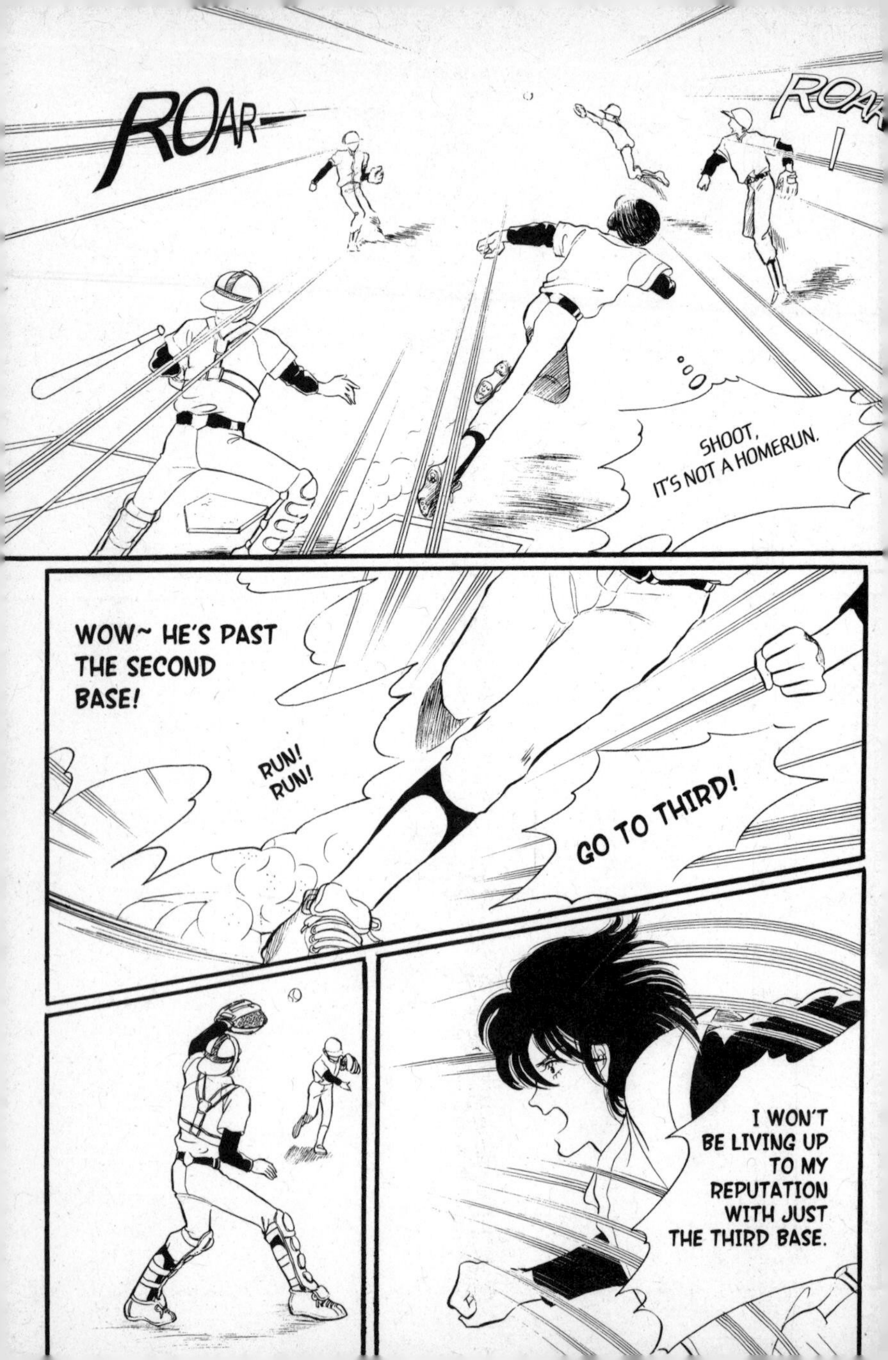
ROAR
ROAR
SHOOT, IT'S NOT A HOMERUN.
WOW~ HE'S PAST THE SECOND BASE!
RUN! RUN!
GO TO THIRD!
I WON'T BE LIVING UP TO MY REPUTATION WITH JUST THE THIRD BASE.

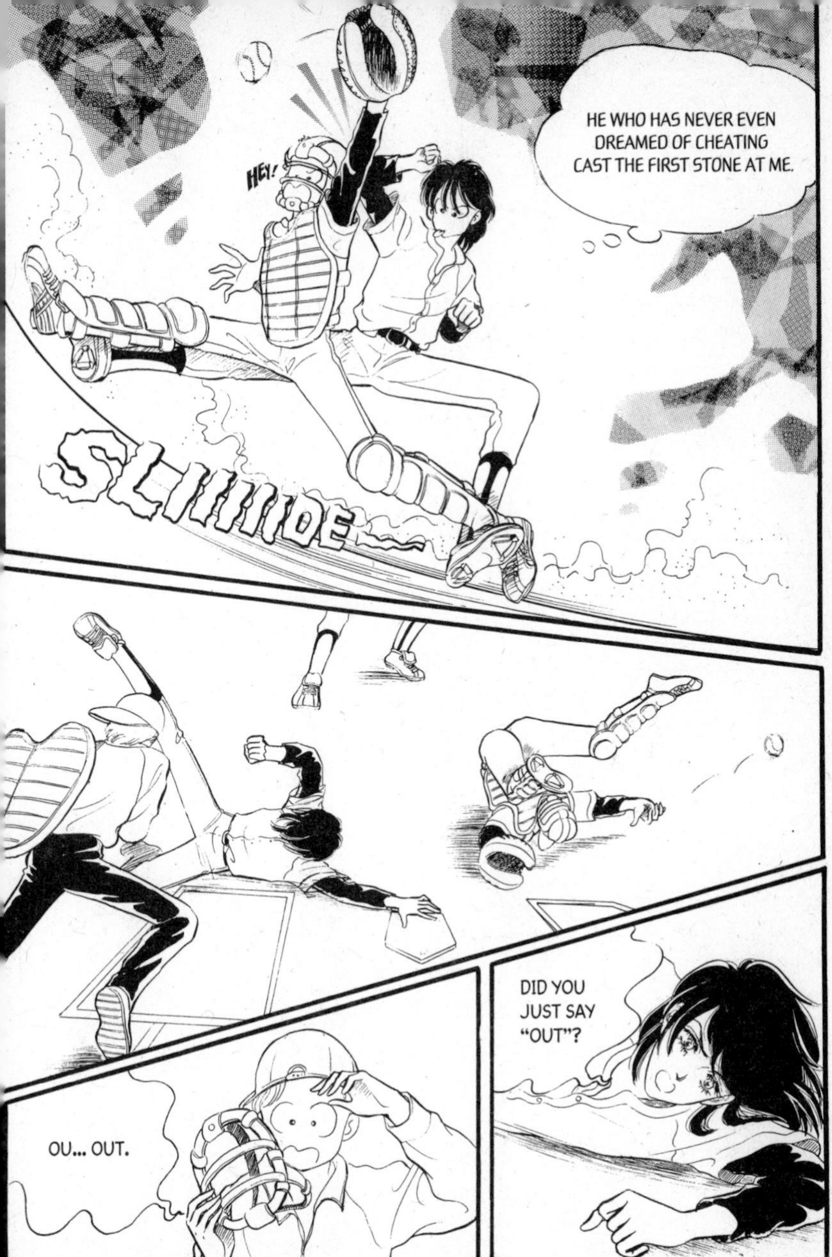
HEY!
HE WHO HAS NEVER EVEN DREAMED OF CHEATING CAST THE FIRST STONE AT ME.
SLIIIIDE
OU... OUT.
DID YOU JUST SAY "OUT"?

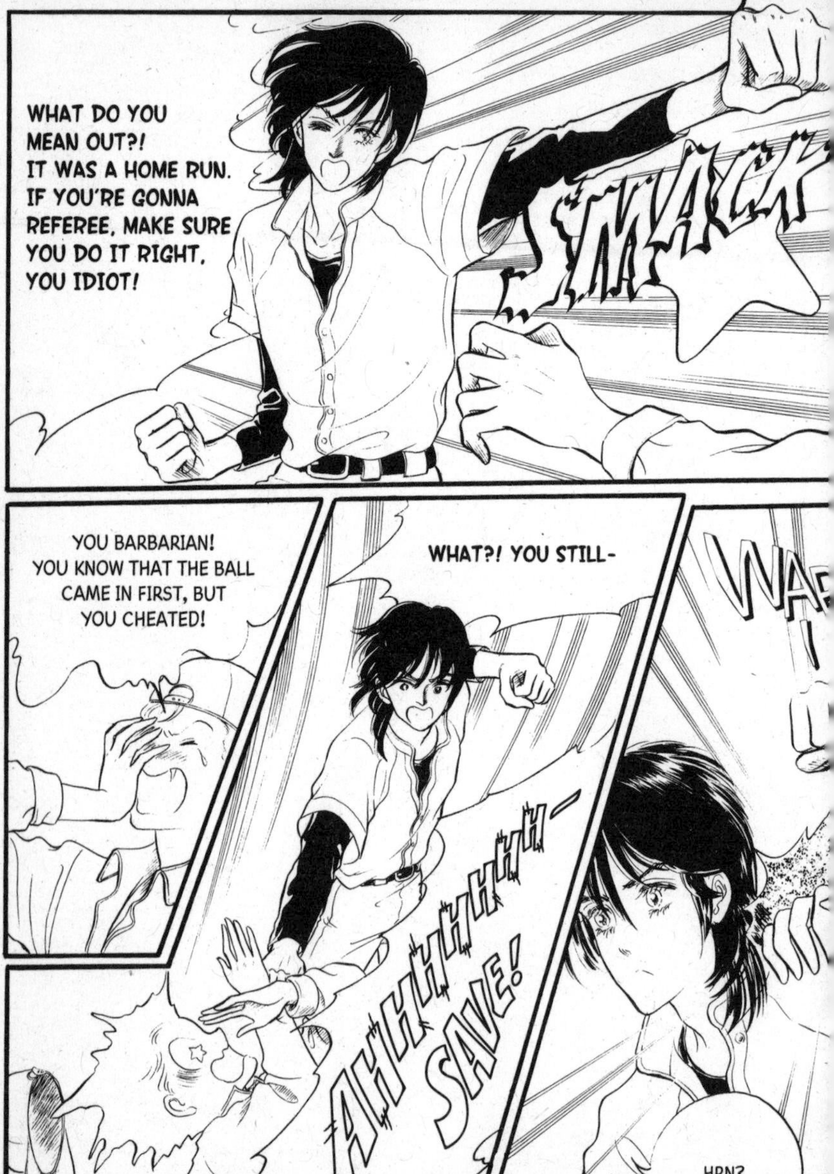
WHAT DO YOU MEAN OUT?! IT WAS A HOME RUN. IF YOU'RE GONNA REFEREE, MAKE SURE YOU DO IT RIGHT, YOU IDIOT!
SMACK
YOU BARBARIAN! YOU KNOW THAT THE BALL CAME IN FIRST, BUT YOU CHEATED!
WHAT?! YOU STILL-
AHHHHHHH-
SAVE!
HRN?

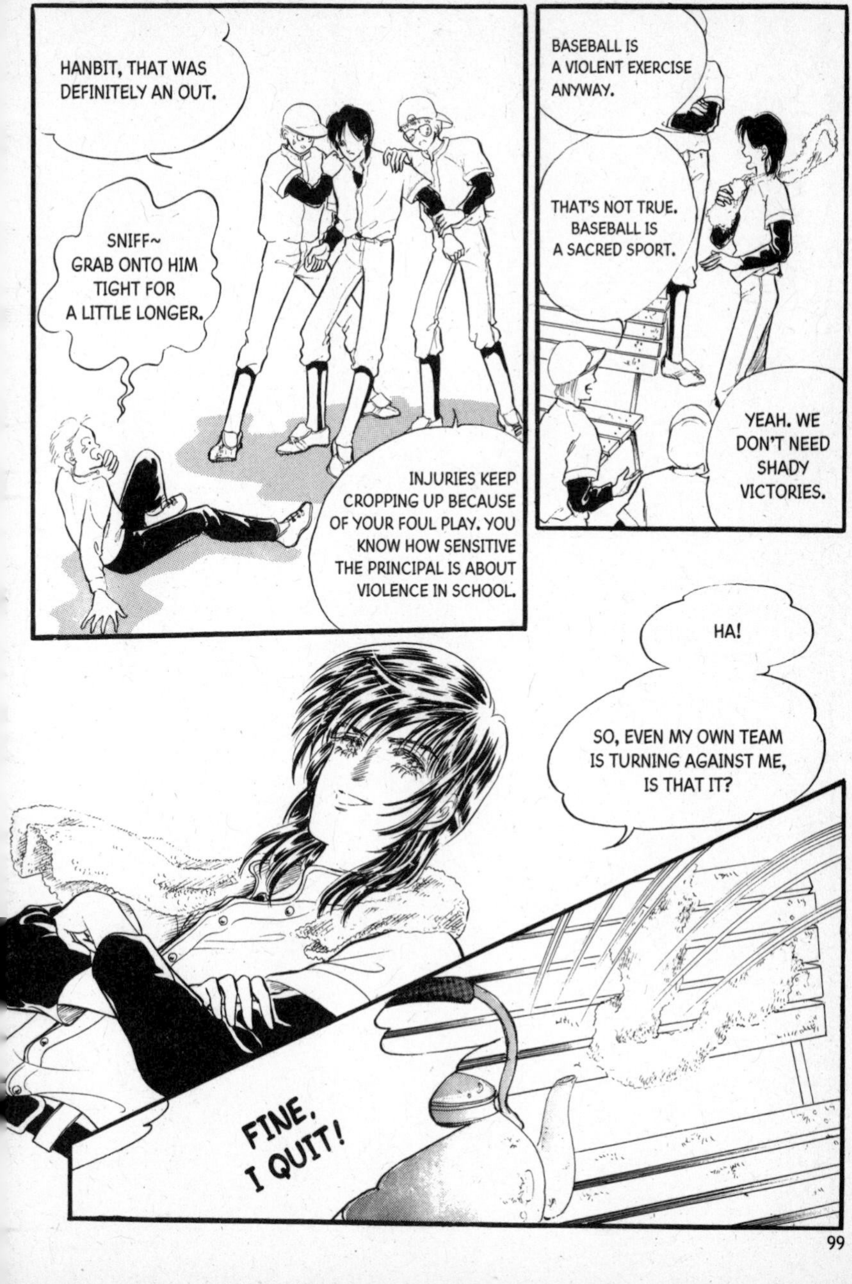
HANBIT, THAT WAS DEFINITELY AN OUT.
SNIFF~ GRAB ONTO HIM TIGHT FOR A LITTLE LONGER.
INJURIES KEEP CROPPING UP BECAUSE OF YOUR FOUL PLAY. YOU KNOW HOW SENSITIVE THE PRINCIPAL IS ABOUT VIOLENCE IN SCHOOL.
BASEBALL IS A VIOLENT EXERCISE ANYWAY.
THAT'S NOT TRUE. BASEBALL IS A SACRED SPORT.
YEAH. WE DON'T NEED SHADY VICTORIES.
HA!
SO, EVEN MY OWN TEAM IS TURNING AGAINST ME, IS THAT IT?
FINE, I QUIT!

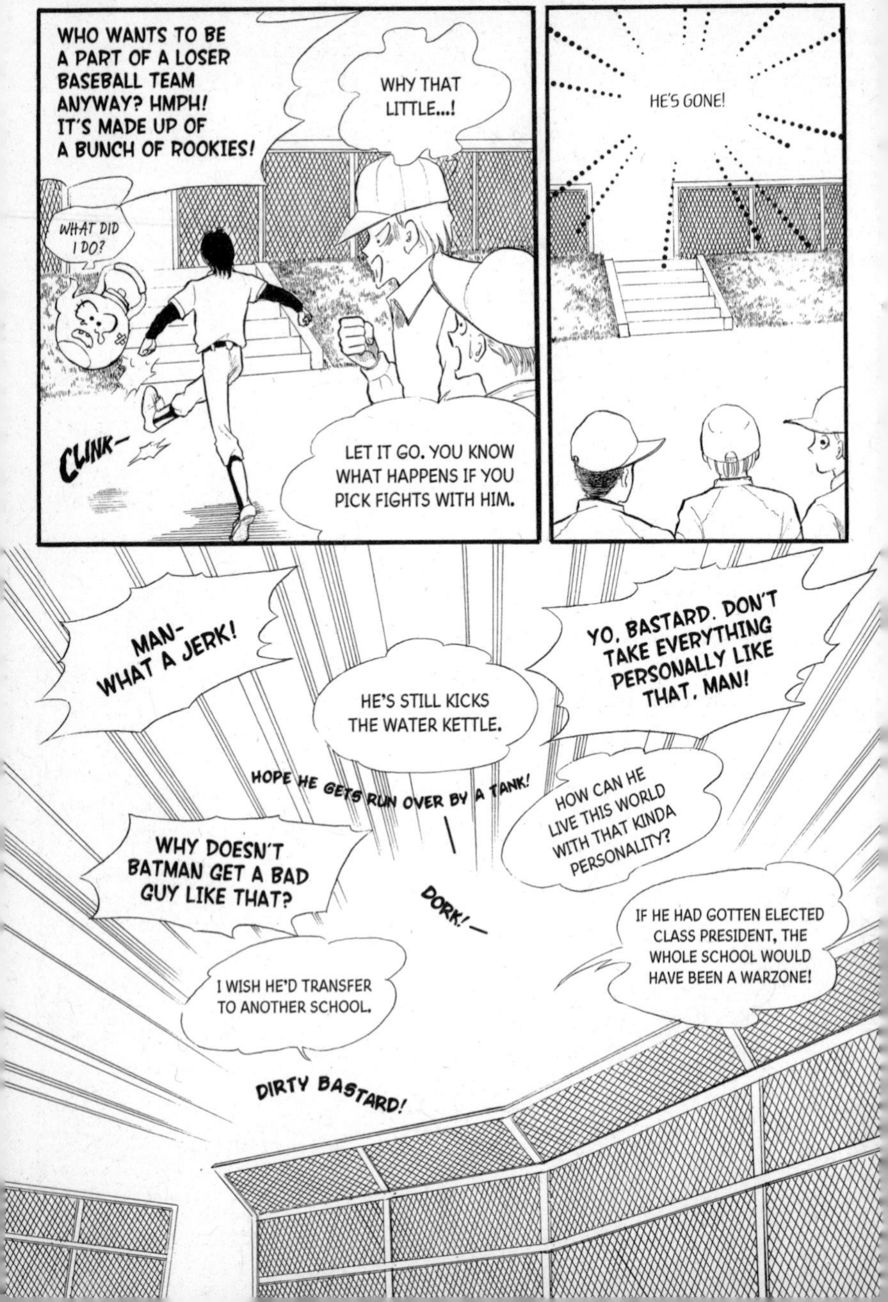
WHO WANTS TO BE A PART OF A LOSER BASEBALL TEAM ANYWAY? HMPH! IT'S MADE UP OF A BUNCH OF ROOKIES!
WHY THAT LITTLE...!
WHAT DID I DO?
CLINK—
LET IT GO. YOU KNOW WHAT HAPPENS IF YOU PICK FIGHTS WITH HIM.
HE'S GONE!
MAN- WHAT A JERK!
HE'S STILL KICKS THE WATER KETTLE.
YO, BASTARD. DON'T TAKE EVERYTHING PERSONALLY LIKE THAT, MAN!
HOPE HE GETS RUN OVER BY A TANK!
HOW CAN HE LIVE THIS WORLD WITH THAT KINDA PERSONALITY?
WHY DOESN'T BATMAN GET A BAD GUY LIKE THAT?
DORK!—
IF HE HAD GOTTEN ELECTED CLASS PRESIDENT, THE WHOLE SCHOOL WOULD HAVE BEEN A WARZONE!
I WISH HE'D TRANSFER TO ANOTHER SCHOOL.
DIRTY BASTARD!

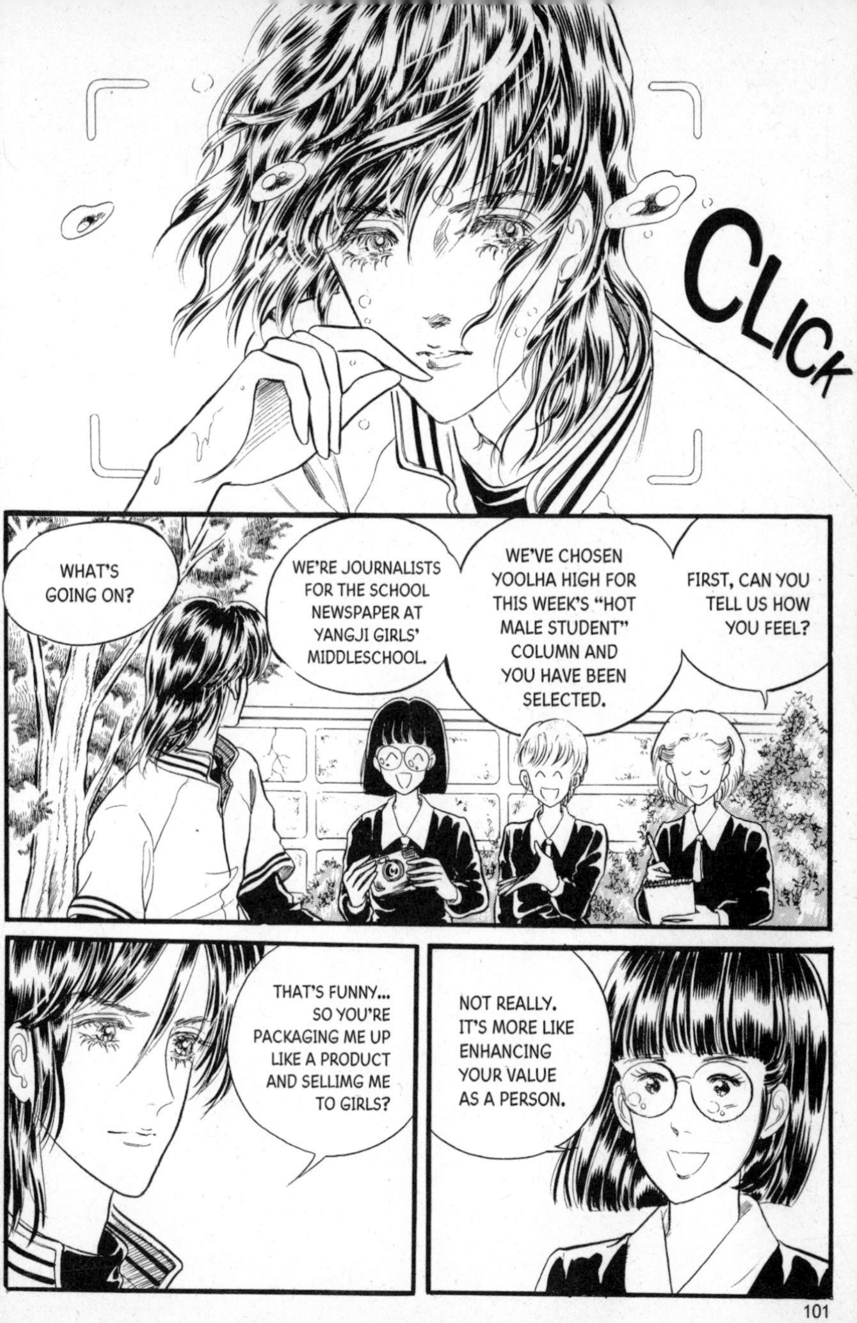
CLICK
WHAT'S GOING ON?
WE'RE JOURNALISTS FOR THE SCHOOL NEWSPAPER AT YANGJI GIRLS' MIDDLESCHOOL.
WE'VE CHOSEN YOOLHA HIGH FOR THIS WEEK'S "HOT MALE STUDENT" COLUMN AND YOU HAVE BEEN SELECTED.
FIRST, CAN YOU TELL US HOW YOU FEEL?
THAT'S FUNNY... SO YOU'RE PACKAGING ME UP LIKE A PRODUCT AND SELLIMG ME TO GIRLS?
NOT REALLY. IT'S MORE LIKE ENHANCING YOUR VALUE AS A PERSON.

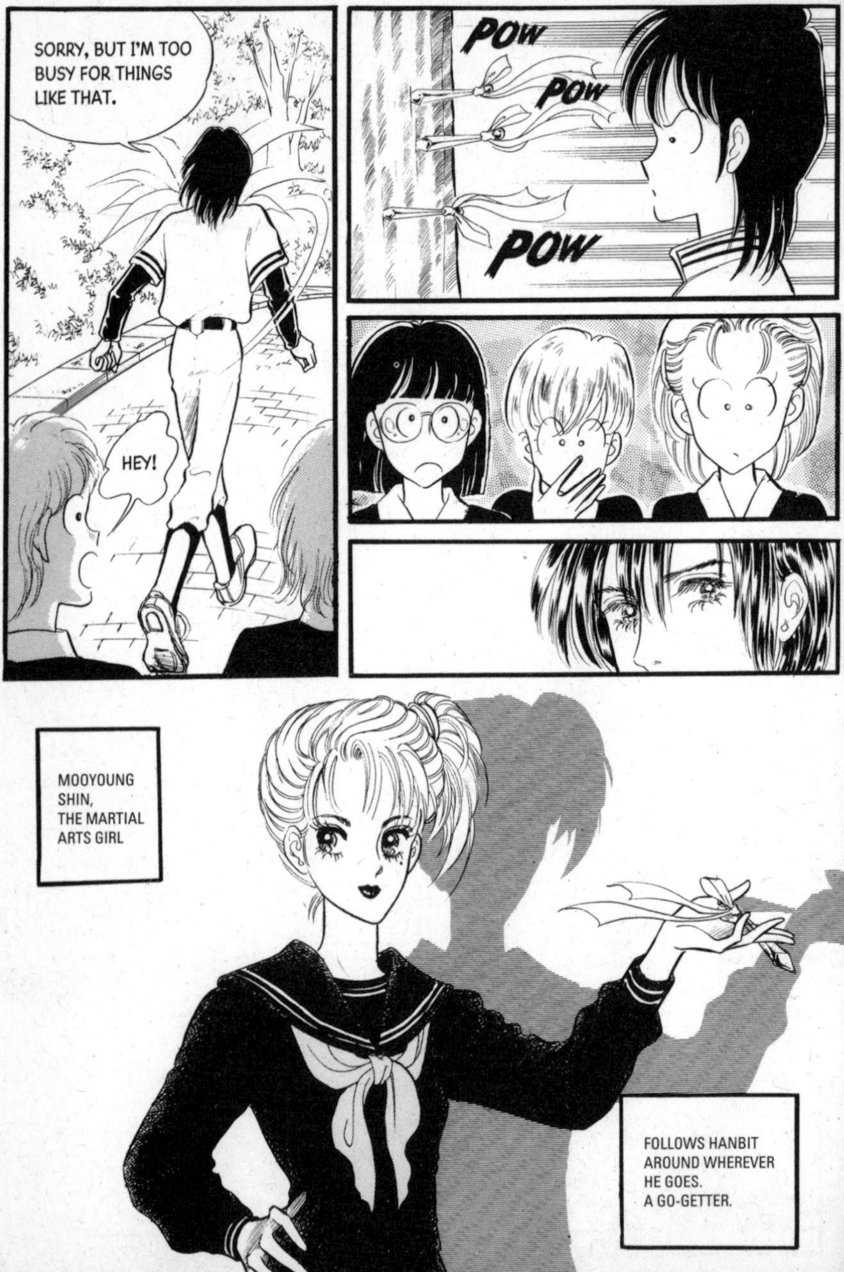
SORRY, BUT I'M TOO BUSY FOR THINGS LIKE THAT.
HEY!
POW
POW
POW
MOOYOUNG SHIN, THE MARTIAL ARTS GIRL
FOLLOWS HANBIT AROUND WHEREVER HE GOES. A GO-GETTER.

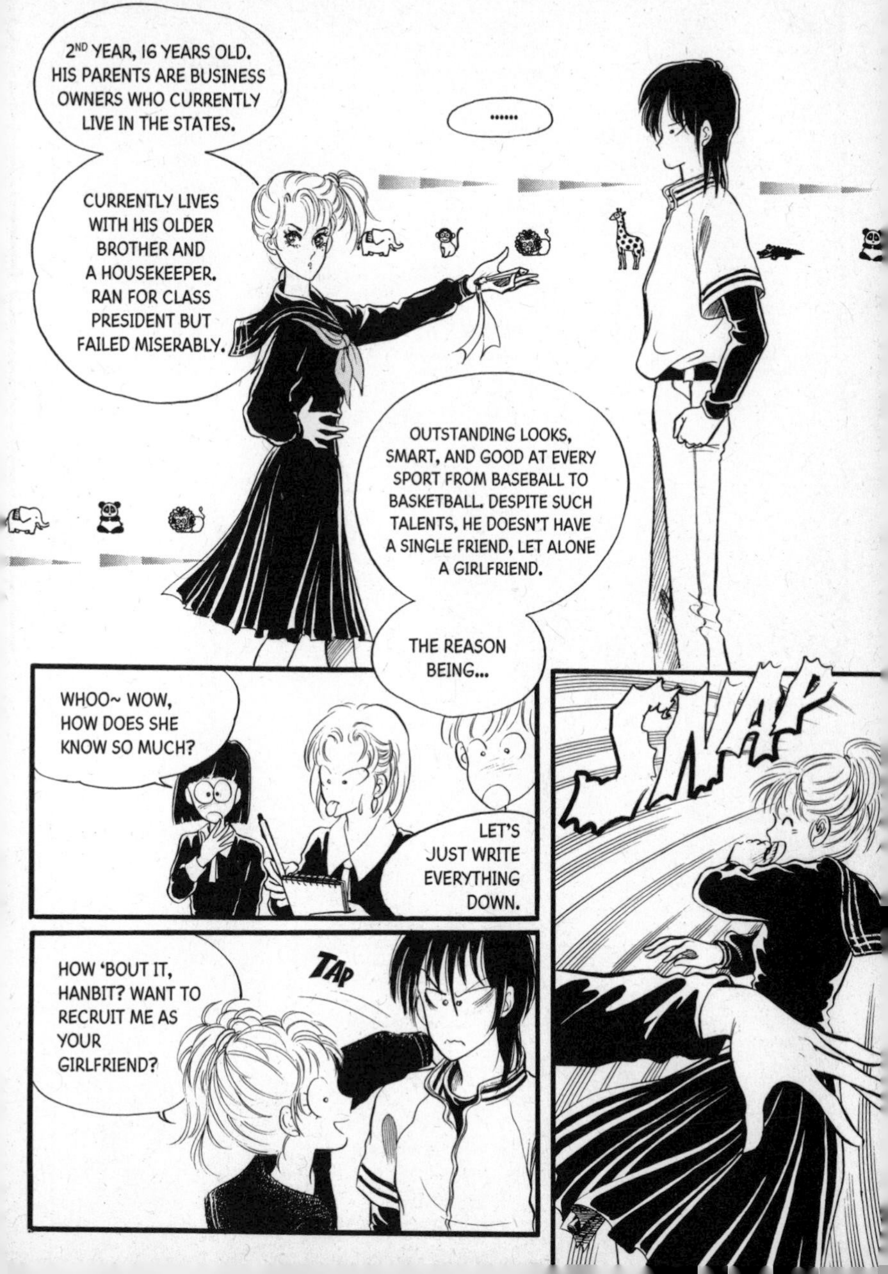
2ND YEAR, 16 YEARS OLD. HIS PARENTS ARE BUSINESS OWNERS WHO CURRENTLY LIVE IN THE STATES.
CURRENTLY LIVES WITH HIS OLDER BROTHER AND A HOUSEKEEPER. RAN FOR CLASS PRESIDENT BUT FAILED MISERABLY.
......
OUTSTANDING LOOKS, SMART, AND GOOD AT EVERY SPORT FROM BASEBALL TO BASKETBALL. DESPITE SUCH TALENTS, HE DOESN'T HAVE A SINGLE FRIEND, LET ALONE A GIRLFRIEND.
THE REASON BEING...
WHOO~ WOW, HOW DOES SHE KNOW SO MUCH?
LET'S JUST WRITE EVERYTHING DOWN.
HOW 'BOUT IT, HANBIT? WANT TO RECRUIT ME AS YOUR GIRLFRIEND?
TAP
SNAP

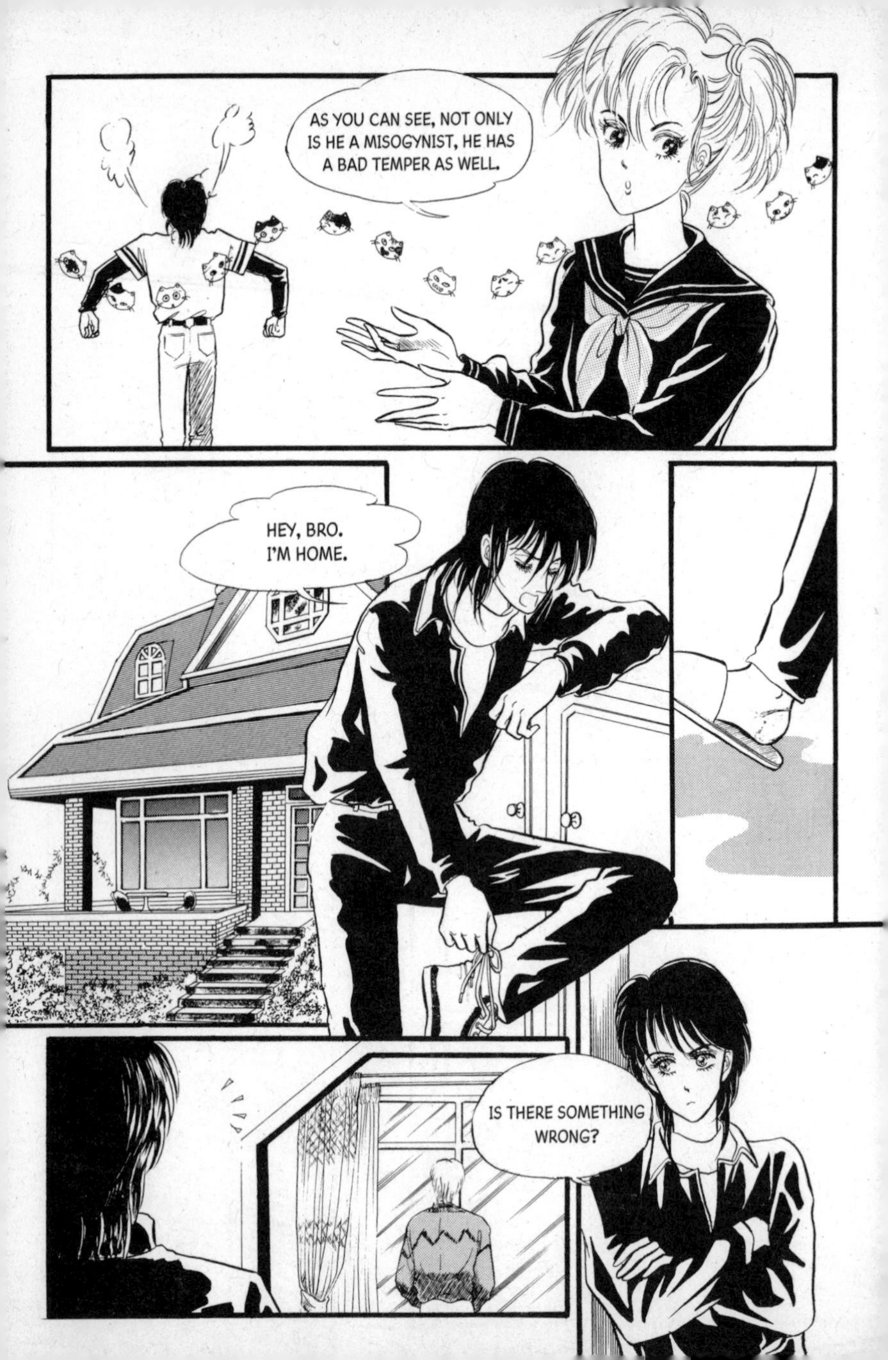
AS YOU CAN SEE, NOT ONLY IS HE A MISOGYNIST, HE HAS A BAD TEMPER AS WELL.
HEY, BRO. I'M HOME.
IS THERE SOMETHING WRONG?

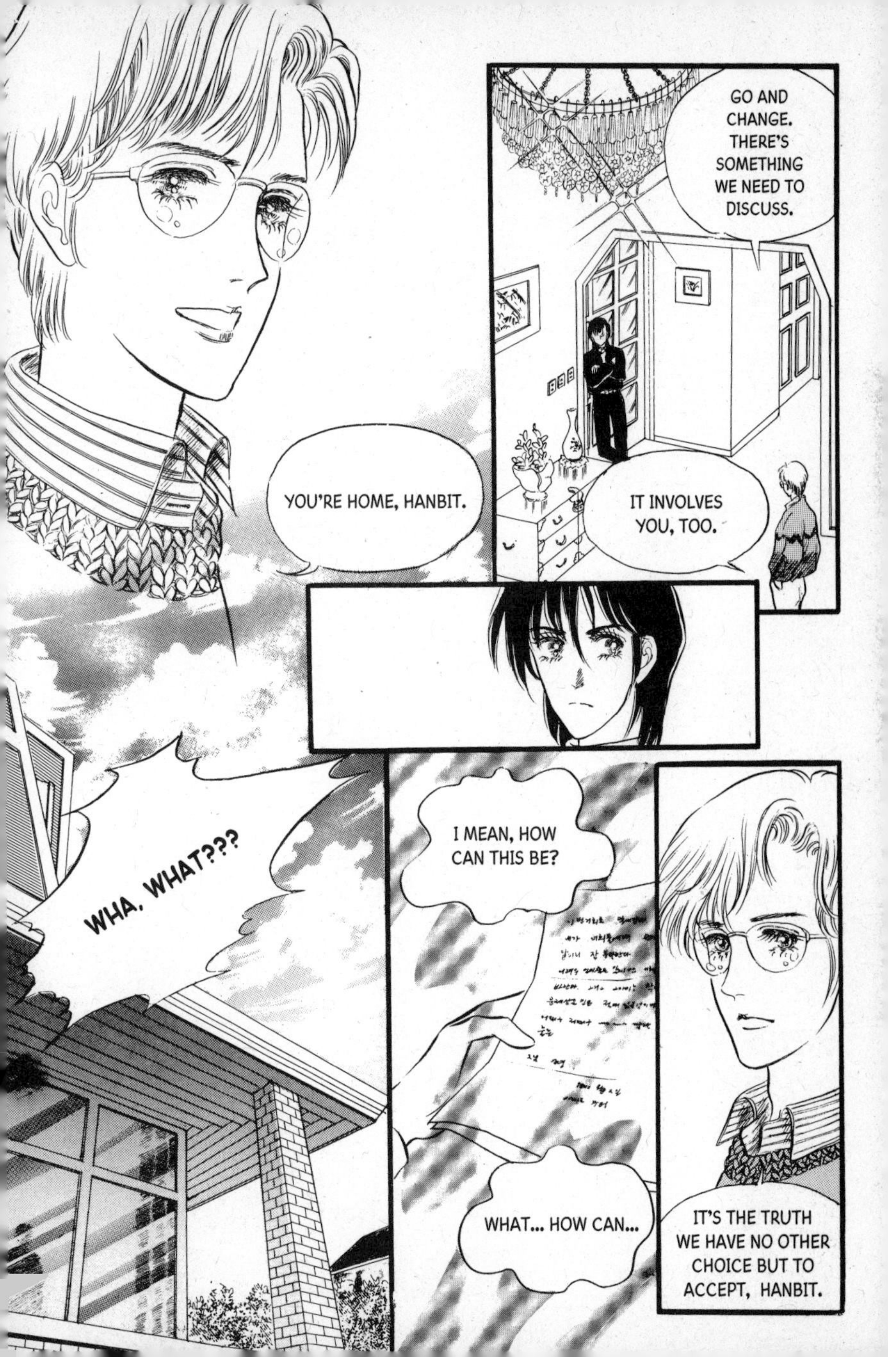
YOU'RE HOME, HANBIT.
GO AND CHANGE. THERE'S SOMETHING WE NEED TO DISCUSS.
IT INVOLVES YOU, TOO.
WHA, WHAT???
I MEAN, HOW CAN THIS BE?
WHAT... HOW CAN...
IT'S THE TRUTH WE HAVE NO OTHER CHOICE BUT TO ACCEPT, HANBIT.

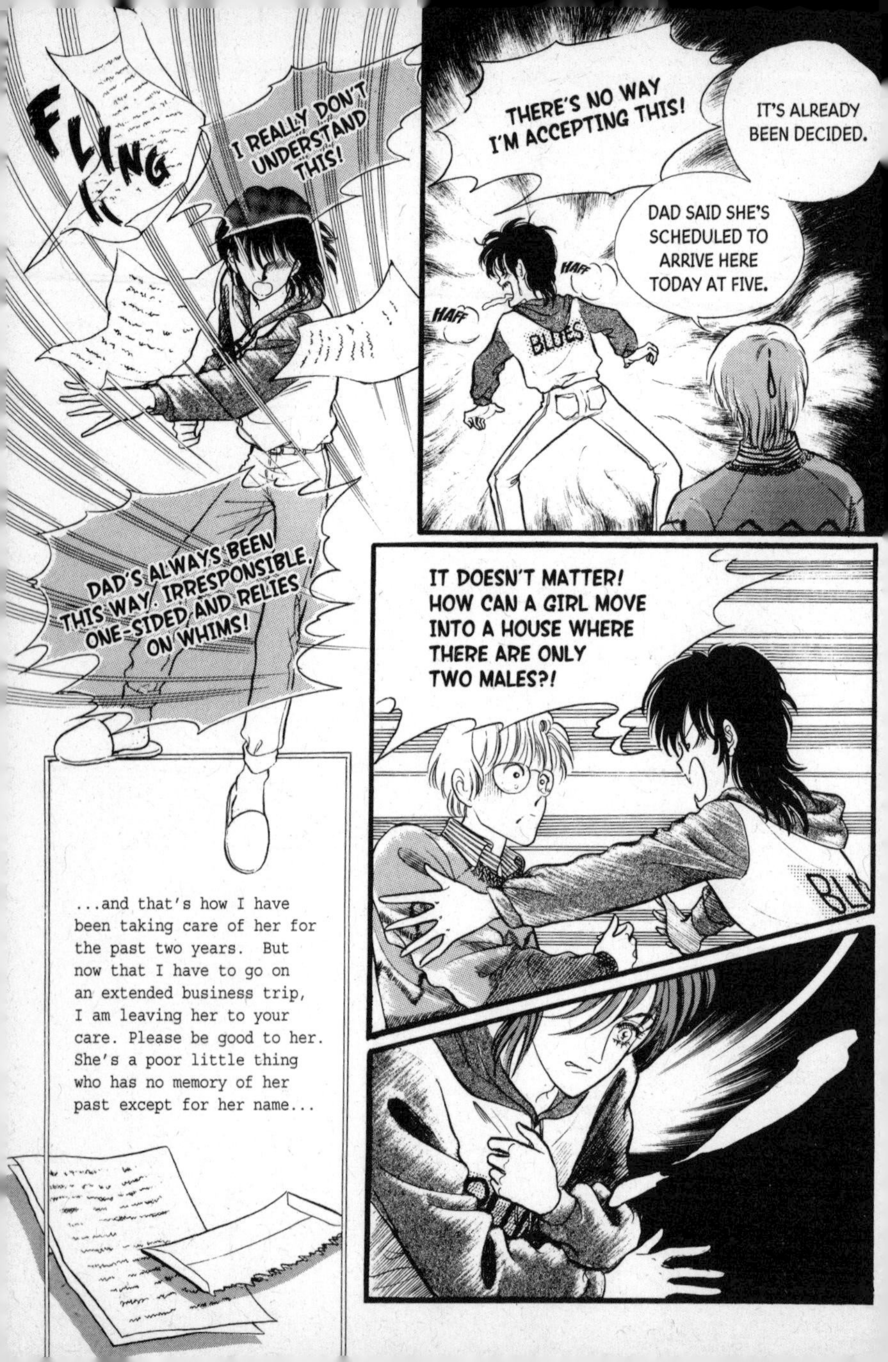
FLING
I REALLY DON'T UNDERSTAND THIS!
DAD'S ALWAYS BEEN THIS WAY. IRRESPONSIBLE, ONE-SIDED AND RELIES ON WHIMS!
...and that's how I have been taking care of her for the past two years. But now that I have to go on an extended business trip, I am leaving her to your care. Please be good to her. She's a poor little thing who has no memory of her past except for her name...
THERE'S NO WAY I'M ACCEPTING THIS!
IT'S ALREADY BEEN DECIDED.
DAD SAID SHE'S SCHEDULED TO ARRIVE HERE TODAY AT FIVE.
HAFF
HAFF
BLUES
IT DOESN'T MATTER! HOW CAN A GIRL MOVE INTO A HOUSE WHERE THERE ARE ONLY TWO MALES?!
BLU

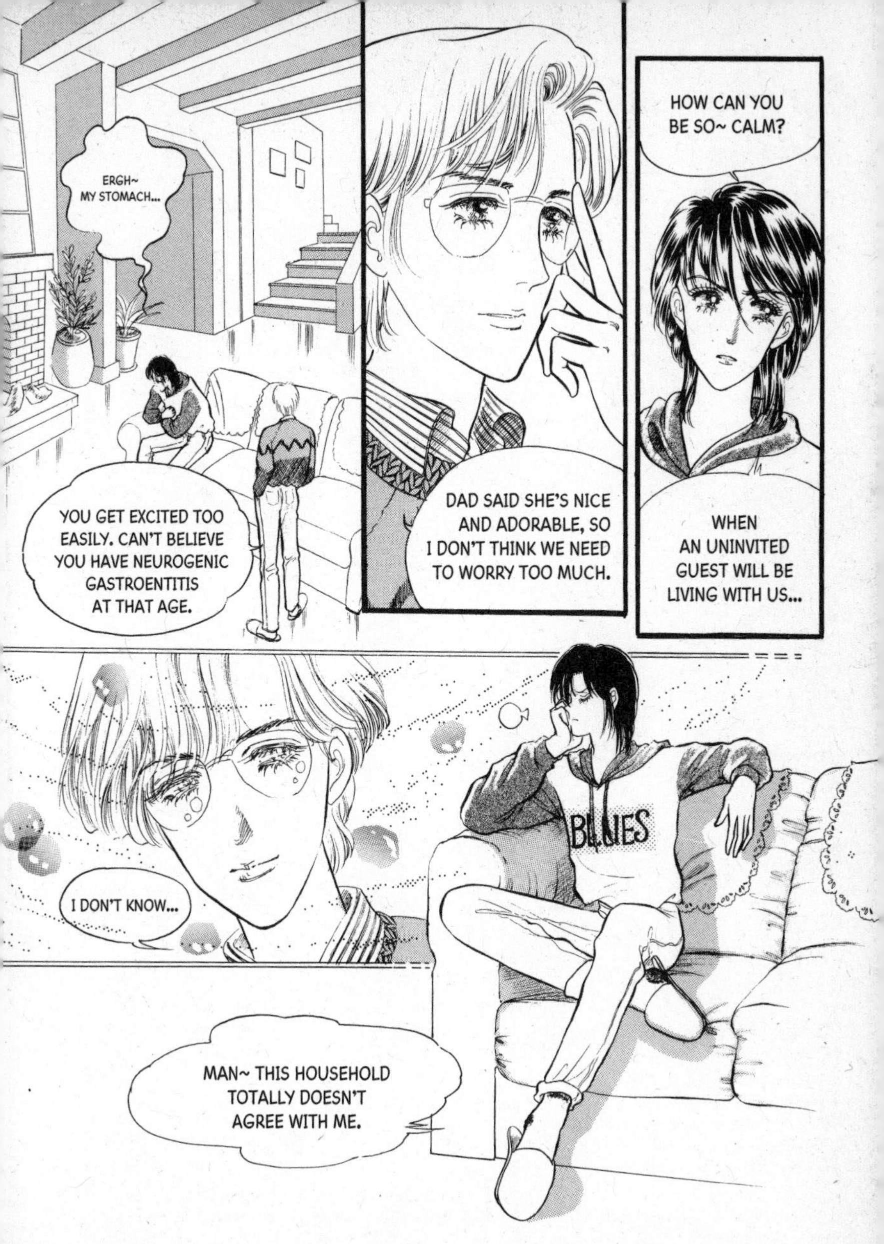
ERGH~ MY STOMACH...
YOU GET EXCITED TOO EASILY. CAN'T BELIEVE YOU HAVE NEUROGENIC GASTROENTITIS AT THAT AGE.
DAD SAID SHE'S NICE AND ADORABLE, SO I DON'T THINK WE NEED TO WORRY TOO MUCH.
HOW CAN YOU BE SO~ CALM?
WHEN AN UNINVITED GUEST WILL BE LIVING WITH US...
I DON'T KNOW...
BLUES
MAN~ THIS HOUSEHOLD TOTALLY DOESN'T AGREE WITH ME.

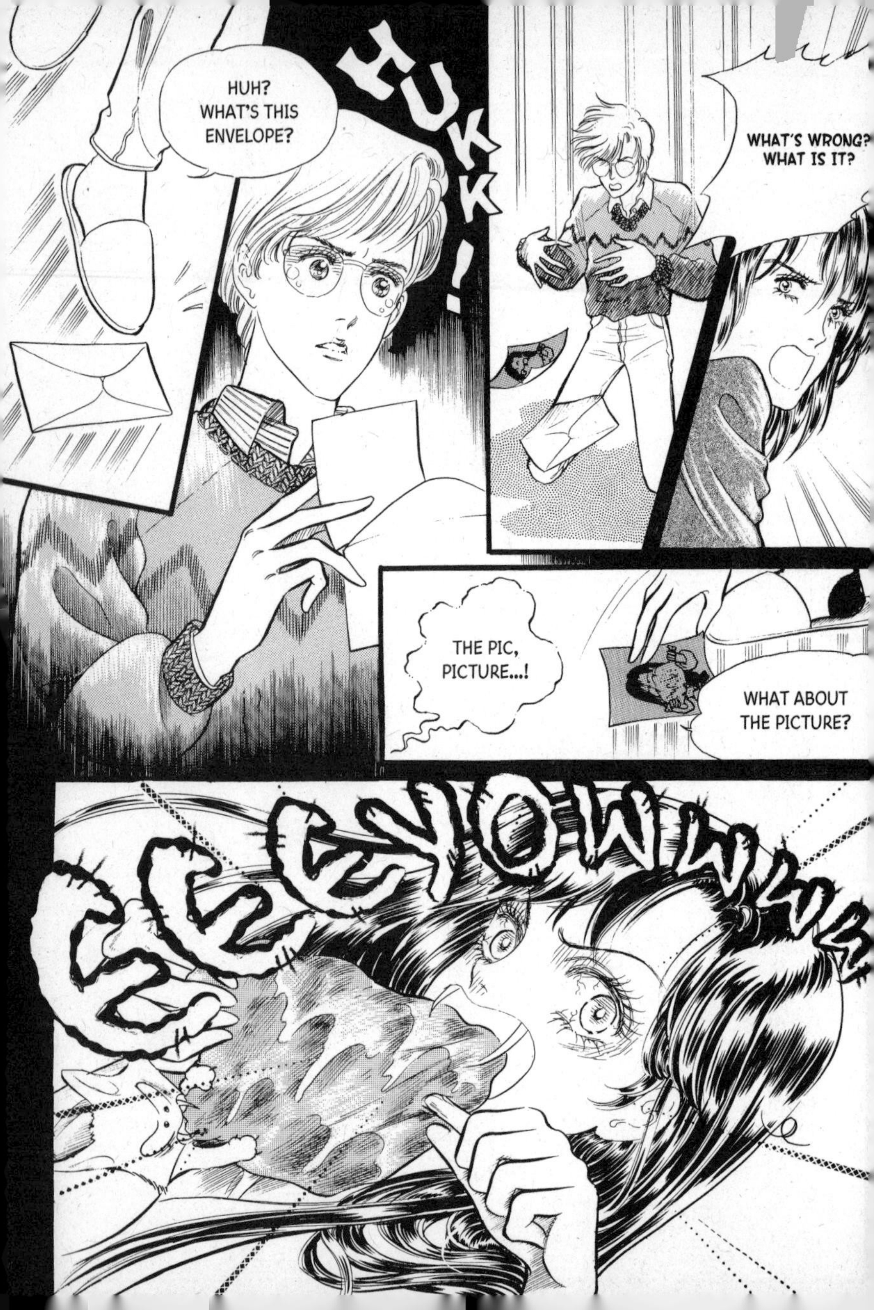
HUH? WHAT'S THIS ENVELOPE?
HUK!
WHAT'S WRONG? WHAT IS IT?
THE PIC, PICTURE...!
WHAT ABOUT THE PICTURE?

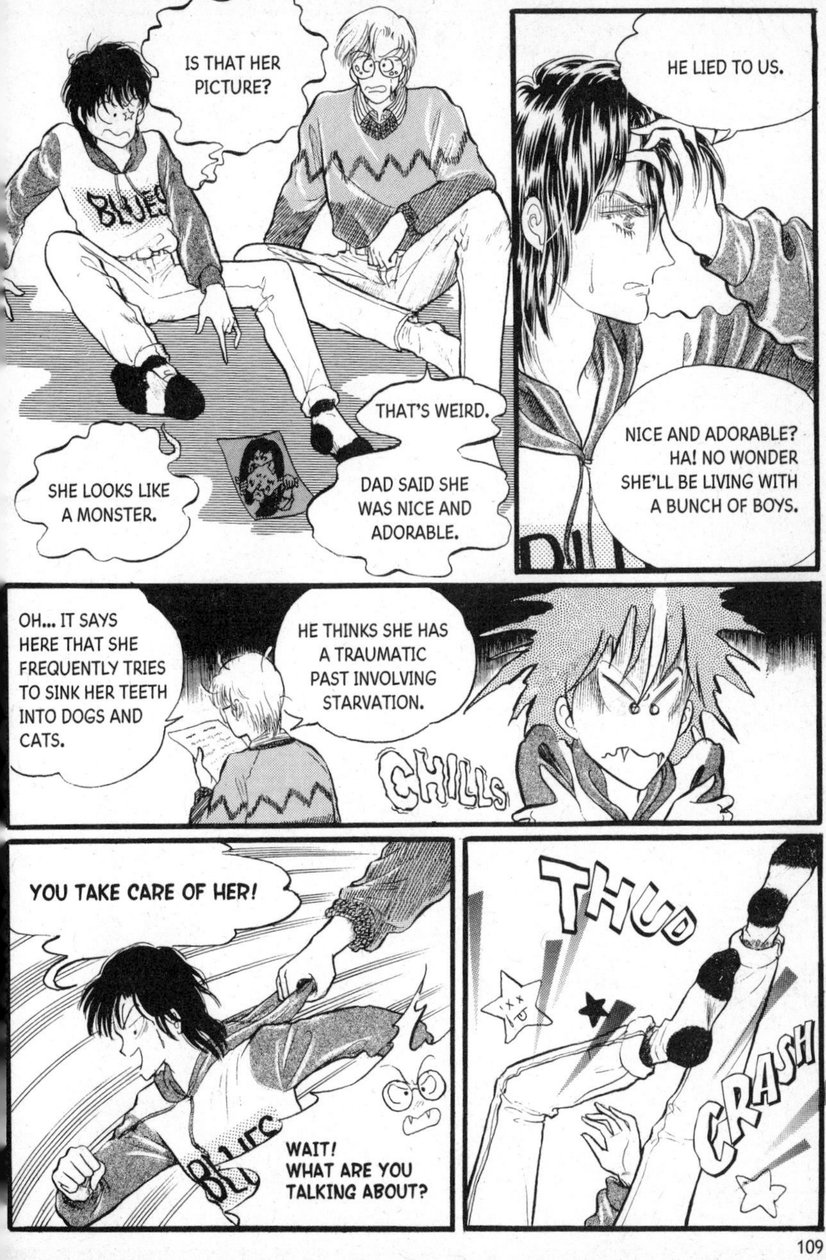
IS THAT HER PICTURE?
THAT'S WEIRD.
SHE LOOKS LIKE A MONSTER.
DAD SAID SHE WAS NICE AND ADORABLE.
HE LIED TO US.
NICE AND ADORABLE? HA! NO WONDER SHE'LL BE LIVING WITH A BUNCH OF BOYS.
OH... IT SAYS HERE THAT SHE FREQUENTLY TRIES TO SINK HER TEETH INTO DOGS AND CATS.
HE THINKS SHE HAS A TRAUMATIC PAST INVOLVING STARVATION.
CHILLS
YOU TAKE CARE OF HER!
WAIT! WHAT ARE YOU TALKING ABOUT?
THUD
CRASH

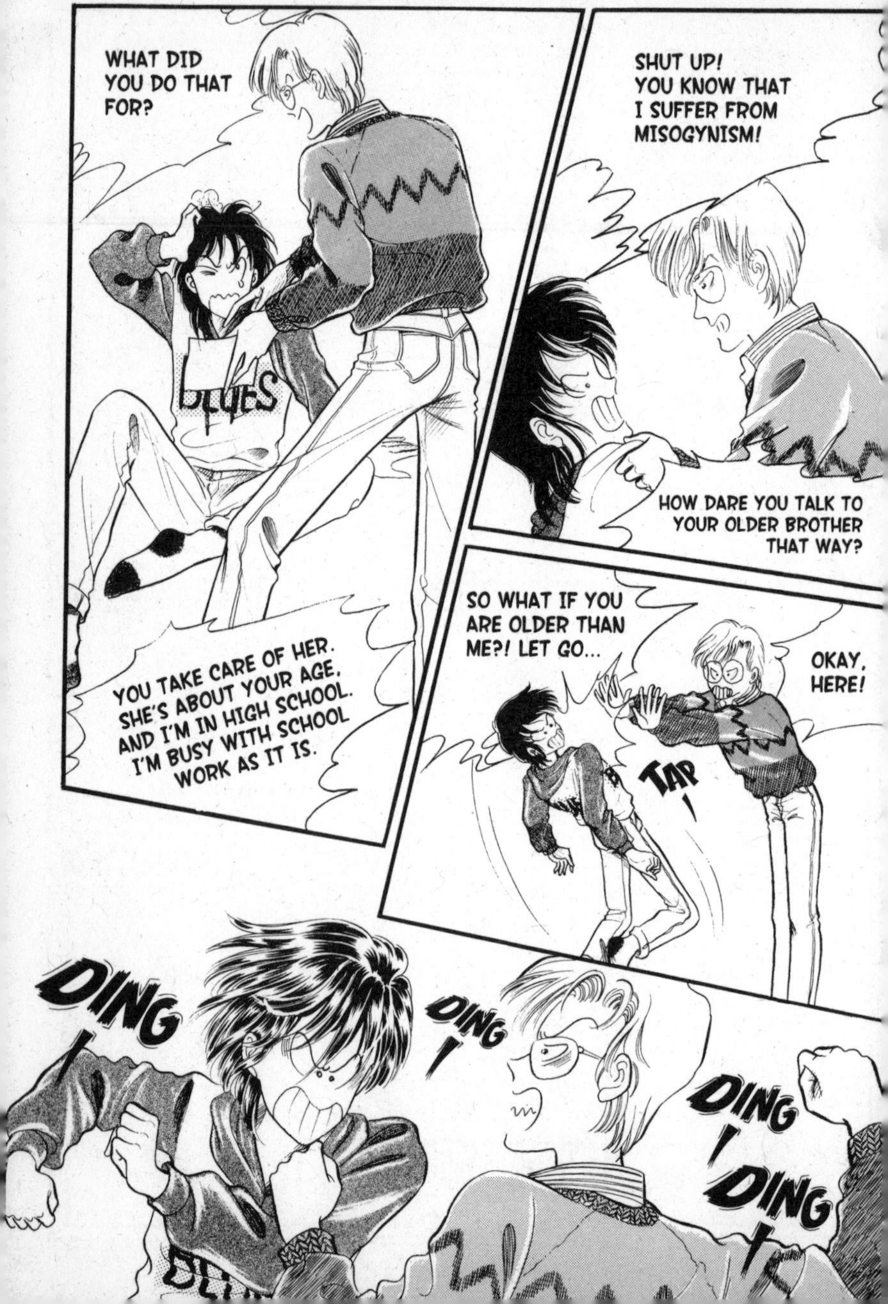
WHAT DID YOU DO THAT FOR?
YOU TAKE CARE OF HER. SHE'S ABOUT YOUR AGE, AND I'M IN HIGH SCHOOL. I'M BUSY WITH SCHOOL WORK AS IT IS.
SHUT UP! YOU KNOW THAT I SUFFER FROM MISOGYNISM!
HOW DARE YOU TALK TO YOUR OLDER BROTHER THAT WAY?
SO WHAT IF YOU ARE OLDER THAN ME?! LET GO...
OKAY, HERE!
TAP
DING
DING
DING
DING

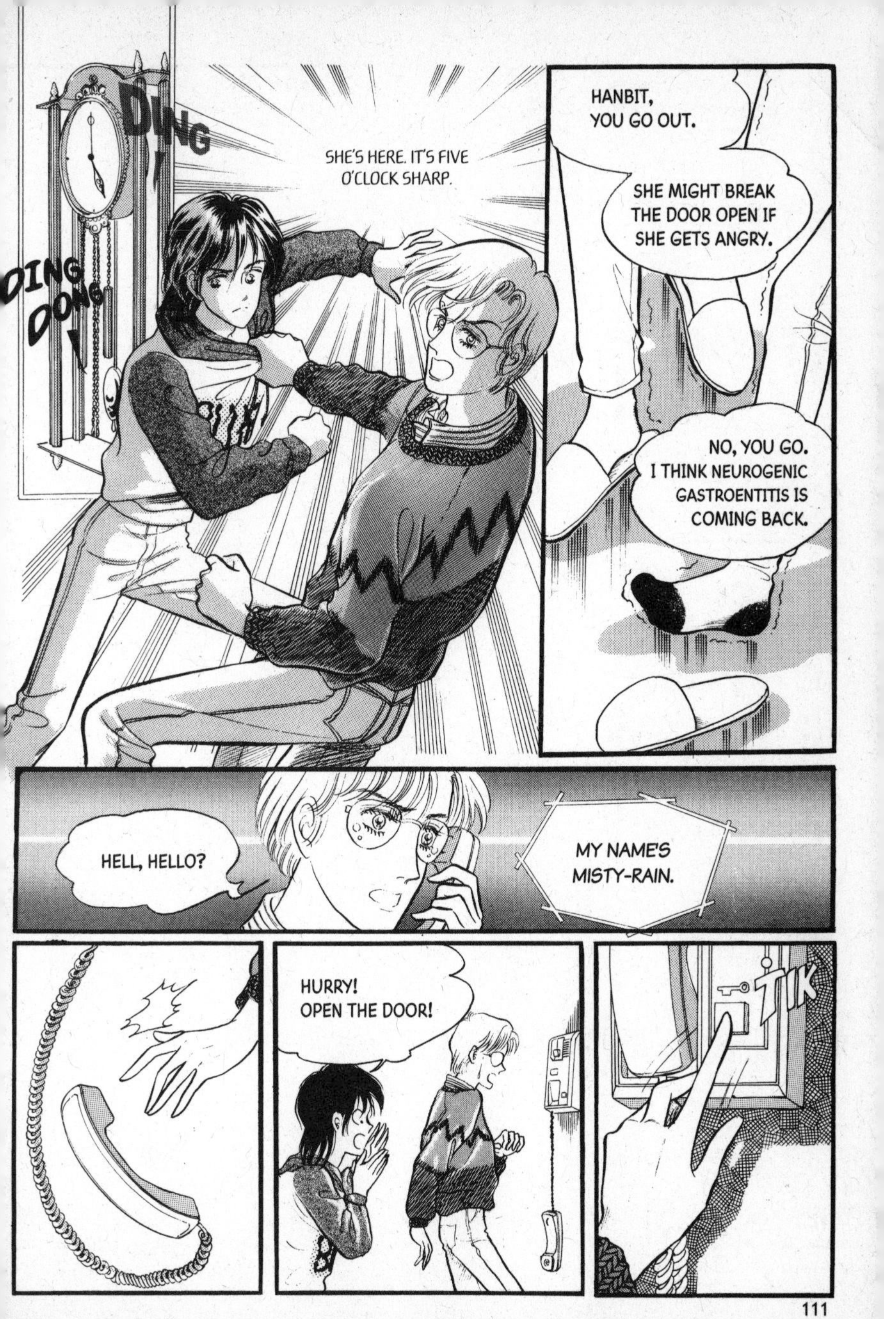
DING
DING DONG
SHE'S HERE. IT'S FIVE O'CLOCK SHARP.
HANBIT, YOU GO OUT.
SHE MIGHT BREAK THE DOOR OPEN IF SHE GETS ANGRY.
NO, YOU GO. I THINK NEUROGENIC GASTROENTITIS IS COMING BACK.
HELL, HELLO?
MY NAME'S MISTY-RAIN.
HURRY! OPEN THE DOOR!
TIK

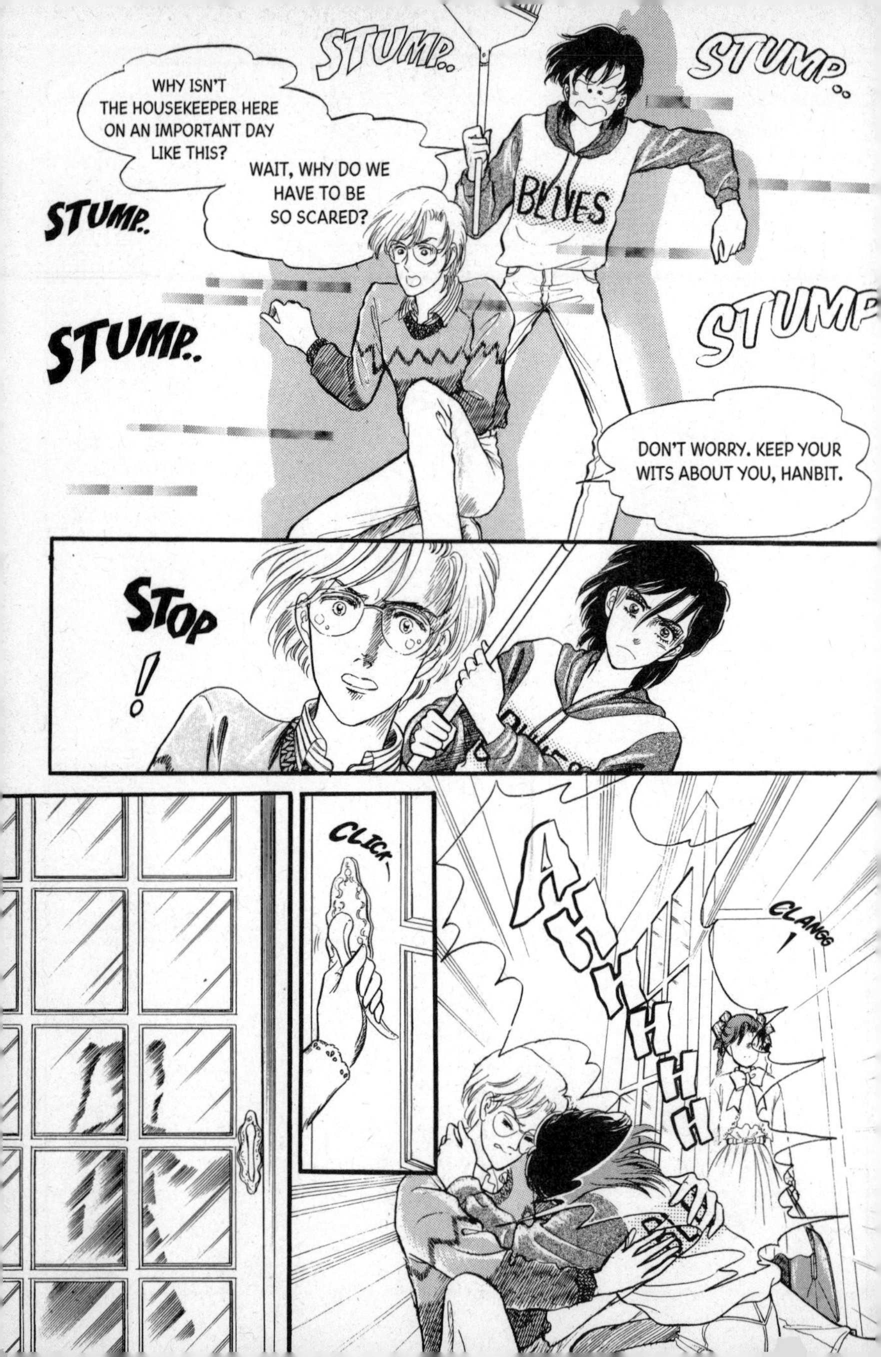
STUMP..
STUMP..
WHY ISN'T THE HOUSEKEEPER HERE ON AN IMPORTANT DAY LIKE THIS?
WAIT, WHY DO WE HAVE TO BE SO SCARED?
STUMP..
STUMP..
STUMP
DON'T WORRY. KEEP YOUR WITS ABOUT YOU, HANBIT.
STOP
!
CLICK-
AHHHHHH
CLANGG
!

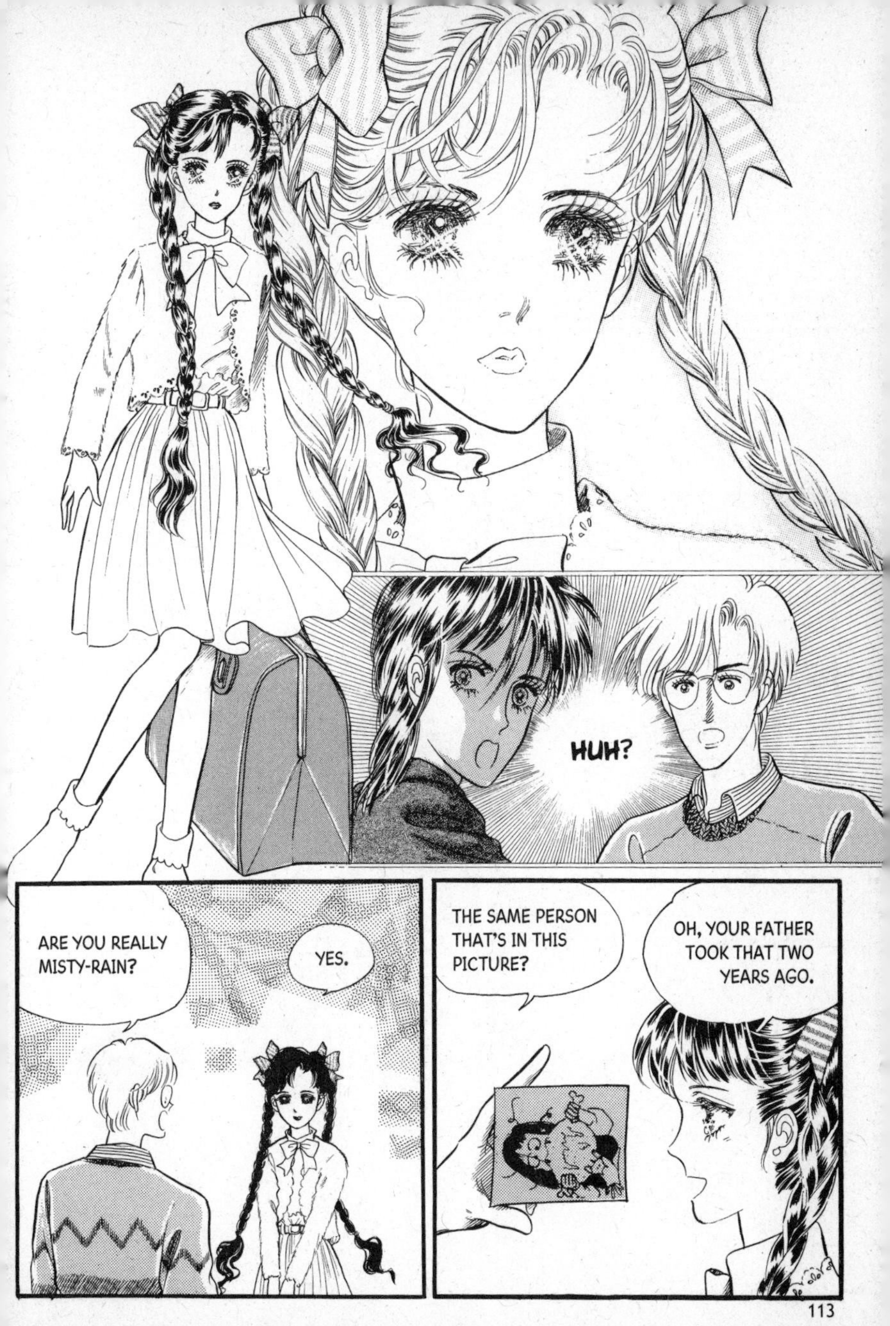
HUH?
ARE YOU REALLY MISTY-RAIN?
YES.
THE SAME PERSON THAT'S IN THIS PICTURE?
OH, YOUR FATHER TOOK THAT TWO YEARS AGO.

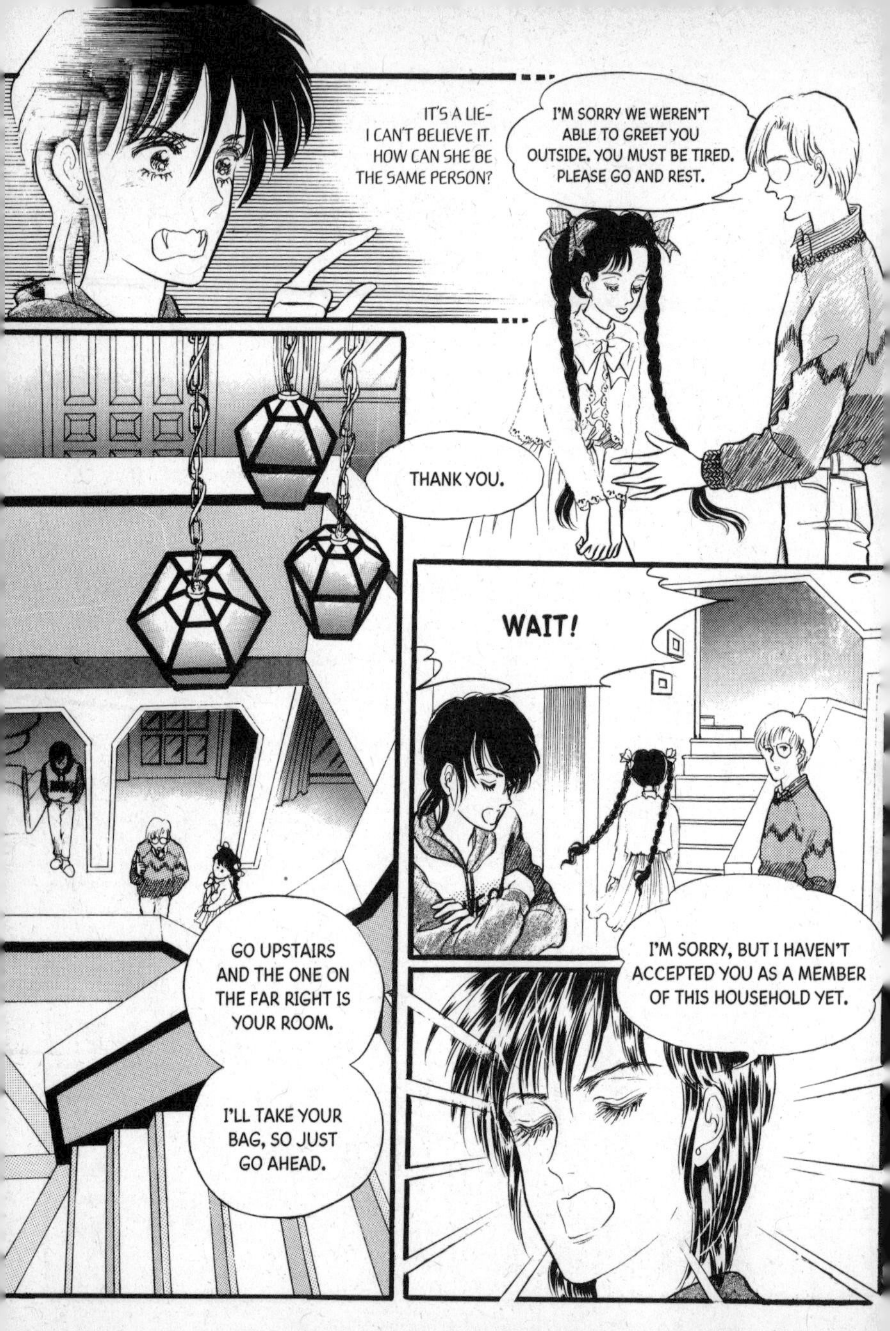
IT'S A LIE- I CAN'T BELIEVE IT. HOW CAN SHE BE THE SAME PERSON?
I'M SORRY WE WEREN'T ABLE TO GREET YOU OUTSIDE. YOU MUST BE TIRED. PLEASE GO AND REST.
GO UPSTAIRS AND THE ONE ON THE FAR RIGHT IS YOUR ROOM.
I'LL TAKE YOUR BAG, SO JUST GO AHEAD.
THANK YOU.
WAIT!
I'M SORRY, BUT I HAVEN'T ACCEPTED YOU AS A MEMBER OF THIS HOUSEHOLD YET.

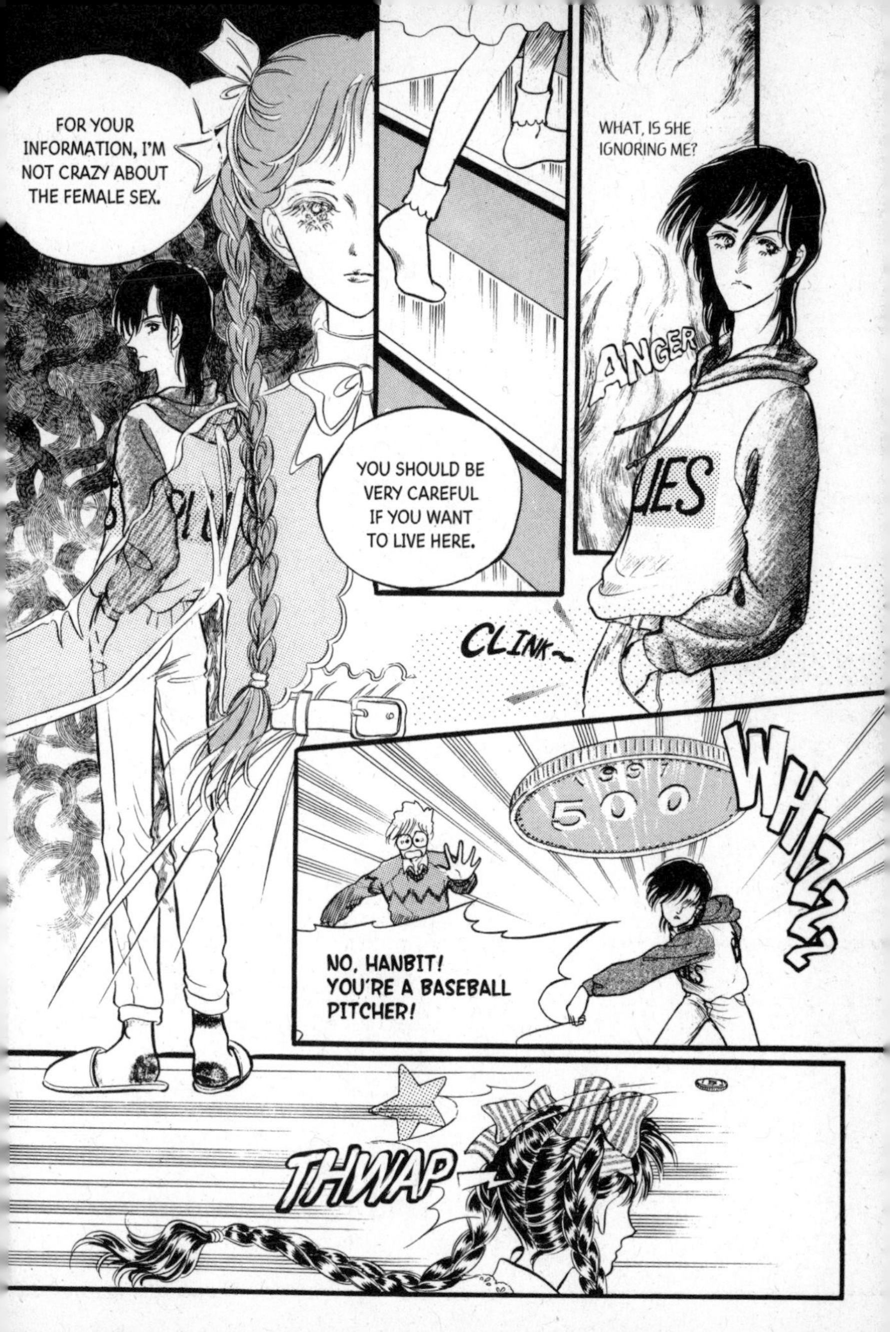
FOR YOUR INFORMATION, I'M NOT CRAZY ABOUT THE FEMALE SEX.
YOU SHOULD BE VERY CAREFUL IF YOU WANT TO LIVE HERE.
WHAT, IS SHE IGNORING ME?
ANGER
CLINK~
500
WHIZZZ
NO, HANBIT! YOU'RE A BASEBALL PITCHER!
THWAP

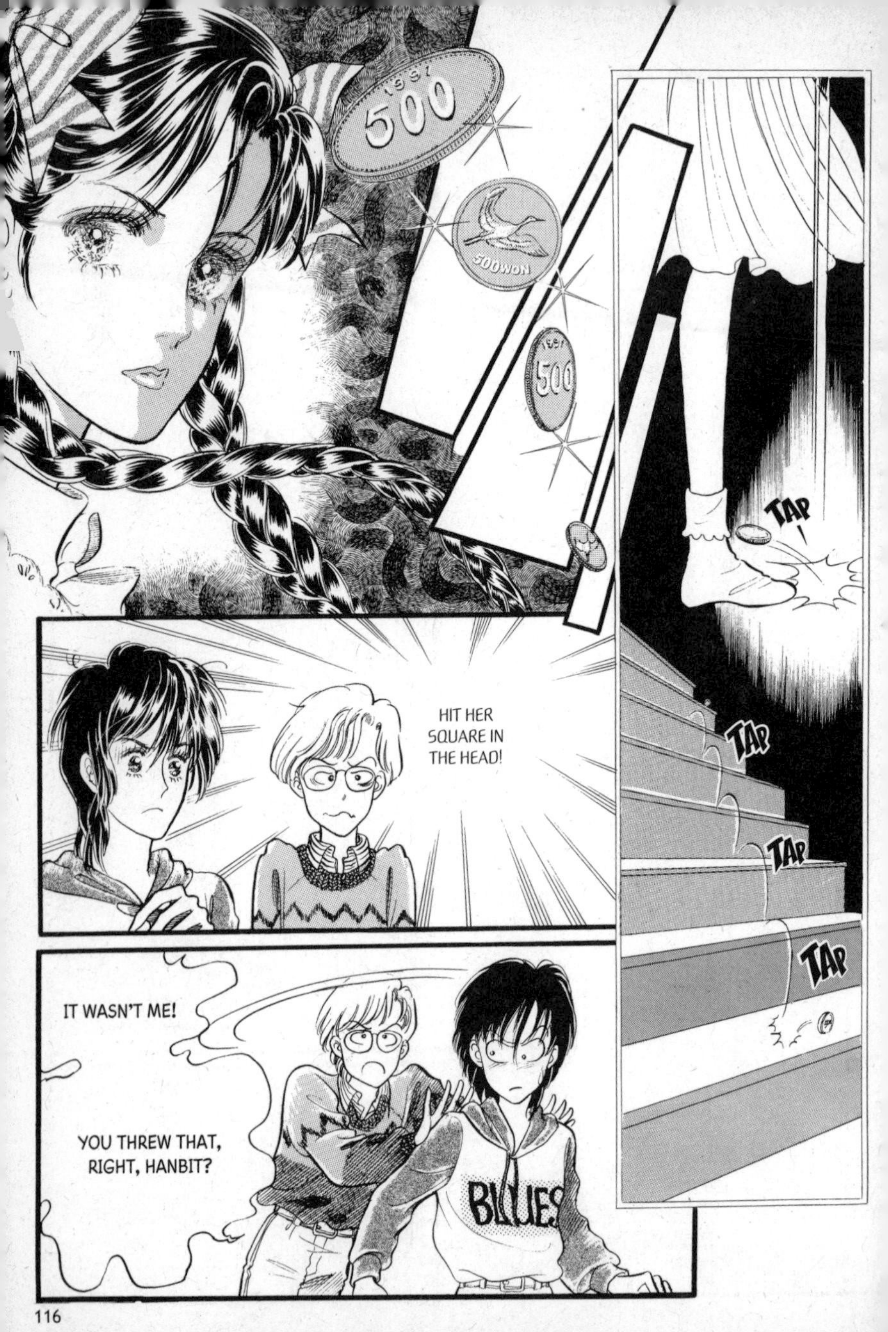
HIT HER SQUARE IN THE HEAD!
IT WASN'T ME!
YOU THREW THAT, RIGHT, HANBIT?
BLUES
TAP
TAP
TAP
TAP

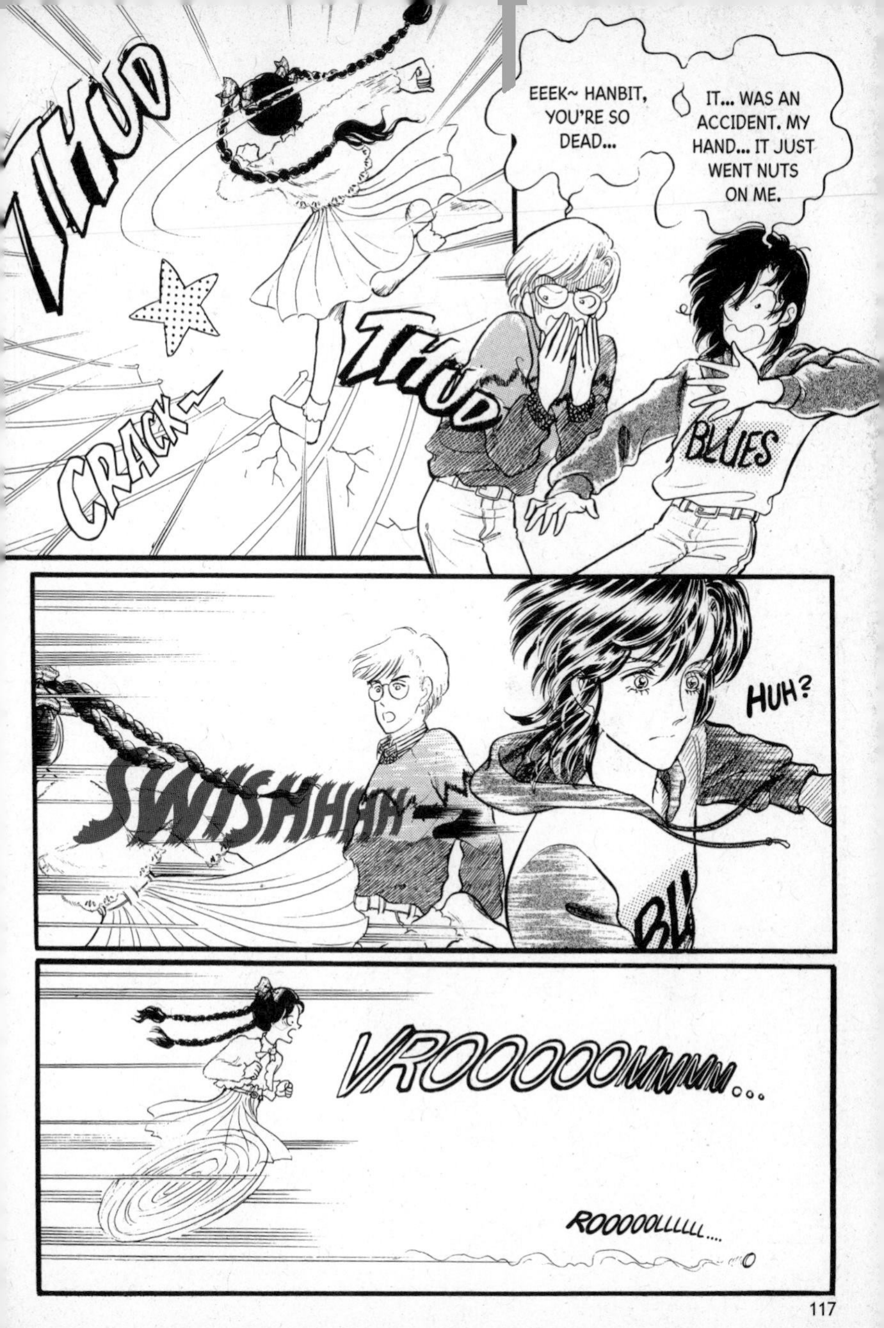
THUD
CRACK~
THUD
EEEK~ HANBIT, YOU'RE SO DEAD...
IT... WAS AN ACCIDENT. MY HAND... IT JUST WENT NUTS ON ME.
BLUES
SWISHHH~
HUH?
VROOOOOOMMMM...
ROOOOOLLLLLL....

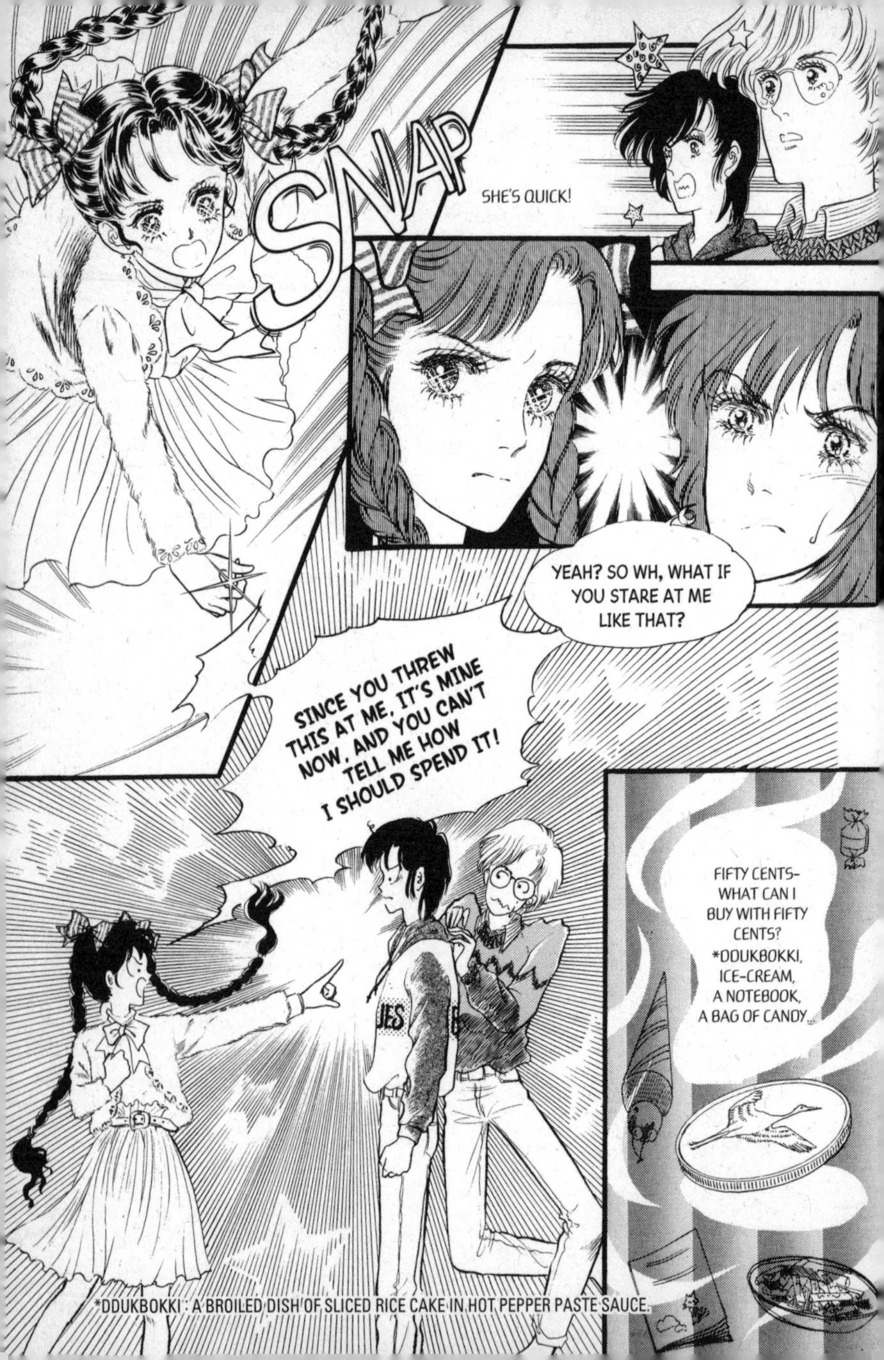
SNAP
SHE'S QUICK!
YEAH? SO WH, WHAT IF YOU STARE AT ME LIKE THAT?
SINCE YOU THREW THIS AT ME, IT'S MINE NOW, AND YOU CAN'T TELL ME HOW I SHOULD SPEND IT!
FIFTY CENTS- WHAT CAN I BUY WITH FIFTY CENTS? *DDUKBOKKI, ICE-CREAM, A NOTEBOOK, A BAG OF CANDY...
*DDUKBOKKI : A BROILED DISH OF SLICED RICE CAKE IN HOT PEPPER PASTE SAUCE.

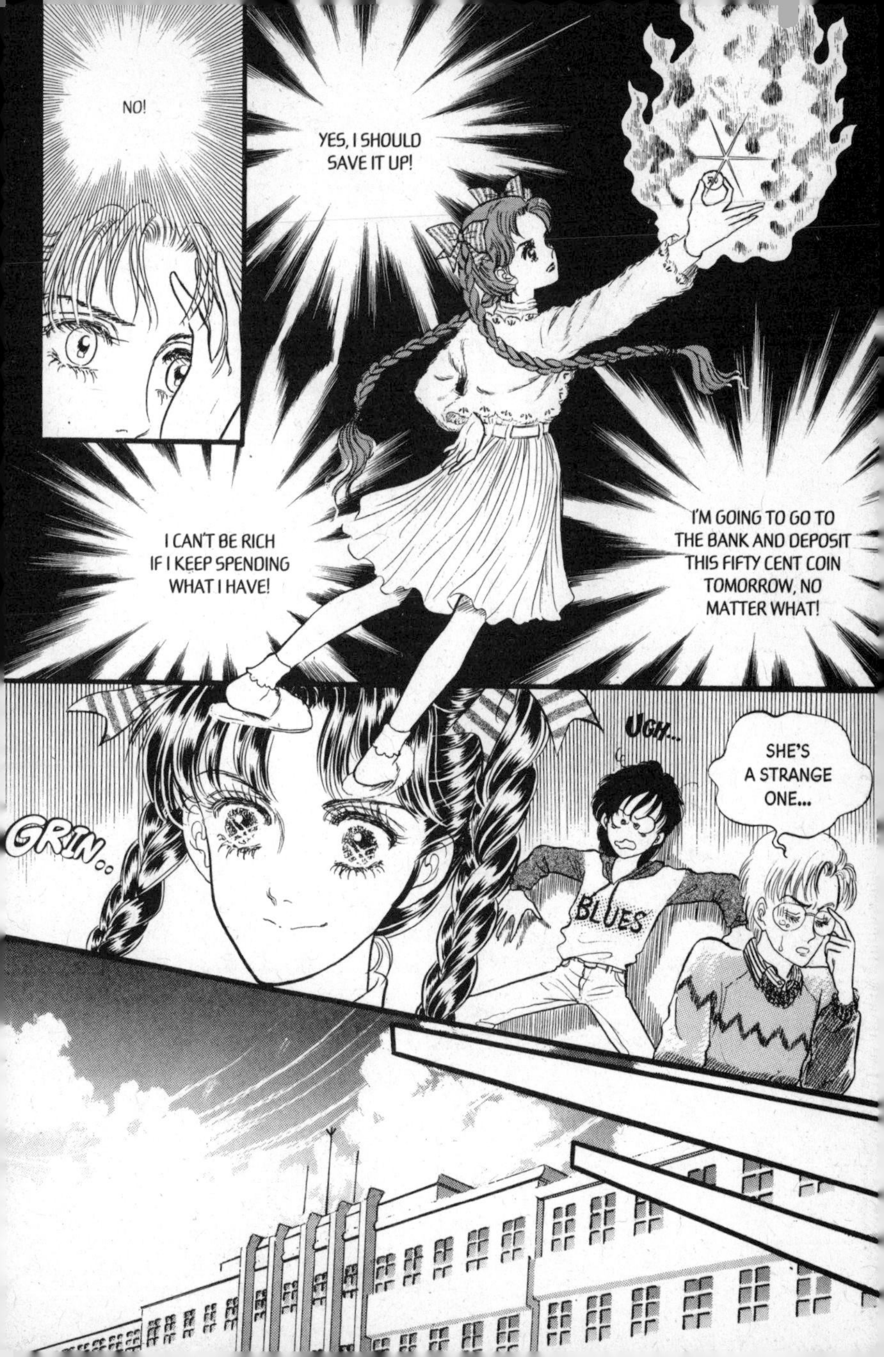
NO!
YES, I SHOULD SAVE IT UP!
I CAN'T BE RICH IF I KEEP SPENDING WHAT I HAVE!
I'M GOING TO GO TO THE BANK AND DEPOSIT THIS FIFTY CENT COIN TOMORROW, NO MATTER WHAT!
GRIN..
UGH...
BLUES
SHE'S A STRANGE ONE...

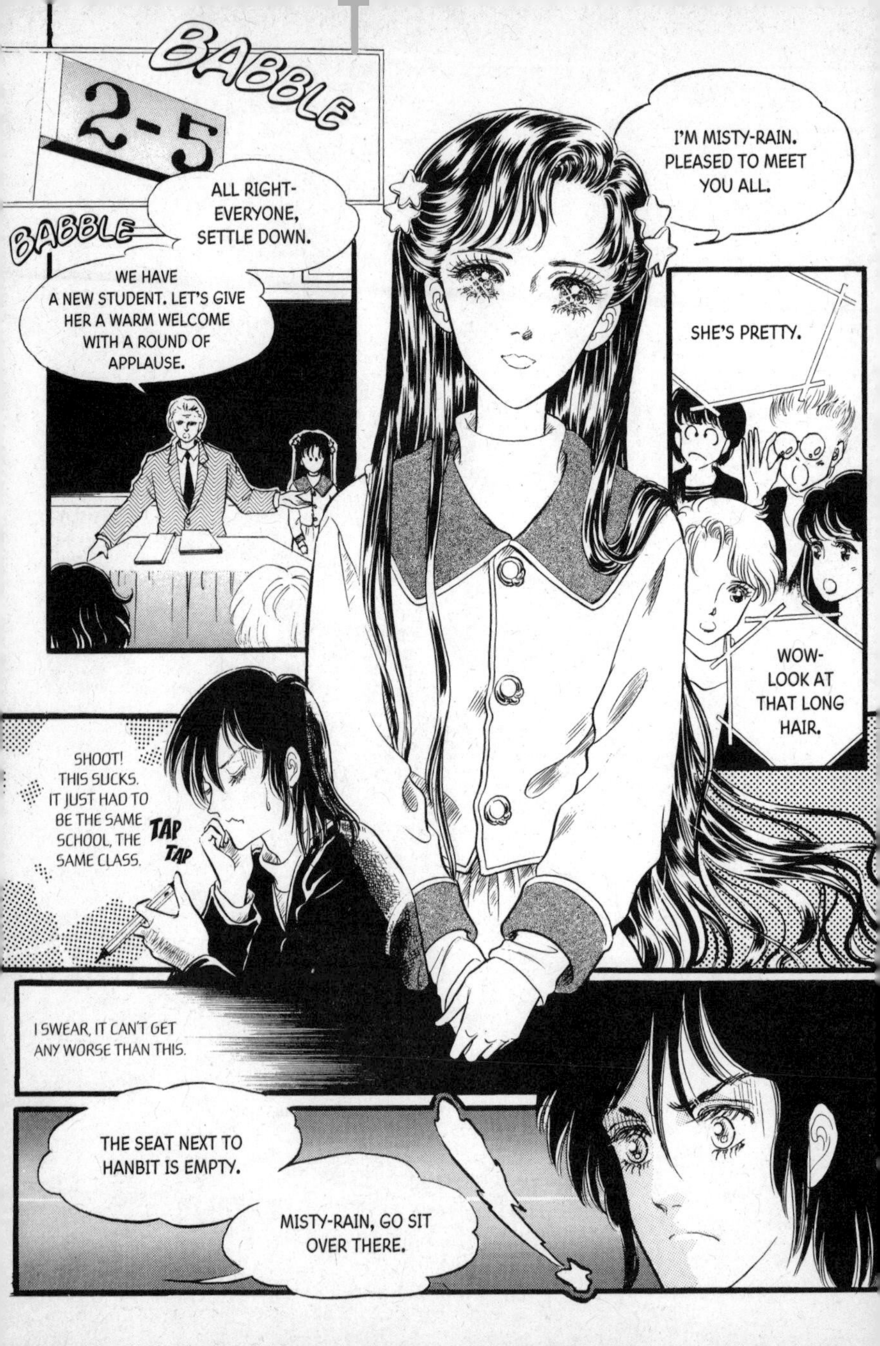
BABBLE
2-5
ALL RIGHT- EVERYONE, SETTLE DOWN.
BABBLE
WE HAVE A NEW STUDENT. LET'S GIVE HER A WARM WELCOME WITH A ROUND OF APPLAUSE.
I'M MISTY-RAIN. PLEASED TO MEET YOU ALL.
SHE'S PRETTY.
WOW- LOOK AT THAT LONG HAIR.
SHOOT! THIS SUCKS. IT JUST HAD TO BE THE SAME SCHOOL, THE SAME CLASS.
TAP TAP
I SWEAR, IT CAN'T GET ANY WORSE THAN THIS.
THE SEAT NEXT TO HANBIT IS EMPTY.
MISTY-RAIN, GO SIT OVER THERE.

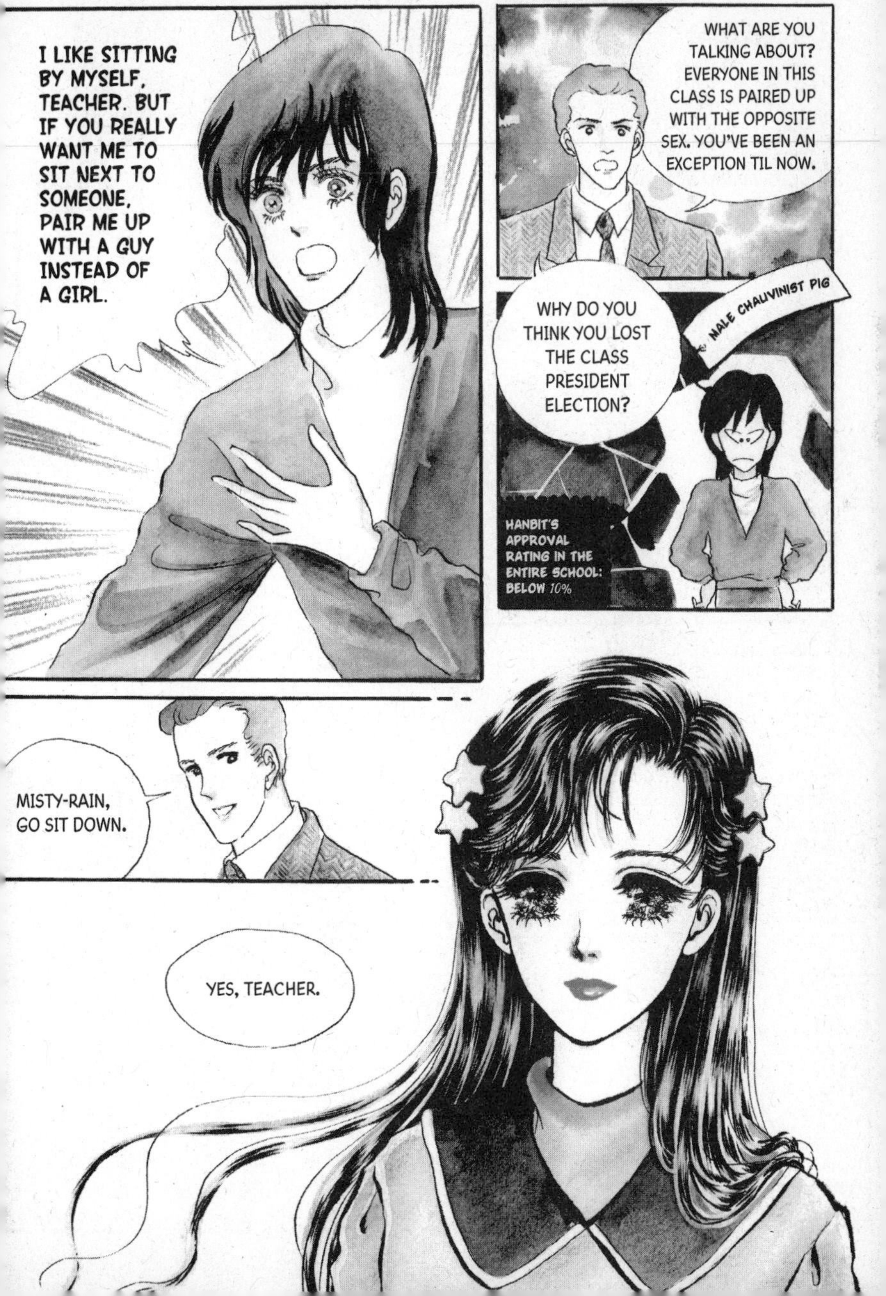
I LIKE SITTING BY MYSELF, TEACHER. BUT IF YOU REALLY WANT ME TO SIT NEXT TO SOMEONE, PAIR ME UP WITH A GUY INSTEAD OF A GIRL.
WHAT ARE YOU TALKING ABOUT? EVERYONE IN THIS CLASS IS PAIRED UP WITH THE OPPOSITE SEX. YOU'VE BEEN AN EXCEPTION TIL NOW.
WHY DO YOU THINK YOU LOST THE CLASS PRESIDENT ELECTION?
MALE CHAUVINIST PIG
HANBIT'S APPROVAL RATING IN THE ENTIRE SCHOOL: BELOW 10%
MISTY-RAIN, GO SIT DOWN.
YES, TEACHER.

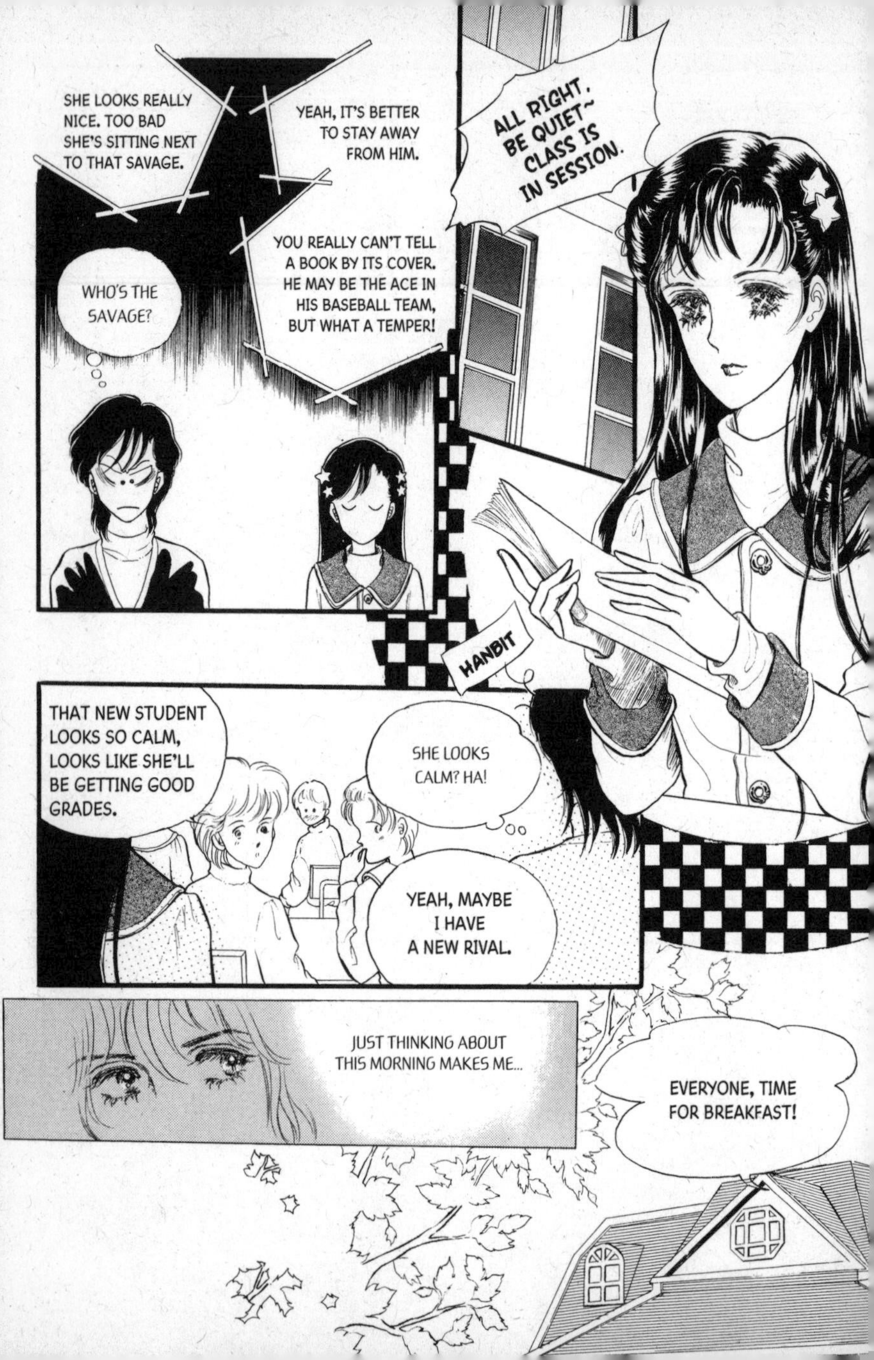
SHE LOOKS REALLY NICE. TOO BAD SHE'S SITTING NEXT TO THAT SAVAGE.
YEAH, IT'S BETTER TO STAY AWAY FROM HIM.
WHO'S THE SAVAGE?
YOU REALLY CAN'T TELL A BOOK BY ITS COVER. HE MAY BE THE ACE IN HIS BASEBALL TEAM, BUT WHAT A TEMPER!
ALL RIGHT. BE QUIET~ CLASS IS IN SESSION.
HANBIT
THAT NEW STUDENT LOOKS SO CALM, LOOKS LIKE SHE'LL BE GETTING GOOD GRADES.
SHE LOOKS CALM? HA!
YEAH, MAYBE I HAVE A NEW RIVAL.
JUST THINKING ABOUT THIS MORNING MAKES ME...
EVERYONE, TIME FOR BREAKFAST!

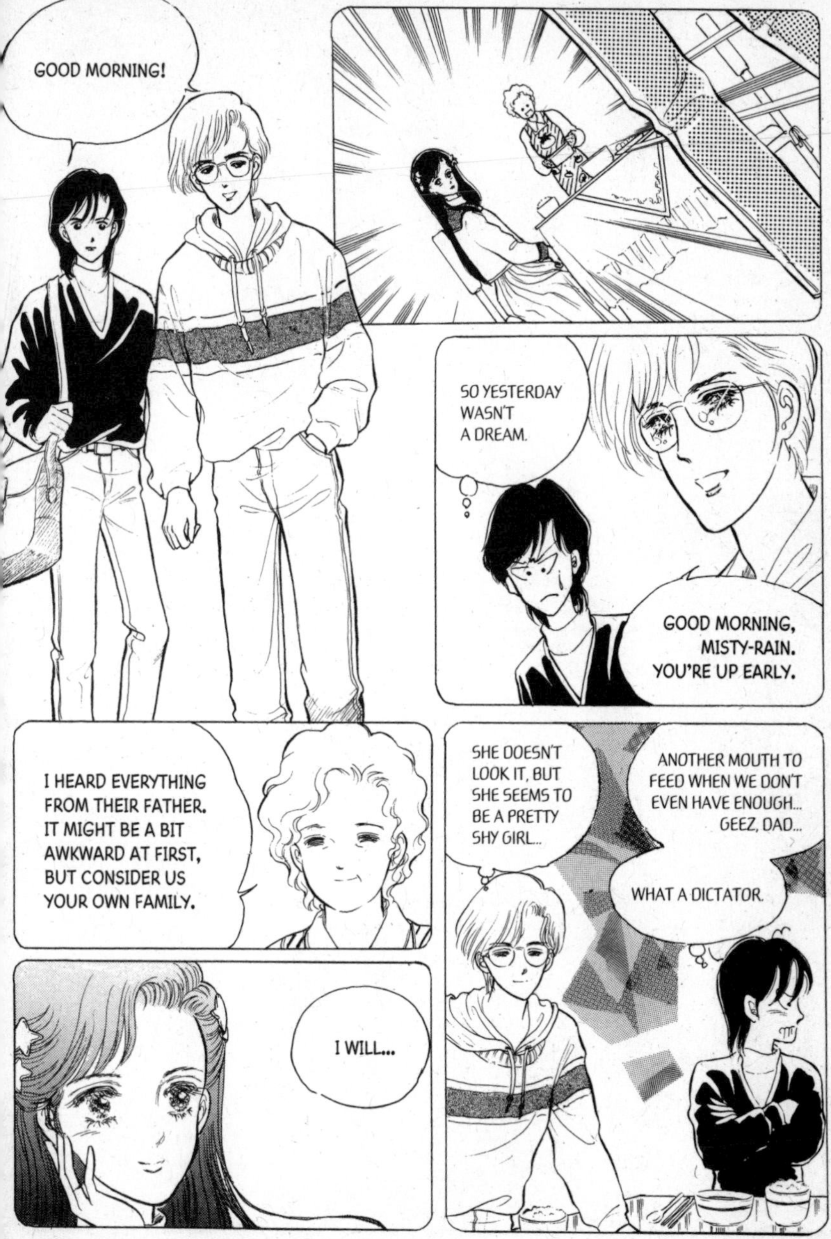
GOOD MORNING!
SO YESTERDAY WASN'T A DREAM.
GOOD MORNING, MISTY-RAIN. YOU'RE UP EARLY.
I HEARD EVERYTHING FROM THEIR FATHER. IT MIGHT BE A BIT AWKWARD AT FIRST, BUT CONSIDER US YOUR OWN FAMILY.
I WILL...
SHE DOESN'T LOOK IT, BUT SHE SEEMS TO BE A PRETTY SHY GIRL...
ANOTHER MOUTH TO FEED WHEN WE DON'T EVEN HAVE ENOUGH... GEEZ, DAD...
WHAT A DICTATOR.

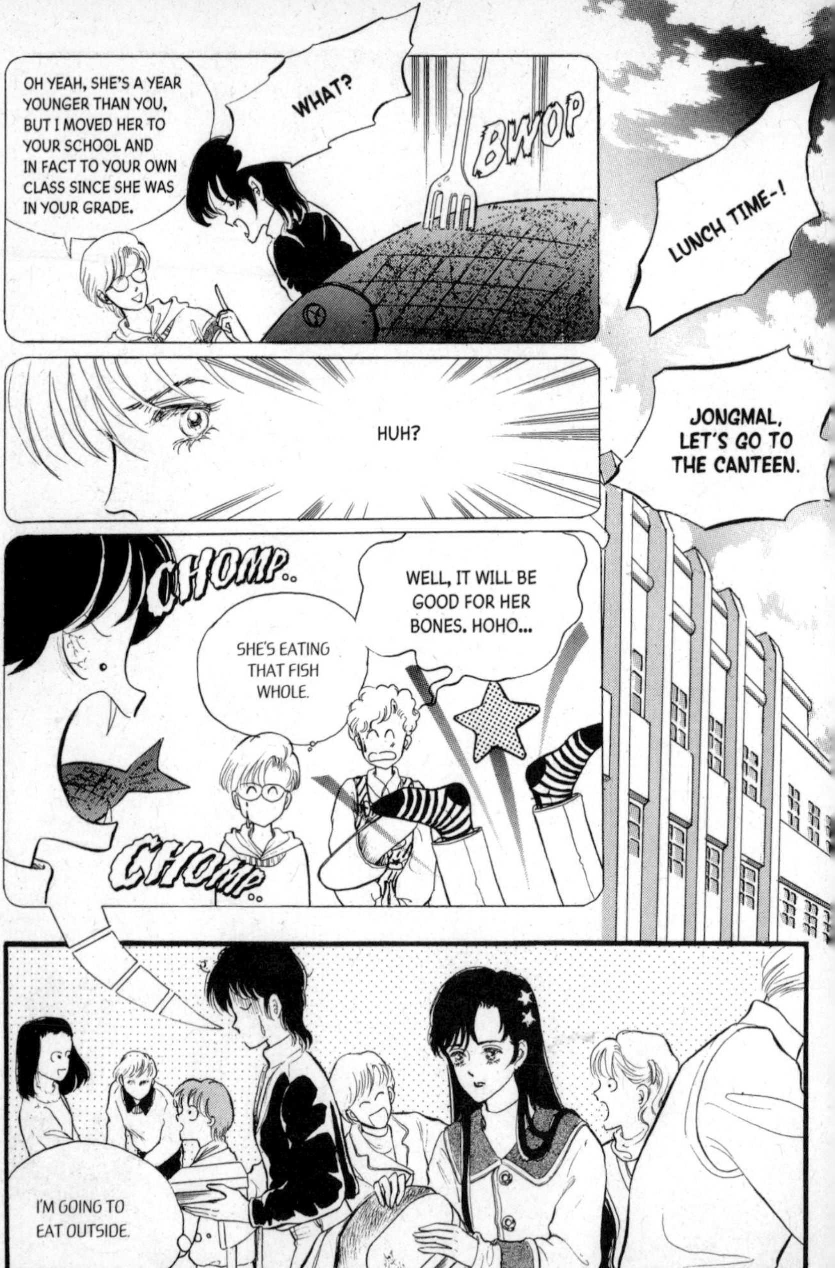
OH YEAH, SHE'S A YEAR YOUNGER THAN YOU, BUT I MOVED HER TO YOUR SCHOOL AND IN FACT TO YOUR OWN CLASS SINCE SHE WAS IN YOUR GRADE.
WHAT?
BWOP
HUH?
CHOMP..
SHE'S EATING THAT FISH WHOLE.
WELL, IT WILL BE GOOD FOR HER BONES. HOHO...
CHOMP..
LUNCH TIME-!
JONGMAL, LET'S GO TO THE CANTEEN.
I'M GOING TO EAT OUTSIDE.

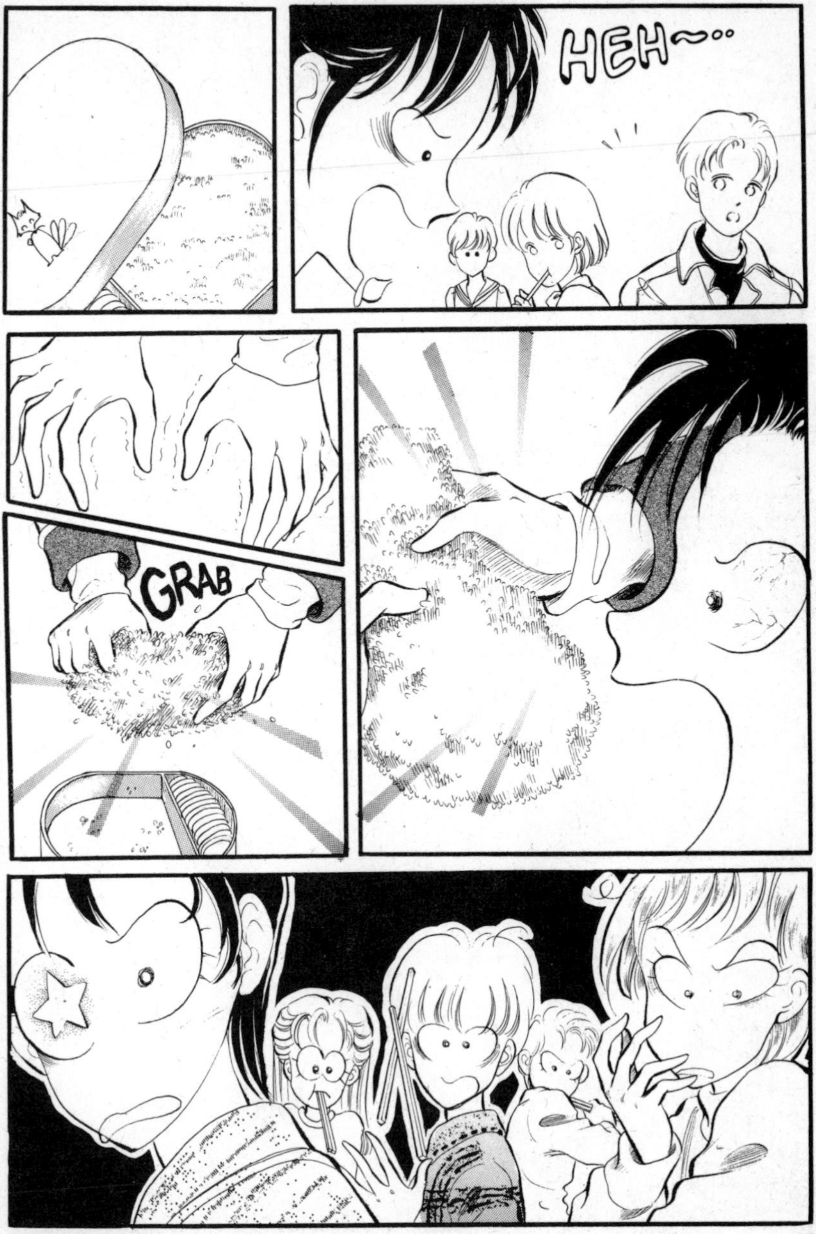
HEH~..
GRAB

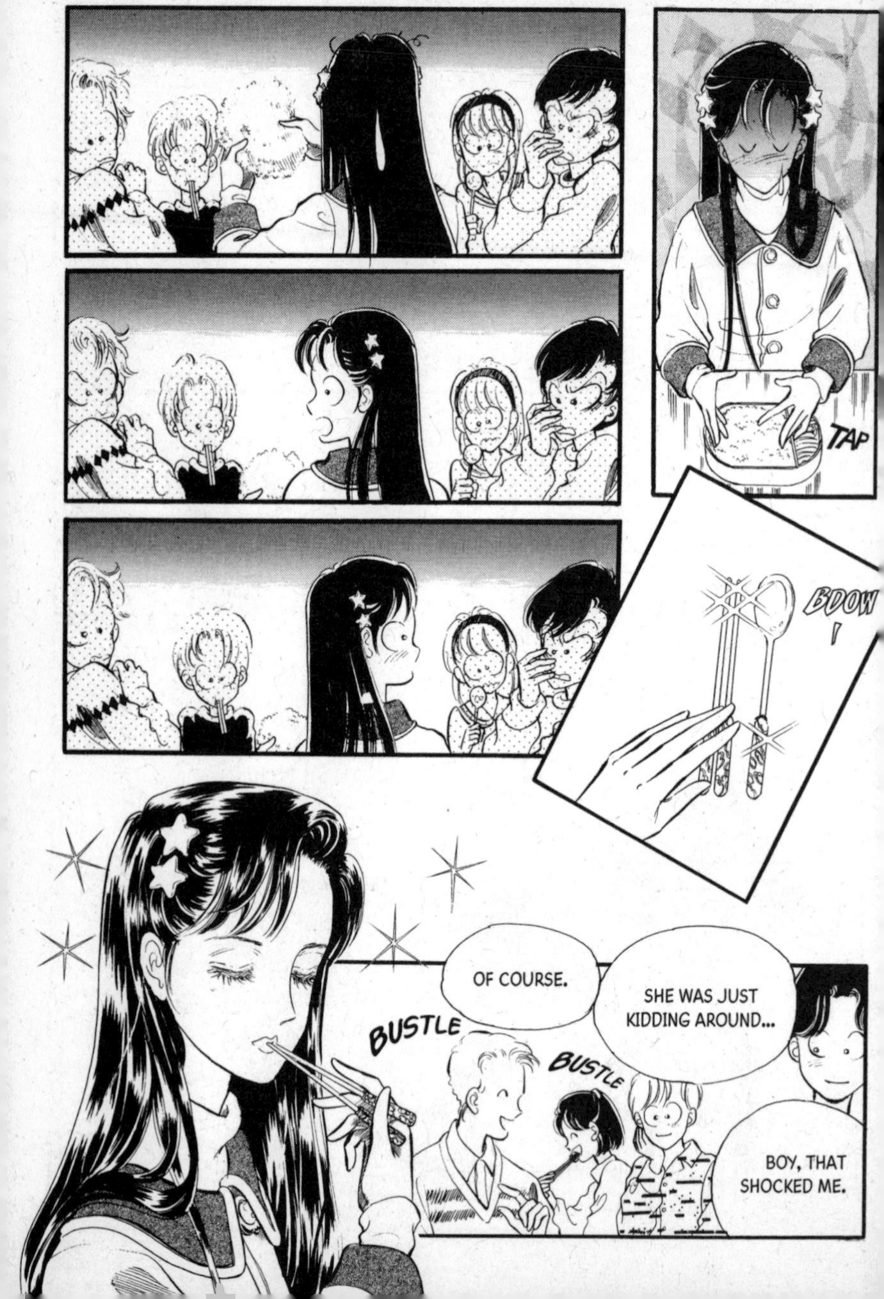
TAP
BDOW
OF COURSE.
BUSTLE
BUSTLE
SHE WAS JUST KIDDING AROUND...
BOY, THAT SHOCKED ME.

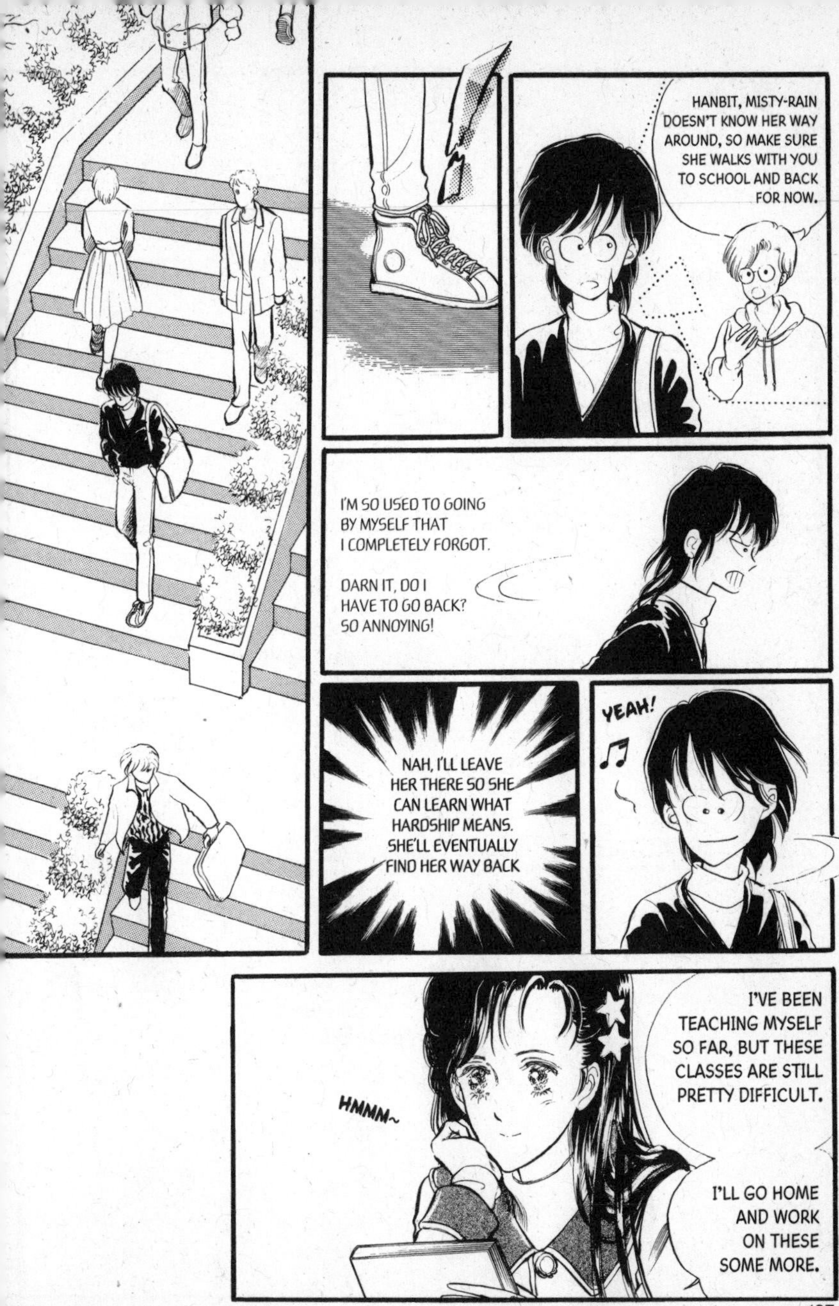
HANBIT, MISTY-RAIN DOESN'T KNOW HER WAY AROUND, SO MAKE SURE SHE WALKS WITH YOU TO SCHOOL AND BACK FOR NOW.
I'M SO USED TO GOING BY MYSELF THAT I COMPLETELY FORGOT.
DARN IT, DO I HAVE TO GO BACK? SO ANNOYING!
NAH, I'LL LEAVE HER THERE SO SHE CAN LEARN WHAT HARDSHIP MEANS. SHE'LL EVENTUALLY FIND HER WAY BACK
YEAH!
I'VE BEEN TEACHING MYSELF SO FAR, BUT THESE CLASSES ARE STILL PRETTY DIFFICULT.
HMMM~
I'LL GO HOME AND WORK ON THESE SOME MORE.

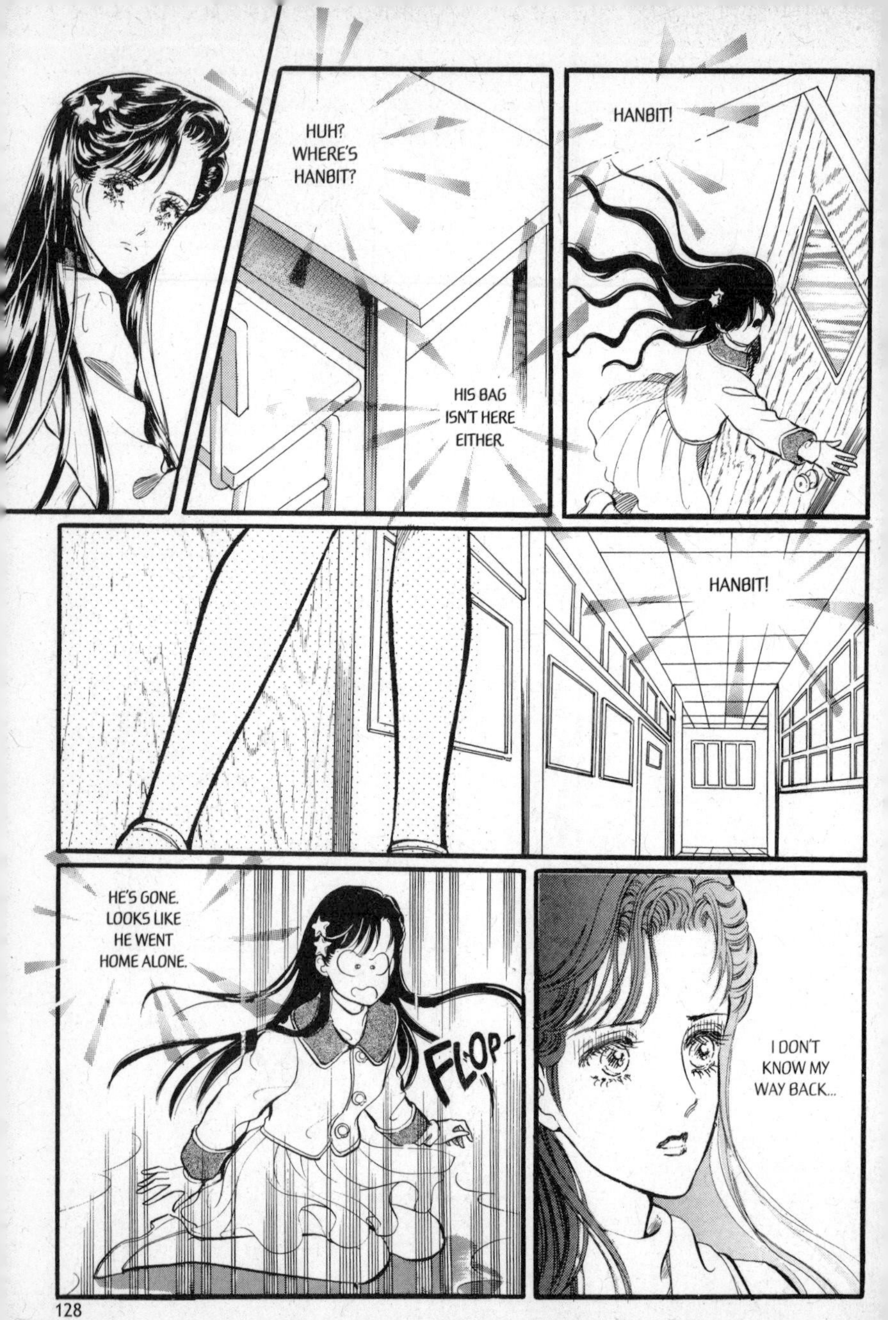
HUH? WHERE'S HANBIT?
HIS BAG ISN'T HERE EITHER.
HANBIT!
HANBIT!
HE'S GONE. LOOKS LIKE HE WENT HOME ALONE.
FLOP
I DON'T KNOW MY WAY BACK...

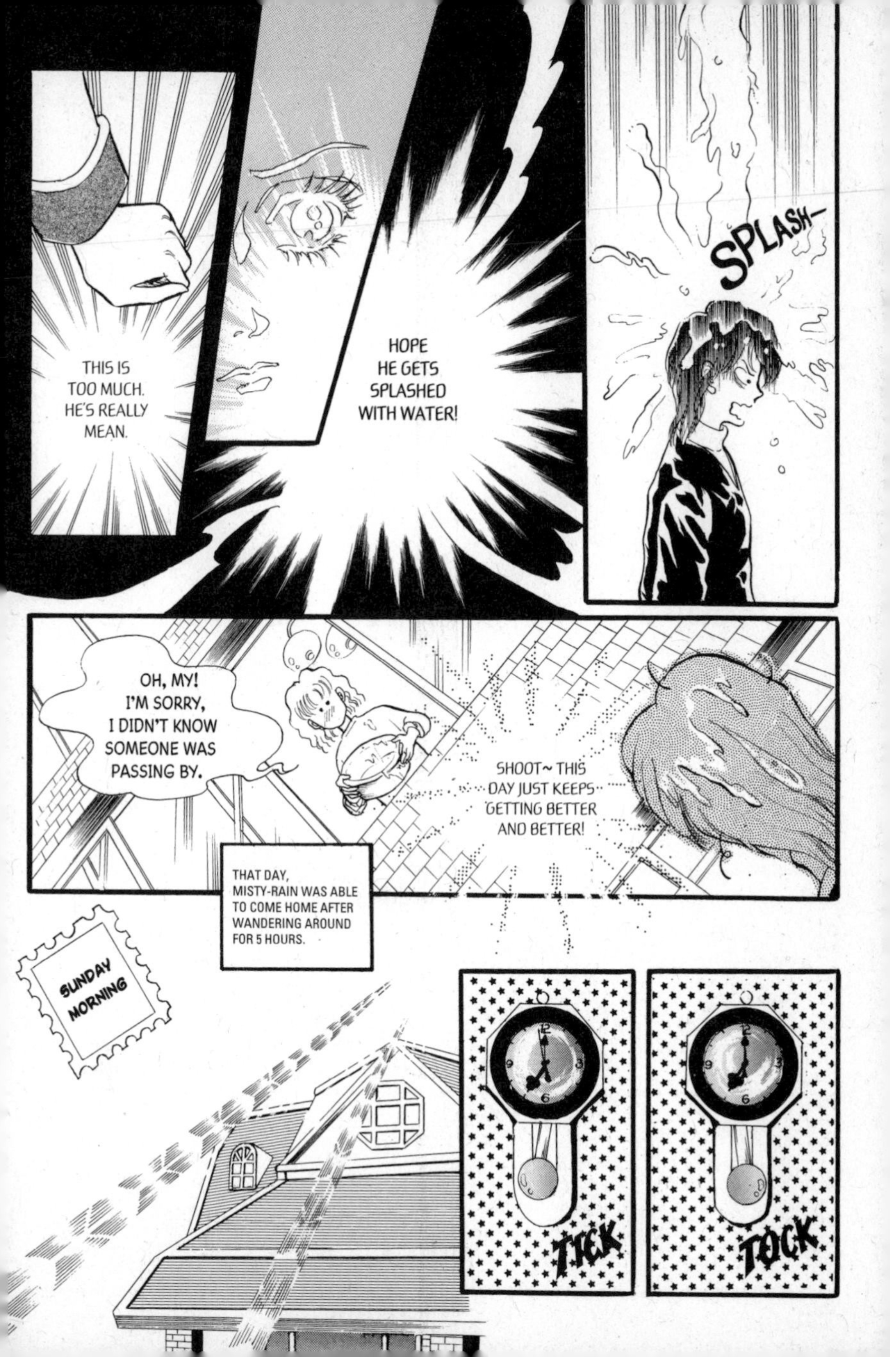
THIS IS TOO MUCH. HE'S REALLY MEAN.
HOPE HE GETS SPLASHED WITH WATER!
SPLASH—
OH, MY! I'M SORRY, I DIDN'T KNOW SOMEONE WAS PASSING BY.
SHOOT~ THIS DAY JUST KEEPS GETTING BETTER AND BETTER!
THAT DAY, MISTY-RAIN WAS ABLE TO COME HOME AFTER WANDERING AROUND FOR 5 HOURS.
SUNDAY MORNING
TICK
TOCK

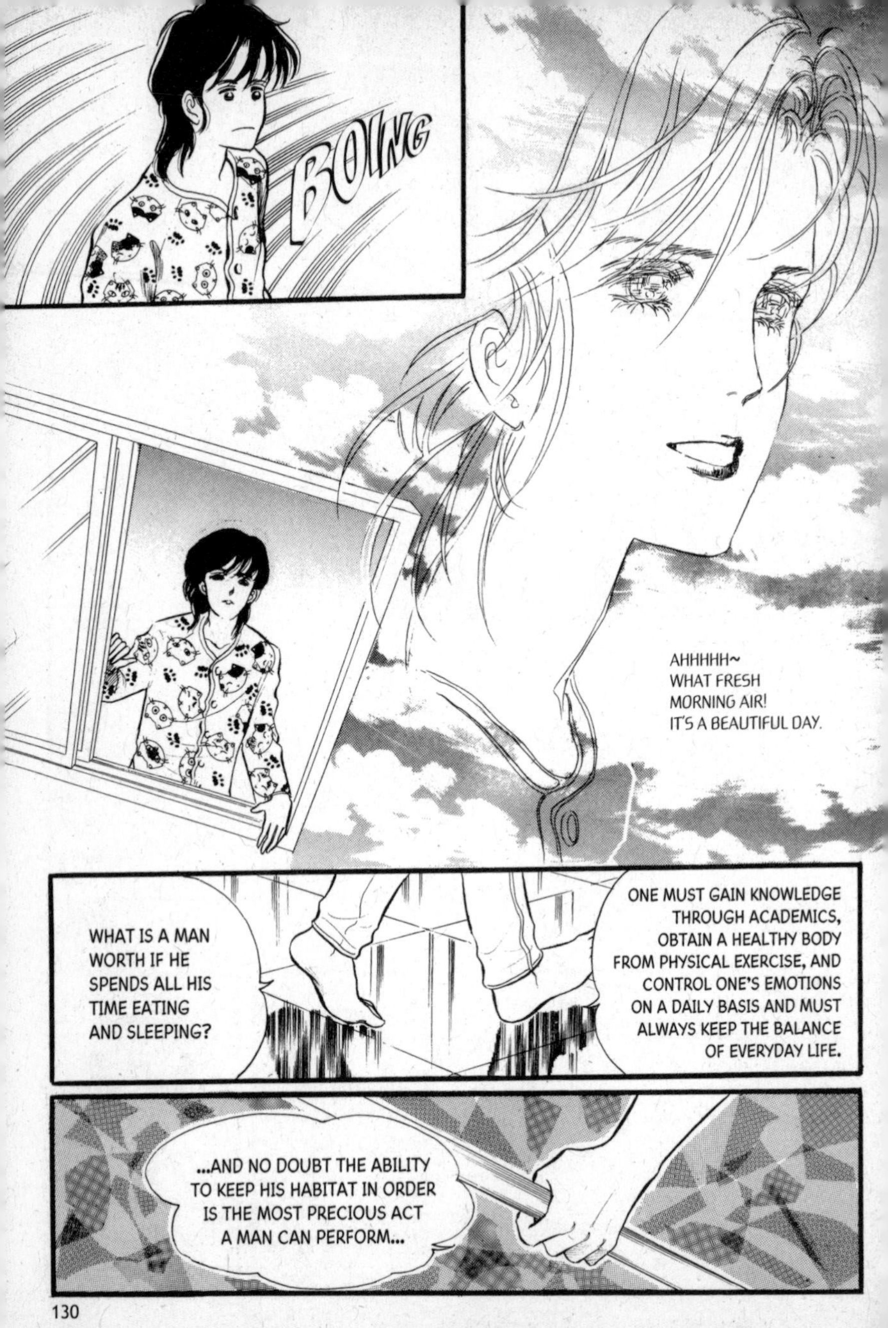
BOING
AHHHHH~ WHAT FRESH MORNING AIR! IT'S A BEAUTIFUL DAY.
ONE MUST GAIN KNOWLEDGE THROUGH ACADEMICS, OBTAIN A HEALTHY BODY FROM PHYSICAL EXERCISE, AND CONTROL ONE'S EMOTIONS ON A DAILY BASIS AND MUST ALWAYS KEEP THE BALANCE OF EVERYDAY LIFE.
WHAT IS A MAN WORTH IF HE SPENDS ALL HIS TIME EATING AND SLEEPING?
...AND NO DOUBT THE ABILITY TO KEEP HIS HABITAT IN ORDER IS THE MOST PRECIOUS ACT A MAN CAN PERFORM...

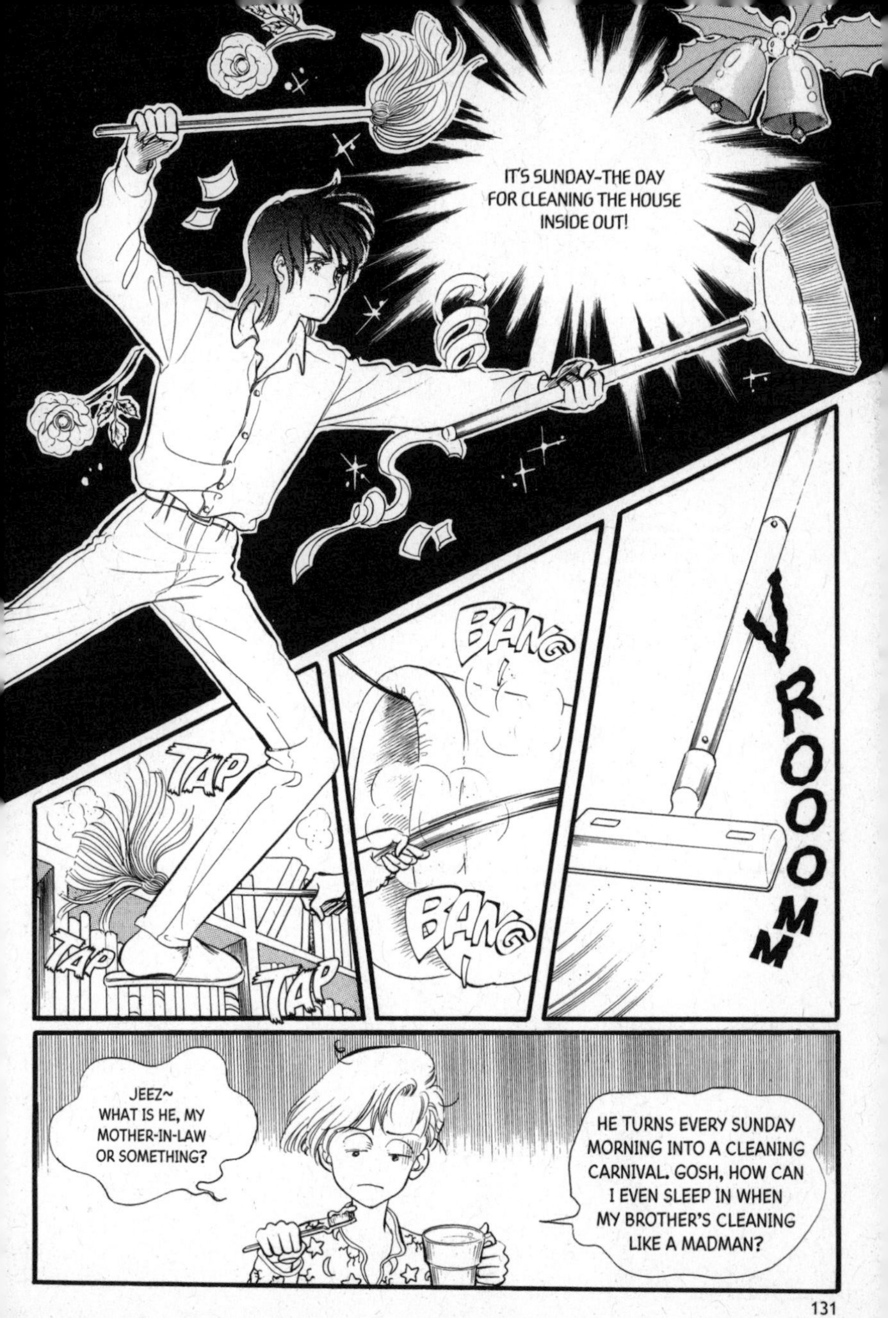
IT'S SUNDAY–THE DAY FOR CLEANING THE HOUSE INSIDE OUT!
TAP
TAP
TAP
BANG
BANG
VROOOMM
JEEZ~ WHAT IS HE, MY MOTHER-IN-LAW OR SOMETHING?
HE TURNS EVERY SUNDAY MORNING INTO A CLEANING CARNIVAL. GOSH, HOW CAN I EVEN SLEEP IN WHEN MY BROTHER'S CLEANING LIKE A MADMAN?

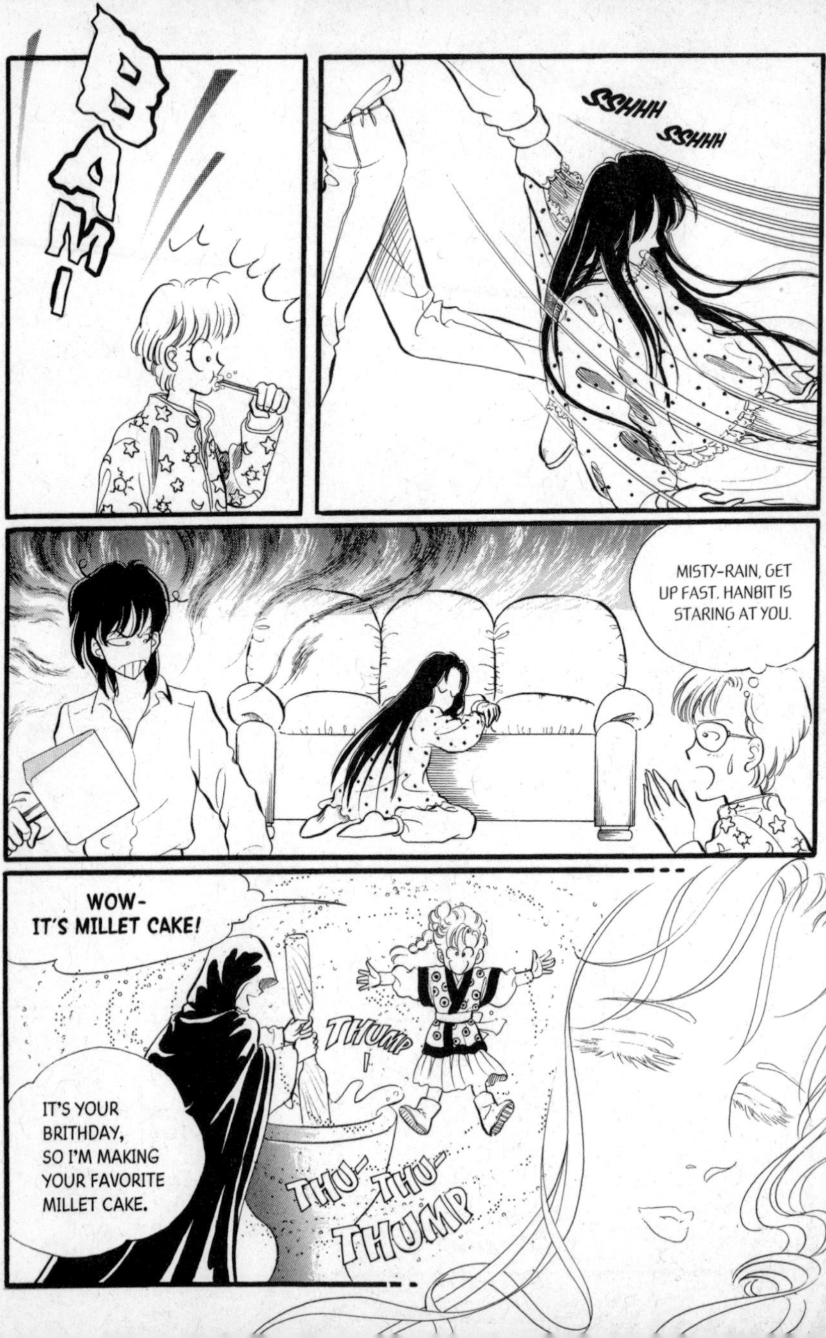
BAM!
SSHHH
SSHHH
MISTY-RAIN, GET UP FAST. HANBIT IS STARING AT YOU.
WOW- IT'S MILLET CAKE!
IT'S YOUR BRITHDAY, SO I'M MAKING YOUR FAVORITE MILLET CAKE.
THUMP!
THU-THU-THUMP

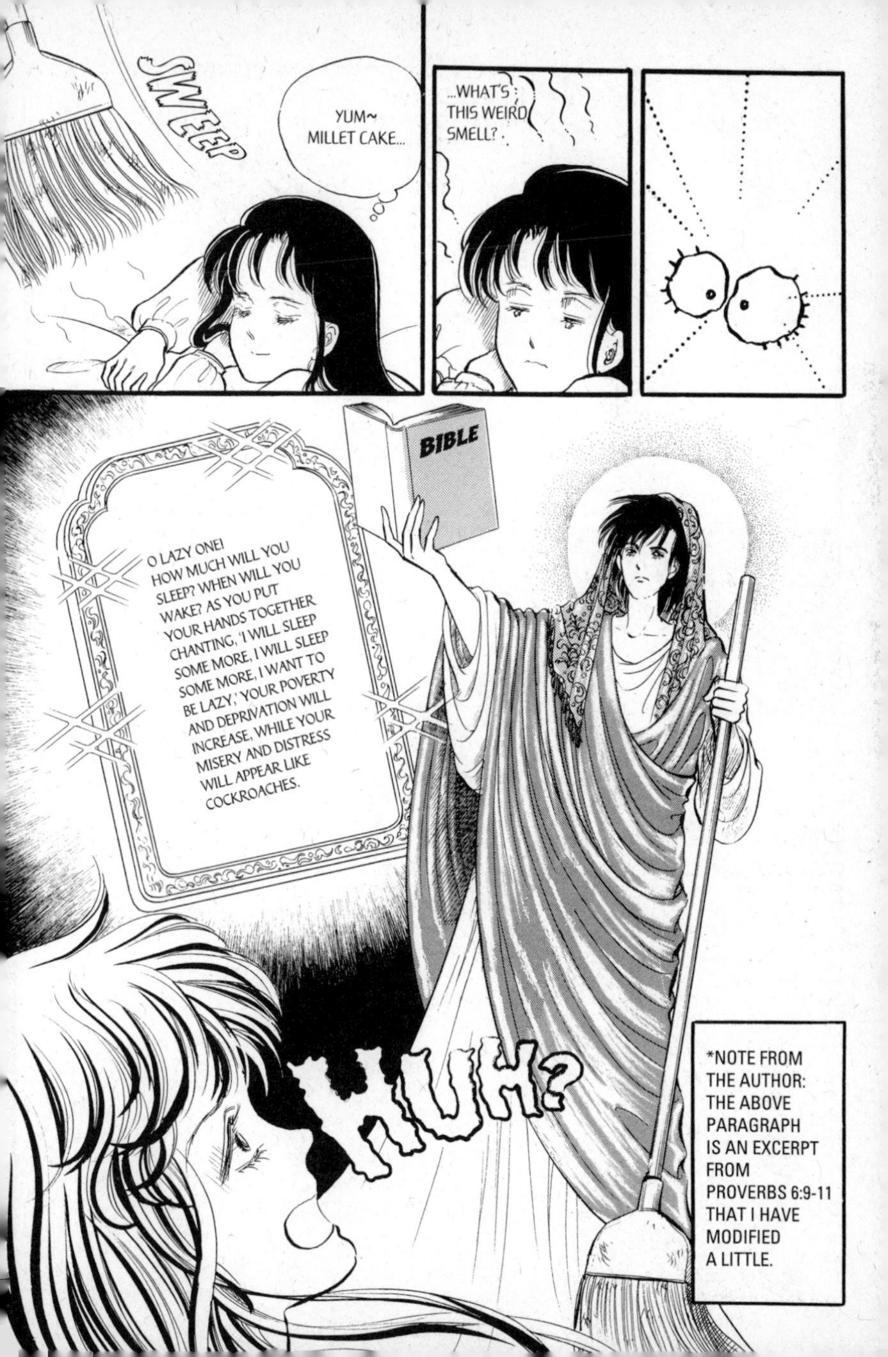
SWEEP
YUM~ MILLET CAKE...
...WHAT'S THIS WEIRD SMELL?
BIBLE
O LAZY ONE! HOW MUCH WILL YOU SLEEP? WHEN WILL YOU WAKE? AS YOU PUT YOUR HANDS TOGETHER CHANTING, 'I WILL SLEEP SOME MORE, I WILL SLEEP SOME MORE, I WANT TO BE LAZY,' YOUR POVERTY AND DEPRIVATION WILL INCREASE, WHILE YOUR MISERY AND DISTRESS WILL APPEAR LIKE COCKROACHES.
HUH?
*NOTE FROM THE AUTHOR: THE ABOVE PARAGRAPH IS AN EXCERPT FROM PROVERBS 6:9-11 THAT I HAVE MODIFIED A LITTLE.

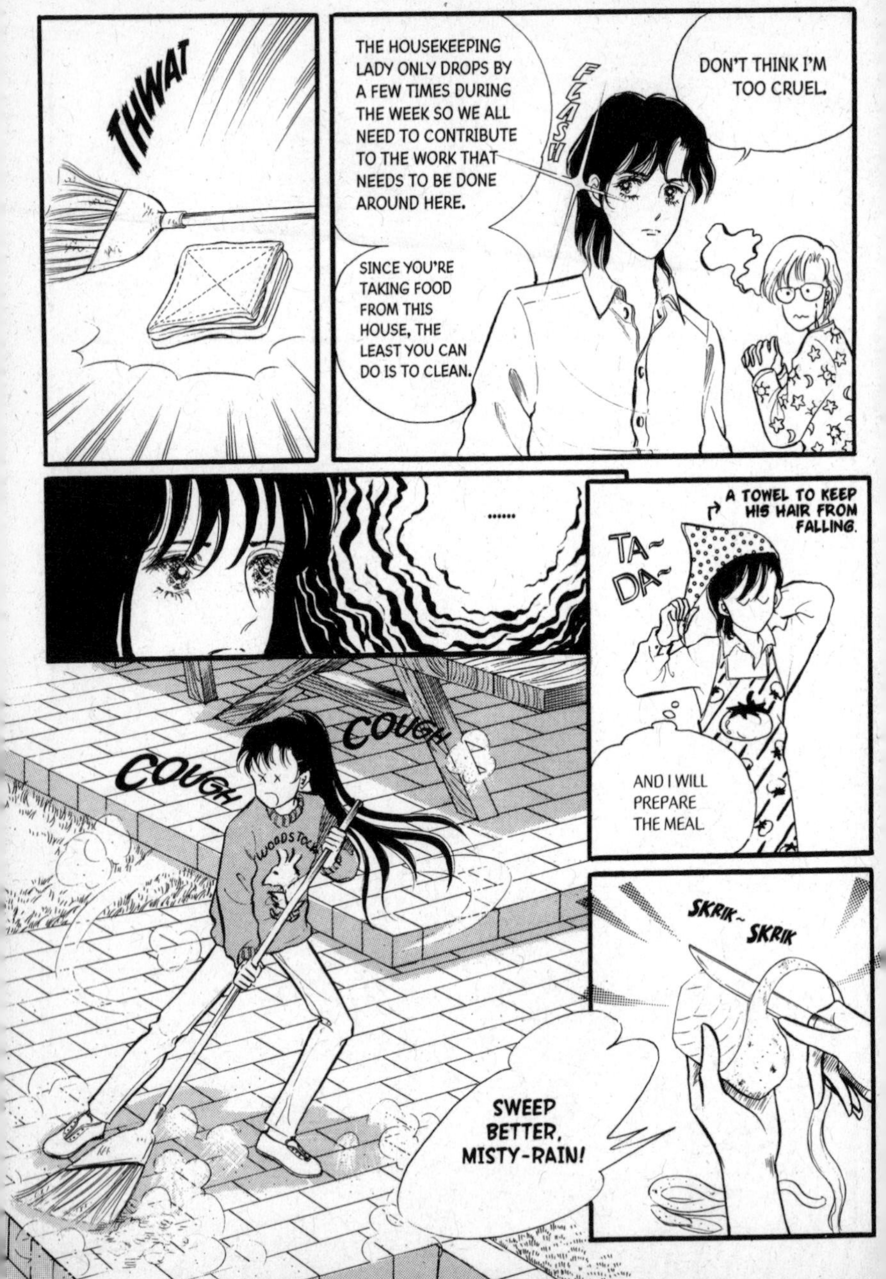
THWAT
THE HOUSEKEEPING LADY ONLY DROPS BY A FEW TIMES DURING THE WEEK SO WE ALL NEED TO CONTRIBUTE TO THE WORK THAT NEEDS TO BE DONE AROUND HERE.
FLASH
SINCE YOU'RE TAKING FOOD FROM THIS HOUSE, THE LEAST YOU CAN DO IS TO CLEAN.
DON'T THINK I'M TOO CRUEL.
......
A TOWEL TO KEEP HIS HAIR FROM FALLING.
TA~ DA~
AND I WILL PREPARE THE MEAL.
COUGH
COUGH
WOODSTOCK
SKRIK~ SKRIK
SWEEP BETTER, MISTY-RAIN!

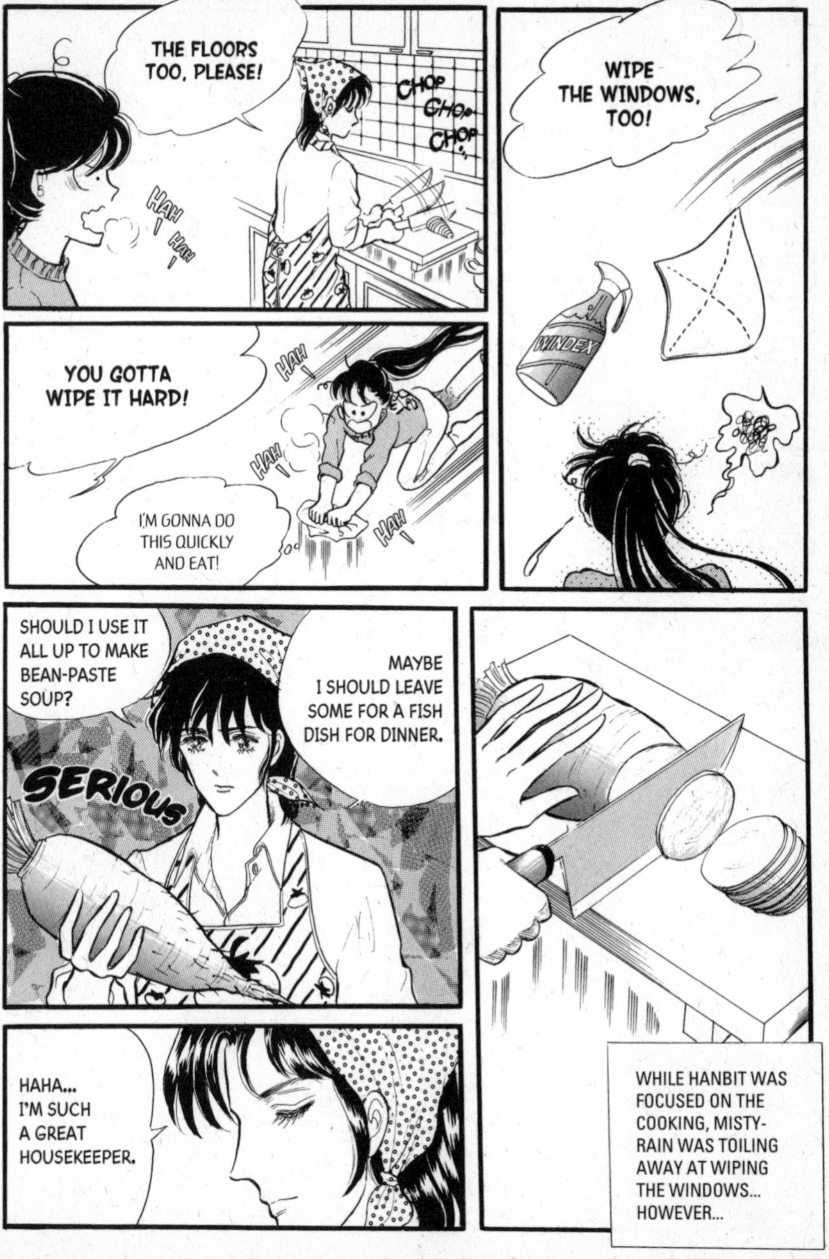

THE FLOORS TOO, PLEASE!
CHOP CHOP CHOP
HAH! HAH!
YOU GOTTA WIPE IT HARD!
HAH HAH HAH
I'M GONNA DO THIS QUICKLY AND EAT!
WIPE THE WINDOWS, TOO!
WINDEX
SHOULD I USE IT ALL UP TO MAKE BEAN-PASTE SOUP?
MAYBE I SHOULD LEAVE SOME FOR A FISH DISH FOR DINNER.
SERIOUS
HAHA... I'M SUCH A GREAT HOUSEKEEPER.
WHILE HANBIT WAS FOCUSED ON THE COOKING, MISTY-RAIN WAS TOILING AWAY AT WIPING THE WINDOWS... HOWEVER...

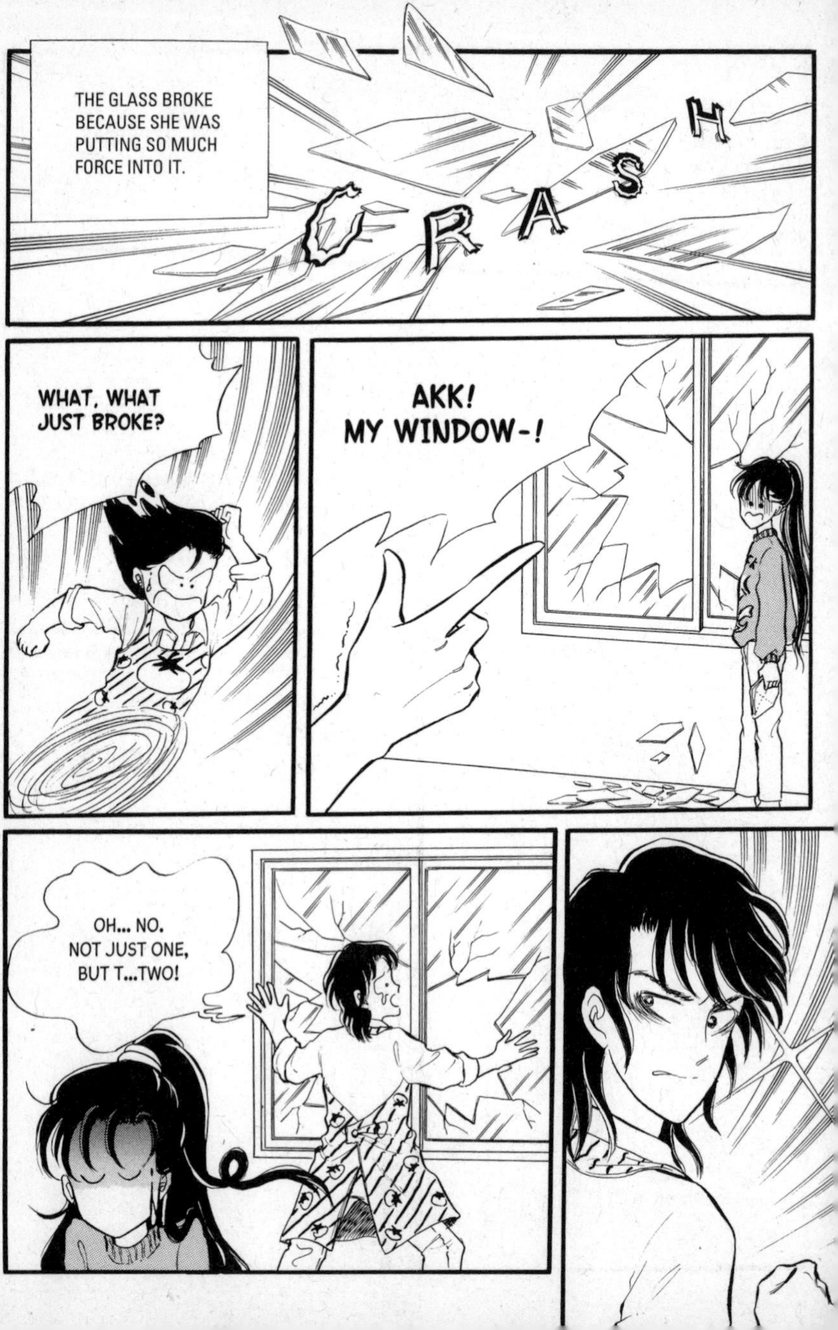
THE GLASS BROKE BECAUSE SHE WAS PUTTING SO MUCH FORCE INTO IT.
CRASH
WHAT, WHAT JUST BROKE?
AKK! MY WINDOW-!
OH... NO. NOT JUST ONE, BUT T...TWO!

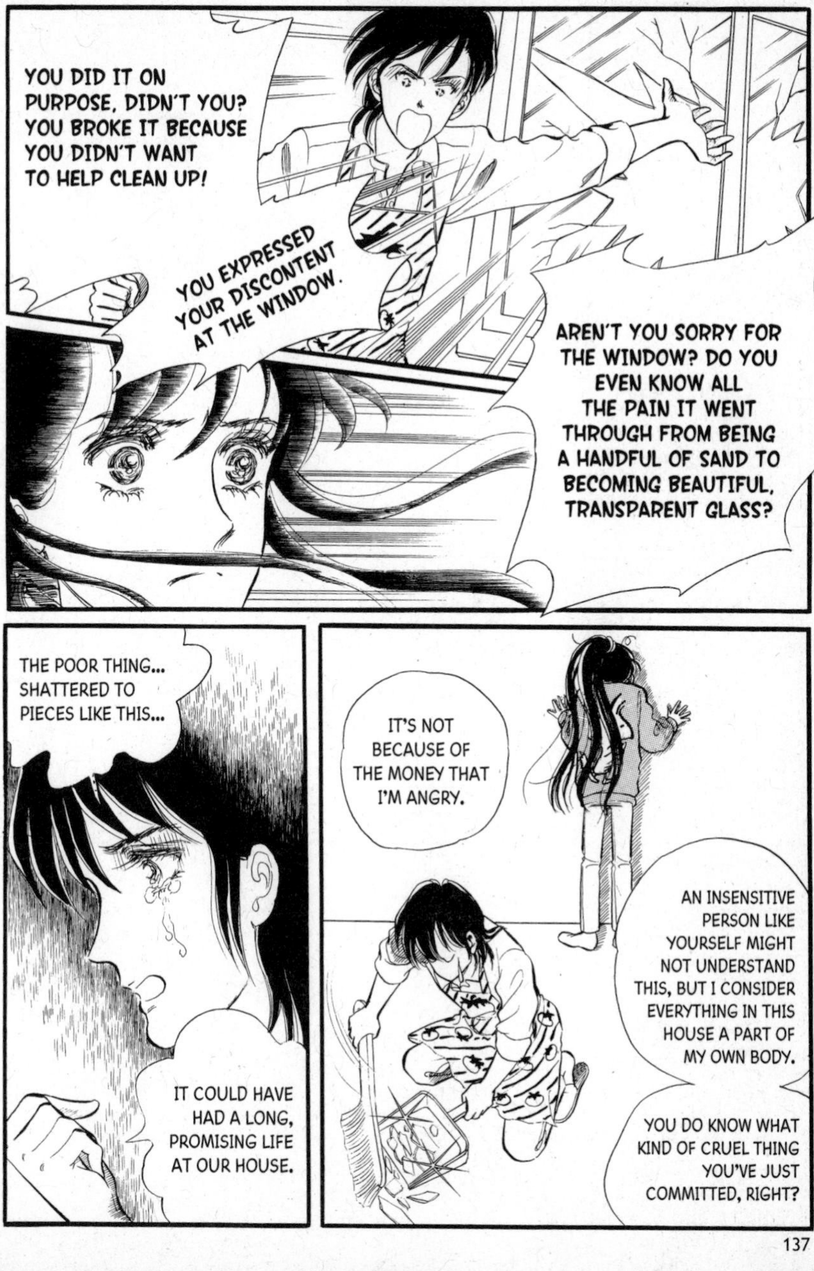
YOU DID IT ON PURPOSE, DIDN'T YOU? YOU BROKE IT BECAUSE YOU DIDN'T WANT TO HELP CLEAN UP!
YOU EXPRESSED YOUR DISCONTENT AT THE WINDOW.
AREN'T YOU SORRY FOR THE WINDOW? DO YOU EVEN KNOW ALL THE PAIN IT WENT THROUGH FROM BEING A HANDFUL OF SAND TO BECOMING BEAUTIFUL, TRANSPARENT GLASS?
THE POOR THING... SHATTERED TO PIECES LIKE THIS...
IT COULD HAVE HAD A LONG, PROMISING LIFE AT OUR HOUSE.
IT'S NOT BECAUSE OF THE MONEY THAT I'M ANGRY.
AN INSENSITIVE PERSON LIKE YOURSELF MIGHT NOT UNDERSTAND THIS, BUT I CONSIDER EVERYTHING IN THIS HOUSE A PART OF MY OWN BODY.
YOU DO KNOW WHAT KIND OF CRUEL THING YOU'VE JUST COMMITTED, RIGHT?

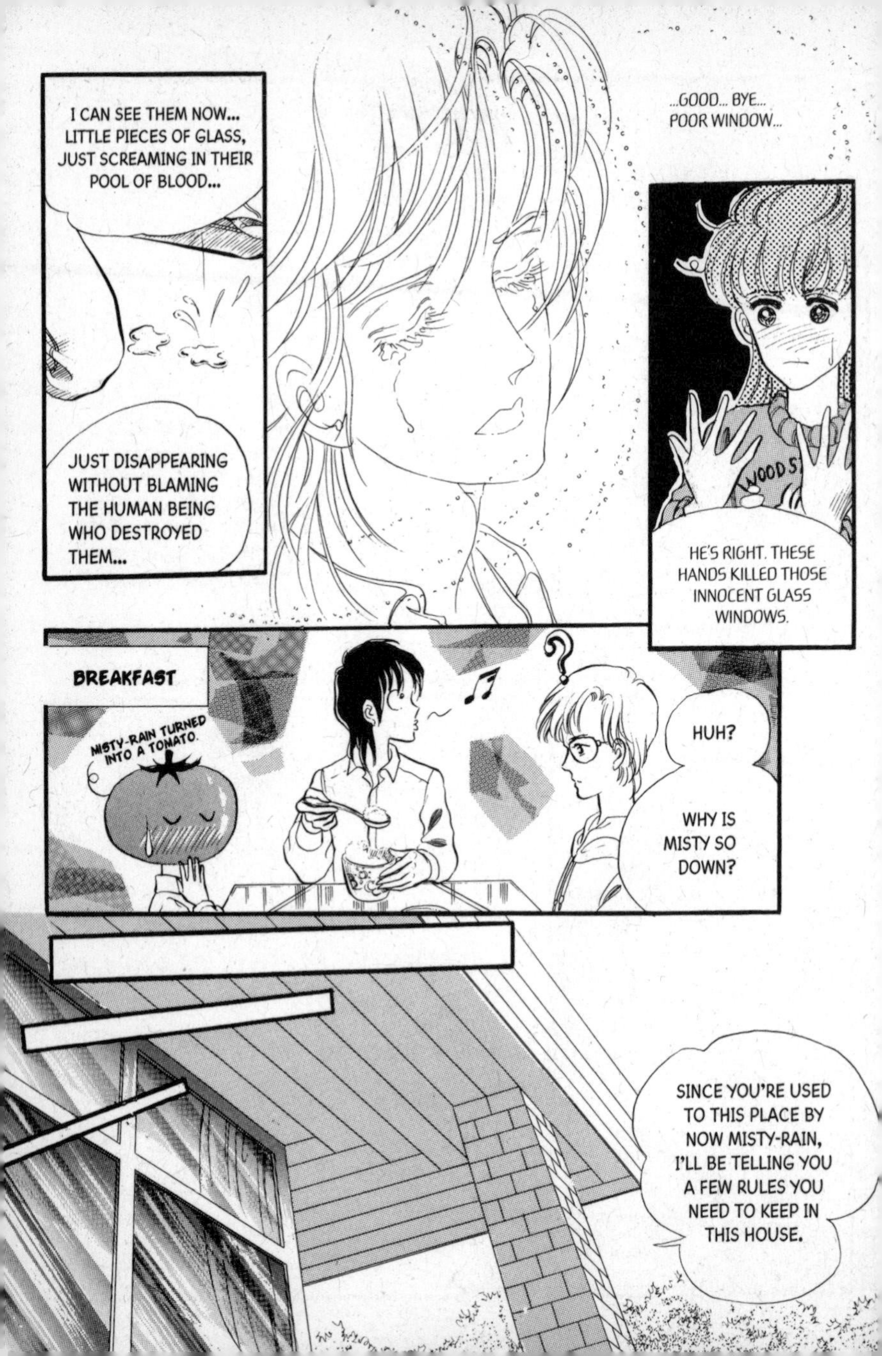
I CAN SEE THEM NOW... LITTLE PIECES OF GLASS, JUST SCREAMING IN THEIR POOL OF BLOOD...
JUST DISAPPEARING WITHOUT BLAMING THE HUMAN BEING WHO DESTROYED THEM...
...GOOD... BYE... POOR WINDOW...
WOODS
HE'S RIGHT. THESE HANDS KILLED THOSE INNOCENT GLASS WINDOWS.
BREAKFAST
MISTY-RAIN TURNED INTO A TOMATO.
HUH?
WHY IS MISTY SO DOWN?
SINCE YOU'RE USED TO THIS PLACE BY NOW MISTY-RAIN, I'LL BE TELLING YOU A FEW RULES YOU NEED TO KEEP IN THIS HOUSE.

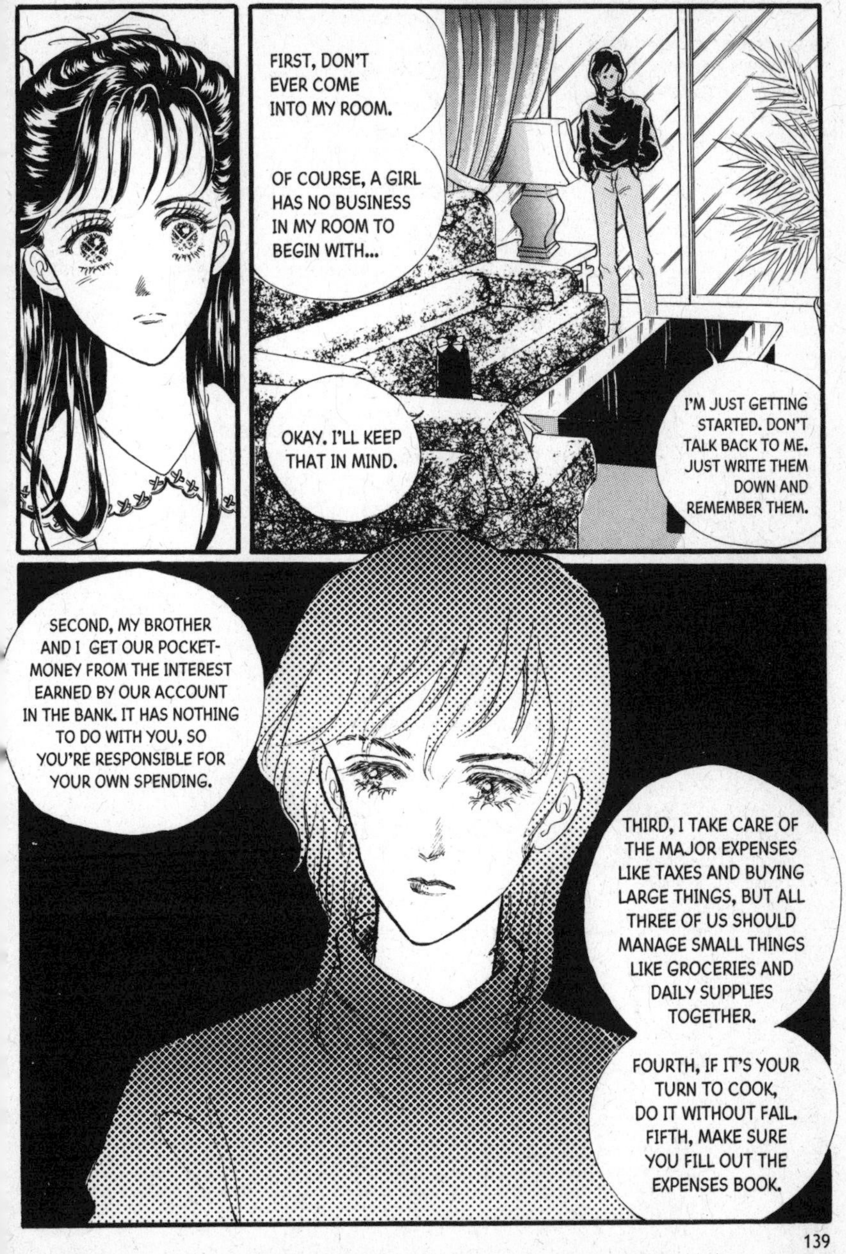
FIRST, DON'T EVER COME INTO MY ROOM.
OF COURSE, A GIRL HAS NO BUSINESS IN MY ROOM TO BEGIN WITH...
OKAY. I'LL KEEP THAT IN MIND.
I'M JUST GETTING STARTED. DON'T TALK BACK TO ME. JUST WRITE THEM DOWN AND REMEMBER THEM.
SECOND, MY BROTHER AND I GET OUR POCKET-MONEY FROM THE INTEREST EARNED BY OUR ACCOUNT IN THE BANK. IT HAS NOTHING TO DO WITH YOU, SO YOU'RE RESPONSIBLE FOR YOUR OWN SPENDING.
THIRD, I TAKE CARE OF THE MAJOR EXPENSES LIKE TAXES AND BUYING LARGE THINGS, BUT ALL THREE OF US SHOULD MANAGE SMALL THINGS LIKE GROCERIES AND DAILY SUPPLIES TOGETHER.
FOURTH, IF IT'S YOUR TURN TO COOK, DO IT WITHOUT FAIL. FIFTH, MAKE SURE YOU FILL OUT THE EXPENSES BOOK.

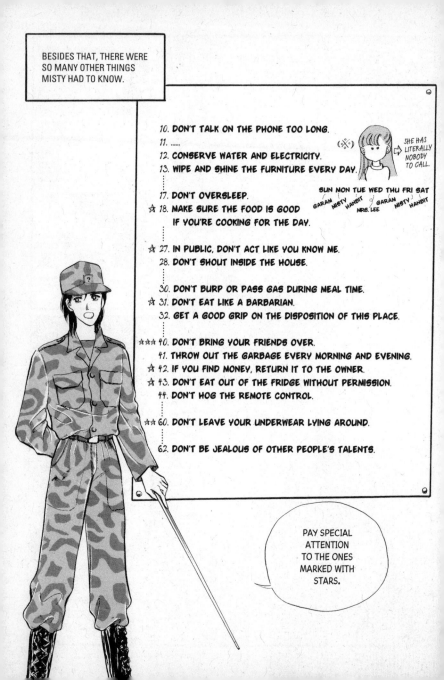

BESIDES THAT, THERE WERE SO MANY OTHER THINGS MISTY HAD TO KNOW.

10. DON'T TALK ON THE PHONE TOO LONG.
11. ......
12. CONSERVE WATER AND ELECTRICITY.
13. WIPE AND SHINE THE FURNITURE EVERY DAY.

SHE HAS LITERALLY NOBODY TO CALL.

17. DON'T OVERSLEEP.
☆ 18. MAKE SURE THE FOOD IS GOOD IF YOU'RE COOKING FOR THE DAY.

SUN	MON	TUE	WED	THU	FRI	SAT
GARAM	MISTY	HANBIT	MRS. LEE	GARAM	MISTY	HANBIT

☆ 27. IN PUBLIC, DON'T ACT LIKE YOU KNOW ME.
28. DON'T SHOUT INSIDE THE HOUSE.

30. DON'T BURP OR PASS GAS DURING MEAL TIME.
☆ 31. DON'T EAT LIKE A BARBARIAN.
32. GET A GOOD GRIP ON THE DISPOSITION OF THIS PLACE.

☆☆☆ 40. DON'T BRING YOUR FRIENDS OVER.
41. THROW OUT THE GARBAGE EVERY MORNING AND EVENING.
☆ 42. IF YOU FIND MONEY, RETURN IT TO THE OWNER.
☆ 43. DON'T EAT OUT OF THE FRIDGE WITHOUT PERMISSION.
44. DON'T HOG THE REMOTE CONTROL.

☆☆ 60. DON'T LEAVE YOUR UNDERWEAR LYING AROUND.

62. DON'T BE JEALOUS OF OTHER PEOPLE'S TALENTS.

PAY SPECIAL ATTENTION TO THE ONES MARKED WITH STARS.

THE UNBEARABLE LIGHTNESS OF HER BEING!

I'M NOT OUT TO GET YOUR OR ANYTHING. MY FATHER HAS DECIDED TO LET YOU STAY WITH HIS SONS, AND SINCE YOU'RE LIVING UNDER OUR ROOF, I BELIEVE THAT YOU SHOULD AT LEAST MAKE SURE YOU FOLLOW ALL THE RULES OF THIS HOUSE...

YOU SHOULDN'T GIVE UP AND JUST LET THINGS BE SIMPLY BECAUSE YOU HAD A VIOLENT AND BARBARIC PAST.

I'M THE BOURGEOIS

YOU'RE 14 ALREADY —OLD ENOUGH TO KNOW WHAT'S GOING ON.

DON'T BLAME SOCIETY BECAUSE YOU'RE POOR AND WERE BORN AN ORPHAN (I'M NOT SURE IF YOU ARE). INSTEAD, ENDURE AND WORK HARD SO YOU CAN LEAD A PRODUCTIVE LIFE. THAT'S ALL I WANT TO SAY TO YOU.

YOU ARE A PROLETARIAT..

...AND THUS SAID HANBIT TO MISTY-RAIN.

ALTHOUGH VERY SELF-CENTERED, WHAT HE SAID WAS VERY CONVINCING TO MISTY-RAIN.

THE PAST

RULES AND ORDERS

ENDURANCE

SOCIAL LIFE

WORK

HE'S SO SMART THAT IT FREAKS ME OUT. I DON'T KNOW MUCH, BUT I THINK HE'S RIGHT IN EVERYTHING.

HANBIT GAVE HER A NEW CONCEPT OF LIFE: "THOUGHT," SOMETHING MISTY-RAIN, SOMEONE WHO'S LIVED HER ENTIRE LIFE WITHOUT THINKING, WAS UNFAMILIAR WITH.

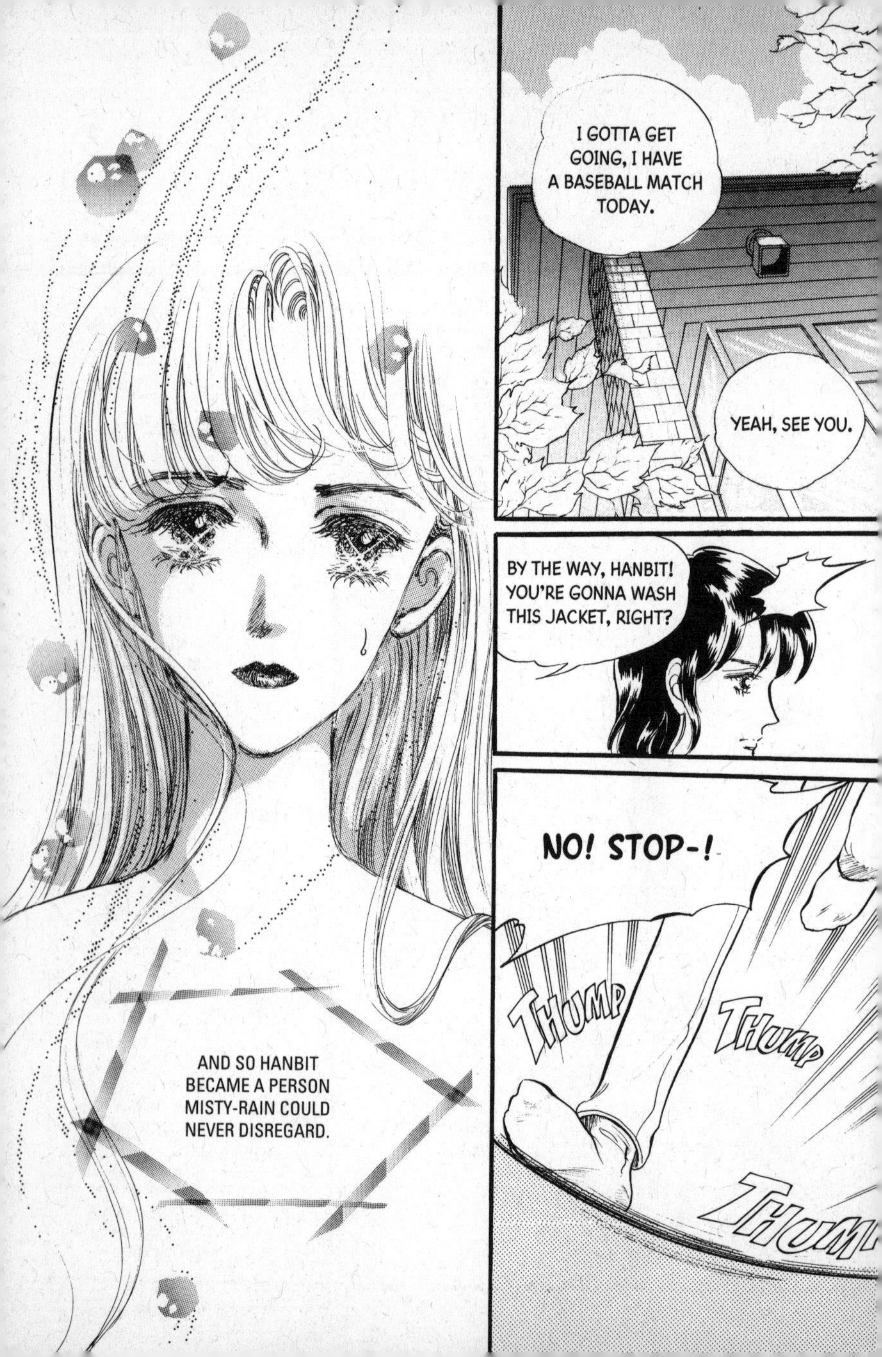
AND SO HANBIT BECAME A PERSON MISTY-RAIN COULD NEVER DISREGARD.
I GOTTA GET GOING, I HAVE A BASEBALL MATCH TODAY.
YEAH, SEE YOU.
BY THE WAY, HANBIT! YOU'RE GONNA WASH THIS JACKET, RIGHT?
NO! STOP-!
THUMP
THUMP
THUM

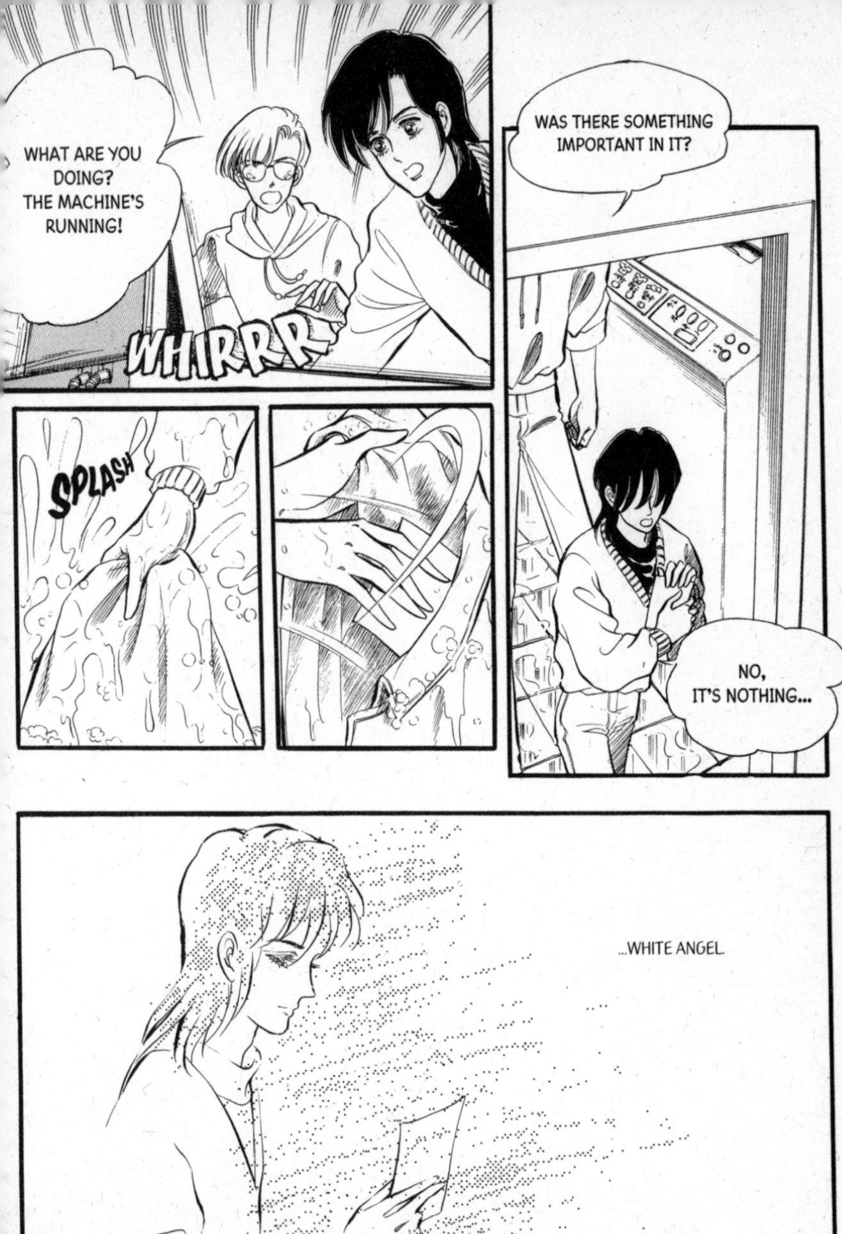
WHAT ARE YOU DOING? THE MACHINE'S RUNNING!
WHIRRR
SPLASH
WAS THERE SOMETHING IMPORTANT IN IT?
NO, IT'S NOTHING...
...WHITE ANGEL.

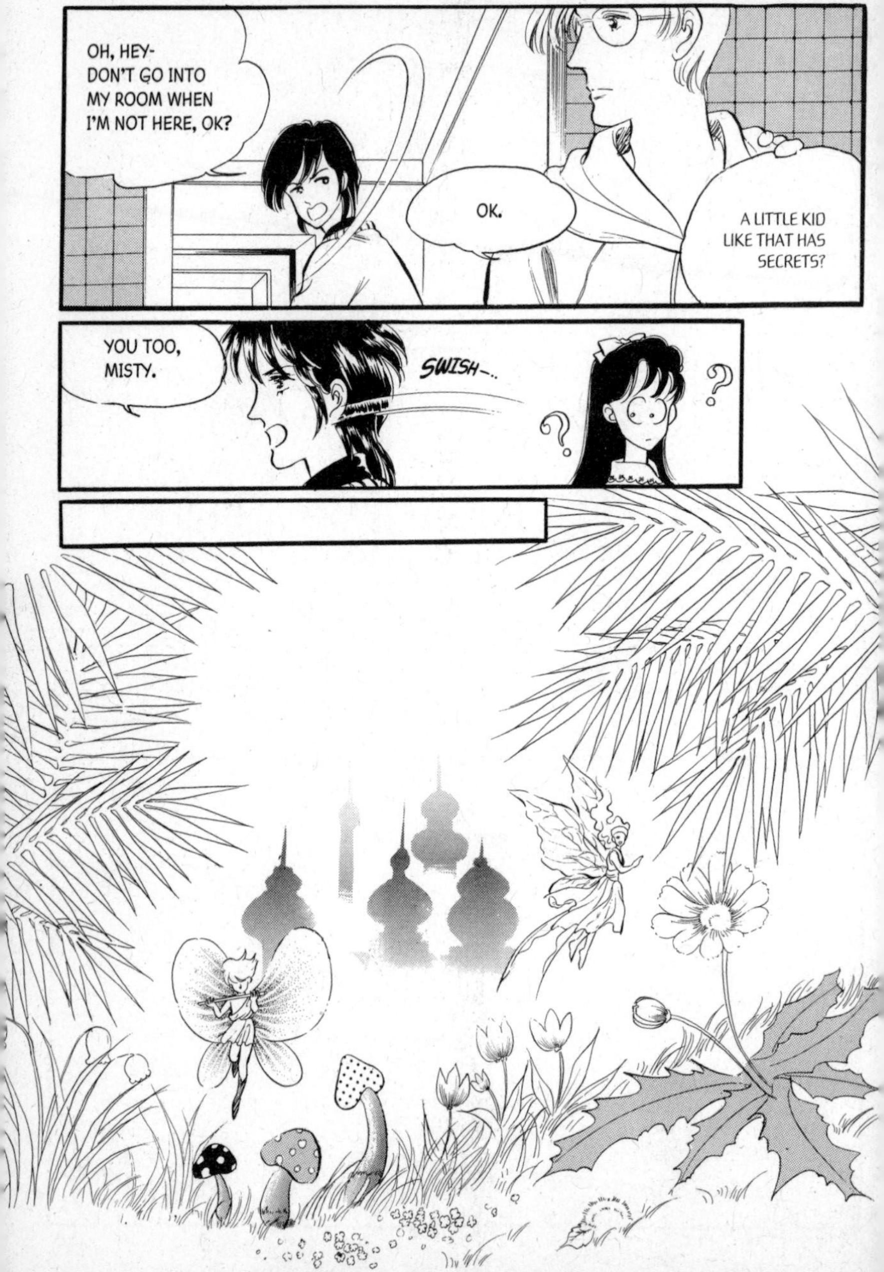
OH, HEY-
DON'T GO INTO MY ROOM WHEN I'M NOT HERE, OK?
OK.
A LITTLE KID LIKE THAT HAS SECRETS?
YOU TOO, MISTY.
SWISH-..
?
?

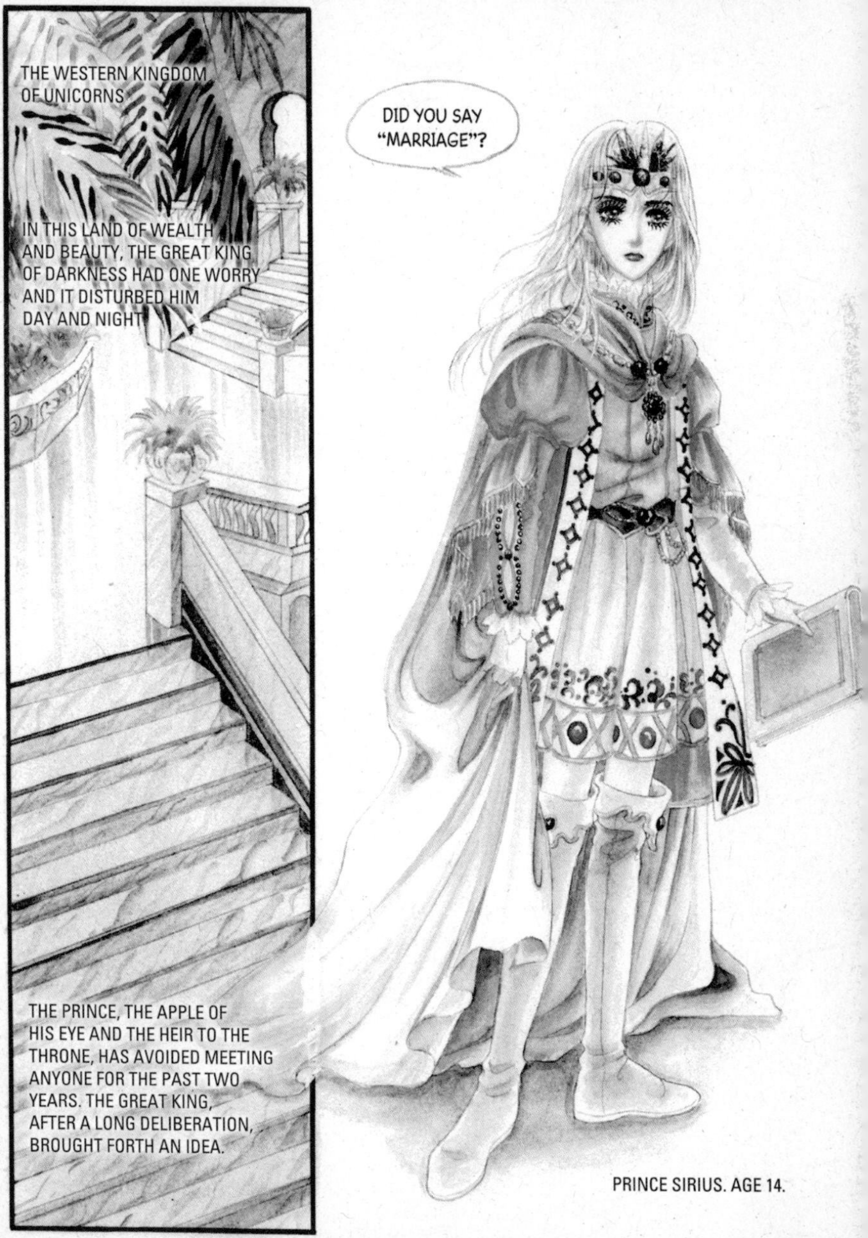
THE WESTERN KINGDOM OF UNICORNS
IN THIS LAND OF WEALTH AND BEAUTY, THE GREAT KING OF DARKNESS HAD ONE WORRY AND IT DISTURBED HIM DAY AND NIGHT
THE PRINCE, THE APPLE OF HIS EYE AND THE HEIR TO THE THRONE, HAS AVOIDED MEETING ANYONE FOR THE PAST TWO YEARS. THE GREAT KING, AFTER A LONG DELIBERATION, BROUGHT FORTH AN IDEA.
DID YOU SAY "MARRIAGE"?
PRINCE SIRIUS. AGE 14.

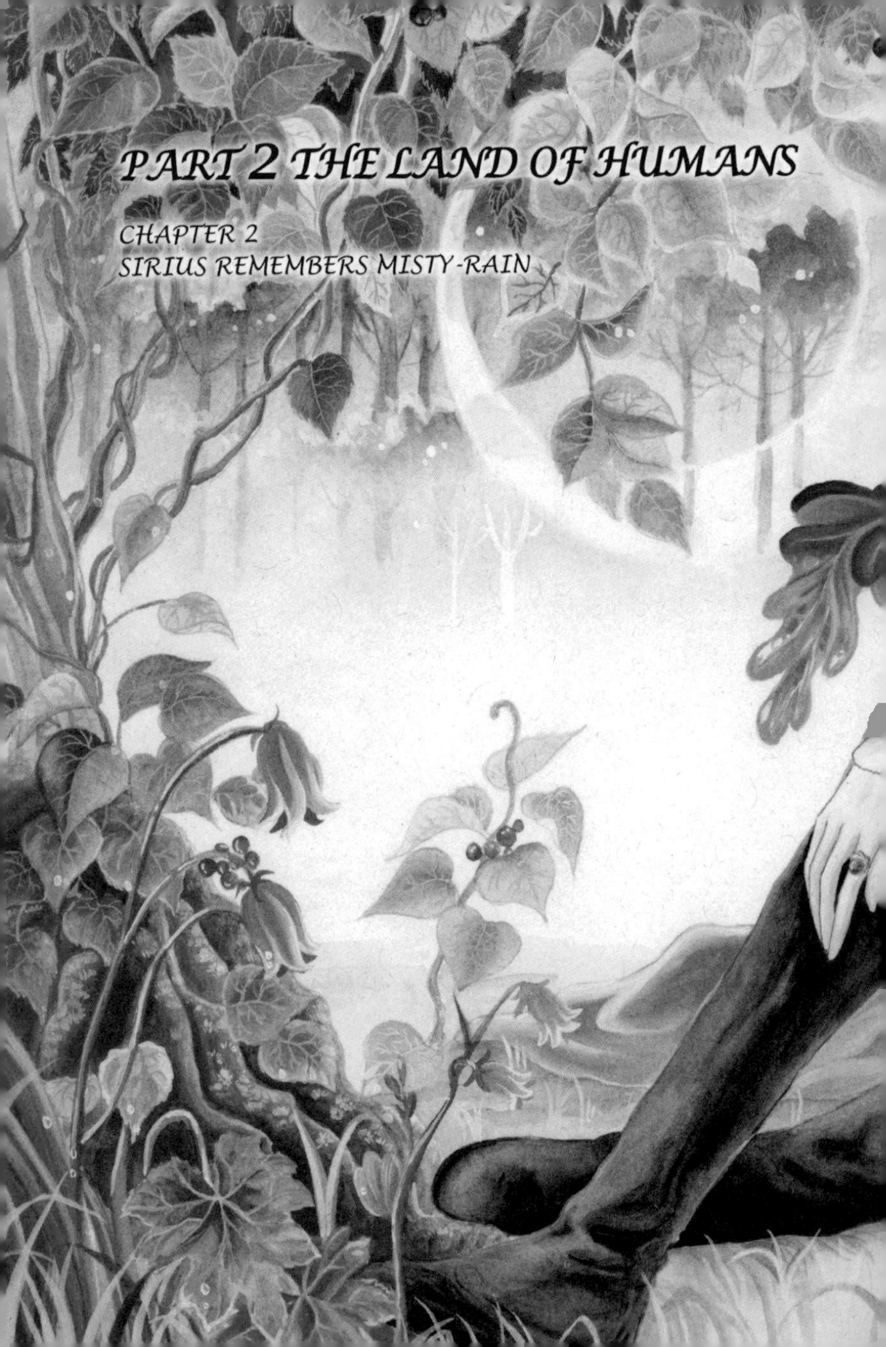
PART 2 THE LAND OF HUMANS
CHAPTER 2
SIRIUS REMEMBERS MISTY-RAIN

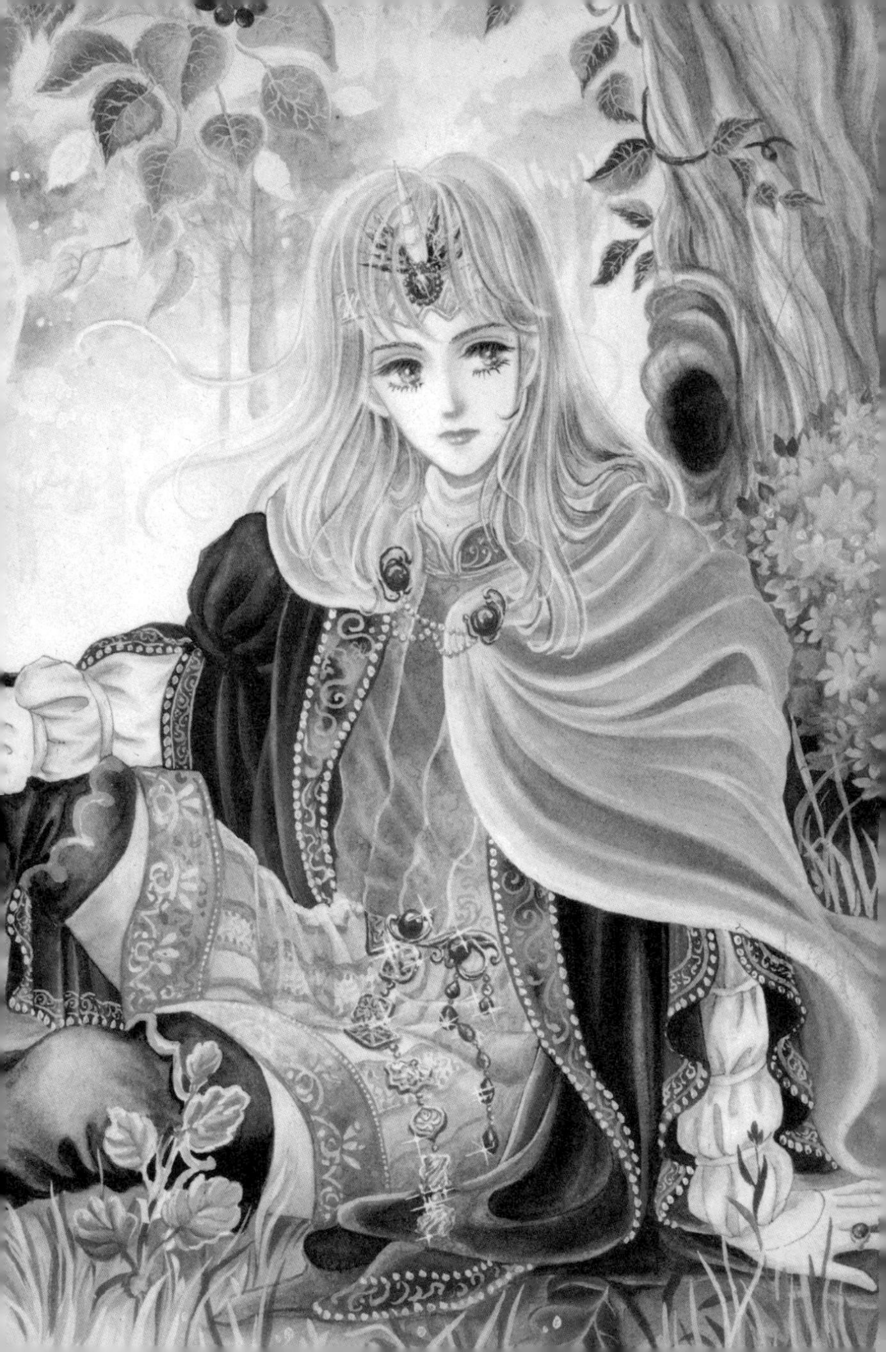

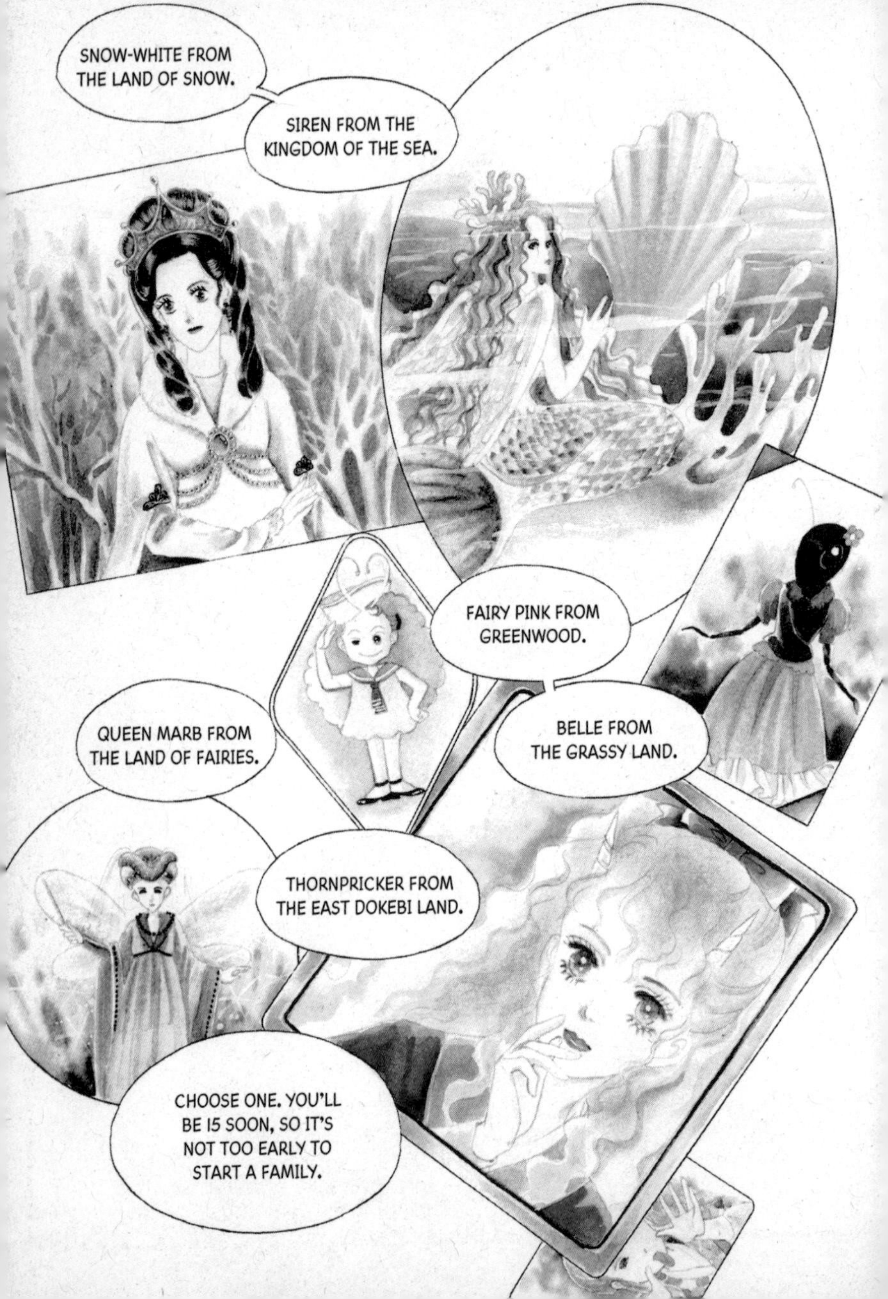
SNOW-WHITE FROM THE LAND OF SNOW.
SIREN FROM THE KINGDOM OF THE SEA.
FAIRY PINK FROM GREENWOOD.
QUEEN MARB FROM THE LAND OF FAIRIES.
BELLE FROM THE GRASSY LAND.
THORNPRICKER FROM THE EAST DOKEBI LAND.
CHOOSE ONE. YOU'LL BE 15 SOON, SO IT'S NOT TOO EARLY TO START A FAMILY.

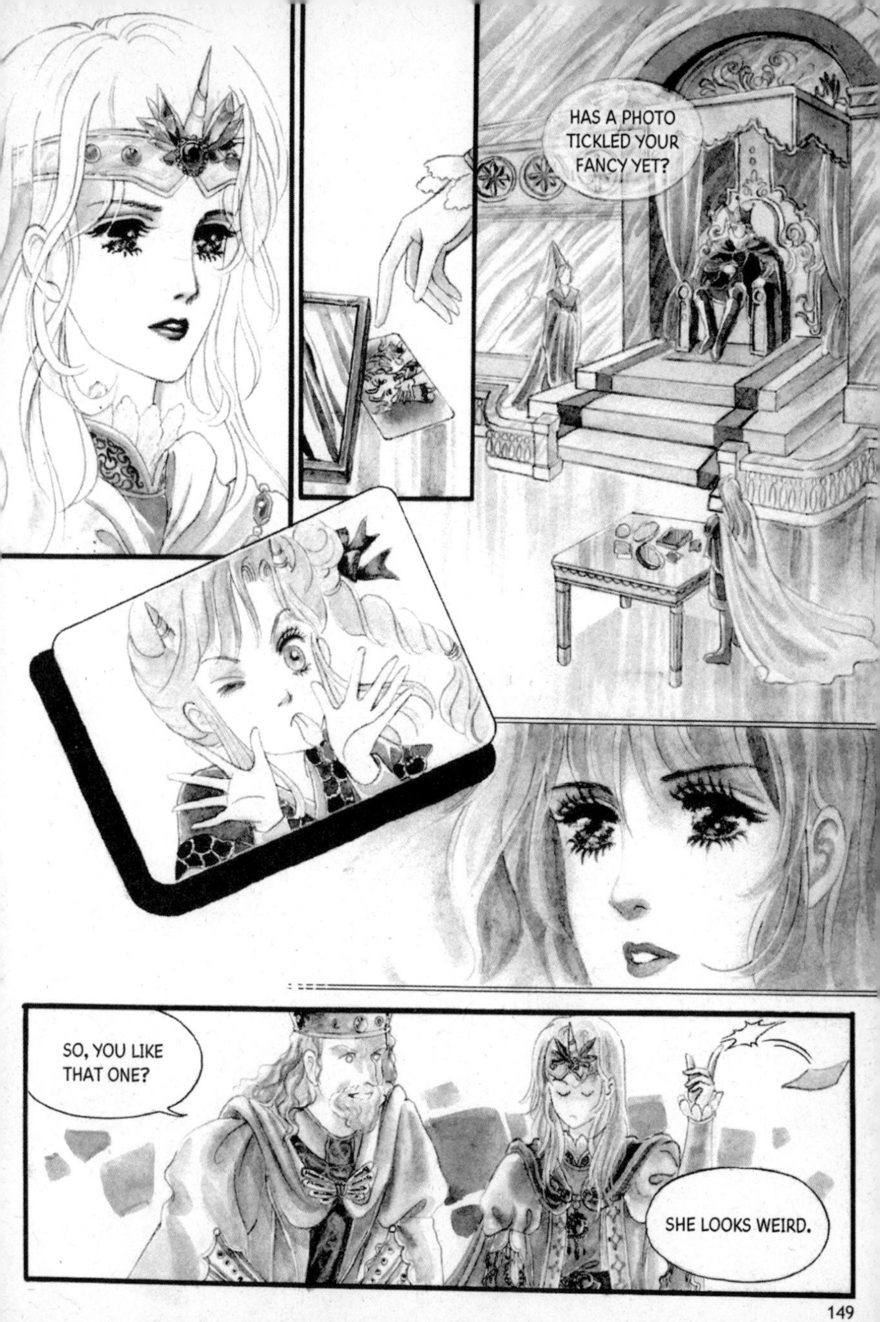
HAS A PHOTO TICKLED YOUR FANCY YET?
SO, YOU LIKE THAT ONE?
SHE LOOKS WEIRD.

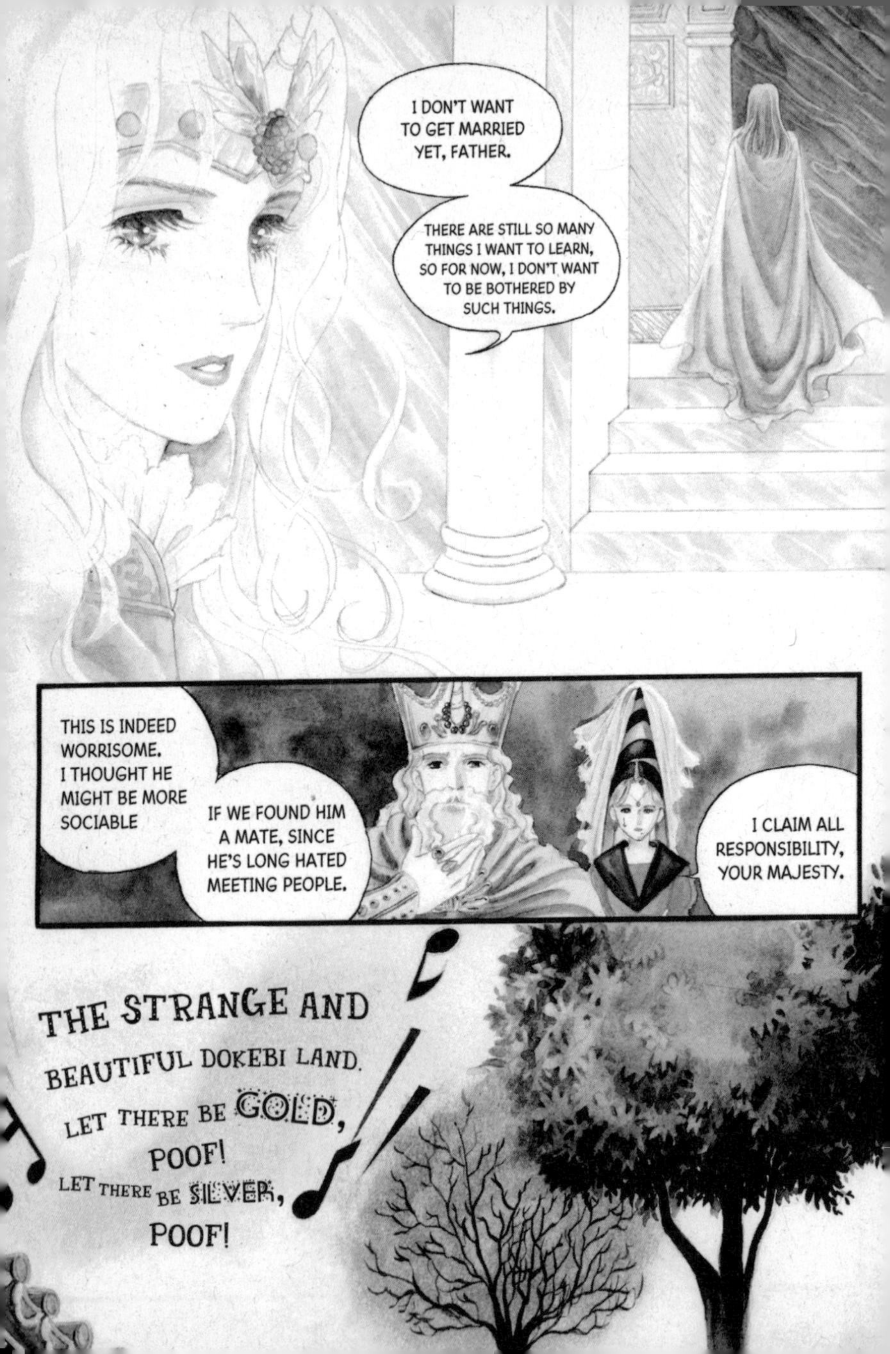
I DON'T WANT TO GET MARRIED YET, FATHER.
THERE ARE STILL SO MANY THINGS I WANT TO LEARN, SO FOR NOW, I DON'T WANT TO BE BOTHERED BY SUCH THINGS.
THIS IS INDEED WORRISOME. I THOUGHT HE MIGHT BE MORE SOCIABLE
IF WE FOUND HIM A MATE, SINCE HE'S LONG HATED MEETING PEOPLE.
I CLAIM ALL RESPONSIBILITY, YOUR MAJESTY.
THE STRANGE AND BEAUTIFUL DOKEBI LAND.
LET THERE BE GOLD, POOF!
LET THERE BE SILVER, POOF!

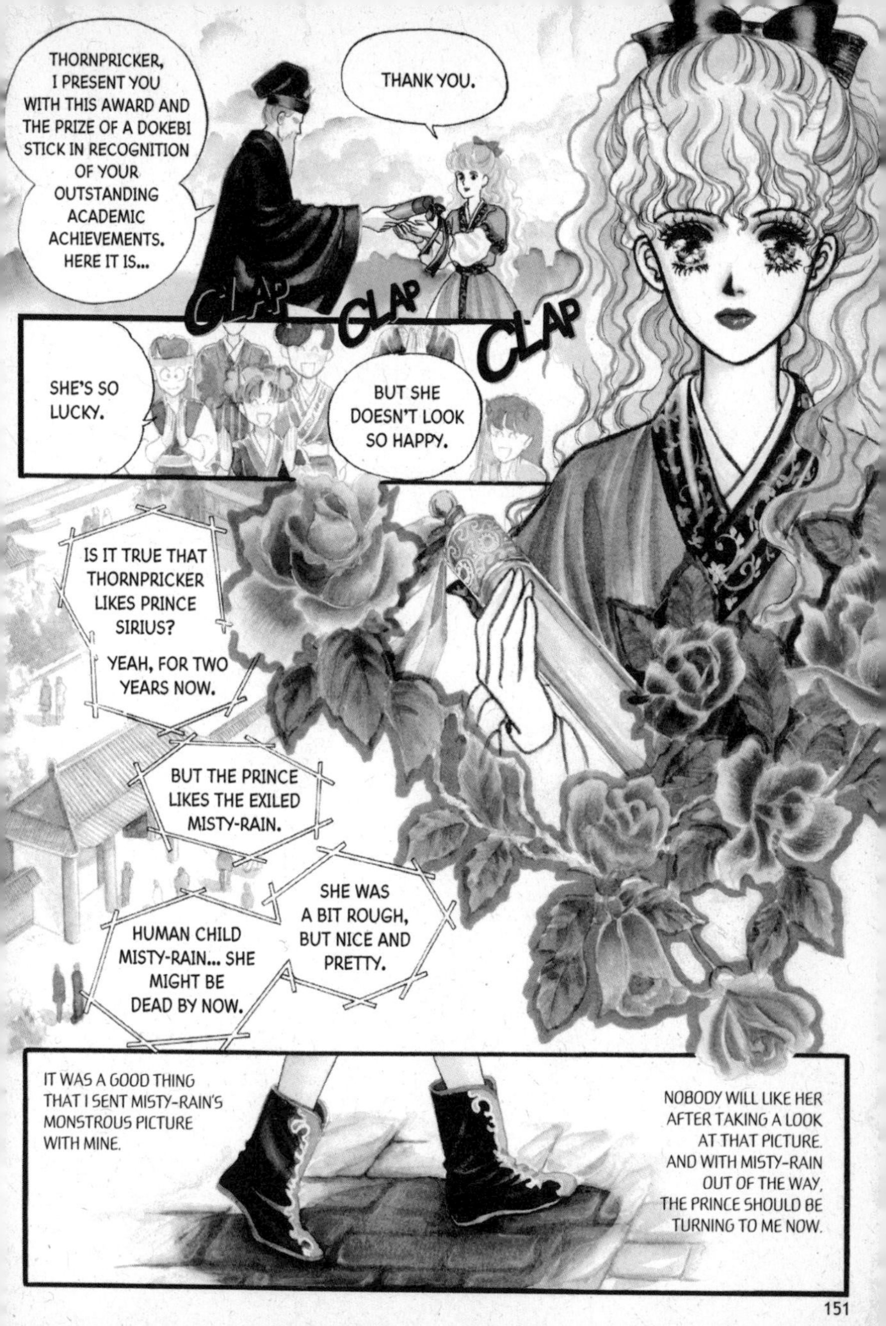
THORNPRICKER, I PRESENT YOU WITH THIS AWARD AND THE PRIZE OF A DOKEBI STICK IN RECOGNITION OF YOUR OUTSTANDING ACADEMIC ACHIEVEMENTS. HERE IT IS...
THANK YOU.
CLAP CLAP CLAP
SHE'S SO LUCKY.
BUT SHE DOESN'T LOOK SO HAPPY.
IS IT TRUE THAT THORNPRICKER LIKES PRINCE SIRIUS?
YEAH, FOR TWO YEARS NOW.
BUT THE PRINCE LIKES THE EXILED MISTY-RAIN.
HUMAN CHILD MISTY-RAIN... SHE MIGHT BE DEAD BY NOW.
SHE WAS A BIT ROUGH, BUT NICE AND PRETTY.
IT WAS A GOOD THING THAT I SENT MISTY-RAIN'S MONSTROUS PICTURE WITH MINE.
NOBODY WILL LIKE HER AFTER TAKING A LOOK AT THAT PICTURE. AND WITH MISTY-RAIN OUT OF THE WAY, THE PRINCE SHOULD BE TURNING TO ME NOW.

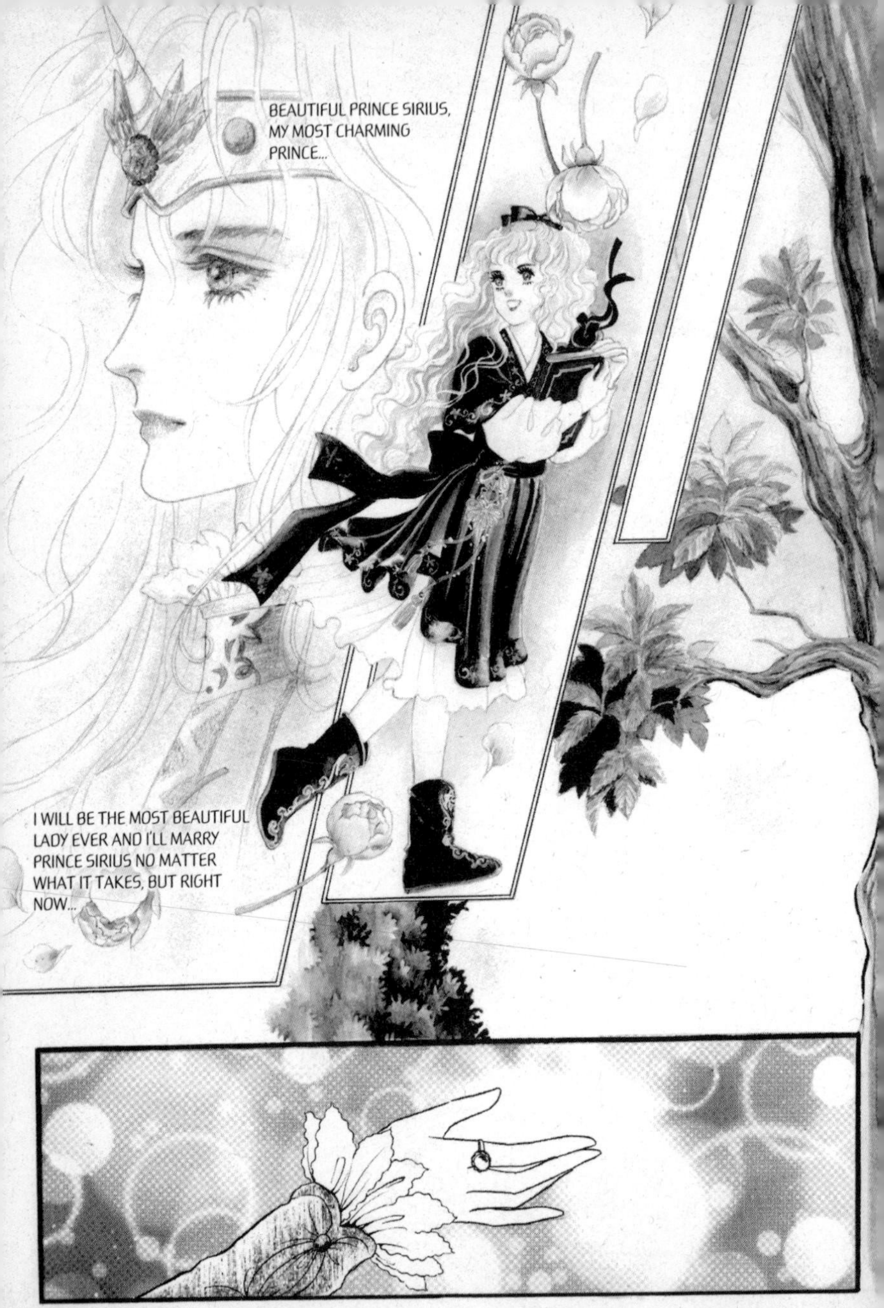
BEAUTIFUL PRINCE SIRIUS, MY MOST CHARMING PRINCE...
I WILL BE THE MOST BEAUTIFUL LADY EVER AND I'LL MARRY PRINCE SIRIUS NO MATTER WHAT IT TAKES, BUT RIGHT NOW...

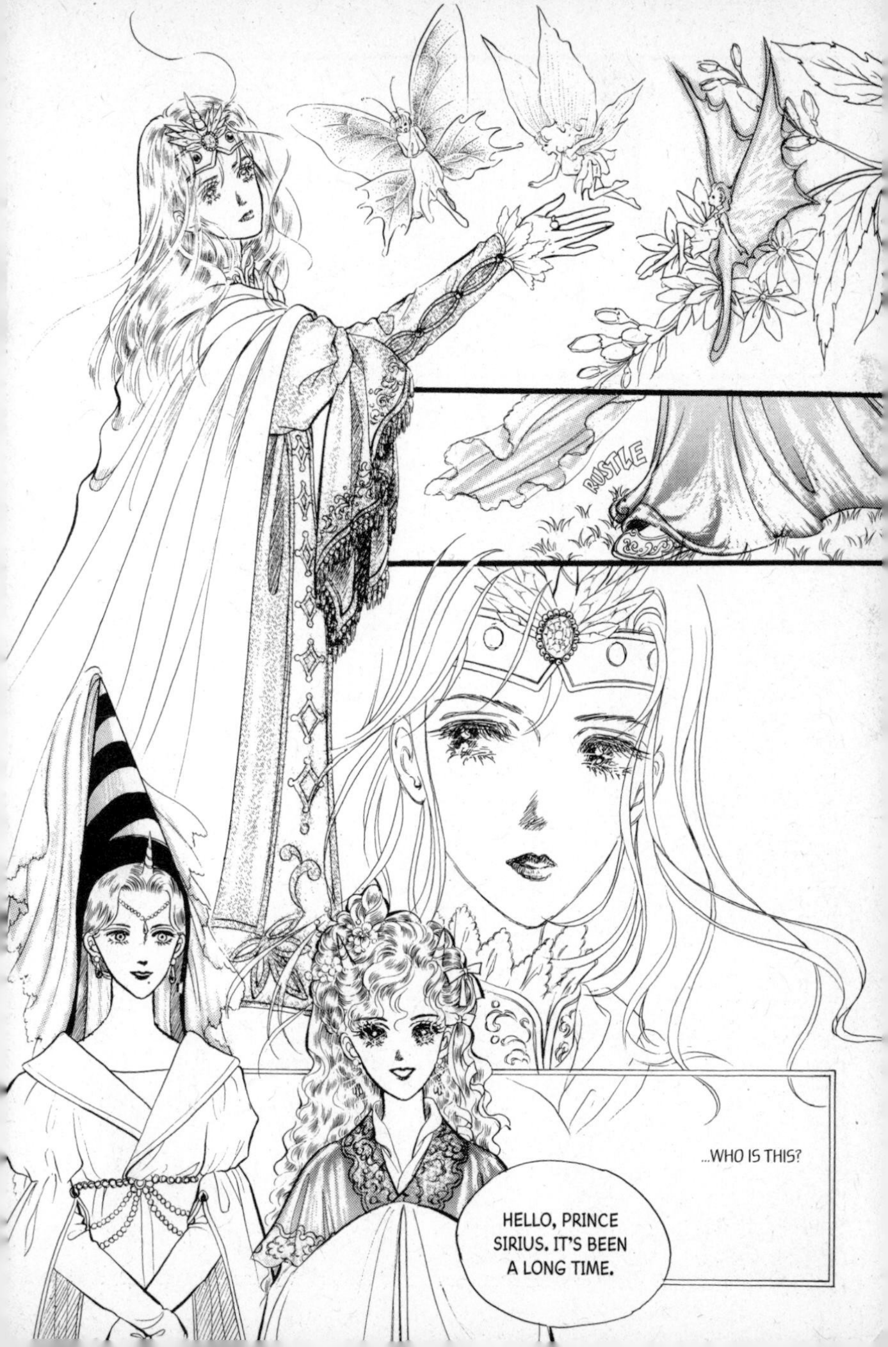
RUSTLE
...WHO IS THIS?
HELLO, PRINCE SIRIUS. IT'S BEEN A LONG TIME.

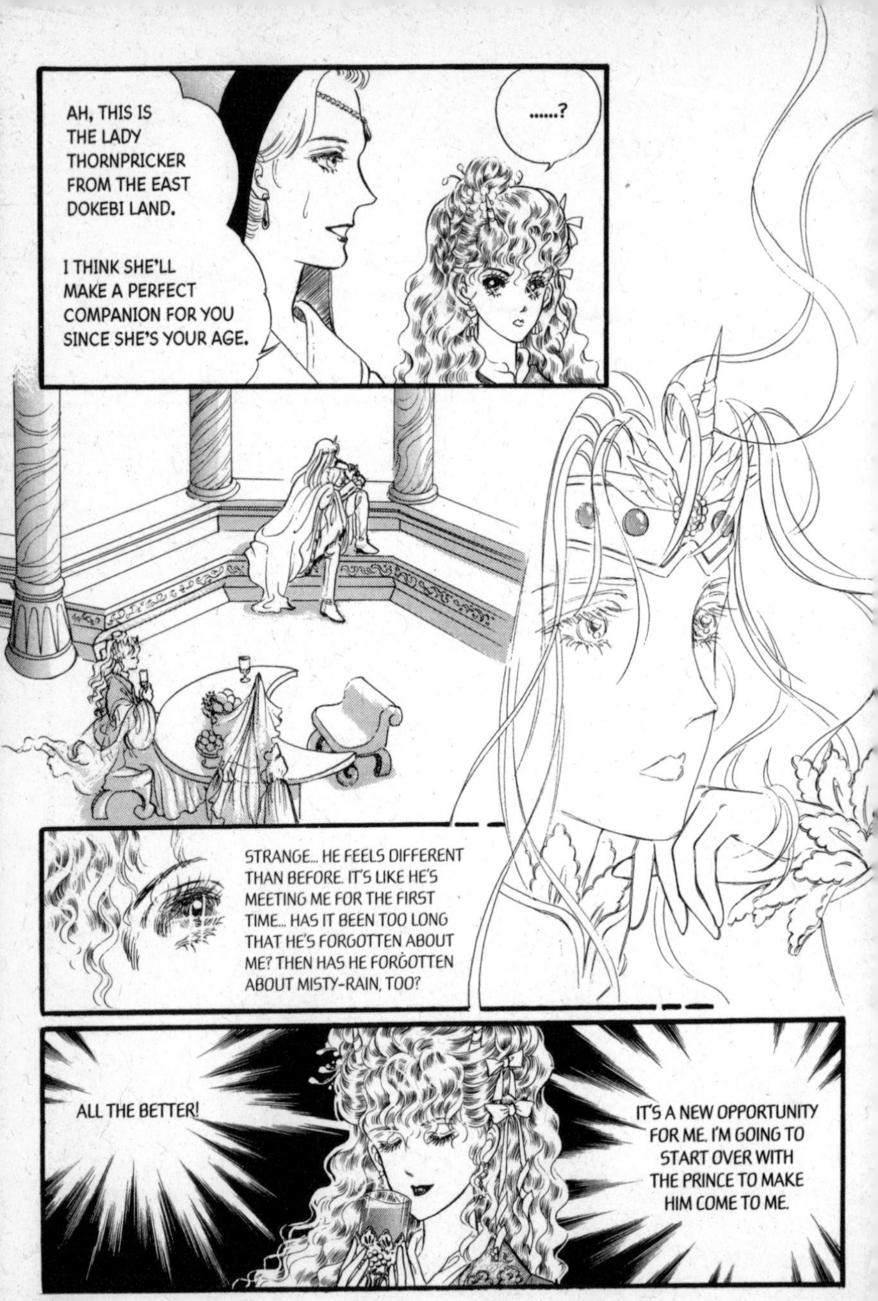
AH, THIS IS THE LADY THORNPRICKER FROM THE EAST DOKEBI LAND.
I THINK SHE'LL MAKE A PERFECT COMPANION FOR YOU SINCE SHE'S YOUR AGE.
......?
STRANGE... HE FEELS DIFFERENT THAN BEFORE. IT'S LIKE HE'S MEETING ME FOR THE FIRST TIME... HAS IT BEEN TOO LONG THAT HE'S FORGOTTEN ABOUT ME? THEN HAS HE FORGOTTEN ABOUT MISTY-RAIN, TOO?
ALL THE BETTER!
IT'S A NEW OPPORTUNITY FOR ME. I'M GOING TO START OVER WITH THE PRINCE TO MAKE HIM COME TO ME.

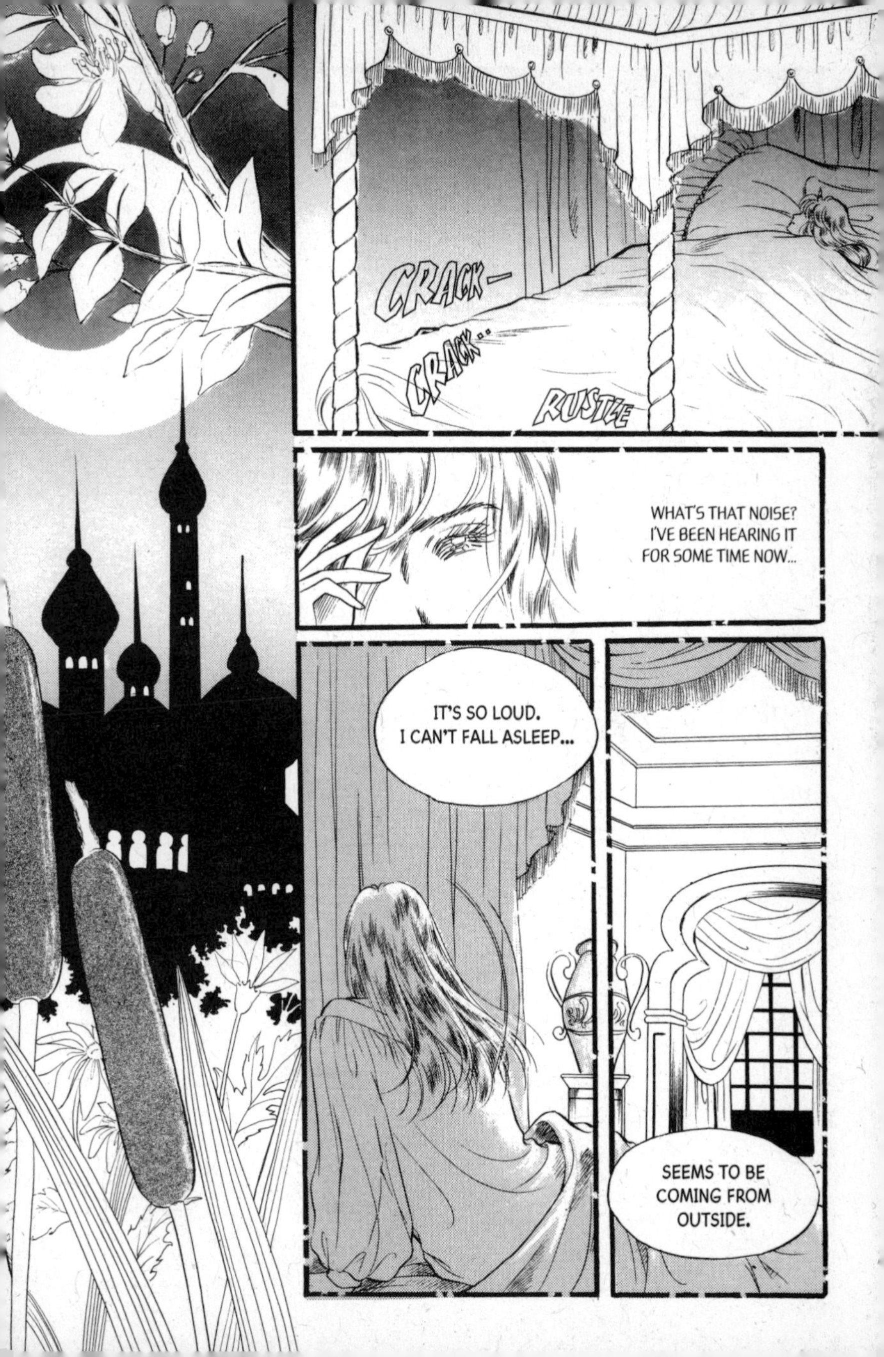
CRACK—
CRACK..
RUSTLE
WHAT'S THAT NOISE? I'VE BEEN HEARING IT FOR SOME TIME NOW...
IT'S SO LOUD. I CAN'T FALL ASLEEP...
SEEMS TO BE COMING FROM OUTSIDE.

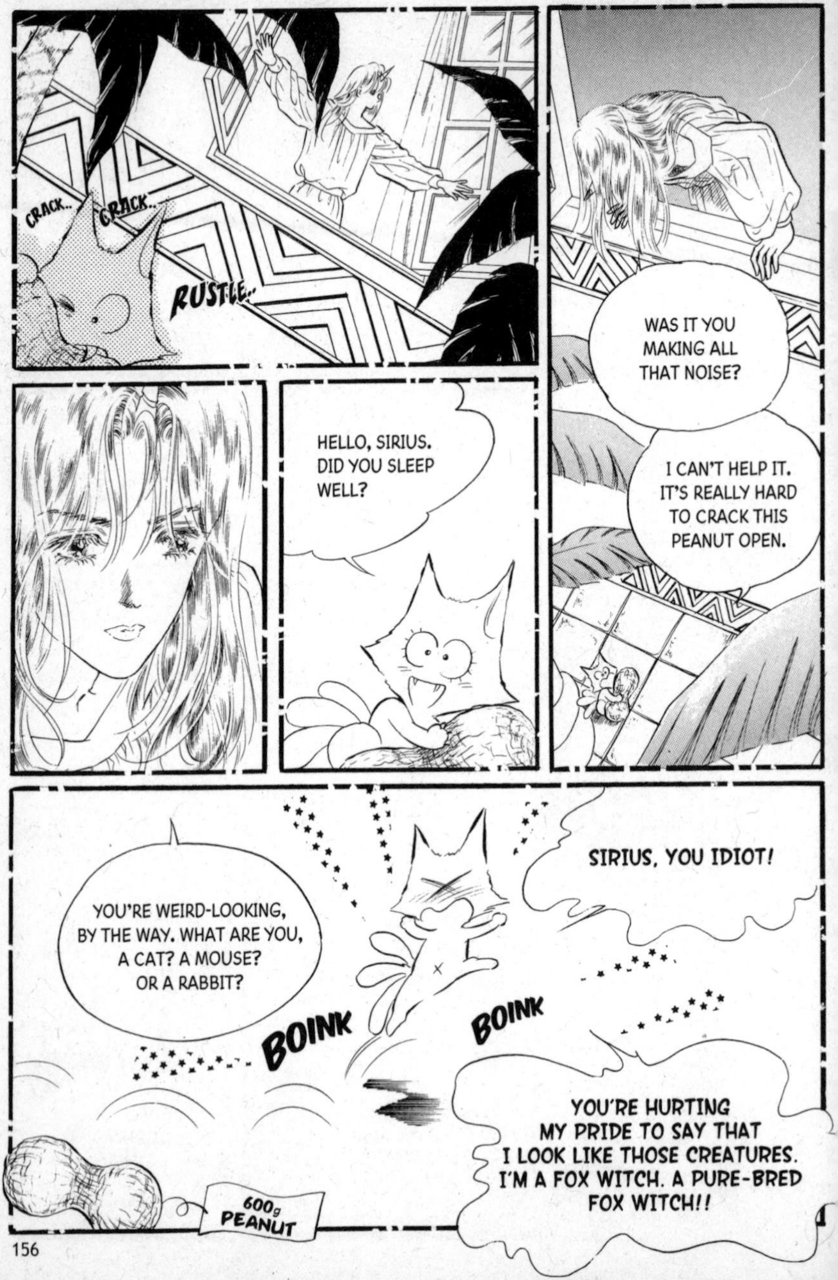
CRACK..
CRACK..
RUSTLE..
HELLO, SIRIUS. DID YOU SLEEP WELL?
WAS IT YOU MAKING ALL THAT NOISE?
I CAN'T HELP IT. IT'S REALLY HARD TO CRACK THIS PEANUT OPEN.
YOU'RE WEIRD-LOOKING, BY THE WAY. WHAT ARE YOU, A CAT? A MOUSE? OR A RABBIT?
SIRIUS, YOU IDIOT!
BOINK
BOINK
YOU'RE HURTING MY PRIDE TO SAY THAT I LOOK LIKE THOSE CREATURES. I'M A FOX WITCH. A PURE-BRED FOX WITCH!!
600g PEANUT

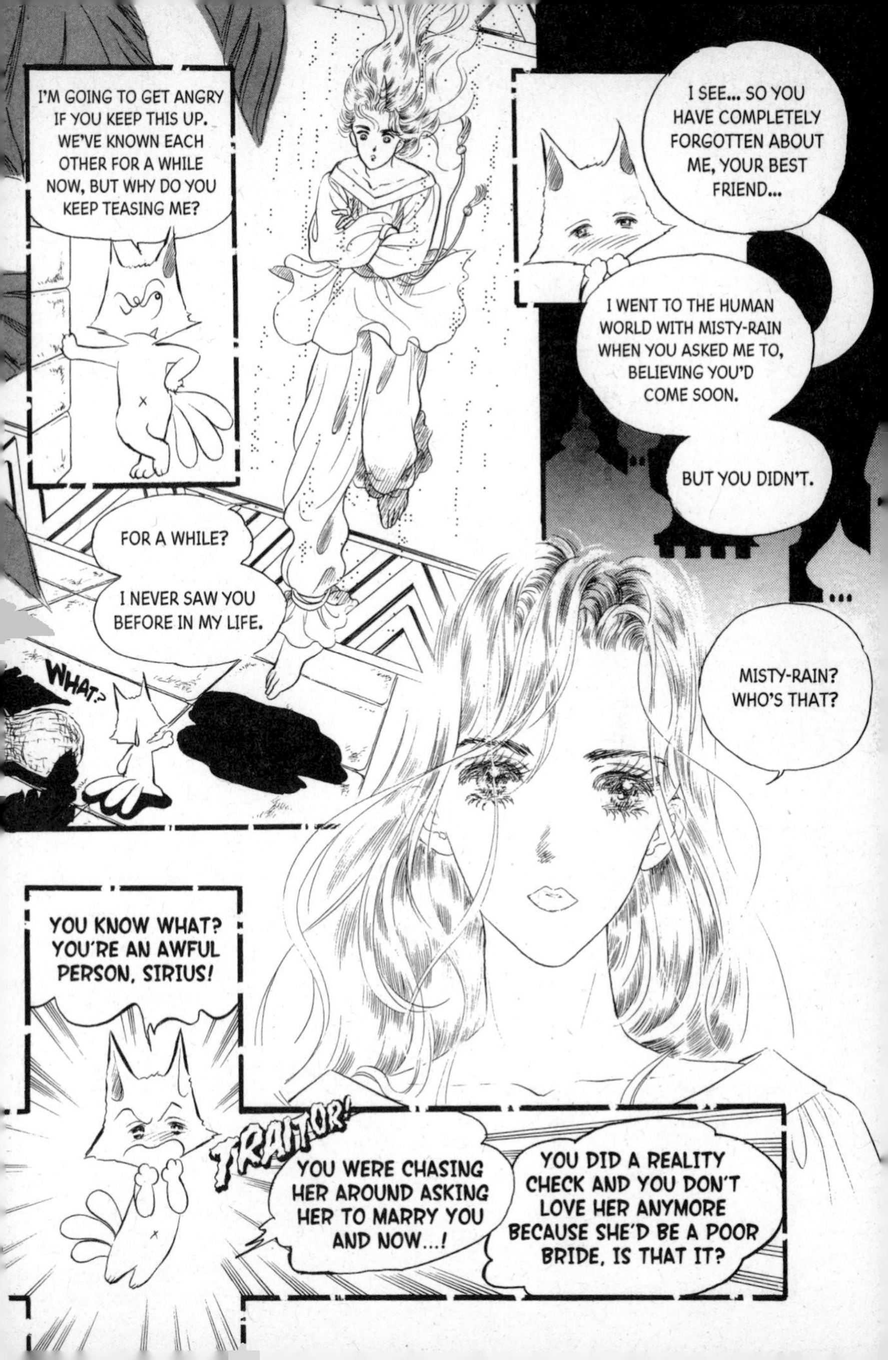

I'M GOING TO GET ANGRY IF YOU KEEP THIS UP. WE'VE KNOWN EACH OTHER FOR A WHILE NOW, BUT WHY DO YOU KEEP TEASING ME?
FOR A WHILE?
I NEVER SAW YOU BEFORE IN MY LIFE.
I SEE... SO YOU HAVE COMPLETELY FORGOTTEN ABOUT ME, YOUR BEST FRIEND...
I WENT TO THE HUMAN WORLD WITH MISTY-RAIN WHEN YOU ASKED ME TO, BELIEVING YOU'D COME SOON.
BUT YOU DIDN'T.
...
WHAT?
MISTY-RAIN? WHO'S THAT?
YOU KNOW WHAT? YOU'RE AN AWFUL PERSON, SIRIUS!
TRAITOR!
YOU WERE CHASING HER AROUND ASKING HER TO MARRY YOU AND NOW...!
YOU DID A REALITY CHECK AND YOU DON'T LOVE HER ANYMORE BECAUSE SHE'D BE A POOR BRIDE, IS THAT IT?

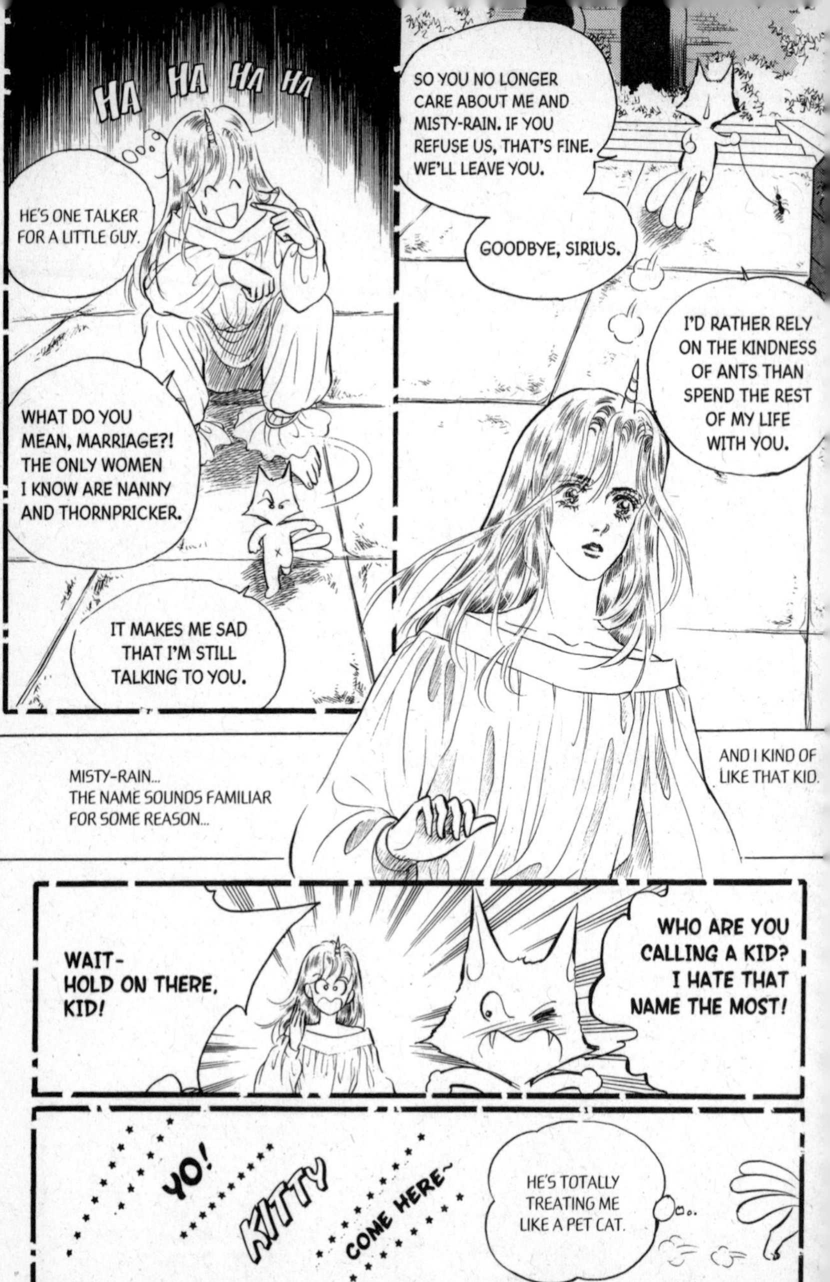
HA HA HA HA
HE'S ONE TALKER FOR A LITTLE GUY.
WHAT DO YOU MEAN, MARRIAGE?! THE ONLY WOMEN I KNOW ARE NANNY AND THORNPRICKER.
IT MAKES ME SAD THAT I'M STILL TALKING TO YOU.
SO YOU NO LONGER CARE ABOUT ME AND MISTY-RAIN. IF YOU REFUSE US, THAT'S FINE. WE'LL LEAVE YOU.
GOODBYE, SIRIUS.
I'D RATHER RELY ON THE KINDNESS OF ANTS THAN SPEND THE REST OF MY LIFE WITH YOU.
MISTY-RAIN... THE NAME SOUNDS FAMILIAR FOR SOME REASON...
AND I KIND OF LIKE THAT KID.
WAIT- HOLD ON THERE, KID!
WHO ARE YOU CALLING A KID? I HATE THAT NAME THE MOST!
YO! KITTY COME HERE~
HE'S TOTALLY TREATING ME LIKE A PET CAT.

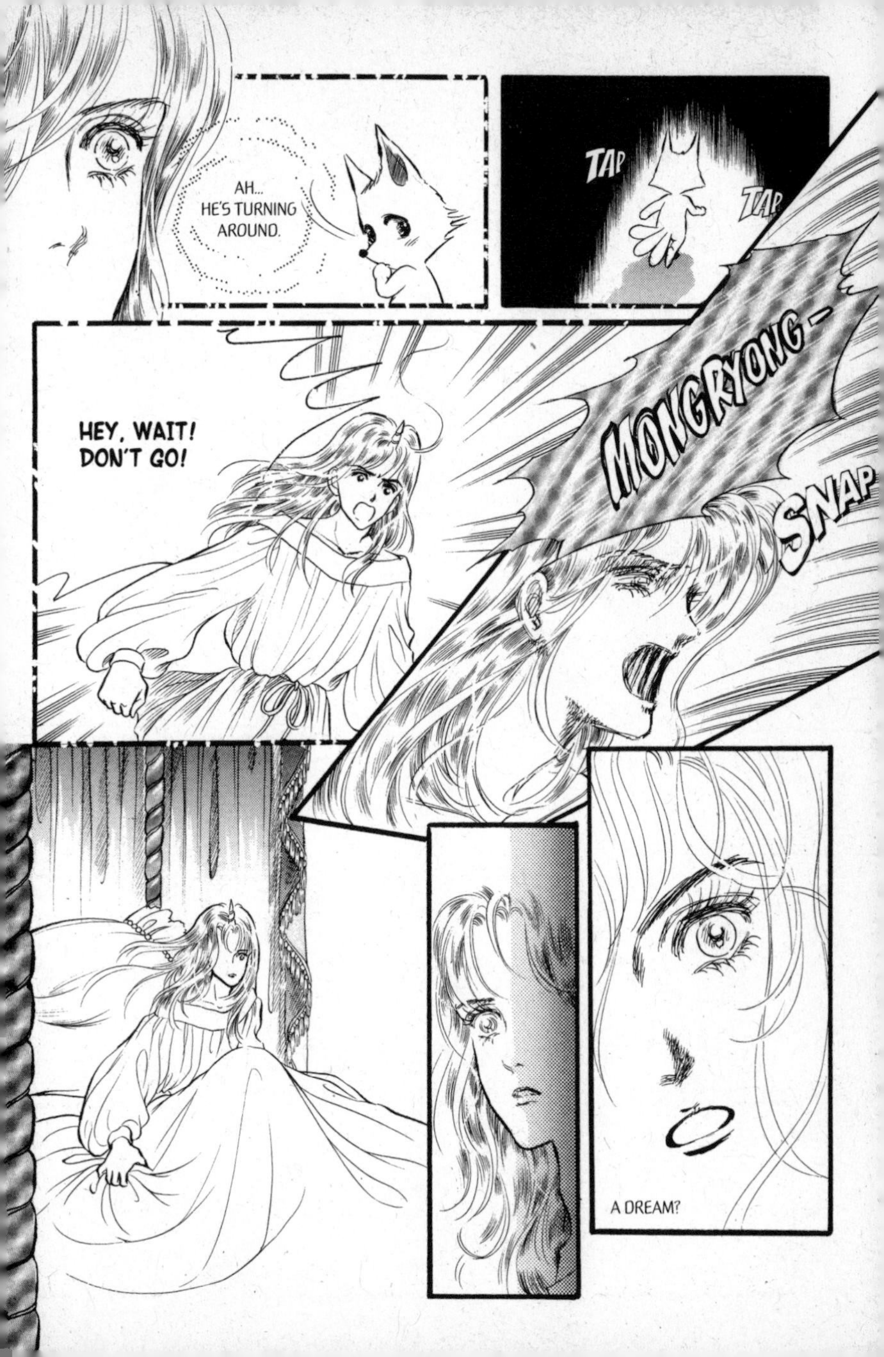
AH... HE'S TURNING AROUND.
TAP
TAP
HEY, WAIT! DON'T GO!
MONGRYONG -
SNAP
A DREAM?

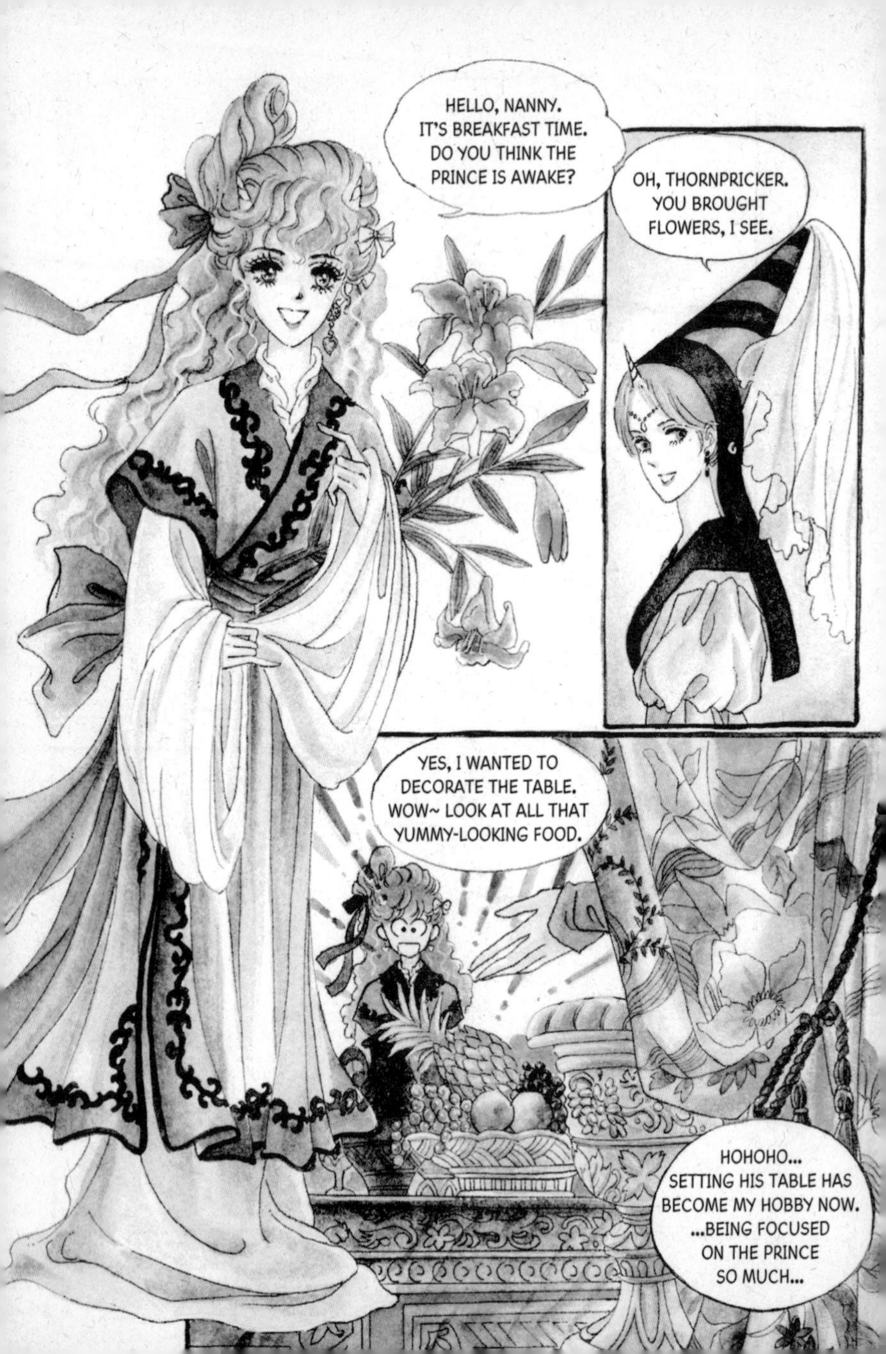
HELLO, NANNY. IT'S BREAKFAST TIME. DO YOU THINK THE PRINCE IS AWAKE?
OH, THORNPRICKER. YOU BROUGHT FLOWERS, I SEE.
YES, I WANTED TO DECORATE THE TABLE. WOW~ LOOK AT ALL THAT YUMMY-LOOKING FOOD.
HOHOHO... SETTING HIS TABLE HAS BECOME MY HOBBY NOW. ...BEING FOCUSED ON THE PRINCE SO MUCH...

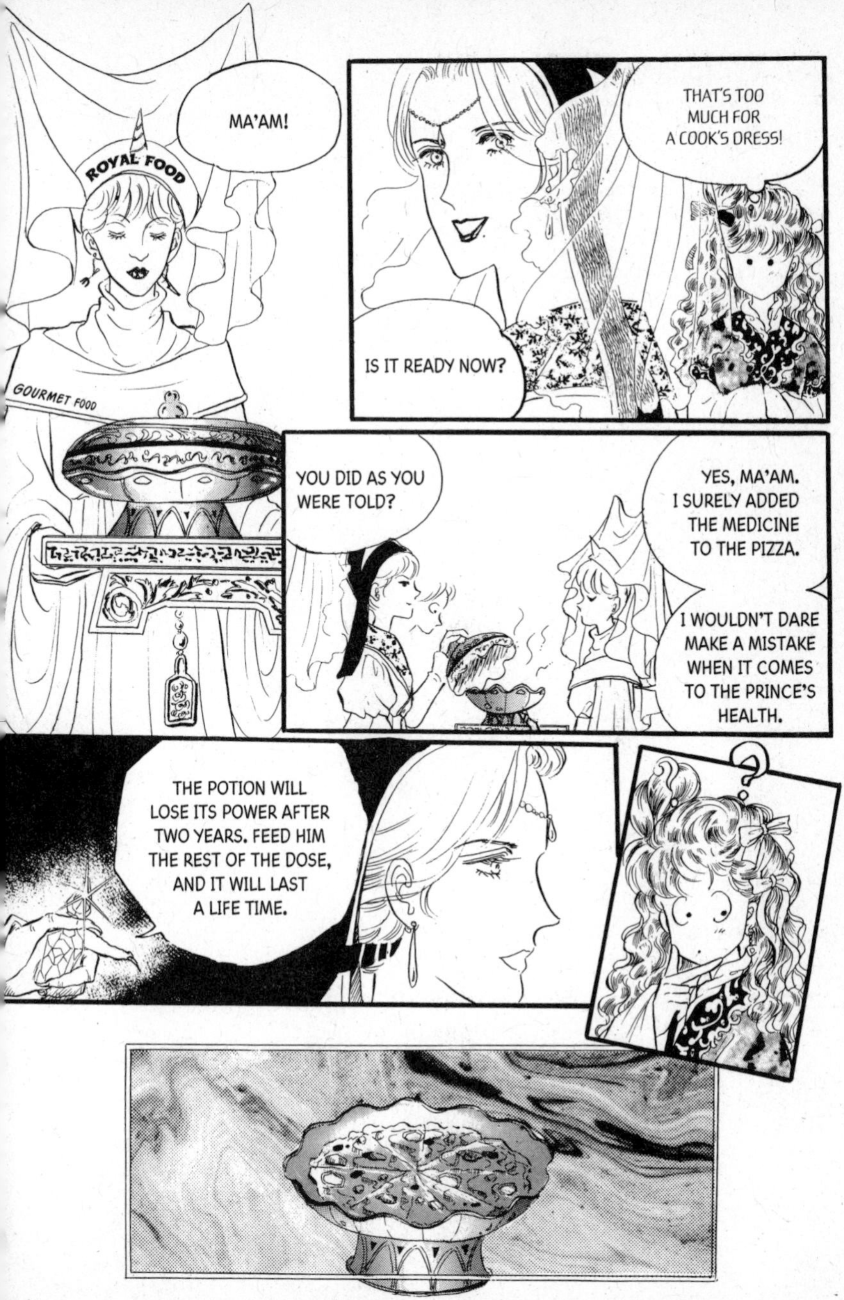
MA'AM!
ROYAL FOOD
GOURMET FOOD
THAT'S TOO MUCH FOR A COOK'S DRESS!
IS IT READY NOW?
YOU DID AS YOU WERE TOLD?
YES, MA'AM. I SURELY ADDED THE MEDICINE TO THE PIZZA.
I WOULDN'T DARE MAKE A MISTAKE WHEN IT COMES TO THE PRINCE'S HEALTH.
THE POTION WILL LOSE ITS POWER AFTER TWO YEARS. FEED HIM THE REST OF THE DOSE, AND IT WILL LAST A LIFE TIME.
?

IT WAS TOO VIVID TO BE A DREAM.
MONGRYONG... MONGRYONG...
THAT NAME JUST SLIPPED OUT OF MY MOUTH...
AS IF I'VE CALLED OUT TO HIM MANY TIMES BEFORE...
IT WAS SO NATURAL...

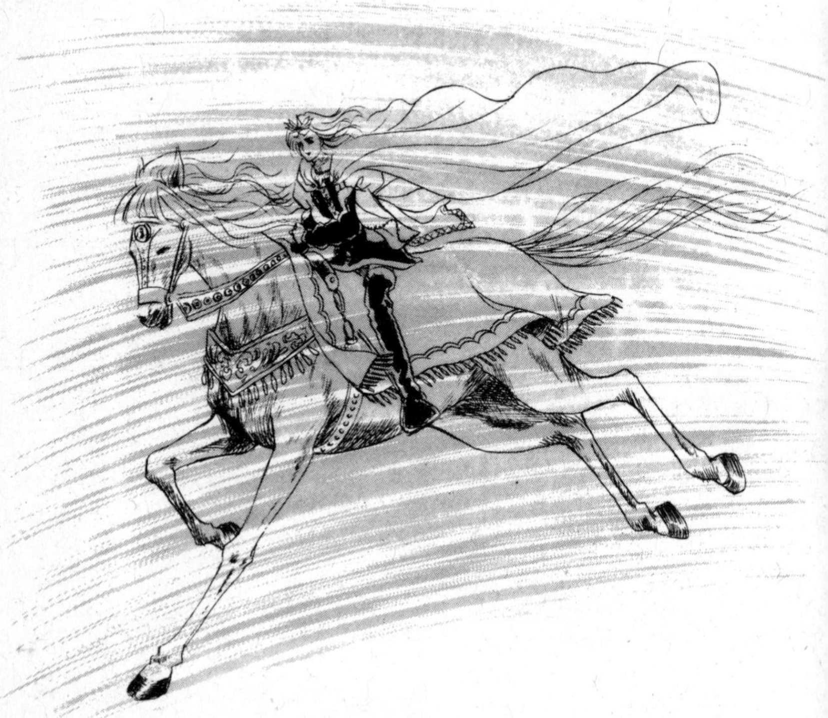

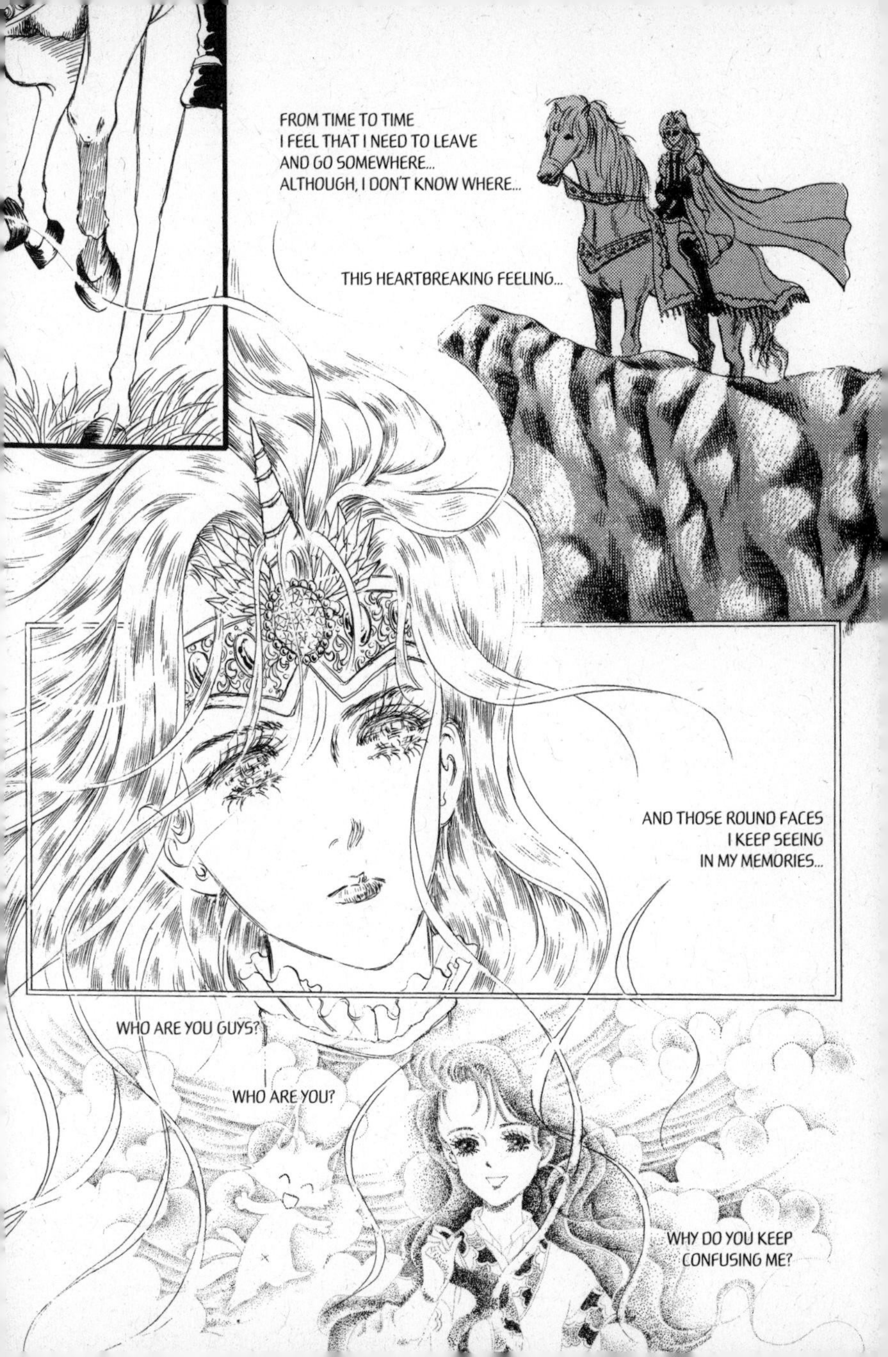
FROM TIME TO TIME
I FEEL THAT I NEED TO LEAVE
AND GO SOMEWHERE...
ALTHOUGH, I DON'T KNOW WHERE...
THIS HEARTBREAKING FEELING...
AND THOSE ROUND FACES
I KEEP SEEING
IN MY MEMORIES...
WHO ARE YOU GUYS?
WHO ARE YOU?
WHY DO YOU KEEP
CONFUSING ME?

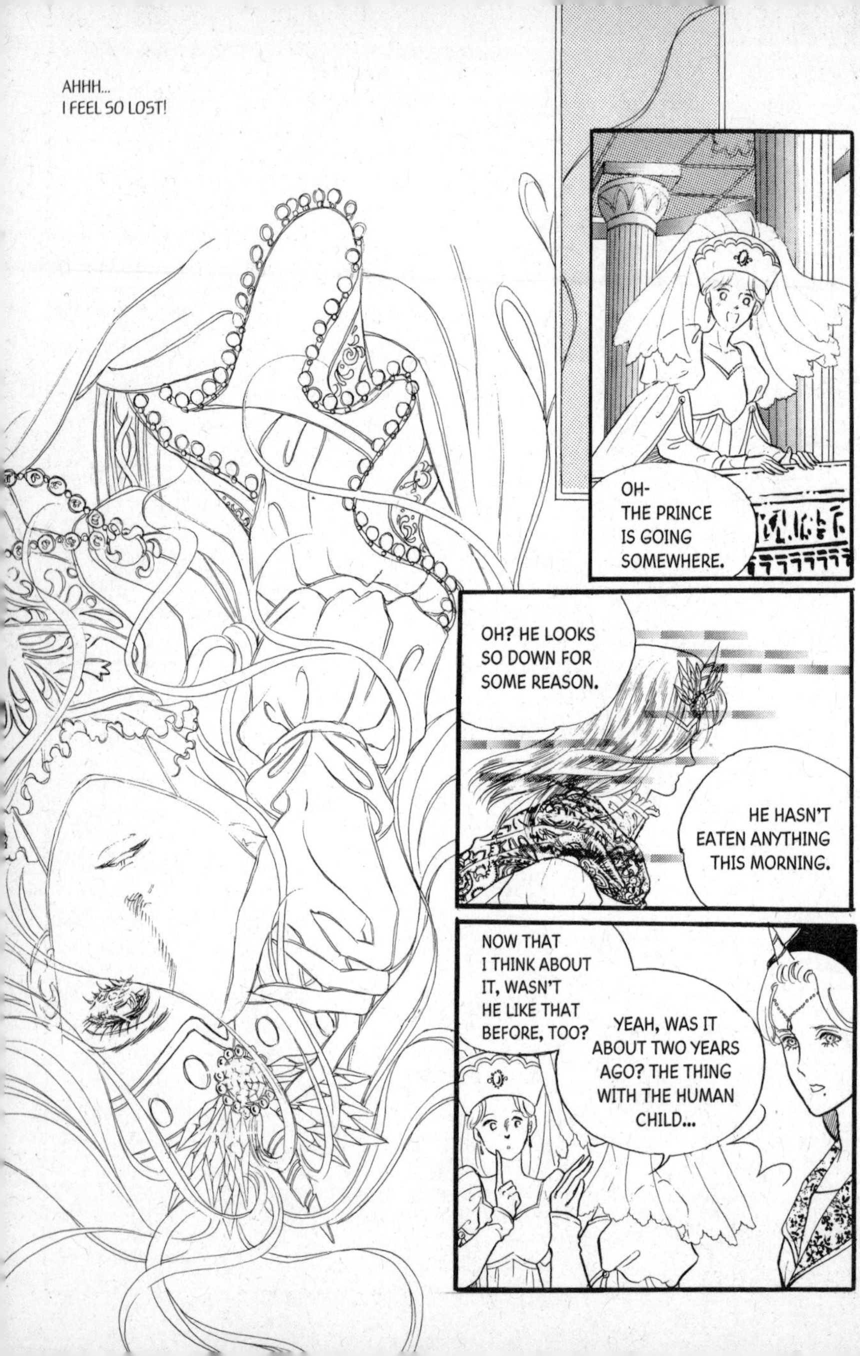
AHHH... I FEEL SO LOST!
OH- THE PRINCE IS GOING SOMEWHERE.
OH? HE LOOKS SO DOWN FOR SOME REASON.
HE HASN'T EATEN ANYTHING THIS MORNING.
NOW THAT I THINK ABOUT IT, WASN'T HE LIKE THAT BEFORE, TOO?
YEAH, WAS IT ABOUT TWO YEARS AGO? THE THING WITH THE HUMAN CHILD...

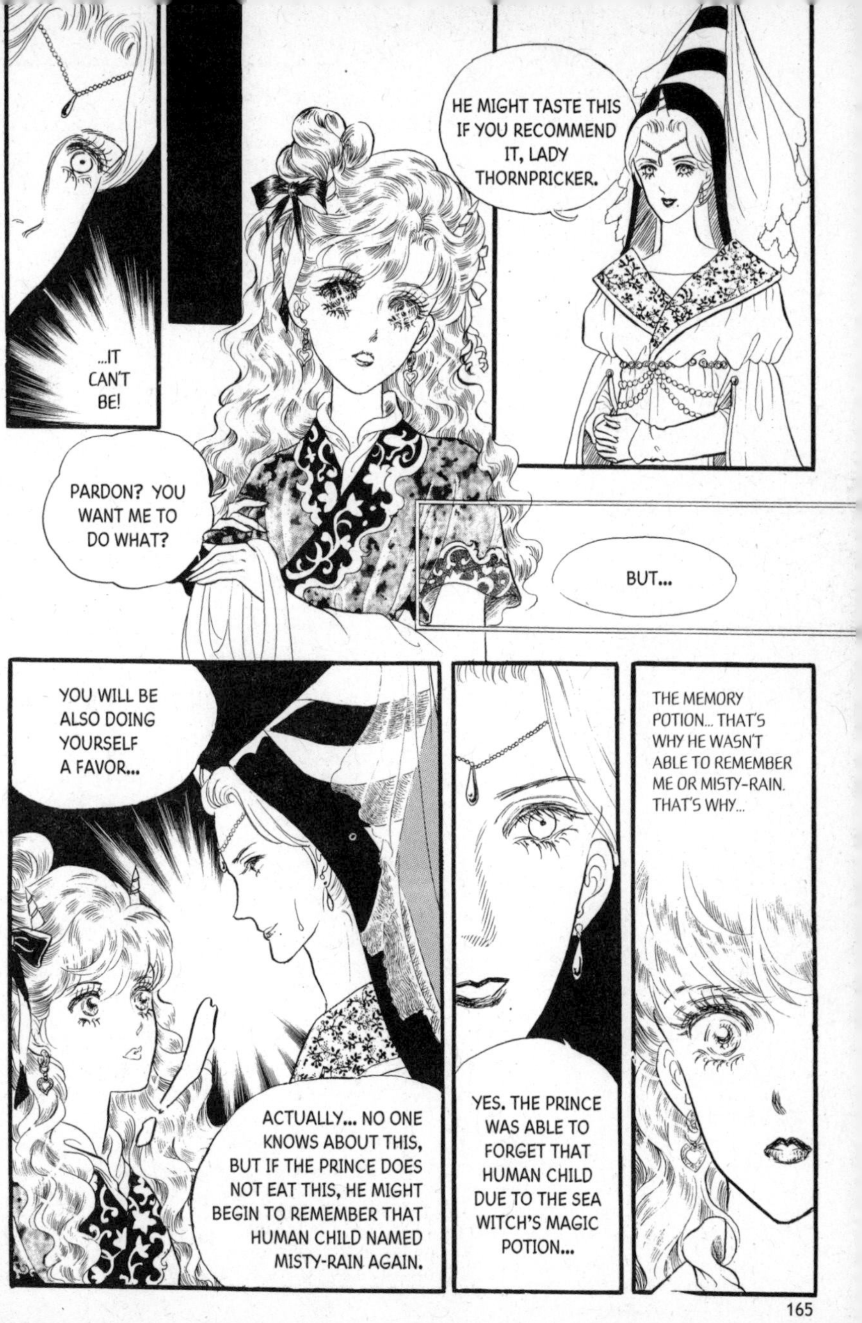
...IT CAN'T BE!
HE MIGHT TASTE THIS IF YOU RECOMMEND IT, LADY THORNPRICKER.
PARDON? YOU WANT ME TO DO WHAT?
BUT...
YOU WILL BE ALSO DOING YOURSELF A FAVOR...
ACTUALLY... NO ONE KNOWS ABOUT THIS, BUT IF THE PRINCE DOES NOT EAT THIS, HE MIGHT BEGIN TO REMEMBER THAT HUMAN CHILD NAMED MISTY-RAIN AGAIN.
YES. THE PRINCE WAS ABLE TO FORGET THAT HUMAN CHILD DUE TO THE SEA WITCH'S MAGIC POTION...
THE MEMORY POTION... THAT'S WHY HE WASN'T ABLE TO REMEMBER ME OR MISTY-RAIN. THAT'S WHY...

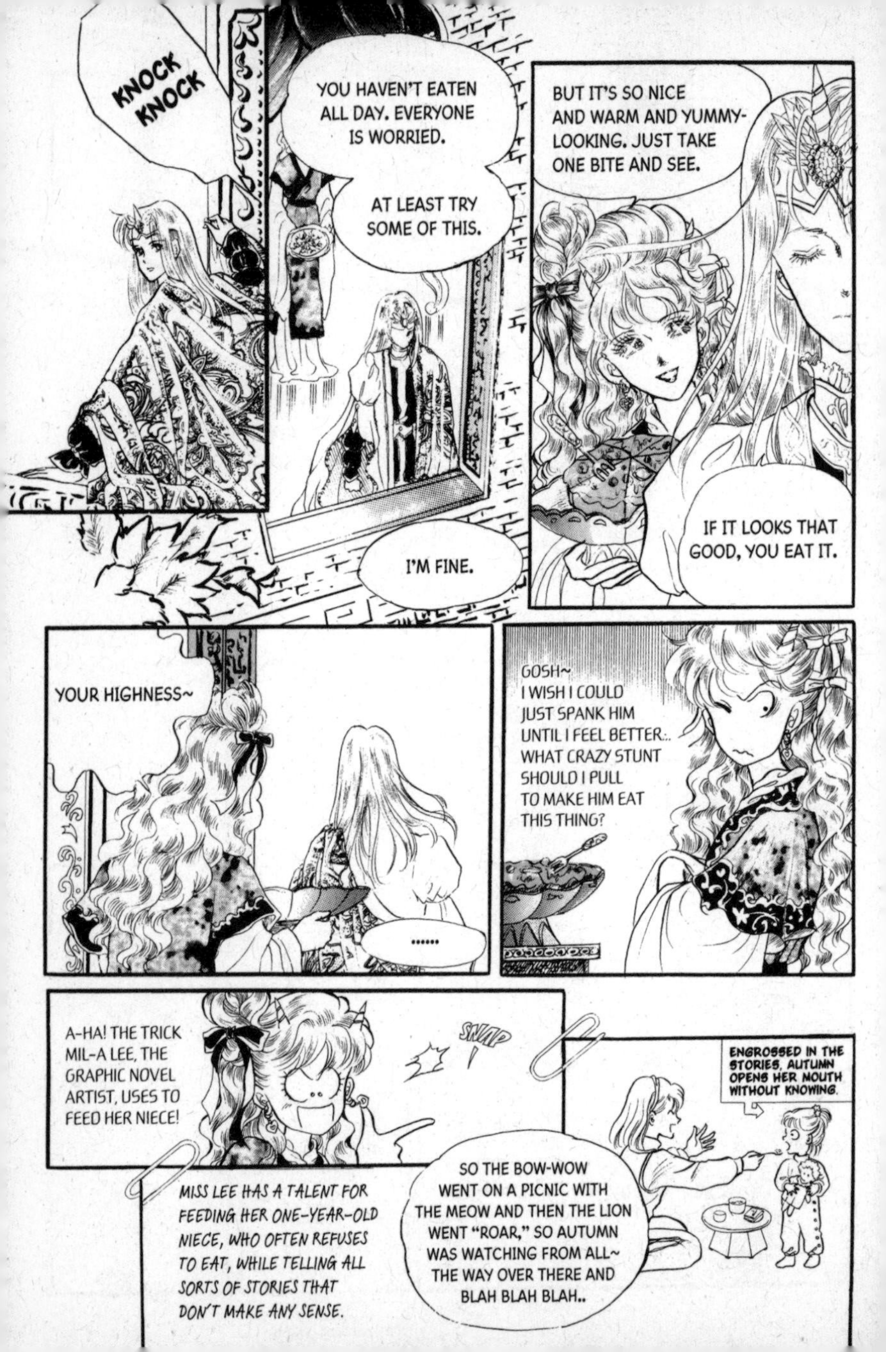
KNOCK KNOCK
YOU HAVEN'T EATEN ALL DAY. EVERYONE IS WORRIED.
AT LEAST TRY SOME OF THIS.
I'M FINE.
BUT IT'S SO NICE AND WARM AND YUMMY-LOOKING. JUST TAKE ONE BITE AND SEE.
IF IT LOOKS THAT GOOD, YOU EAT IT.
YOUR HIGHNESS~
......
GOSH~ I WISH I COULD JUST SPANK HIM UNTIL I FEEL BETTER.. WHAT CRAZY STUNT SHOULD I PULL TO MAKE HIM EAT THIS THING?
A-HA! THE TRICK MIL-A LEE, THE GRAPHIC NOVEL ARTIST, USES TO FEED HER NIECE!
SNAP
ENGROSSED IN THE STORIES, AUTUMN OPENS HER MOUTH WITHOUT KNOWING.
MISS LEE HAS A TALENT FOR FEEDING HER ONE-YEAR-OLD NIECE, WHO OFTEN REFUSES TO EAT, WHILE TELLING ALL SORTS OF STORIES THAT DON'T MAKE ANY SENSE.
SO THE BOW-WOW WENT ON A PICNIC WITH THE MEOW AND THEN THE LION WENT "ROAR," SO AUTUMN WAS WATCHING FROM ALL~ THE WAY OVER THERE AND BLAH BLAH BLAH..

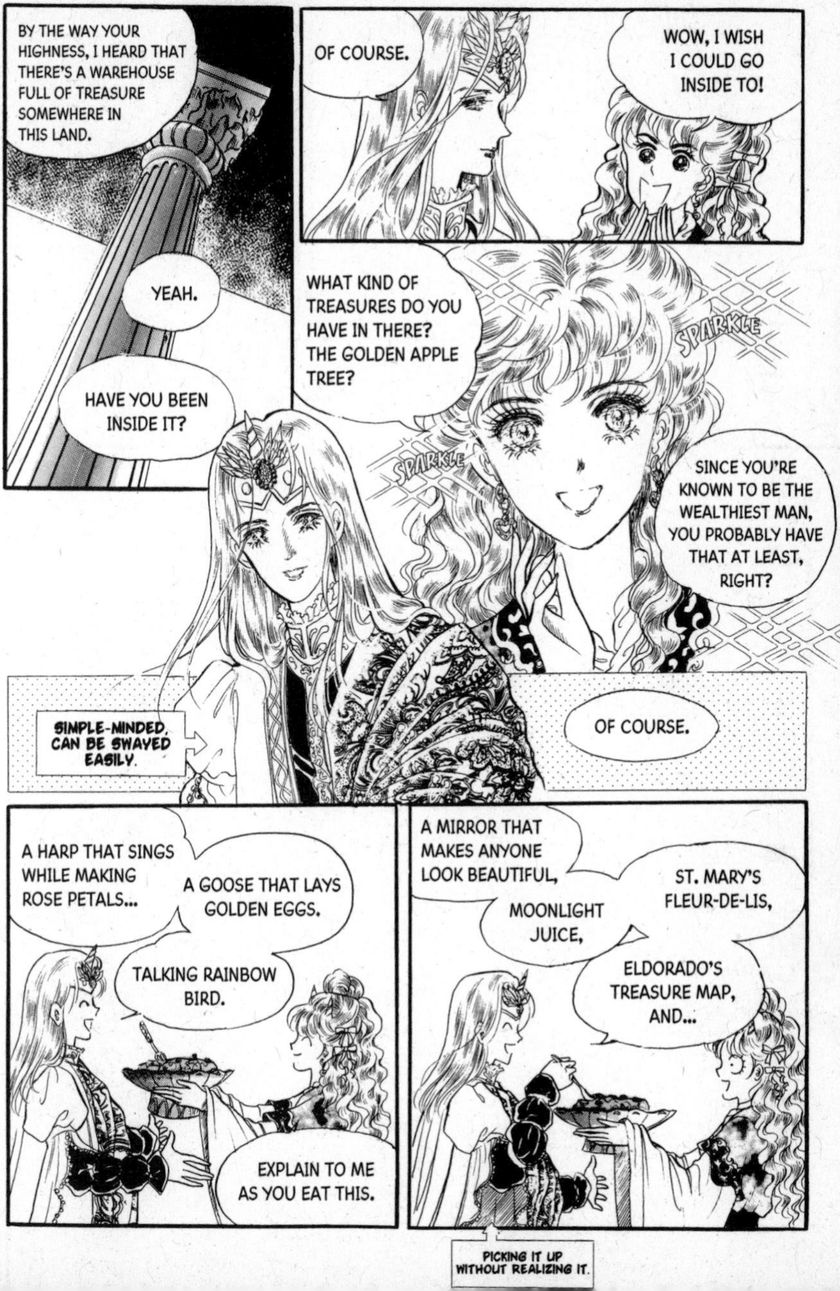
BY THE WAY YOUR HIGHNESS, I HEARD THAT THERE'S A WAREHOUSE FULL OF TREASURE SOMEWHERE IN THIS LAND.
YEAH.
HAVE YOU BEEN INSIDE IT?
OF COURSE.
WOW, I WISH I COULD GO INSIDE TO!
WHAT KIND OF TREASURES DO YOU HAVE IN THERE? THE GOLDEN APPLE TREE?
SPARKLE
SPARKLE
SINCE YOU'RE KNOWN TO BE THE WEALTHIEST MAN, YOU PROBABLY HAVE THAT AT LEAST, RIGHT?
SIMPLE-MINDED, CAN BE SWAYED EASILY.
OF COURSE.
A HARP THAT SINGS WHILE MAKING ROSE PETALS...
A GOOSE THAT LAYS GOLDEN EGGS.
TALKING RAINBOW BIRD.
EXPLAIN TO ME AS YOU EAT THIS.
A MIRROR THAT MAKES ANYONE LOOK BEAUTIFUL,
MOONLIGHT JUICE,
ST. MARY'S FLEUR-DE-LIS,
ELDORADO'S TREASURE MAP, AND...
PICKING IT UP WITHOUT REALIZING IT.

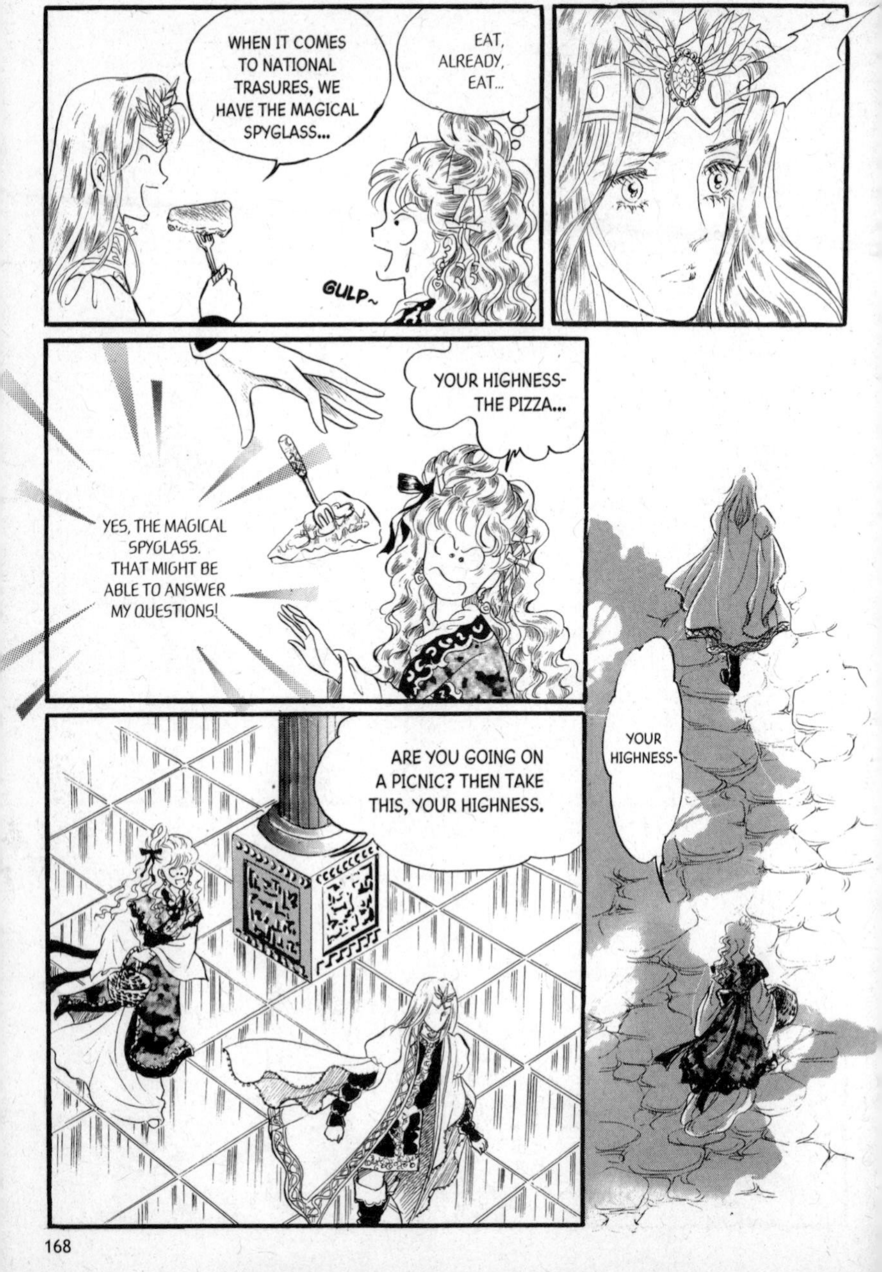
WHEN IT COMES TO NATIONAL TRASURES, WE HAVE THE MAGICAL SPYGLASS...
EAT, ALREADY, EAT...
GULP~
YOUR HIGHNESS- THE PIZZA...
YES, THE MAGICAL SPYGLASS. THAT MIGHT BE ABLE TO ANSWER MY QUESTIONS!
ARE YOU GOING ON A PICNIC? THEN TAKE THIS, YOUR HIGHNESS.
YOUR HIGHNESS-

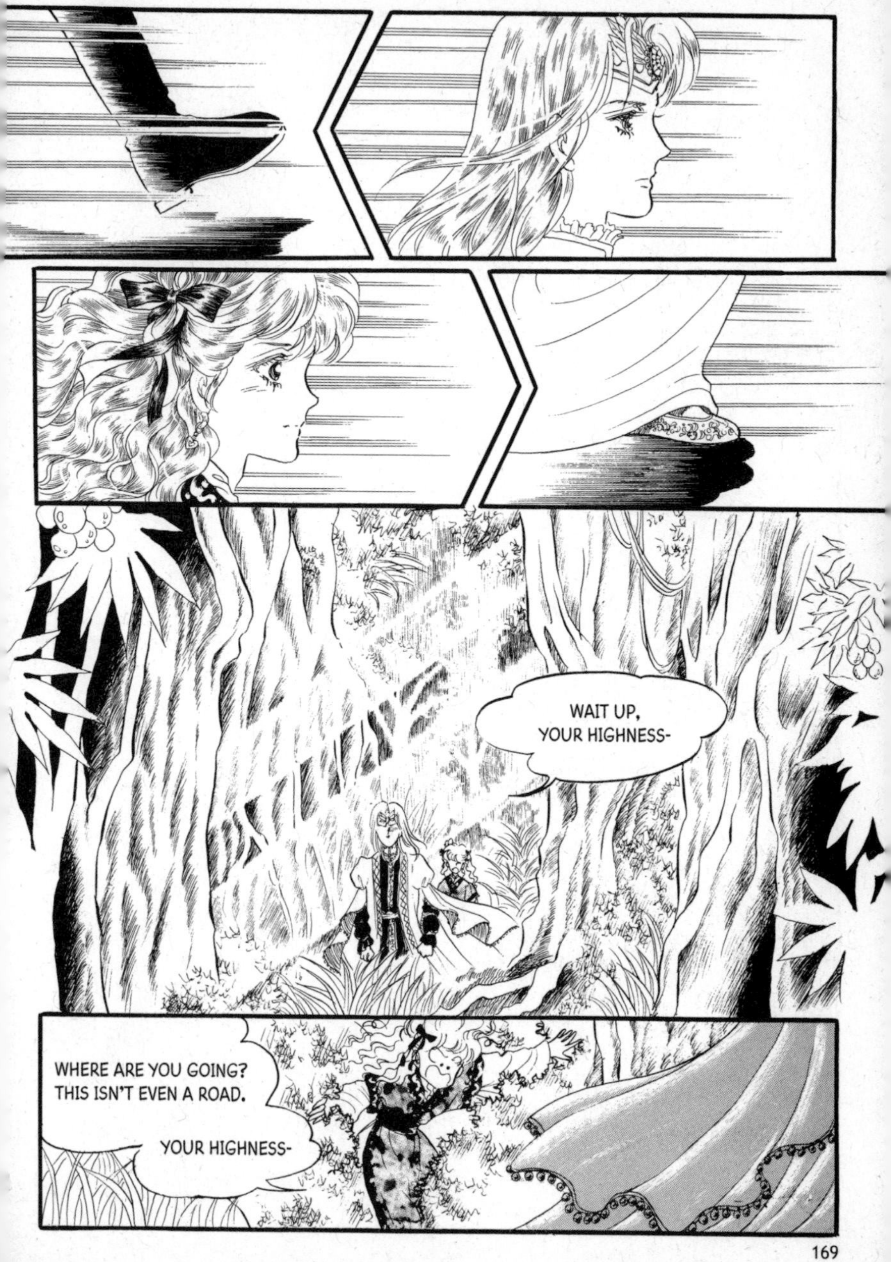
WAIT UP, YOUR HIGHNESS-
WHERE ARE YOU GOING? THIS ISN'T EVEN A ROAD.
YOUR HIGHNESS-

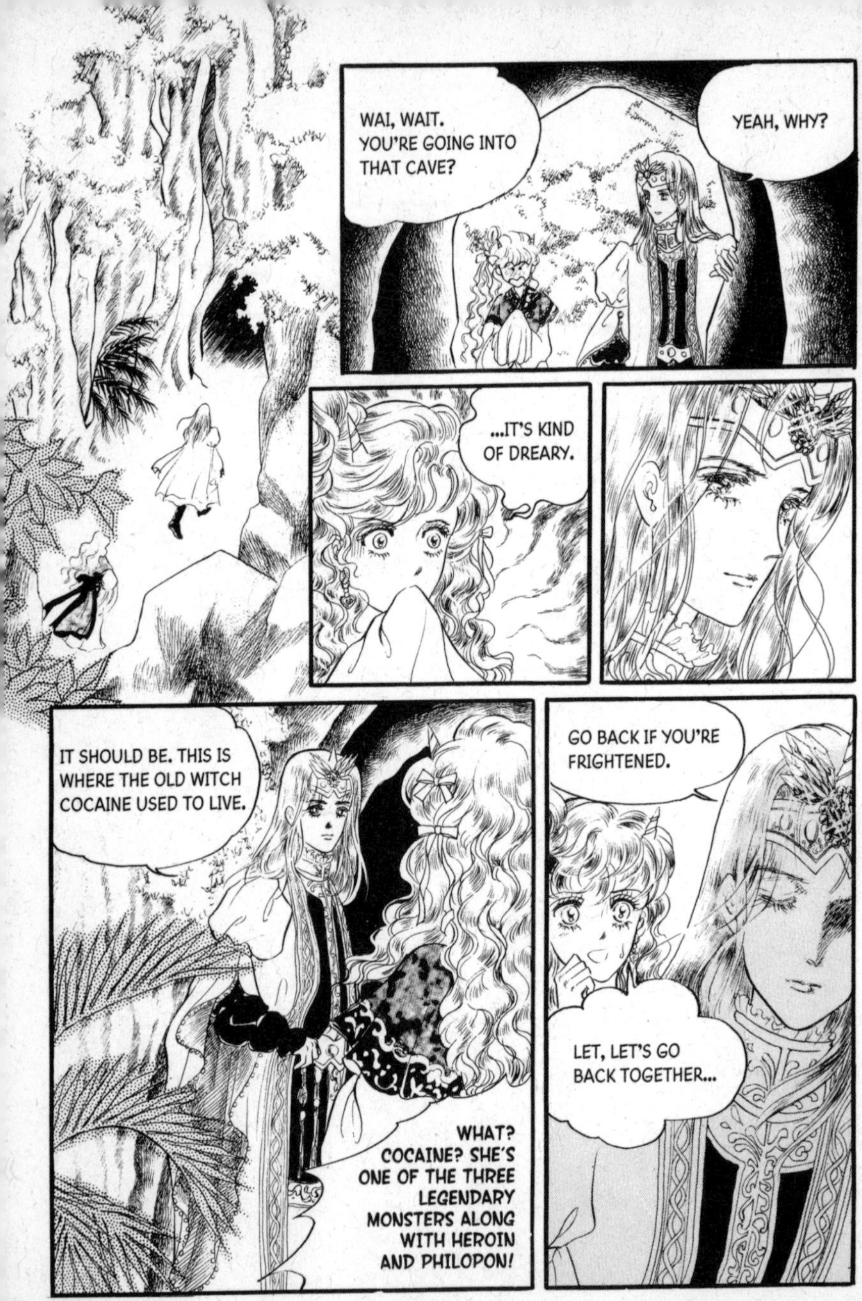
WAI, WAIT. YOU'RE GOING INTO THAT CAVE?
YEAH, WHY?
...IT'S KIND OF DREARY.
IT SHOULD BE. THIS IS WHERE THE OLD WITCH COCAINE USED TO LIVE.
WHAT? COCAINE? SHE'S ONE OF THE THREE LEGENDARY MONSTERS ALONG WITH HEROIN AND PHILOPON!
GO BACK IF YOU'RE FRIGHTENED.
LET, LET'S GO BACK TOGETHER...

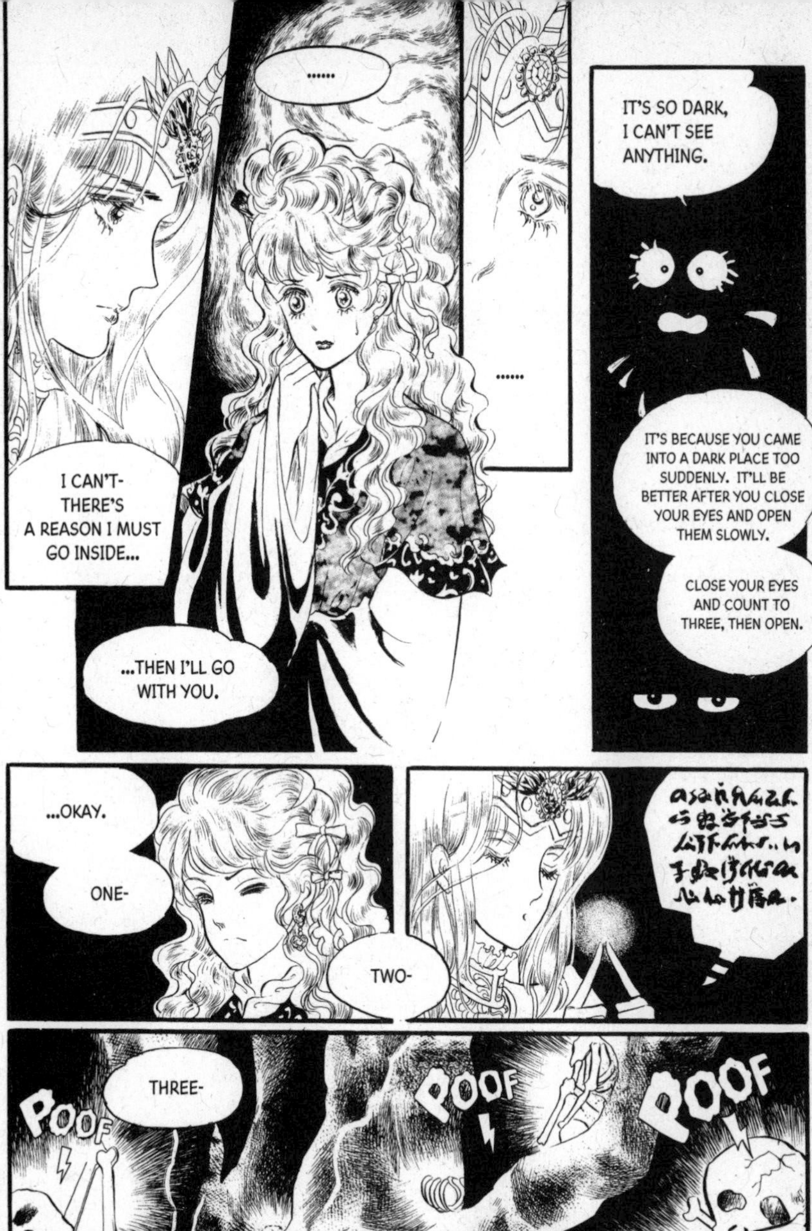
I CAN'T- THERE'S A REASON I MUST GO INSIDE...
......
...THEN I'LL GO WITH YOU.
......
IT'S SO DARK, I CAN'T SEE ANYTHING.
IT'S BECAUSE YOU CAME INTO A DARK PLACE TOO SUDDENLY. IT'LL BE BETTER AFTER YOU CLOSE YOUR EYES AND OPEN THEM SLOWLY.
CLOSE YOUR EYES AND COUNT TO THREE, THEN OPEN.
...OKAY.
ONE-
TWO-
THREE-
POOF
POOF
POOF

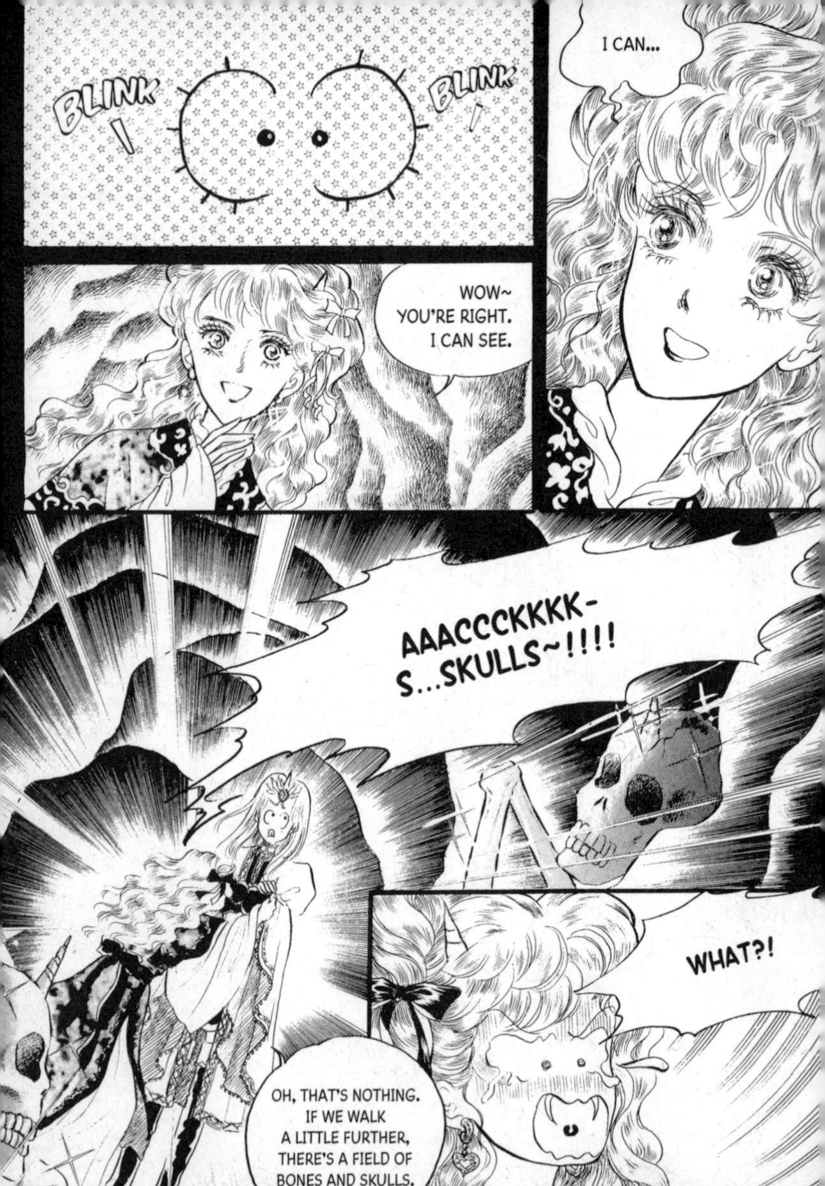
BLINK
BLINK
WOW~ YOU'RE RIGHT. I CAN SEE.
I CAN...
AAACCCKKKK-
S...SKULLS~!!!!
OH, THAT'S NOTHING. IF WE WALK A LITTLE FURTHER, THERE'S A FIELD OF BONES AND SKULLS.
WHAT?!

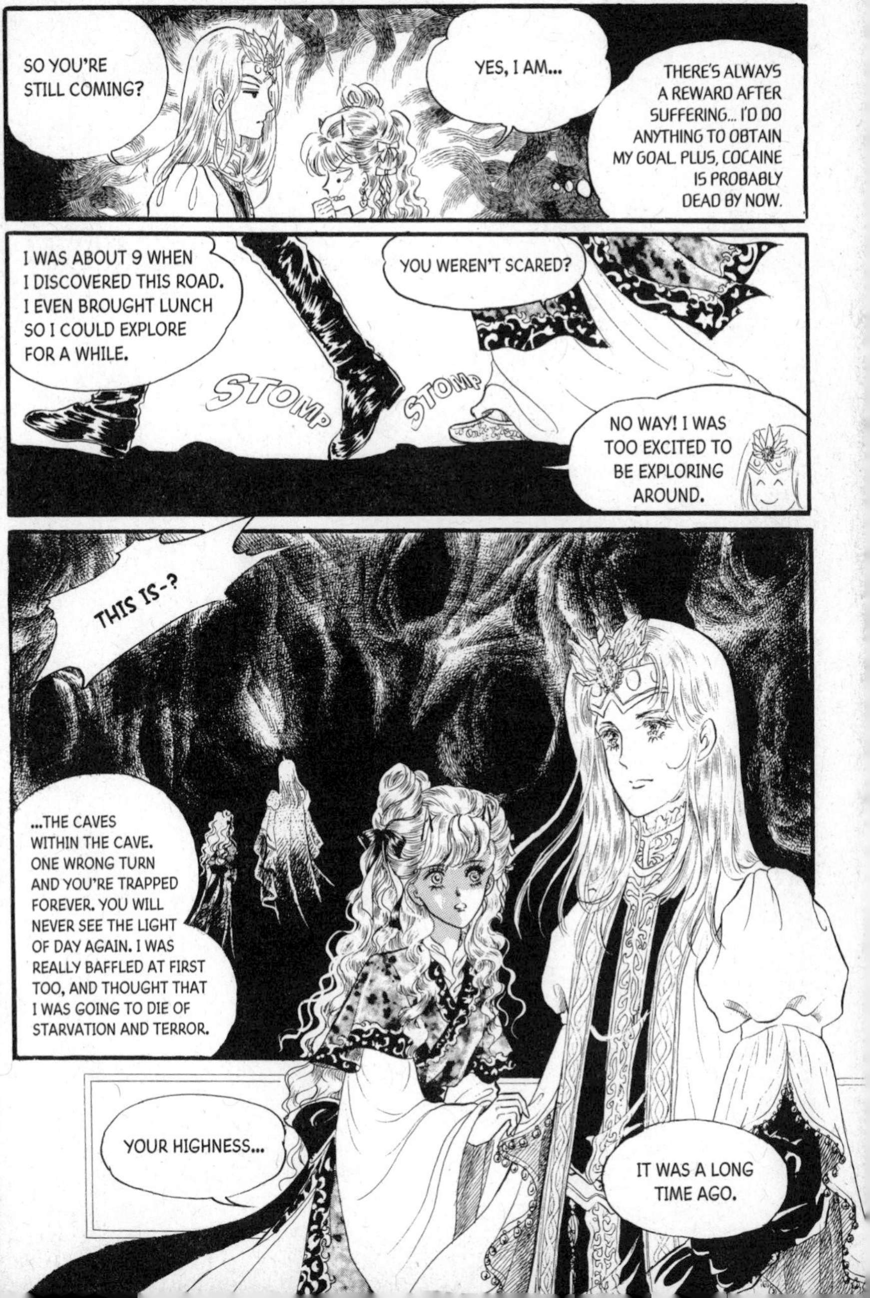
SO YOU'RE STILL COMING?
YES, I AM...
THERE'S ALWAYS A REWARD AFTER SUFFERING... I'D DO ANYTHING TO OBTAIN MY GOAL. PLUS, COCAINE IS PROBABLY DEAD BY NOW.
I WAS ABOUT 9 WHEN I DISCOVERED THIS ROAD. I EVEN BROUGHT LUNCH SO I COULD EXPLORE FOR A WHILE.
STOMP
STOMP
YOU WEREN'T SCARED?
NO WAY! I WAS TOO EXCITED TO BE EXPLORING AROUND.
THIS IS-?
...THE CAVES WITHIN THE CAVE. ONE WRONG TURN AND YOU'RE TRAPPED FOREVER. YOU WILL NEVER SEE THE LIGHT OF DAY AGAIN. I WAS REALLY BAFFLED AT FIRST TOO, AND THOUGHT THAT I WAS GOING TO DIE OF STARVATION AND TERROR.
YOUR HIGHNESS...
IT WAS A LONG TIME AGO.

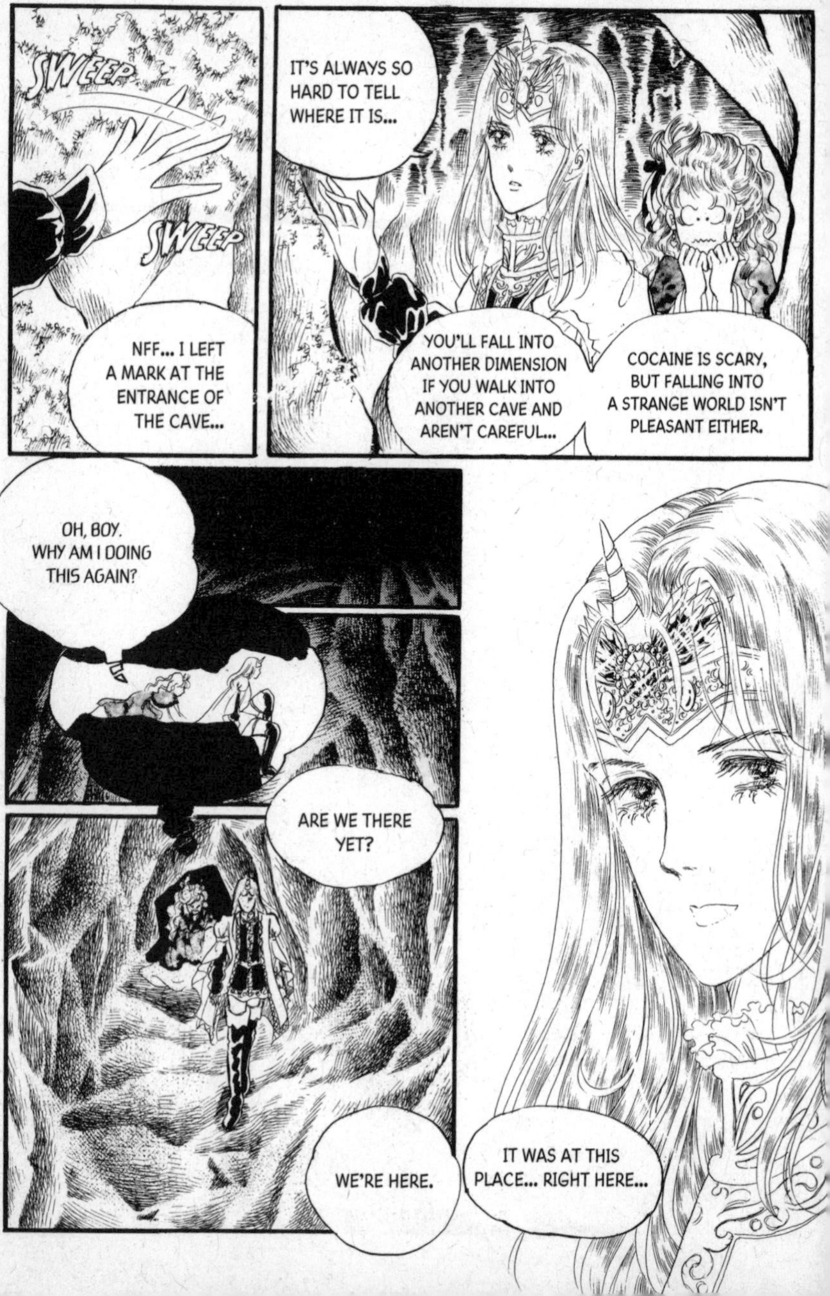
SWEEP
SWEEP
NFF... I LEFT A MARK AT THE ENTRANCE OF THE CAVE...
IT'S ALWAYS SO HARD TO TELL WHERE IT IS...
YOU'LL FALL INTO ANOTHER DIMENSION IF YOU WALK INTO ANOTHER CAVE AND AREN'T CAREFUL...
COCAINE IS SCARY, BUT FALLING INTO A STRANGE WORLD ISN'T PLEASANT EITHER.
OH, BOY. WHY AM I DOING THIS AGAIN?
ARE WE THERE YET?
WE'RE HERE.
IT WAS AT THIS PLACE... RIGHT HERE...

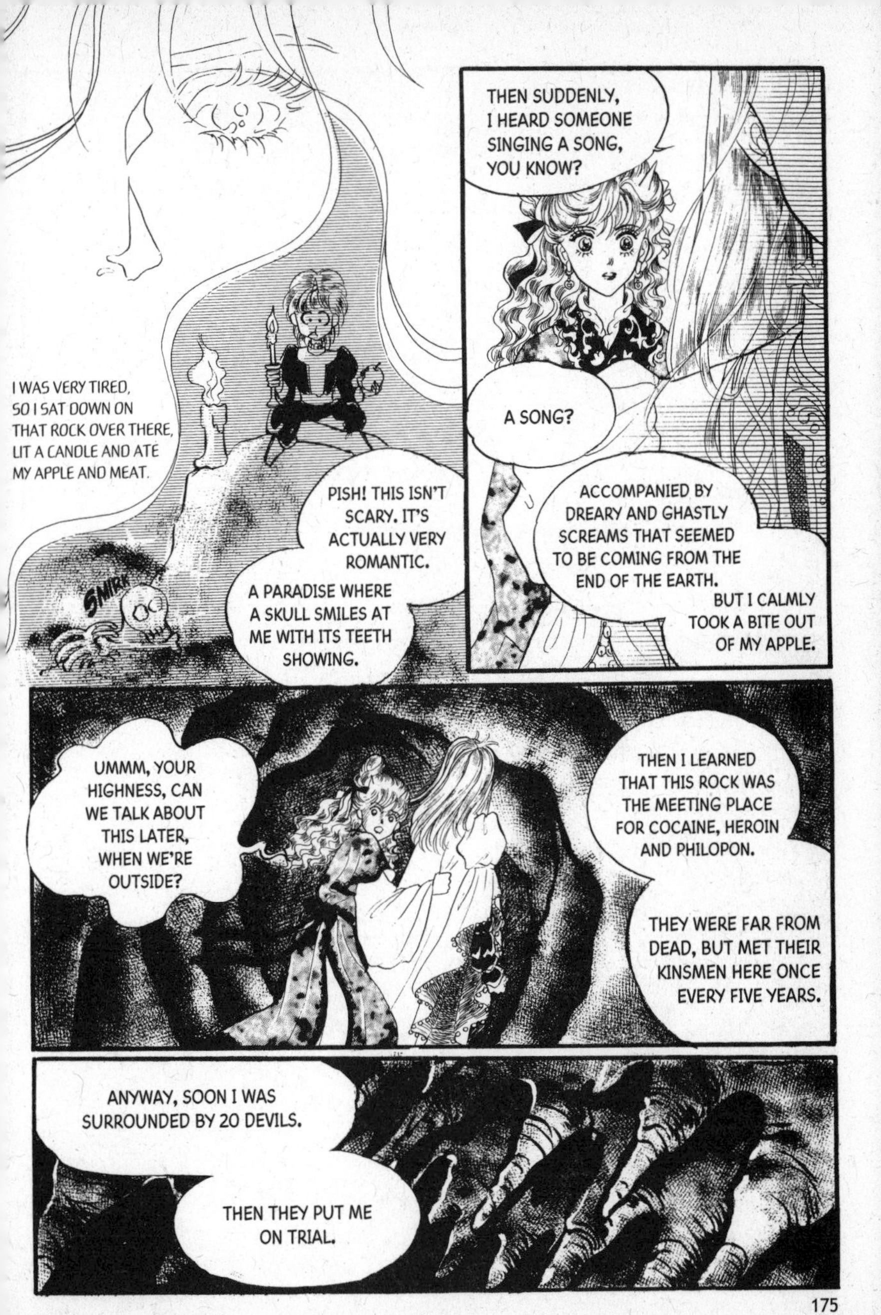
I WAS VERY TIRED, SO I SAT DOWN ON THAT ROCK OVER THERE, LIT A CANDLE AND ATE MY APPLE AND MEAT.
PISH! THIS ISN'T SCARY. IT'S ACTUALLY VERY ROMANTIC.
A PARADISE WHERE A SKULL SMILES AT ME WITH ITS TEETH SHOWING.
SMIRK
THEN SUDDENLY, I HEARD SOMEONE SINGING A SONG, YOU KNOW?
A SONG?
ACCOMPANIED BY DREARY AND GHASTLY SCREAMS THAT SEEMED TO BE COMING FROM THE END OF THE EARTH.
BUT I CALMLY TOOK A BITE OUT OF MY APPLE.
UMMM, YOUR HIGHNESS, CAN WE TALK ABOUT THIS LATER, WHEN WE'RE OUTSIDE?
THEN I LEARNED THAT THIS ROCK WAS THE MEETING PLACE FOR COCAINE, HEROIN AND PHILOPON.
THEY WERE FAR FROM DEAD, BUT MET THEIR KINSMEN HERE ONCE EVERY FIVE YEARS.
ANYWAY, SOON I WAS SURROUNDED BY 20 DEVILS.
THEN THEY PUT ME ON TRIAL.

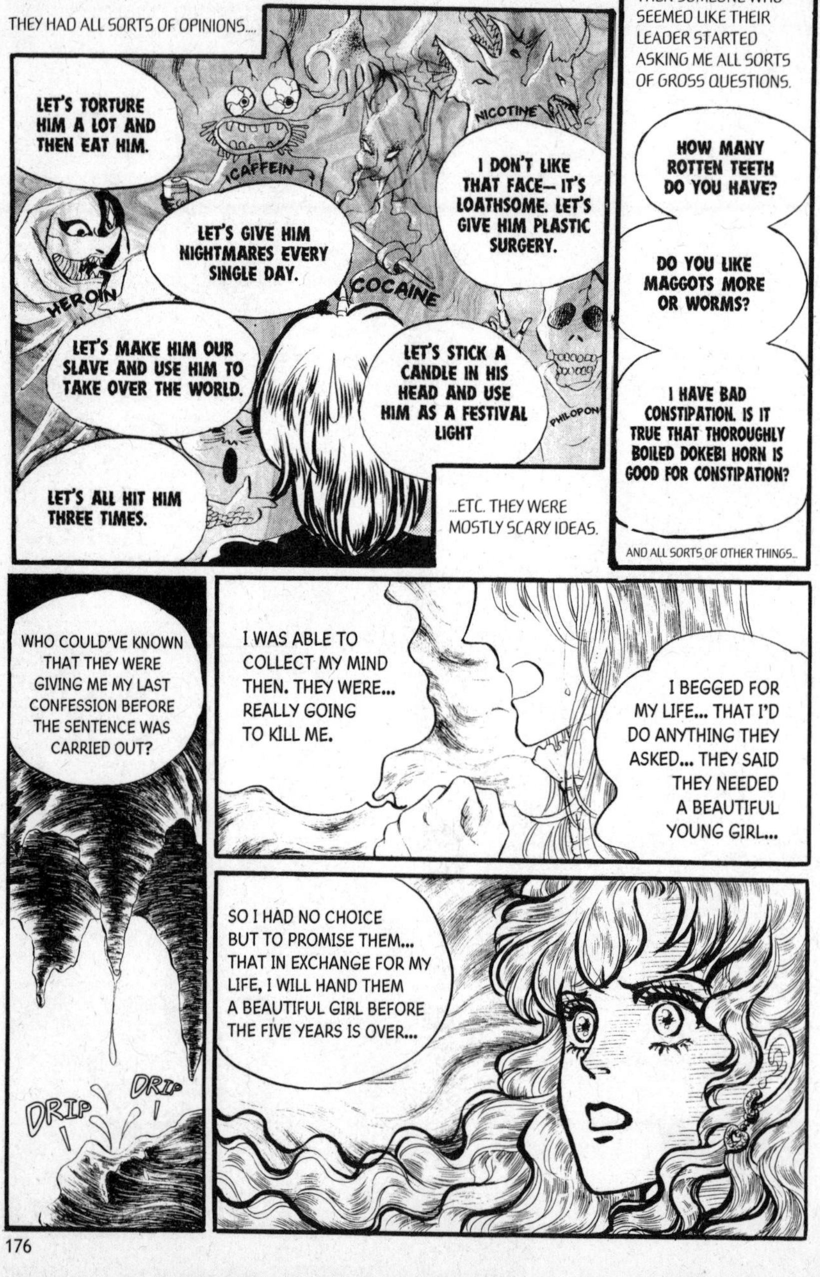
THEY HAD ALL SORTS OF OPINIONS....
LET'S TORTURE HIM A LOT AND THEN EAT HIM.
CAFFEIN
NICOTINE
LET'S GIVE HIM NIGHTMARES EVERY SINGLE DAY.
I DON'T LIKE THAT FACE— IT'S LOATHSOME. LET'S GIVE HIM PLASTIC SURGERY.
HEROIN
COCAINE
LET'S MAKE HIM OUR SLAVE AND USE HIM TO TAKE OVER THE WORLD.
LET'S STICK A CANDLE IN HIS HEAD AND USE HIM AS A FESTIVAL LIGHT
PHILOPON
LET'S ALL HIT HIM THREE TIMES.
...ETC. THEY WERE MOSTLY SCARY IDEAS.
THEN SOMEONE WHO SEEMED LIKE THEIR LEADER STARTED ASKING ME ALL SORTS OF GROSS QUESTIONS.
HOW MANY ROTTEN TEETH DO YOU HAVE?
DO YOU LIKE MAGGOTS MORE OR WORMS?
I HAVE BAD CONSTIPATION. IS IT TRUE THAT THOROUGHLY BOILED DOKEBI HORN IS GOOD FOR CONSTIPATION?
AND ALL SORTS OF OTHER THINGS...
WHO COULD'VE KNOWN THAT THEY WERE GIVING ME MY LAST CONFESSION BEFORE THE SENTENCE WAS CARRIED OUT?
DRIP
DRIP
I WAS ABLE TO COLLECT MY MIND THEN. THEY WERE... REALLY GOING TO KILL ME.
I BEGGED FOR MY LIFE... THAT I'D DO ANYTHING THEY ASKED... THEY SAID THEY NEEDED A BEAUTIFUL YOUNG GIRL...
SO I HAD NO CHOICE BUT TO PROMISE THEM... THAT IN EXCHANGE FOR MY LIFE, I WILL HAND THEM A BEAUTIFUL GIRL BEFORE THE FIVE YEARS IS OVER...

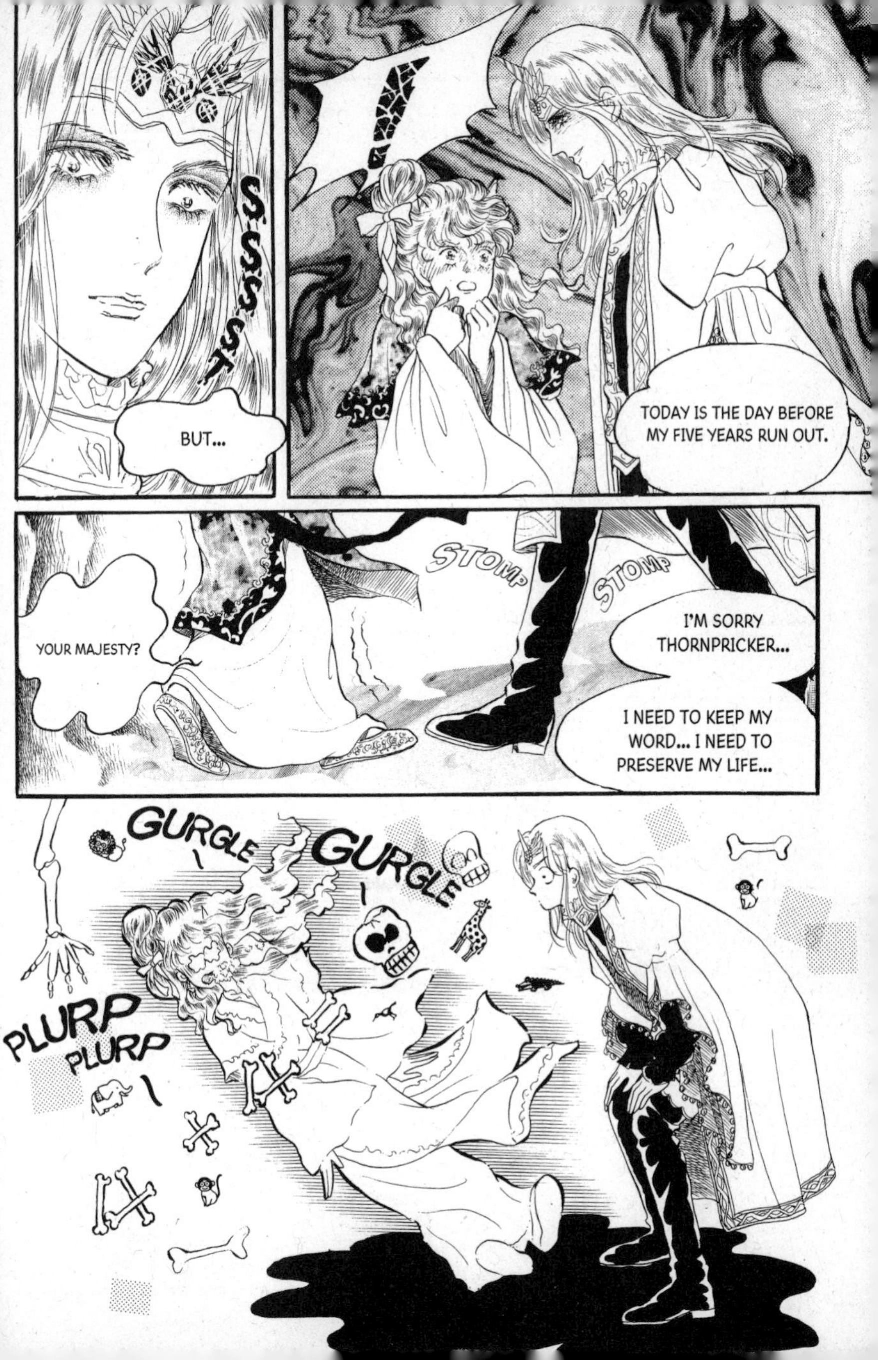
SSSST
BUT...
TODAY IS THE DAY BEFORE MY FIVE YEARS RUN OUT.
YOUR MAJESTY?
STOMP
STOMP
I'M SORRY THORNPRICKER...
I NEED TO KEEP MY WORD... I NEED TO PRESERVE MY LIFE...
GURGLE
GURGLE
PLURP
PLURP

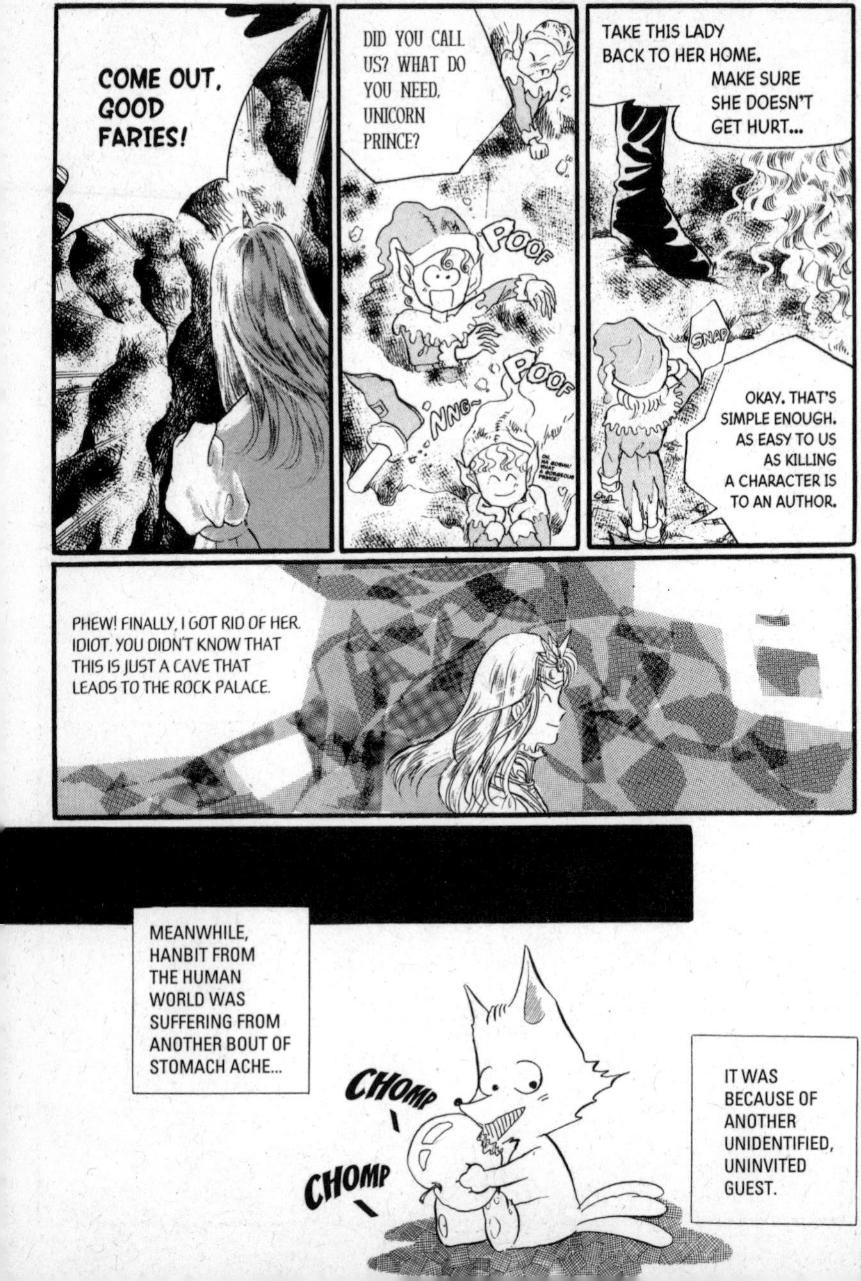
COME OUT, GOOD FARIES!
DID YOU CALL US? WHAT DO YOU NEED, UNICORN PRINCE?
POOF
POOF
NNG~
TAKE THIS LADY BACK TO HER HOME.
MAKE SURE SHE DOESN'T GET HURT...
SNAP
OKAY. THAT'S SIMPLE ENOUGH. AS EASY TO US AS KILLING A CHARACTER IS TO AN AUTHOR.
PHEW! FINALLY, I GOT RID OF HER. IDIOT. YOU DIDN'T KNOW THAT THIS IS JUST A CAVE THAT LEADS TO THE ROCK PALACE.
MEANWHILE, HANBIT FROM THE HUMAN WORLD WAS SUFFERING FROM ANOTHER BOUT OF STOMACH ACHE...
CHOMP
CHOMP
IT WAS BECAUSE OF ANOTHER UNIDENTIFIED, UNINVITED GUEST.

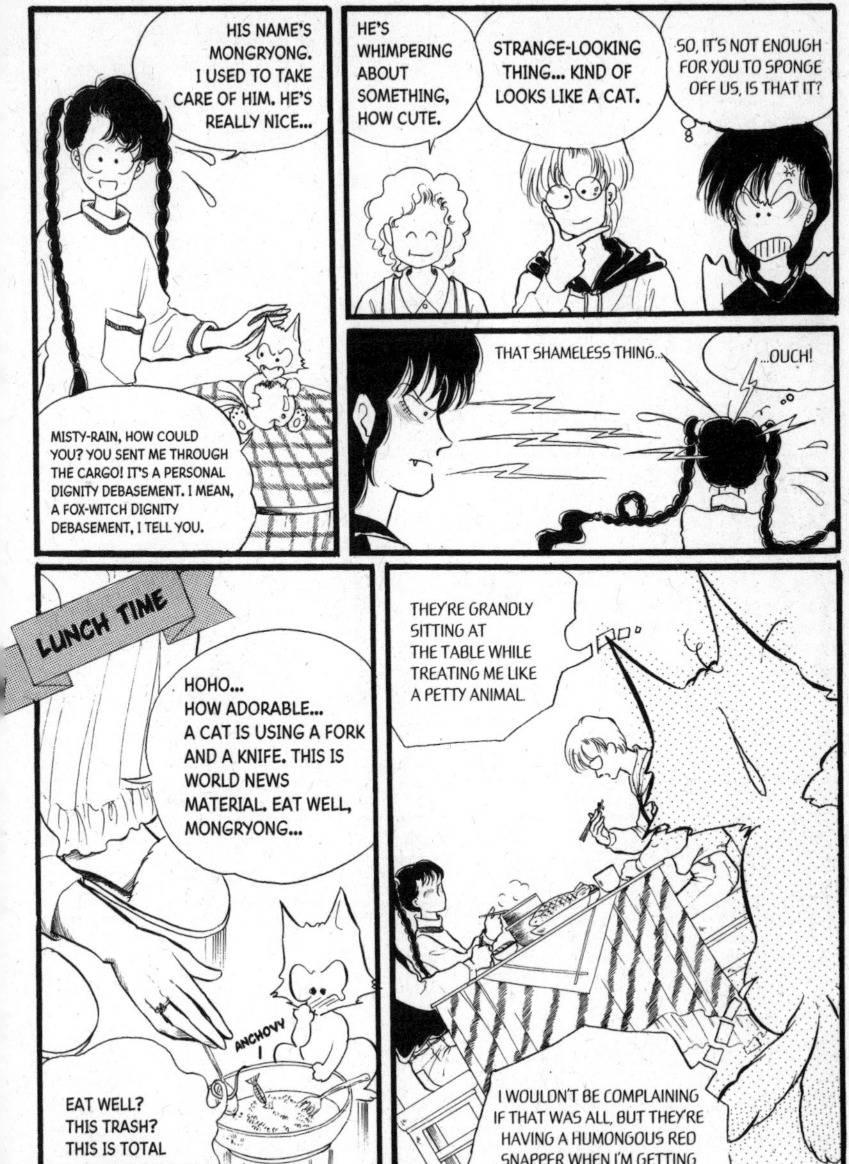
HIS NAME'S MONGRYONG. I USED TO TAKE CARE OF HIM. HE'S REALLY NICE...
MISTY-RAIN, HOW COULD YOU? YOU SENT ME THROUGH THE CARGO! IT'S A PERSONAL DIGNITY DEBASEMENT. I MEAN, A FOX-WITCH DIGNITY DEBASEMENT, I TELL YOU.
HE'S WHIMPERING ABOUT SOMETHING, HOW CUTE.
STRANGE-LOOKING THING... KIND OF LOOKS LIKE A CAT.
SO, IT'S NOT ENOUGH FOR YOU TO SPONGE OFF US, IS THAT IT?
THAT SHAMELESS THING...
...OUCH!
LUNCH TIME
HOHO... HOW ADORABLE... A CAT IS USING A FORK AND A KNIFE. THIS IS WORLD NEWS MATERIAL. EAT WELL, MONGRYONG...
ANCHOVY
EAT WELL? THIS TRASH? THIS IS TOTAL DISCRIMINATION!
THEY'RE GRANDLY SITTING AT THE TABLE WHILE TREATING ME LIKE A PETTY ANIMAL.
I WOULDN'T BE COMPLAINING IF THAT WAS ALL, BUT THEY'RE HAVING A HUMONGOUS RED SNAPPER WHEN I'M GETTING THIS ONE LOUSY ANCHOVY? SO FREAKING CHEAP!

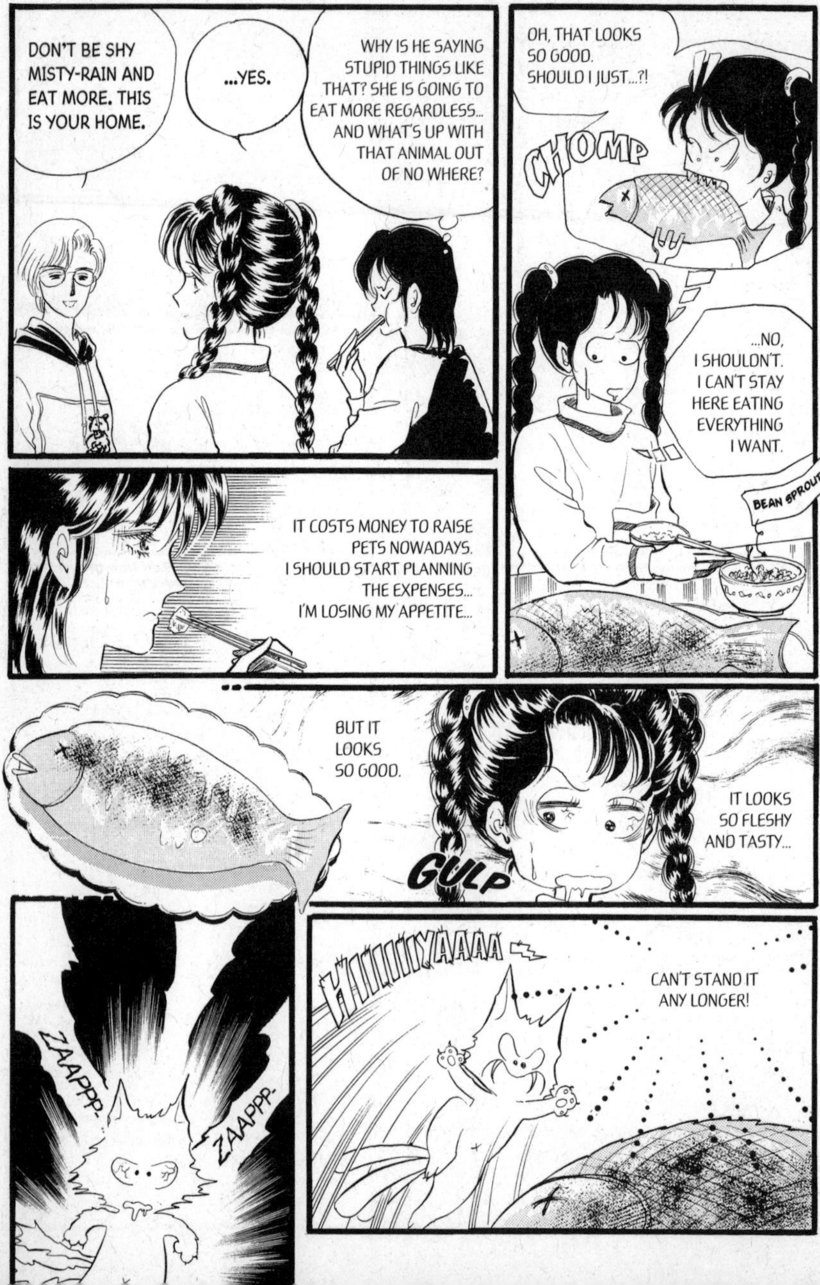
DON'T BE SHY MISTY-RAIN AND EAT MORE. THIS IS YOUR HOME.
...YES.
WHY IS HE SAYING STUPID THINGS LIKE THAT? SHE IS GOING TO EAT MORE REGARDLESS... AND WHAT'S UP WITH THAT ANIMAL OUT OF NO WHERE?
IT COSTS MONEY TO RAISE PETS NOWADAYS. I SHOULD START PLANNING THE EXPENSES... I'M LOSING MY APPETITE...
OH, THAT LOOKS SO GOOD. SHOULD I JUST...?!
CHOMP
...NO, I SHOULDN'T. I CAN'T STAY HERE EATING EVERYTHING I WANT.
BEAN SPROUT
BUT IT LOOKS SO GOOD.
GULP
IT LOOKS SO FLESHY AND TASTY...
ZAAPPP-
ZAAPPP-
HIIIIIYAAAA
CAN'T STAND IT ANY LONGER!

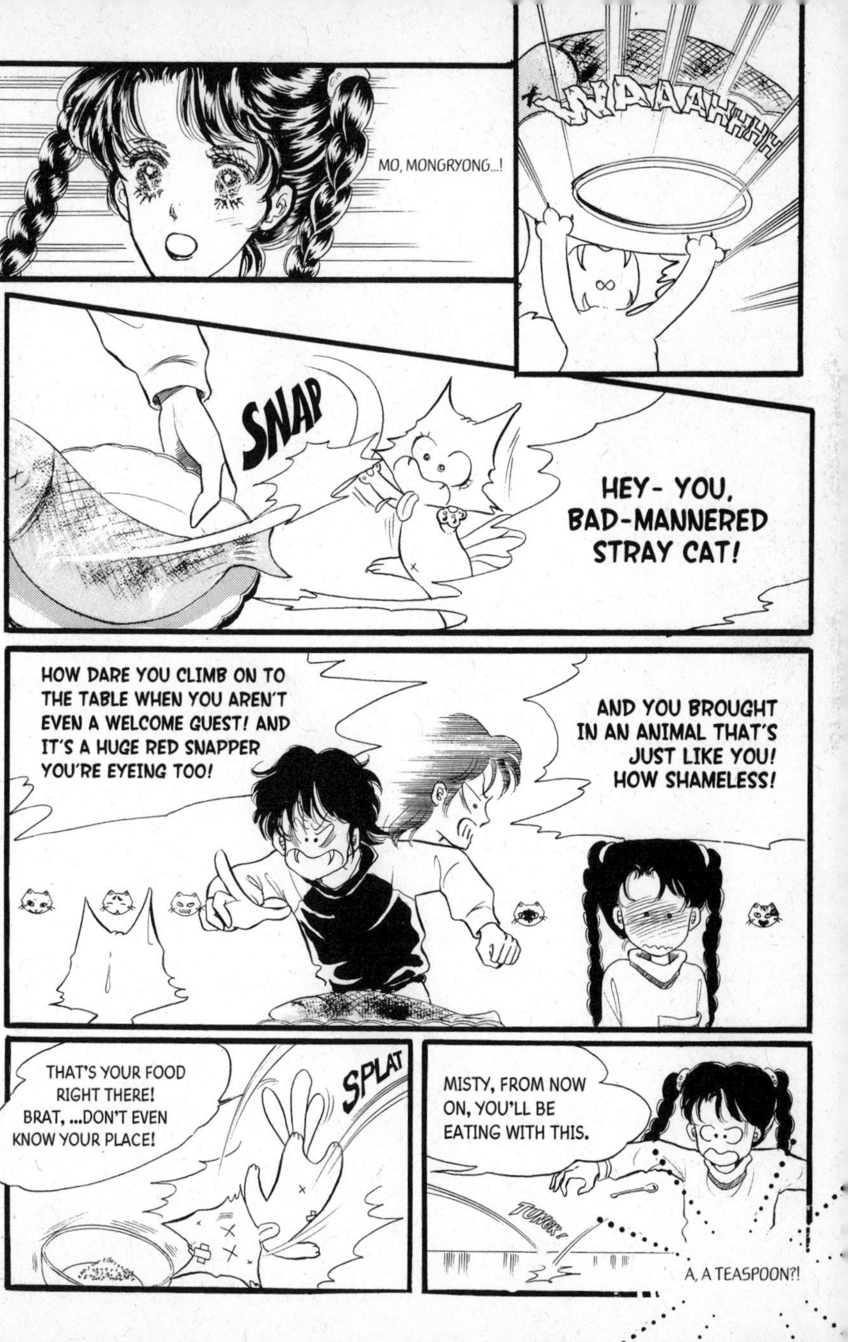
MO, MONGRYONG...!
NYAAAAHHHH
SNAP
HEY- YOU, BAD-MANNERED STRAY CAT!
HOW DARE YOU CLIMB ON TO THE TABLE WHEN YOU AREN'T EVEN A WELCOME GUEST! AND IT'S A HUGE RED SNAPPER YOU'RE EYEING TOO!
AND YOU BROUGHT IN AN ANIMAL THAT'S JUST LIKE YOU! HOW SHAMELESS!
THAT'S YOUR FOOD RIGHT THERE! BRAT, ...DON'T EVEN KNOW YOUR PLACE!
SPLAT
MISTY, FROM NOW ON, YOU'LL BE EATING WITH THIS.
TUNCK!
A, A TEASPOON?!

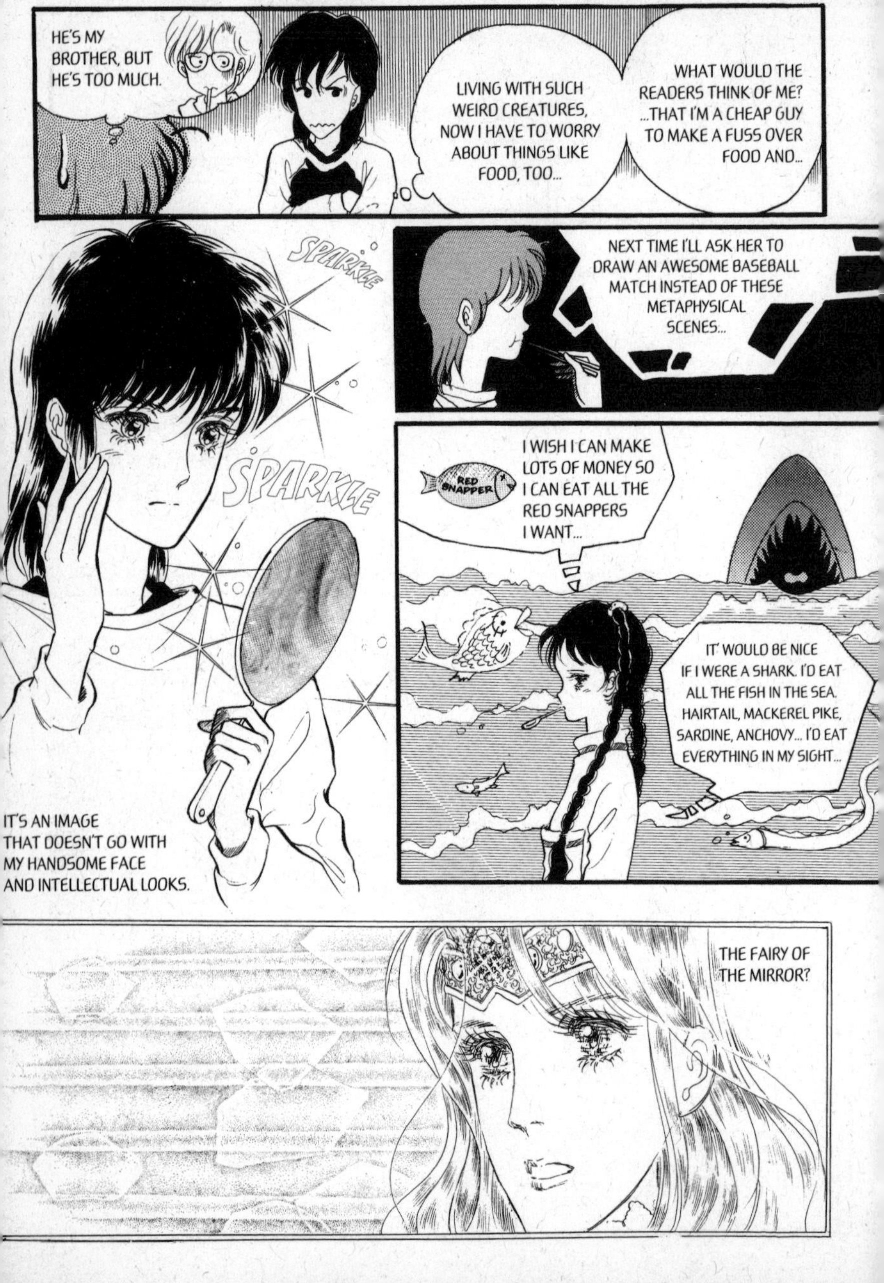
HE'S MY BROTHER, BUT HE'S TOO MUCH.
LIVING WITH SUCH WEIRD CREATURES, NOW I HAVE TO WORRY ABOUT THINGS LIKE FOOD, TOO...
WHAT WOULD THE READERS THINK OF ME? ...THAT I'M A CHEAP GUY TO MAKE A FUSS OVER FOOD AND...
SPARKLE
SPARKLE
IT'S AN IMAGE THAT DOESN'T GO WITH MY HANDSOME FACE AND INTELLECTUAL LOOKS.
NEXT TIME I'LL ASK HER TO DRAW AN AWESOME BASEBALL MATCH INSTEAD OF THESE METAPHYSICAL SCENES...
RED SNAPPER
I WISH I CAN MAKE LOTS OF MONEY SO I CAN EAT ALL THE RED SNAPPERS I WANT...
IT WOULD BE NICE IF I WERE A SHARK. I'D EAT ALL THE FISH IN THE SEA. HAIRTAIL, MACKEREL PIKE, SARDINE, ANCHOVY... I'D EAT EVERYTHING IN MY SIGHT...
THE FAIRY OF THE MIRROR?

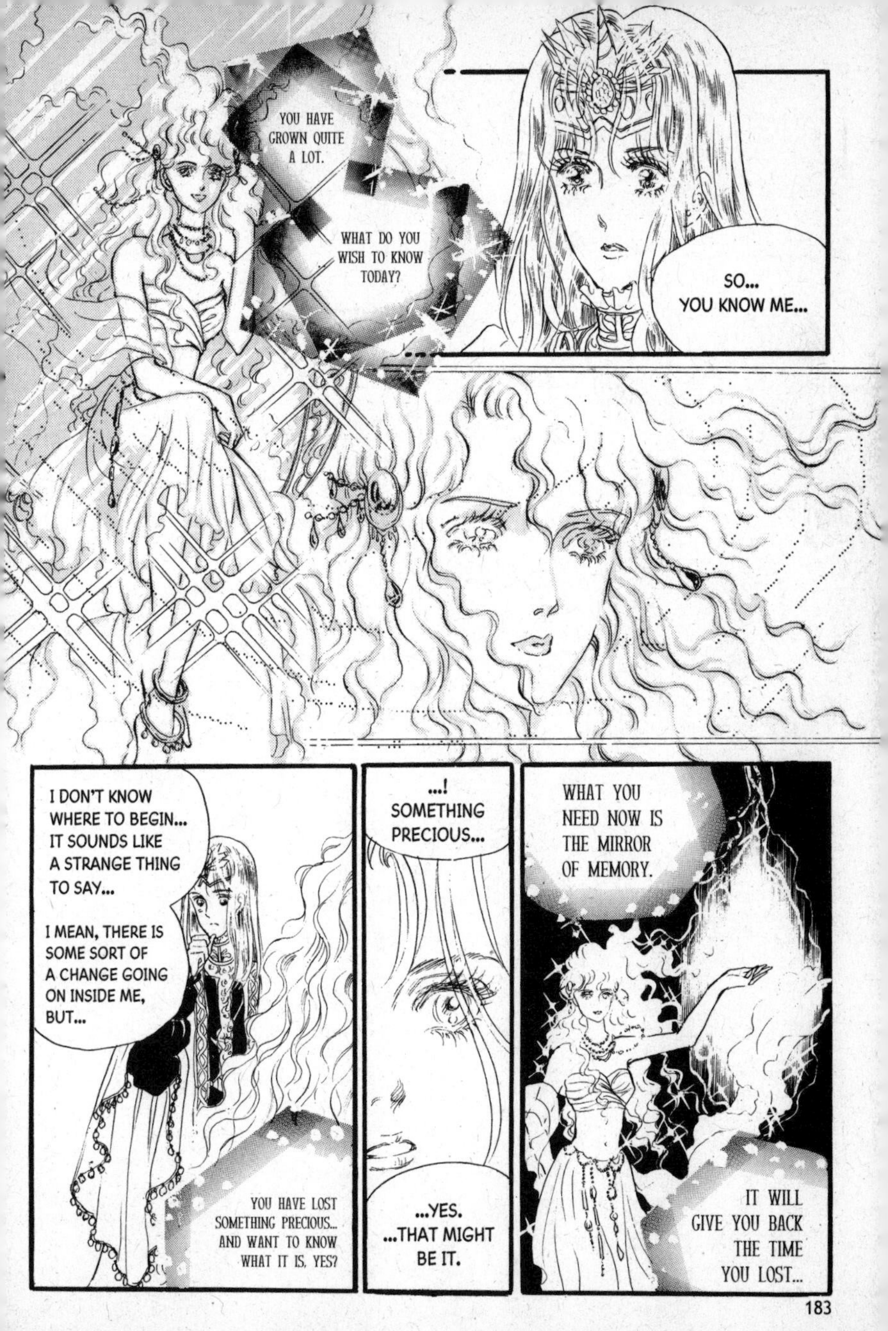
YOU HAVE GROWN QUITE A LOT.
WHAT DO YOU WISH TO KNOW TODAY?
SO... YOU KNOW ME...
I DON'T KNOW WHERE TO BEGIN... IT SOUNDS LIKE A STRANGE THING TO SAY...
I MEAN, THERE IS SOME SORT OF A CHANGE GOING ON INSIDE ME, BUT...
YOU HAVE LOST SOMETHING PRECIOUS... AND WANT TO KNOW WHAT IT IS, YES?
...! SOMETHING PRECIOUS...
...YES. ...THAT MIGHT BE IT.
WHAT YOU NEED NOW IS THE MIRROR OF MEMORY.
IT WILL GIVE YOU BACK THE TIME YOU LOST...

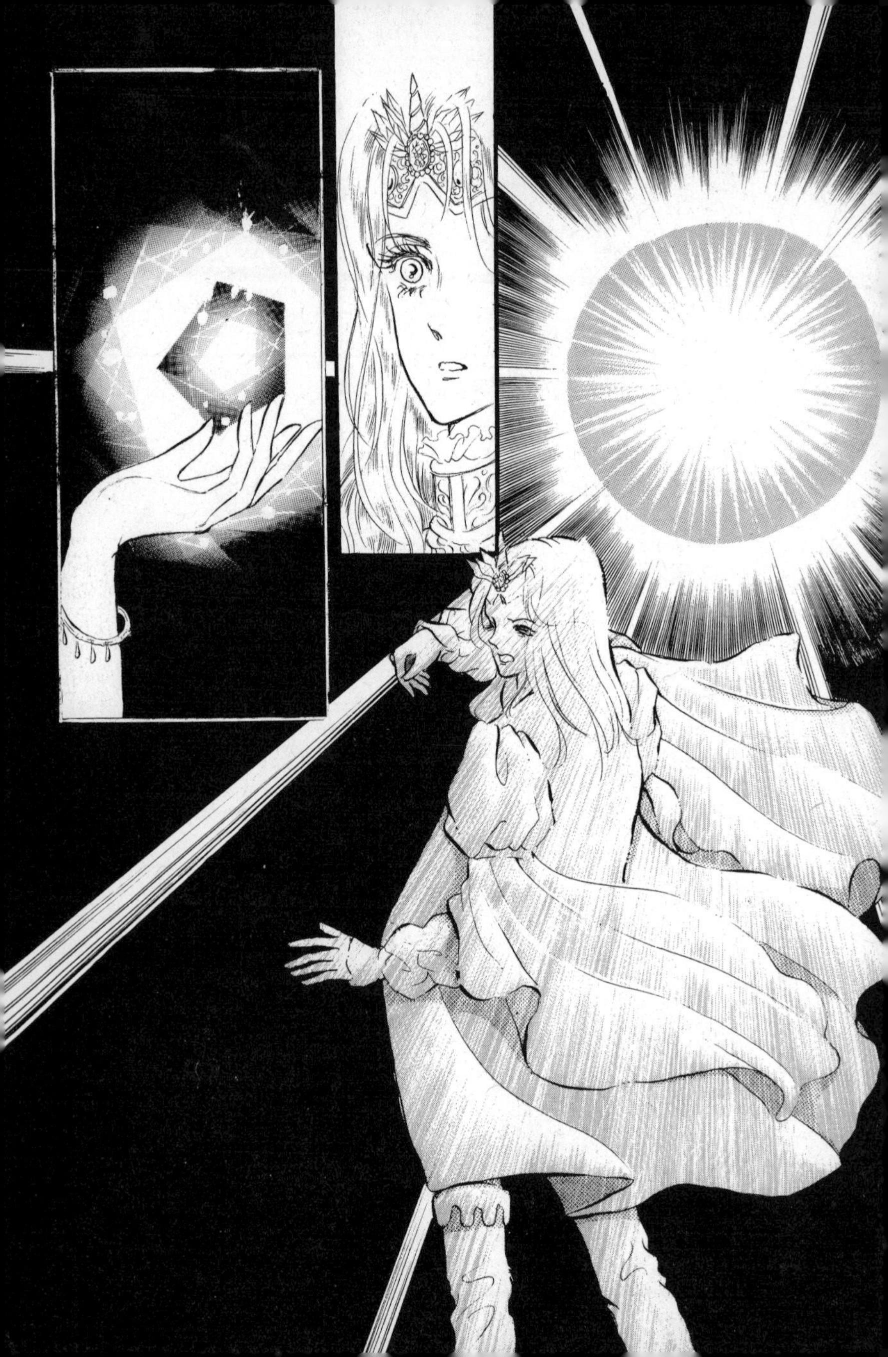

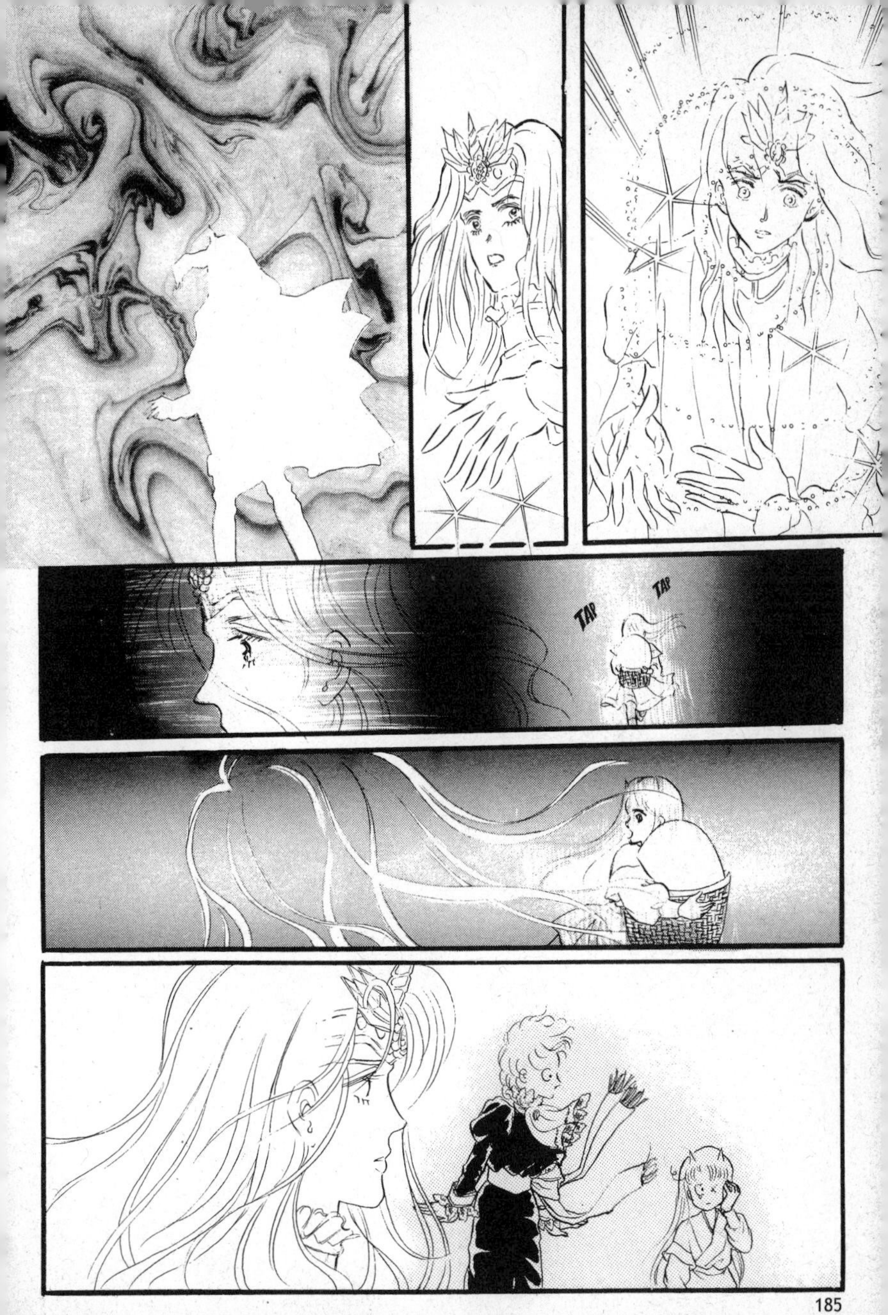
TAP
TAP

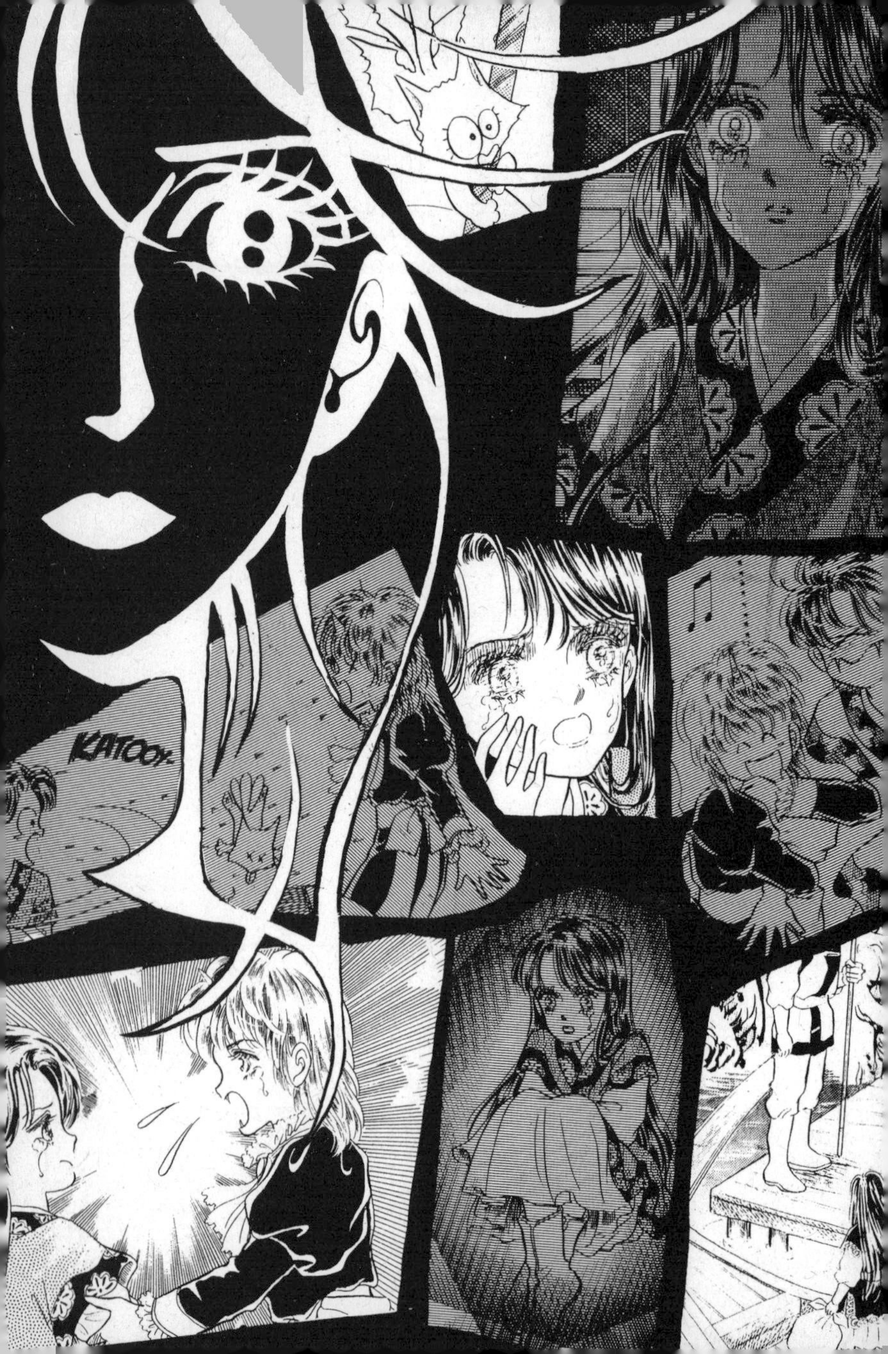
KATOOT

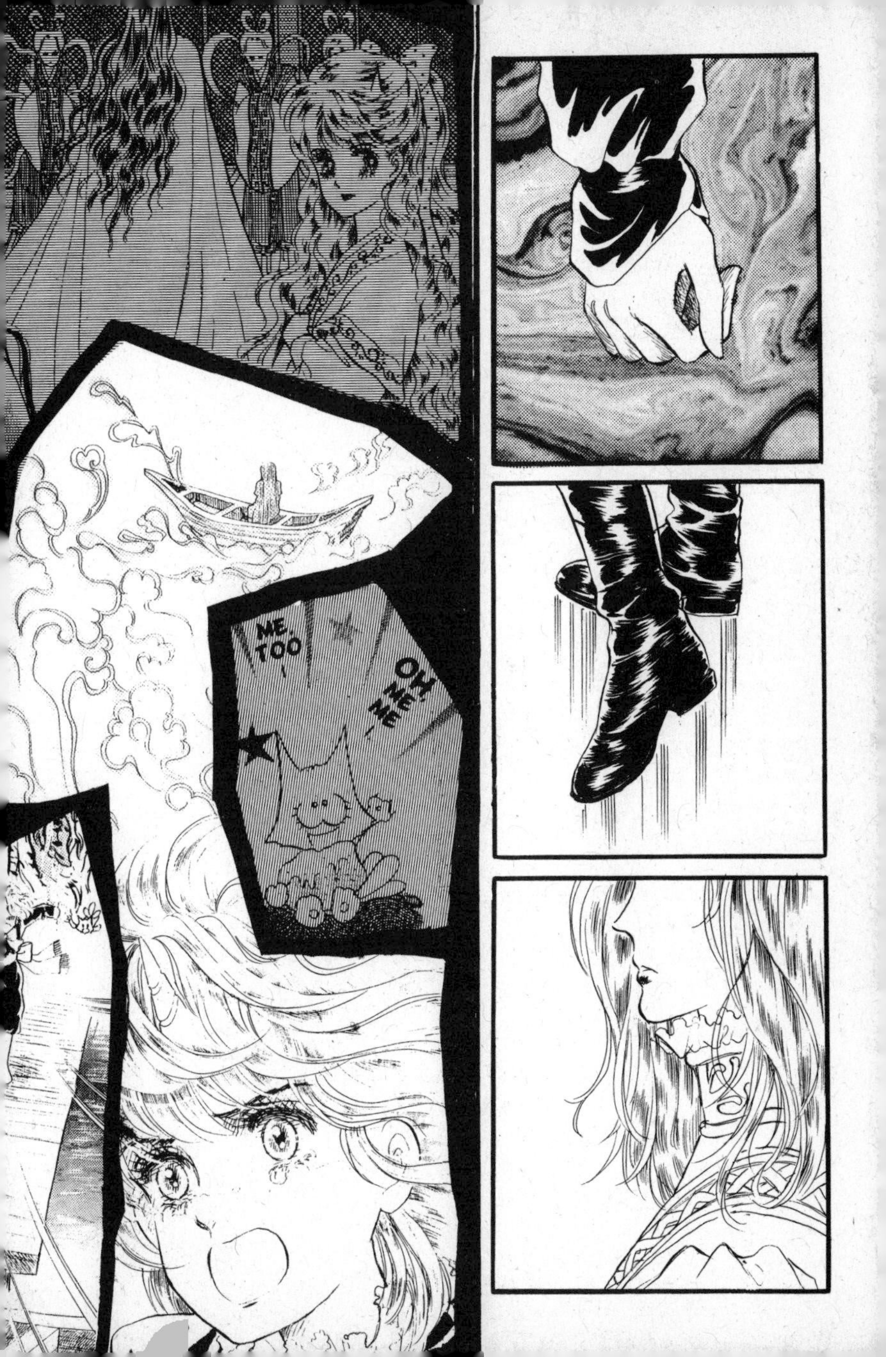
ME, TOO!
OH! ME! ME!

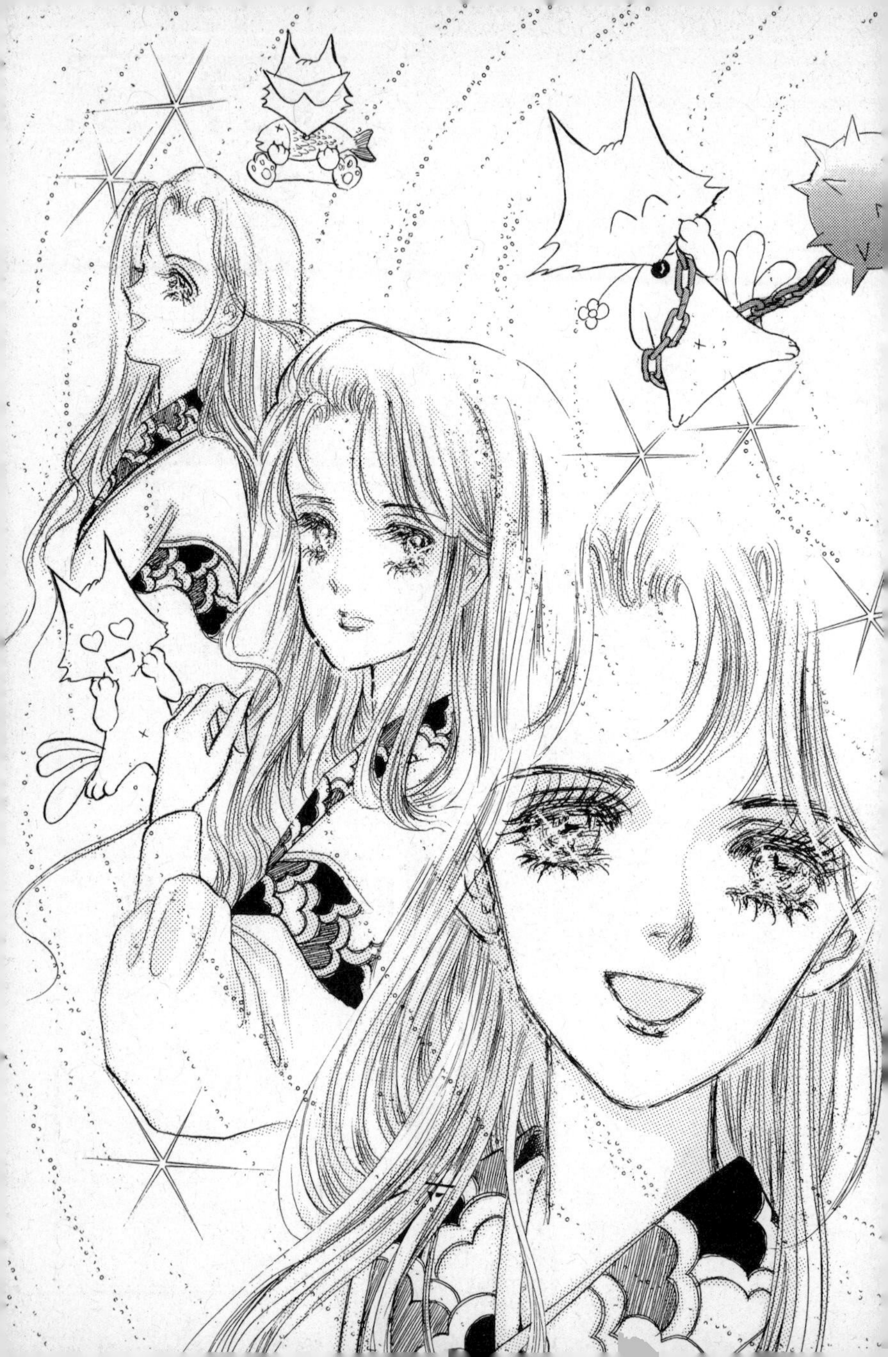

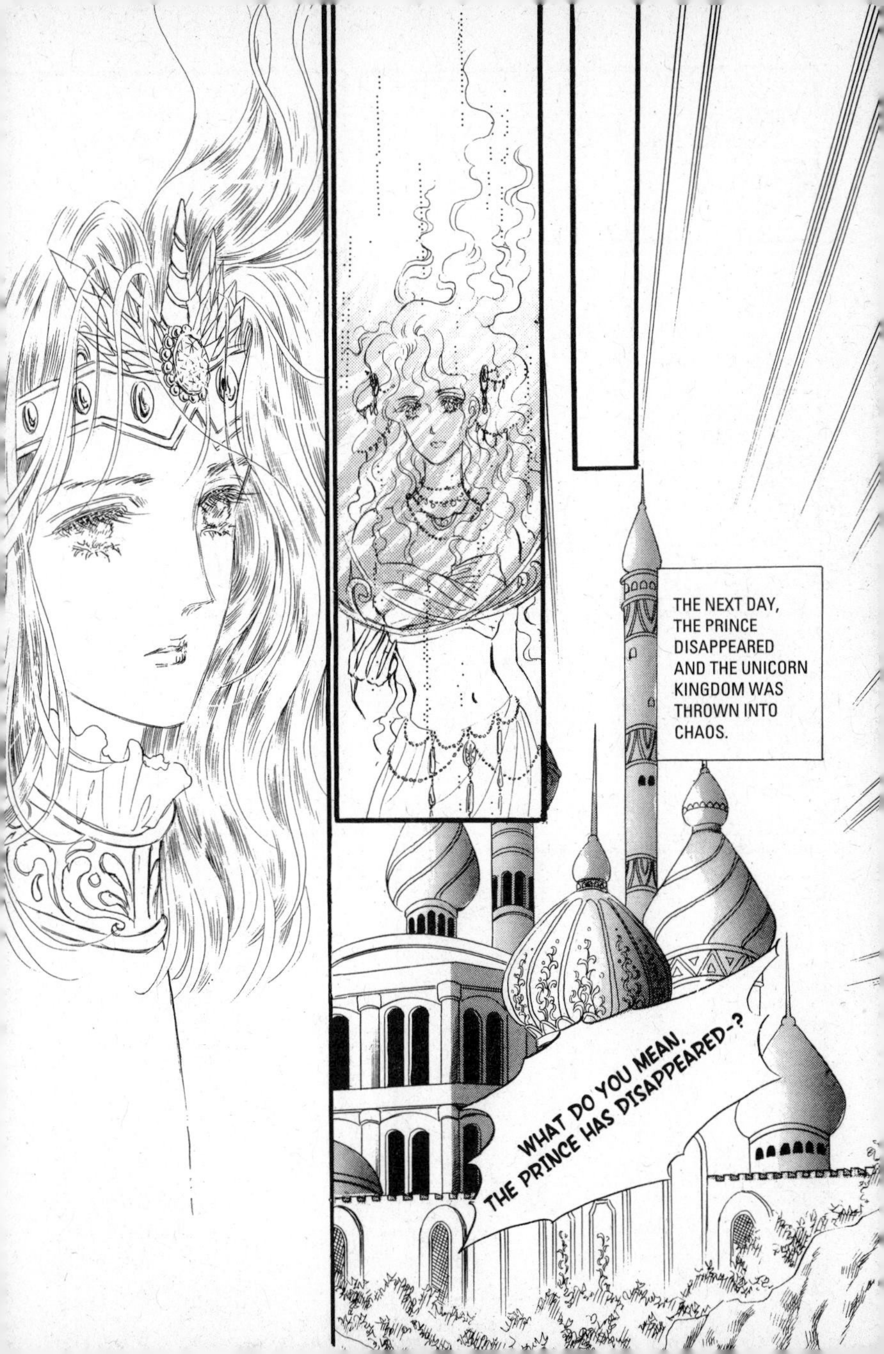
THE NEXT DAY, THE PRINCE DISAPPEARED AND THE UNICORN KINGDOM WAS THROWN INTO CHAOS.
WHAT DO YOU MEAN, THE PRINCE HAS DISAPPEARED-?

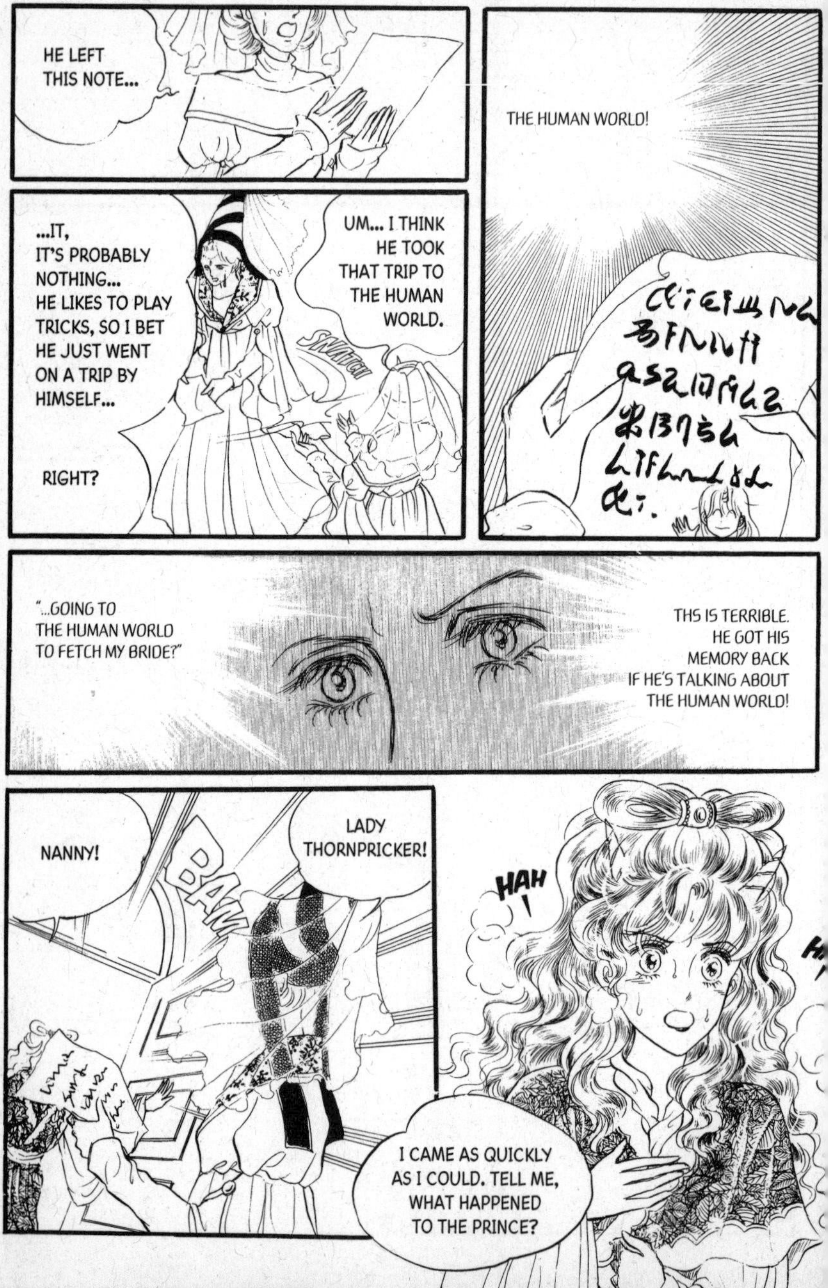
HE LEFT THIS NOTE...
...IT, IT'S PROBABLY NOTHING... HE LIKES TO PLAY TRICKS, SO I BET HE JUST WENT ON A TRIP BY HIMSELF...
RIGHT?
UM... I THINK HE TOOK THAT TRIP TO THE HUMAN WORLD.
SNATCH
THE HUMAN WORLD!
"...GOING TO THE HUMAN WORLD TO FETCH MY BRIDE?"
THS IS TERRIBLE. HE GOT HIS MEMORY BACK IF HE'S TALKING ABOUT THE HUMAN WORLD!
NANNY!
BAM
LADY THORNPRICKER!
HAH!
I CAME AS QUICKLY AS I COULD. TELL ME, WHAT HAPPENED TO THE PRINCE?

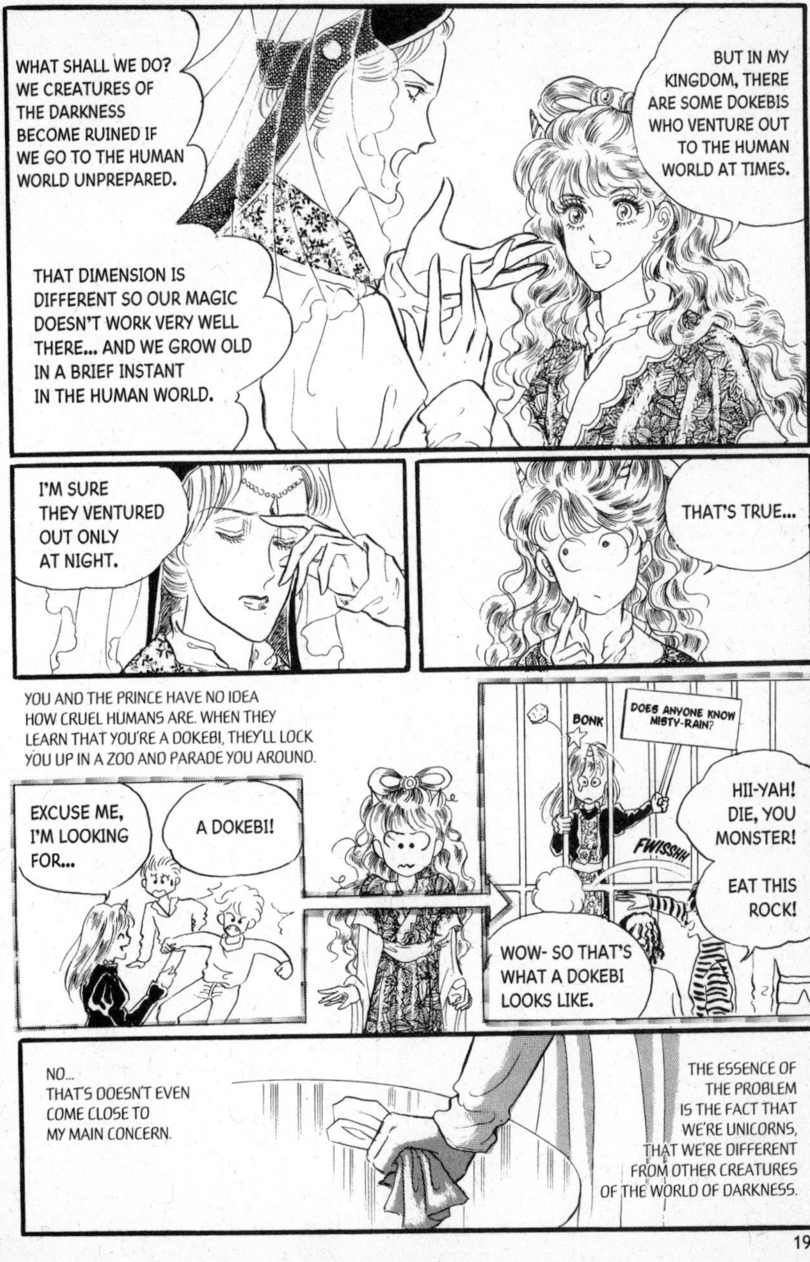
WHAT SHALL WE DO? WE CREATURES OF THE DARKNESS BECOME RUINED IF WE GO TO THE HUMAN WORLD UNPREPARED.
BUT IN MY KINGDOM, THERE ARE SOME DOKEBIS WHO VENTURE OUT TO THE HUMAN WORLD AT TIMES.
THAT DIMENSION IS DIFFERENT SO OUR MAGIC DOESN'T WORK VERY WELL THERE... AND WE GROW OLD IN A BRIEF INSTANT IN THE HUMAN WORLD.
I'M SURE THEY VENTURED OUT ONLY AT NIGHT.
THAT'S TRUE...
YOU AND THE PRINCE HAVE NO IDEA HOW CRUEL HUMANS ARE. WHEN THEY LEARN THAT YOU'RE A DOKEBI, THEY'LL LOCK YOU UP IN A ZOO AND PARADE YOU AROUND.
EXCUSE ME, I'M LOOKING FOR...
A DOKEBI!
BONK
DOES ANYONE KNOW MISTY-RAIN?
HII-YAH! DIE, YOU MONSTER!
FWISSHH
EAT THIS ROCK!
WOW- SO THAT'S WHAT A DOKEBI LOOKS LIKE.
NO... THAT'S DOESN'T EVEN COME CLOSE TO MY MAIN CONCERN.
THE ESSENCE OF THE PROBLEM IS THE FACT THAT WE'RE UNICORNS, THAT WE'RE DIFFERENT FROM OTHER CREATURES OF THE WORLD OF DARKNESS.

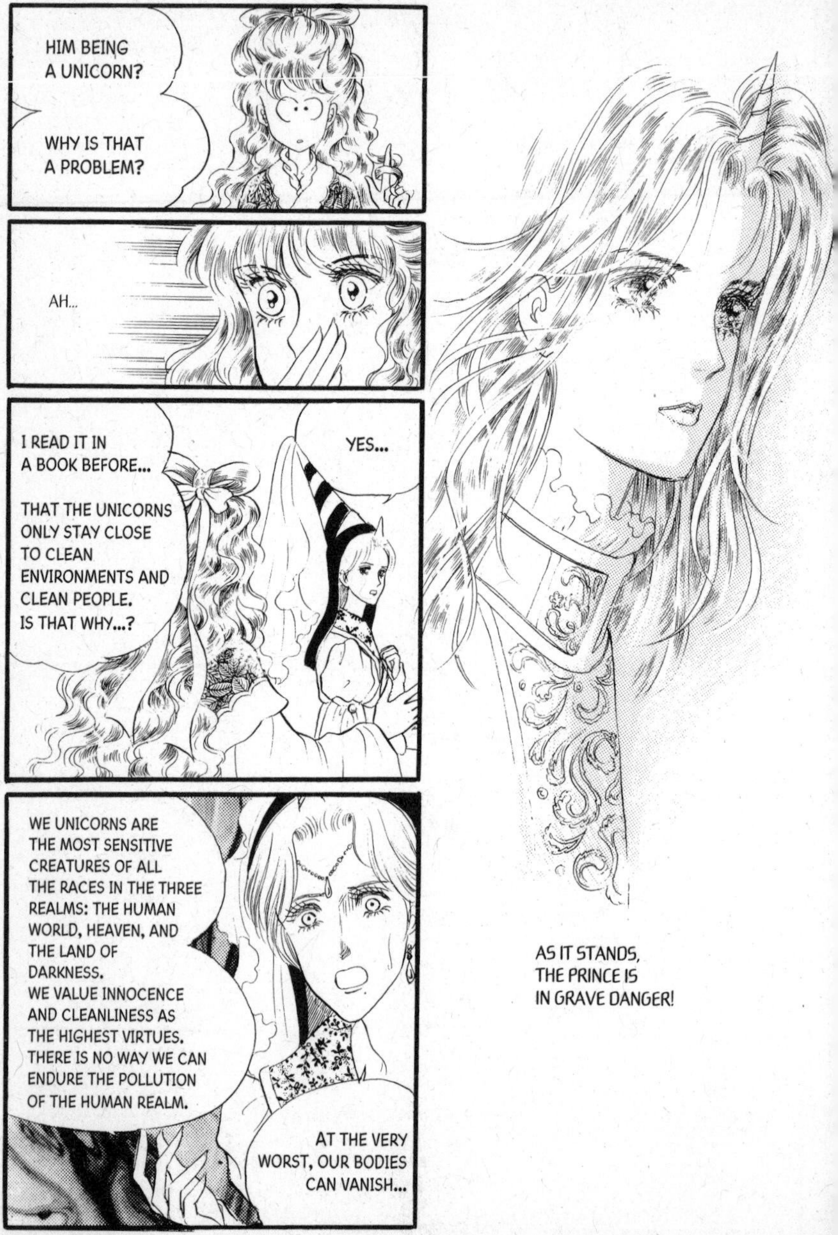
HIM BEING
A UNICORN?
WHY IS THAT
A PROBLEM?
AH...
I READ IT IN
A BOOK BEFORE...
THAT THE UNICORNS
ONLY STAY CLOSE
TO CLEAN
ENVIRONMENTS AND
CLEAN PEOPLE.
IS THAT WHY...?
YES...
WE UNICORNS ARE
THE MOST SENSITIVE
CREATURES OF ALL
THE RACES IN THE THREE
REALMS: THE HUMAN
WORLD, HEAVEN, AND
THE LAND OF
DARKNESS.
WE VALUE INNOCENCE
AND CLEANLINESS AS
THE HIGHEST VIRTUES.
THERE IS NO WAY WE CAN
ENDURE THE POLLUTION
OF THE HUMAN REALM.
AT THE VERY
WORST, OUR BODIES
CAN VANISH...
AS IT STANDS,
THE PRINCE IS
IN GRAVE DANGER!

THE END
To be continued in volume 3 available August 2006.

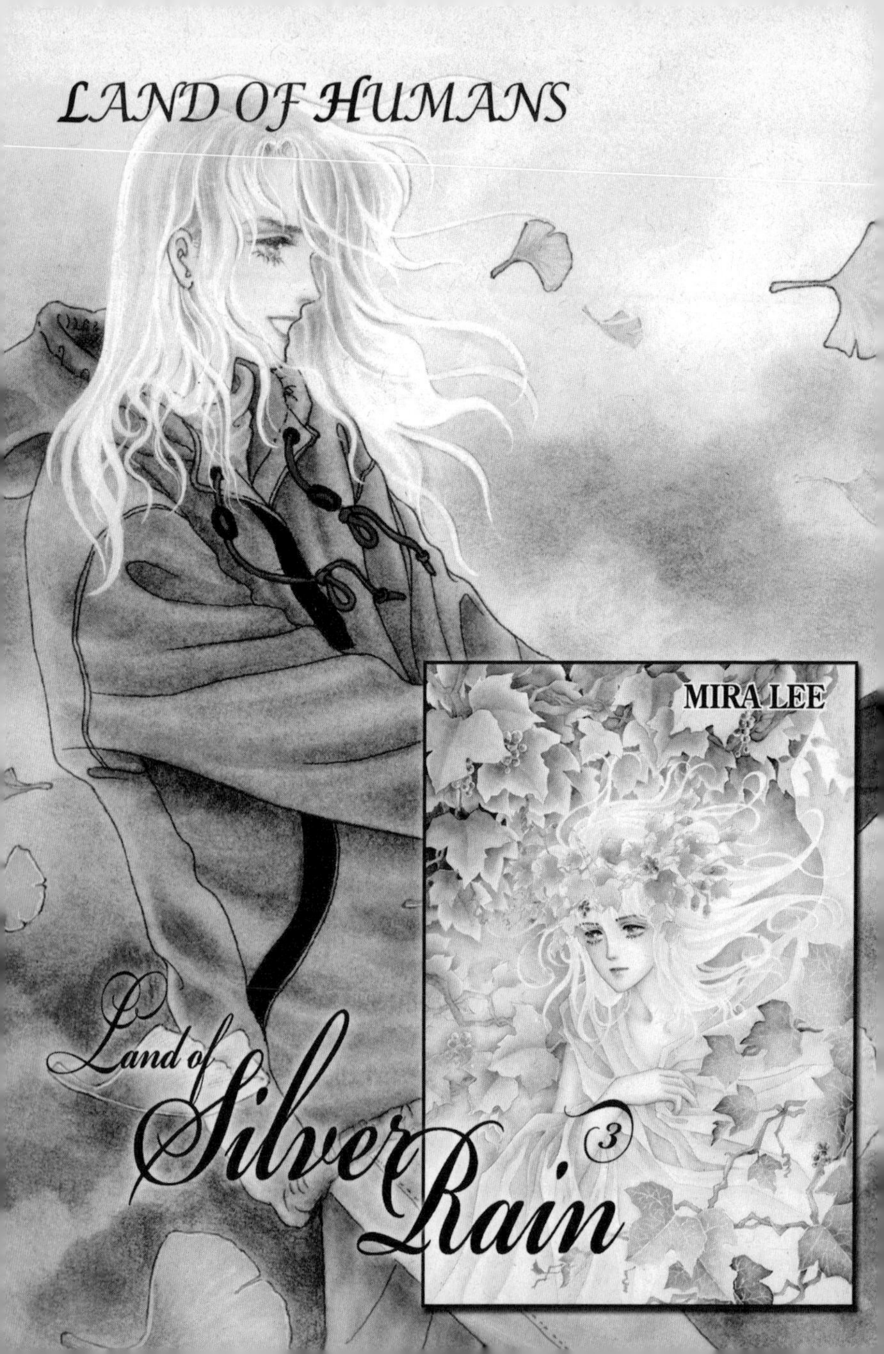

LAND OF HUMANS
MIRA LEE
Land of Silver Rain
3

Land of Silver Rain

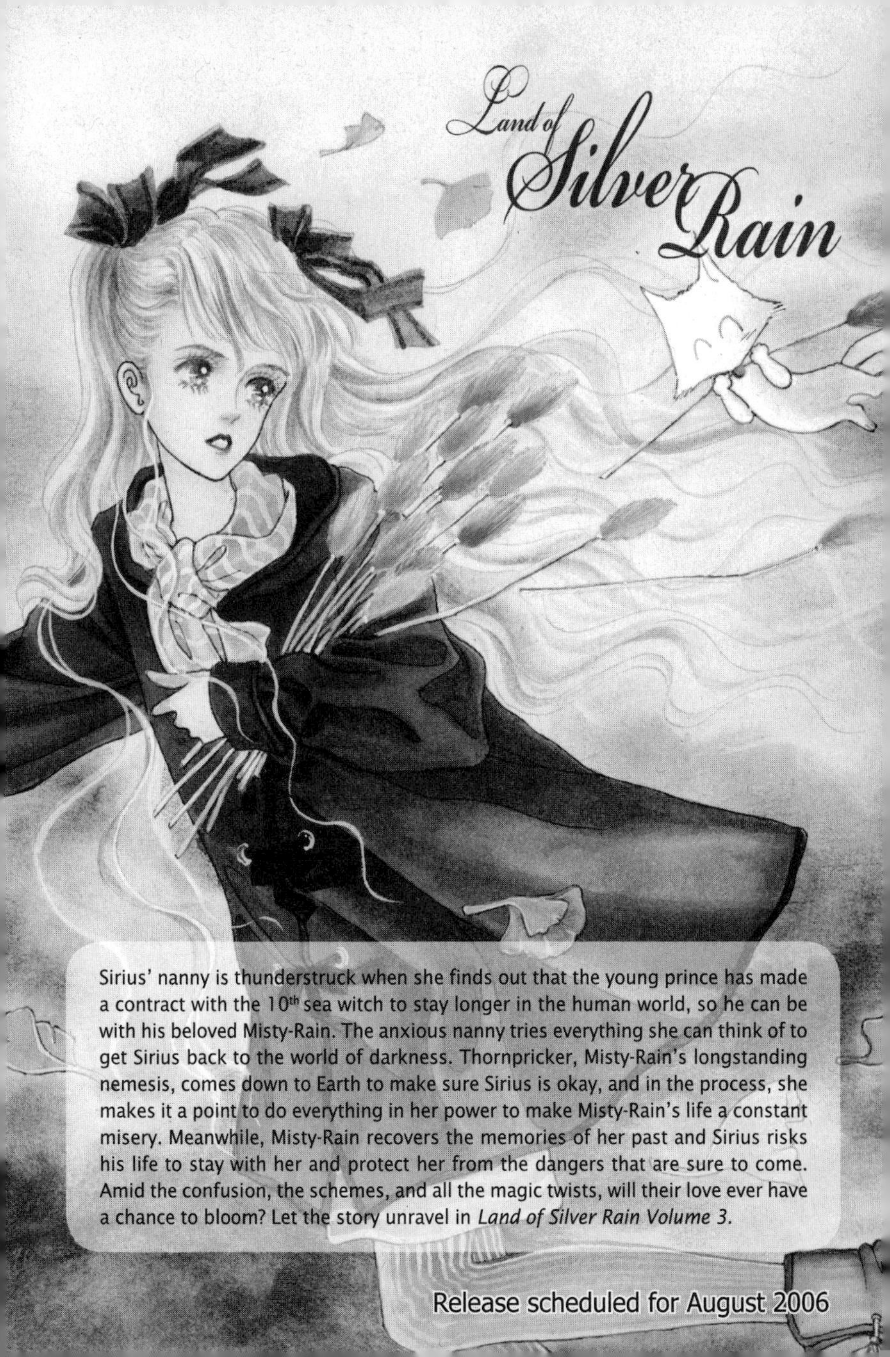

Sirius' nanny is thunderstruck when she finds out that the young prince has made a contract with the 10th sea witch to stay longer in the human world, so he can be with his beloved Misty-Rain. The anxious nanny tries everything she can think of to get Sirius back to the world of darkness. Thornpricker, Misty-Rain's longstanding nemesis, comes down to Earth to make sure Sirius is okay, and in the process, she makes it a point to do everything in her power to make Misty-Rain's life a constant misery. Meanwhile, Misty-Rain recovers the memories of her past and Sirius risks his life to stay with her and protect her from the dangers that are sure to come. Amid the confusion, the schemes, and all the magic twists, will their love ever have a chance to bloom? Let the story unravel in *Land of Silver Rain Volume 3.*

Release scheduled for August 2006

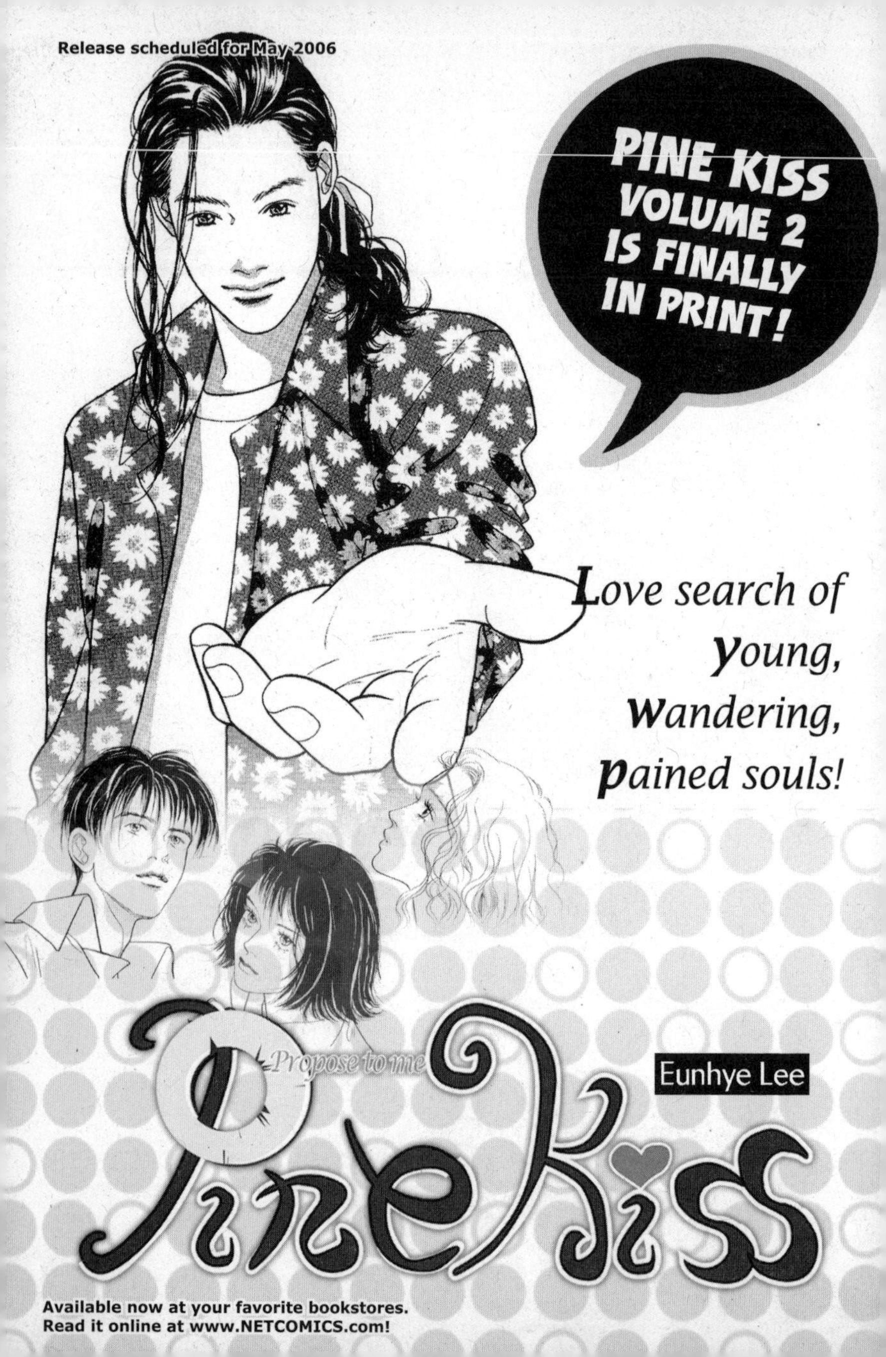
Release scheduled for May 2006
PINE KISS VOLUME 2 IS FINALLY IN PRINT!
Love search of young, wandering, pained souls!
Propose to me
Pine Kiss
Eunhye Lee
Available now at your favorite bookstores.
Read it online at www.NETCOMICS.com!

Release scheduled for June 2006
Dokebi Bride
2
MARLEY
Two shockingly new style graphic novels and their second volumes are scheduled for
release in June 2006!!
Korea's most talked-about new series in 2005!
One of the most acclaimed stories in recent years!
CAN'T LOSE YOU
2
A fast-paced, riveting tale of lovers who can't lose each other even at the risk of their lives!
Available now at your favorite bookstores.
Read it online at www.NETCOMICS.com!
WANN

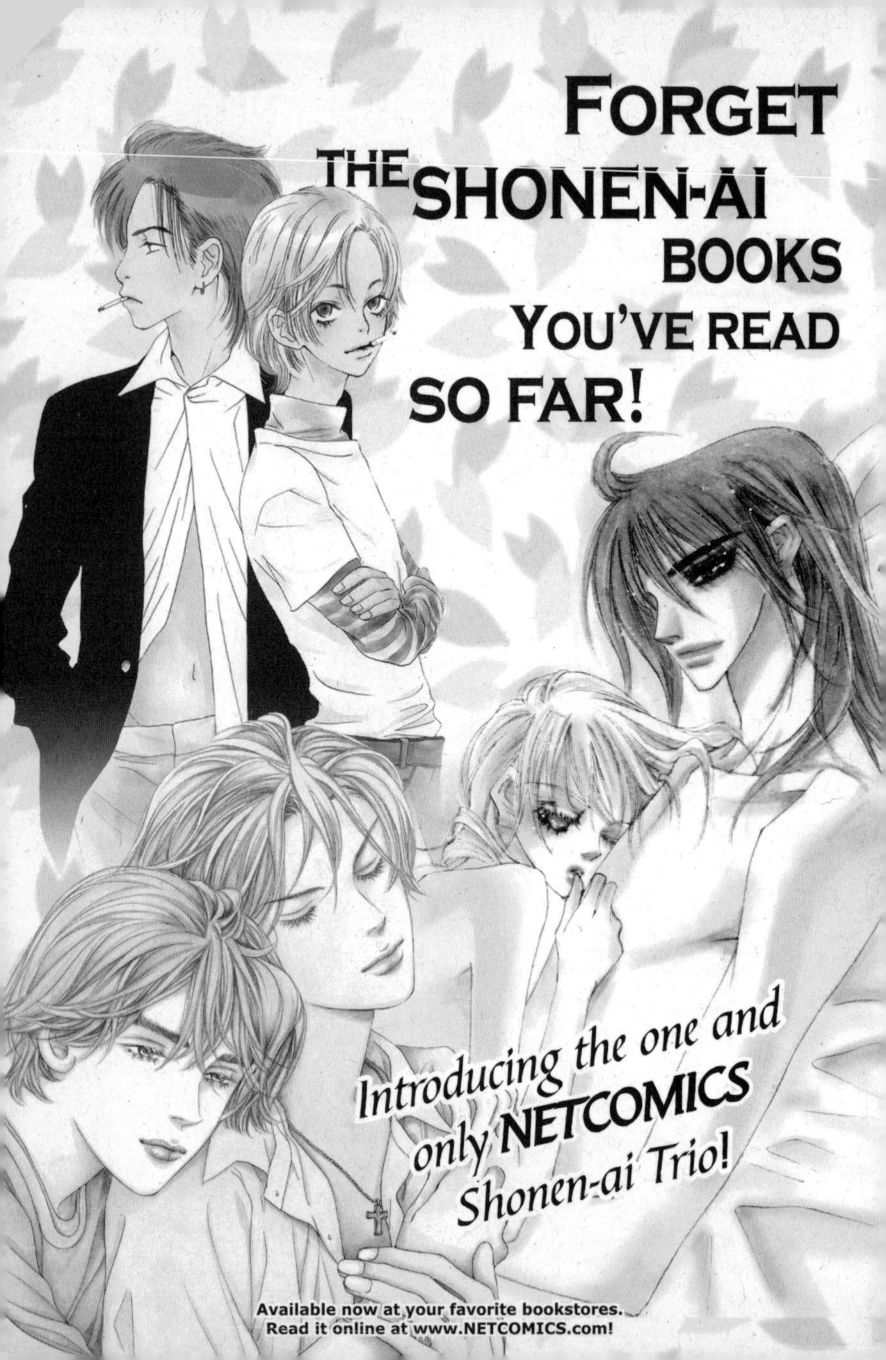

FORGET
THE SHONEN-AI
BOOKS
YOU'VE READ
SO FAR!
Introducing the one and
only NETCOMICS
Shonen-ai Trio!
Available now at your favorite bookstores.
Read it online at www.NETCOMICS.com!